"*Learning Strategies for Sustainable Organisations* Bryan Hopkins provides professionals in business, management, and sustainability with a comprehensive and authoritative account of learning as the source of resilience and sustainability in the volatile, uncertain, complex and ambiguous world of the 21st century."

—Eugene Sadler-Smith, *Professor, Surrey Business School, University of Surrey, UK*

"In a world where many organisations pay lip service to sustainability, *Learning Strategies for Sustainable Organisations* is a must read for businesses serious about sustainability. Full of thought-provoking questions, strategies and knowledge, this book accelerates our understanding of the sustainability agenda and how to create critical and transformative initiatives."

—Helen Routledge, *CEO, Totem Learning, UK*

"There are many books on sustainability or organisations or learning and some which combine two out of the three, but *Learning Strategies for Sustainable Organisations* is the first to bring all three together in a coherent manner. The sustainability challenge is mightily complex and where it is difficult to see the wood for the trees. But Bryan Hopkins examines many trees and shows how they can work together as a wood through systems thinking. And in particular he charts a path through the wood that is recommended reading for all concerned with devising learning strategies for organisations that can help them face up to the sustainability challenge."

—Andy Lane, *Professor of Environmental Systems, The Open University, UK*

"Bryan Hopkins has what it takes to have written a book with profound insights into what to do in developing *Learning Strategies for Sustainable Organisations*. He is a critically reflexive systems thinker and practitioner with well-developed systems literacy and a high level of systemic sensibility, all garnered from life-experience, including self-motivated formal study underpinned by professional, experiential learning."

—Ray Ison, *Professor of Systems, The Open University, UK*

Learning Strategies for Sustainable Organisations

Learning Strategies for Sustainable Organisations explores sustainability in the context of organisational practice and its implications for learning.

Based on a systems thinking approach, it provides a thorough grounding in the principles of systems thinking and tools that can be used to help implement sustainability-focused learning strategies. Increasingly, organisations are recognising the importance of adapting their practices to become more sustainable. Drawing on the Agenda 2030 Sustainable Development Goals as a framework, new knowledge, skills and attitudes are required to help provide products and services that align with changing social and ecological environments and better serve the communities of which they are a part. This book is a practical guide showing how to facilitate sustainability learning and development within organisations, explaining how to identify gaps in current practice, take into account different contexts and perspectives about what sustainability means, and evaluate results following implementation. Learning resources include chapter summaries, illustrations, reflection points, mind maps and further reading.

Written by an independent performance and learning consultant with extensive experience working with international organisations, this book provides a necessary toolkit for human resource development directors, training managers, chief sustainability officers and management consultants specialising in sustainable development.

Bryan Hopkins is a learning and development consultant with over 30 years of work experience with private and public sector organisations within the United Kingdom and internationally to design, deliver and evaluate learning and development programmes. The bulk of his work is with United Nations agencies on humanitarian and development projects, and he has collaborated on a number of projects related to climate change and sustainability.

Routledge Studies in Sustainable Development

This series uniquely brings together original and cutting-edge research on sustainable development. The books in this series tackle difficult and important issues in sustainable development including: values and ethics; sustainability in higher education; climate compatible development; resilience; capitalism and de-growth; sustainable urban development; gender and participation; and well-being.

Drawing on a wide range of disciplines, the series promotes interdisciplinary research for an international readership. The series was recommended in the *Guardian*'s suggested reads on development and the environment.

A New World-System
From Chaos to Sustainability
Donald G. Reid

Buen Vivir as an Alternative to Sustainable Development
Lessons from Ecuador
Natasha Chassagne

Beyond the Blue Economy
Creative Industries and Sustainable Development in Small Island Developing States
Peter Rudge

The Politics of the Sustainable Development Goals
Legitimacy, Responsibility, and Accountability
Magdalena Bexell and Kristina Jönsson

Ecological Limits of Development
Living with the Sustainable Development Goals
Kaitlin Kish and Stephen Quilley

Learning Strategies for Sustainable Organisations
Bryan Hopkins

For more information about this series, please visit: www.routledge.com/Routledge-Studies-in-Sustainable-Development/book-series/RSSD

Learning Strategies for Sustainable Organisations

Bryan Hopkins

Cover image: Bryan Hopkins

First published 2022
by Routledge
4 Park Square, Milton Park, Abingdon, Oxon OX14 4RN

and by Routledge
605 Third Avenue, New York, NY 10158

Routledge is an imprint of the Taylor & Francis Group, an informa business

© 2022 Bryan Hopkins

The right of Bryan Hopkins to be identified as author of this work has been asserted in accordance with sections 77 and 78 of the Copyright, Designs and Patents Act 1988.

All rights reserved. No part of this book may be reprinted or reproduced or utilised in any form or by any electronic, mechanical, or other means, now known or hereafter invented, including photocopying and recording, or in any information storage or retrieval system, without permission in writing from the publishers.

Trademark notice: Product or corporate names may be trademarks or registered trademarks, and are used only for identification and explanation without intent to infringe.

British Library Cataloguing-in-Publication Data
A catalogue record for this book is available from the British Library

Library of Congress Cataloging-in-Publication Data
Names: Hopkins, Bryan, 1954- author.
Title: Learning strategies for sustainable organisations / Bryan Hopkins.
Description: New York, NY : Routledge, 2022. | Series: Routledge studies in sustainable development | Includes bibliographical references and index.
Identifiers: LCCN 2021052406 (print) | LCCN 2021052407 (ebook) |
ISBN 9781032110691 (hardback) | ISBN 9781032110707 (paperback) |
ISBN 9781003218296 (ebook)
Subjects: LCSH: Organizational learning. | Organizational change. | Organizational effectiveness.
Classification: LCC HD58.82 .H67 2022 (print) | LCC HD58.82 (ebook) |
DDC 658.3/124—dc23/eng/20220105
LC record available at https://lccn.loc.gov/2021052406
LC ebook record available at https://lccn.loc.gov/2021052407

ISBN: 978-1-032-11069-1 (hbk)
ISBN: 978-1-032-11070-7 (pbk)
ISBN: 978-1-003-21829-6 (ebk)

DOI: 10.4324/9781003218296

Typeset in Bembo
by codeMantra

To all our children and grandchildren.

Contents

List of figures — xi
List of tables — xv
Cover illustration — xvii
Preface — xix
Acknowledgements — xxi
Permissions — xxiii
Acronyms and abbreviations — xxv

Introduction — 1

1 Sustainability: development of a concept — 10

2 Systems thinking, complexity and sustainability — 35

3 The political economy of sustainability — 74

4 The sustainable organisation — 98

5 Developing a learning strategy 1: what to learn — 142

6 Developing a learning strategy 2: how people learn — 166

7 Developing a learning strategy 3: designing formal learning — 204

8 Developing a learning strategy 4: informal learning and the learning environment — 231

9 Preparing the final strategy — 245

10 Evaluating learning about sustainability — 247

11 Reflecting on learning about learning — 268

Index — 273

Figures

I.1	Chapters in the book	5
1.1	Map of Chapter 1	10
1.2	Timeline showing the development of the concept of sustainability	11
1.3	The 17 Sustainable Development Goals	13
1.4	Great Acceleration graph showing primary energy use	16
1.5	The planetary boundaries (2015 update)	21
1.6	Key points covered in this chapter	30
2.1	Map of Chapter 2	35
2.2	Rich picture for the Sheffield tree maintenance story	39
2.3	The system for managing Sheffield's trees	40
2.4	The updated system map with the media	40
2.5	Updated system map with the police	41
2.6	Updated system map with residents in the system	41
2.7	Influence diagram for the tree management system	44
2.8	Contractual negotiations as a feedback loop	45
2.9	Basic feedback loop	45
2.10	The social construction of knowledge	46
2.11	The interrelationships, perspectives and boundary judgements nexus	49
2.12	Organisation as an open system	51
2.13	Causal flow diagram for population and food per capita	59
2.14	Causal flow diagram showing the impact of services	60
2.15	Projection in world population to 2100	61
2.16	Causal flow loop for the tragedy of the commons	61
2.17	Causal flow loop for the importance of learning about sustainability	62
2.18	The Viable System Model	64
2.19	Key points in this chapter	68
2.20	Causal flow diagram for the collapse of complex societies	70
2.21	Causal flow diagram for the professional development of experts	70
3.1	Map of Chapter 3	74
3.2	CO_2 emissions by world region	75
3.3	Representation of the Kuznets curve	76
3.4	Influence diagram showing the possible impact of neoliberal policies on social sustainability	77
3.5	The Environmental Kuznets Curve	78
3.6	System map and influences in the neoliberal economic system	80
3.7	The future of economic growth	84

3.8	The structure of doughnut economics	88
3.9	Organisation system maps in a sustainable economy	90
3.10	Key points in this chapter	93
4.1	Map of Chapter 4	98
4.2	An organisation as an open system	100
4.3	The development of the organisational sustainability concept	101
4.4	System map for stockholder theory	104
4.5	System map for a social contract view of organisations	105
4.6	Institutional theory as a spiral dynamic	107
4.7	Feedback processes influencing the institutional landscape	107
4.8	System map including social and natural environments	109
4.9	Drivers for sustainability and learning implications of theories of the firm	111
4.10	Tensions between economic, social and environmental sustainability in a political economy landscape	112
4.11	Querying the impact of organisational activities on planetary boundaries	118
4.12	The de-bureaucratisation of the organisation	123
4.13	Single loop learning	125
4.14	Single and double loop learning	125
4.15	Levels of engagement in organisational sustainability	127
4.16	Key points in this chapter	135
5.1	The structure of Chapters 5–11	142
5.2	Map of Chapter 5	143
5.3	Habermas' conception of knowledge interests	145
5.4	The Habermas learning space triangle	146
5.5	Relationships between competence, competency and KSA	152
5.6	Appreciation of the flow of sustainability and its implications for learning	162
5.7	Key points in this chapter	163
6.1	Map of Chapter 6	166
6.2	Mechanisms for learning	167
6.3	Kolb's experiential learning cycle	169
6.4	Shared experiential learning	170
6.5	Experiential learning as a spiral of increasing awareness	171
6.6	Knowledge conversion	171
6.7	The 4I model with action and place	172
6.8	Factors influencing learning about sustainability	174
6.9	Elements of organisational culture and employee significance	175
6.10	The European Corporate Sustainability Framework	177
6.11	Bonding, bridging and bracing ties	180
6.12	Defensive routines minimising the need to change	182
6.13	The Graves levels of existence model	185
6.14	Multiple identities of an individual	187
6.15	Concept map of factors potentially influencing learning effectiveness	195
6.16	Key points in this chapter	199
7.1	Map of Chapter 7	204

7.2	Principles of adult learning	205
7.3	The learning space triangle with unitarist learning approaches	216
7.4	The learning space for action learning	217
7.5	Key points in this chapter	228
8.1	Map of Chapter 8	231
8.2	Key points in this chapter	242
10.1	Map of Chapter 9	247
10.2	Learning needs assessment and evaluation as a feedback mechanism	250
10.3	Causal flow diagram showing organisational constraints on evaluation	250
10.4	A logic model for SFL theory of change	255
10.5	Reviewing the evidence for making a contribution claim	258
10.6	The Behaviour Engineering Model as an influence diagram	261
10.7	The Behaviour Engineering Model as a causal flow diagram	262
10.8	Key points in this chapter	265
11.1	Map of Chapter 11	268

Tables

1.1	Environmental sustainability targets in the SDGs	23
1.2	Social sustainability targets in the SDGs	26
1.3	Economic sustainability targets in the SDGs	29
2.1	VSM systems	64
2.2	Boundary categories within CSH	67
4.1	Examples of activities furthering organisational sustainability	103
4.2	Implications for management across different strategies for sustainability	130
4.3	Internal and external considerations of the sustainability dimensions	136
5.1	Baseline conditions for the LNA	149
5.2	Learning content at the organisational level for each VSM system	156
5.3	Learning content at the team level for each VSM system	157
5.4	Learning content at the individual level for each VSM system	158
5.5	Questions to ask about decisions on learning content	160
6.1	Questions to ask about decisions on learning mechanisms	196
7.1	Questions to ask about decisions on principles for formal learning	225
8.1	Questions to ask about decisions on informal learning	239
9.1	Translating boundary judgements to strategy statements	246
10.1	Evaluation questions for clarifying high-level decisions	256

Cover illustration

The illustration on the front cover shows the author's daughter and grandchildren looking towards a cement factory in Castleton, Derbyshire.
   Credit: Bryan Hopkins
   Globally, cement production accounts for 7% of annual anthropogenic carbon dioxide emissions.

Preface

In 2018, as I dabbled with the idea of semi-retirement and pulled back on the amount of paid work I was doing as a learning and development consultant in the humanitarian and development sectors, I decided to start a part-time PhD. It made sense as a logical progression of studies that I had done over the years, the BSc in mechanical engineering, the MScs in development studies and systems thinking, and various professional development courses. It would also make sense as an academically rigorous way of pulling together the work that I did on training evaluation with my interest in systems thinking, so that I would end up with a thesis proposing a "systems thinking-based methodology for evaluating organisational training programmes".

I started work on this with the Open University in early 2019. I read all the academic articles I could find about training evaluation, but my supervisors advised me to "go up a level of abstraction" to read more widely about organisational learning. So I started to look at other perspectives on how people learnt, on alternative thinking about the role of Human Resource Development (HRD), and in particular at papers talking about the wider responsibilities that HRD have or should have to employees, to the societies where they lived, and to the environments they inhabited.

At the same time, my wife and I were looking after our two small grandchildren once a week: Tober was born in 2016 and Oona in 2018, and as we played and read books together, I thought about the world they would grow into and what that would be like. We were involved with Extinction Rebellion in our home city of Sheffield, attending demonstrations in London in October 2019, and I also worked on consultancy projects about forest management and climate change adaptation. These factors all combined to give me a feeling that spending six years working on a narrowly defined academic thesis that probably only a handful of people would read to tick something off on my qualification bucket list was perhaps not the best use of the time left to me.

So at the end of 2020, I decided to discontinue my PhD studies and take my huge pile of academic papers about sustainable, green, societal, holistic and critical HRD, economic, social and environmental sustainability, formal and informal learning, systems thinking and complexity theory, and weave them together into a practitioner-oriented book that could help HRD professionals make sense of sustainability and sustainability professionals make sense of learning.

The research that I had done had not revealed any comparable texts. While there were quite a few books and academic papers about how to approach sustainability in higher education or the school system, there seemed to be nothing aimed at HRD professionals. So I hope that in some small way this book will help promote the sustainability agenda and will provide new ways of thinking about how people can learn about sustainability in the work that they do and in the communities where they live.

Bryan Hopkins
October 2021

Acknowledgements

First of all, I must offer my thanks to my former PhD supervisors at the Open University, Professor Andy Lane, Martin Reynolds and Rupesh Shah—without their encouragement and advice to read wider, I would not have explored the range of research needed in order to pull the contents of this book together.

Related to that, I must offer thanks to the group of "study buddies" with whom I have shared ideas and from whom I have drawn encouragement over the lifetime of this book: in alphabetical order, Barbara Schmidt-Abbey, Dr Helen Wilding, Houda Khayame, Joan O'Donnell and Pauline Roberts.

Thanks also to colleagues and friends who read drafts and commented: Paul Carnell, Dr Janet Curran, Dr Karine Nohr and Catherine Russ.

I also owe many thanks to people who willingly gave their time to share valuable thoughts about subjects covered in this book. In alphabetical order:

- Fozia Parveen, Head of Social Value, ISG Ltd
- Gail Francis, Strategic Director at RE-AMP
- Helen Routledge, CEO, Totem Learning Ltd
- Dr Karen Watkins, Professor, Learning, Leadership & Organization Development, Department of Lifelong Education, Administration & Policy, The University of Georgia
- Melanie Campbell, Systems Practitioner and Ordinand in the Church of England
- Natalie Wilkinson, Head of Responsibility at NG Bailey
- Rob Hubbard, CEO, LAS (LearningAge Solutions Ltd)
- Rob Powell, Director, Pro-Bono & Corporate Responsibility, Weil, Gotshal & Manges (London) LLP

Finally, major thanks to my wife, Helen, for her patience, support and encouragement and willingness to read through the entire book multiple times!

Permissions

I would like to thank the United Nations' Department of Global Communications (https://www.un.org/sustainabledevelopment/) for permission to use the Sustainable Development Goals graphic (Figure 1.3) and should stress that the content of this publication has not been approved by the United Nations and does not reflect the views of the United Nations or its officials or the Member States.

Figure 1.5 has been downloaded from the Stockholm Resilience Centre website (https://www.stockholmresilience.org/research/planetary-boundaries.html).

Figure 2.15 has been downloaded from https://OurWorldinData.org, licensed under CC-BY 4.0.

Figure 3.2 has been downloaded from https://OurWorldinData.org, licensed under CC-BY.

Figure 3.8 has been downloaded from https://doughnuteconomics.org/tools-and-stories/65, licensed under CC-BY-SA 4.0.

Acronyms and abbreviations

3BL	Triple Bottom Line
AER	After-Event Review
BEM	Behavior Engineering Model
CAS	Complex Adaptive Systems
CoP	Community of Practice
CR	Corporate Responsibility
CS	Corporate Sustainability
CSH	Critical Systems Heuristics
CSR	Corporate Social Responsibility
CSV	Creating Shared Value
ECSF	European Corporate Sustainability Framework
ESD	Education for Sustainable Development
FSSD	Framework for Strategic Sustainable Development
GDP	Gross Domestic Product
GRI	Global Reporting Initiative
HR	Human Resources
HRD	Human Resources Development
HRM	Human Resources Management
ILO	International Labour Organization
ISD	Instructional Systems Design
KSA	Knowledge Skills and Attitude
LNA	Learning Needs Assessment
NEF	New Economics Foundation
NGO	Non-Governmental Organisation
OECD	Organisation for Economic Co-operation and Development
OEM	Organisational Elements Model
O-T-P	Organisation—Task—Person
POSIWID	Purpose of a System Is What It Does
RBV	Resource-Based View
ROI	Return On Investment
SCC	Social Cost of Carbon
SD	System Dynamics
SDG	Sustainable Development Goal
SES	Socio-environmental System
SFL	Sustainability-Focused Learning

SHRM	Strategic Human Resource Management
SNA	Social Network Analysis
TBL	Triple Bottom Line
UNCED	United Nations Conference on Environment and Development
UNCHE	United Nations Conference on the Human Environment
UNCSD	United Nations Conference on Sustainable Development
UNEP	United Nations Environment Programme
UNESCO	United Nations Education, Scientific and Cultural Organization
UNSD	United Nations Sustainable Development
VSM	Viable System Model
VUCA	Volatility, Uncertainty, Complexity, Ambiguity
WCED	World Commission on Environment and Development

Introduction

Why this book?

In the 1950s, as the global mayhem of World War 2 started to fade into history, the industrialised countries around whom the conflict had centred started to use the technologies developed as weapons of war to build peacetime economies. Cars, aeroplanes, telephones, nuclear power, exotic chemicals—all of these and more fed the baby boom generation, and as the years of apparent peace continued, there developed a sense that things could only get better.

By the early years of the 21st century, enough data had been gathered about global human activity to be able to construct a number of graphs which showed how the 1950s marked a noticeable turning point in human impact on planet Earth. The so-called "hockey stick" curves in these graphs showed a dramatic increase in such things as the number of journeys taken by motor vehicles, the use of telephones, the amount of fertilisers being used on agricultural land, and of course, the levels of carbon dioxide in the atmosphere. What has become known as the "Great Acceleration" had started.[1]

Ever-increasing numbers are not a problem where tending to infinity is a mathematical possibility, but this is not the case on a finite sphere of rock moving through the universe. The Earth has a limited quantity of natural resources in terms of the raw materials which can be extracted in order to keep economic and technological development progressing in the way the Great Acceleration is seeing. Although the use of renewable energy sources has shown a way in which one of these limitations may possibly be (temporarily) overcome, these technologies rely on the extraction of raw materials which are themselves in limited supply.

At the same time, there is an increasing awareness that while economic and technological development may have been effective in helping to overcome many of the traditional problems which humanity has faced in living on the Earth, such as keeping warm and ensuring sufficient food supplies, the methods used to enable this to happen have started to cause problems of their own. Climate change is "widespread, rapid and intensifying" according to an Intergovernmental Panel on Climate Change (IPCC) report in August 2021.[2] Atmospheric pollution caused by burning fossil fuels causes lung disease and reduces life expectancy, even in wealthy countries, where at the end of the 20th century, people are starting to take it for granted that they would live longer and longer as time went by. Then, in 2020 came the COVID-19 pandemic. Although at the time of writing the origins of the virus are still not clear, there is strong evidence that it is an indirect result of environmental degradation, resulting from the same activities that led to diseases such as AIDS, SARS and Ebola crossing the species divide into humans.[3]

DOI: 10.4324/9781003218296-1

Although the social and environmental impacts of increased economic activity have been apparent in poorer parts of the world for decades, Western societies, perhaps drugged by the comforts that technology offers, have been largely complacent about this trend. For a long time, concerns about environmental degradation were limited to often disparaged "environmentalists" and minority publications such as Rachel Carson's *Silent Spring* and Ernst Schumacher's *Small is Beautiful*. Concerns about the negative impact of technology on societies were dismissed as left-wing grumbling by the increasingly confident neoliberal political economists of the late 20th century. However, as guardians of global concern, the United Nations had long recognised the growing nature of these concerns, and in 1987 its landmark publication *Our Common Future* propelled the word "sustainability" into greater prominence, articulating the idea that present generations have a responsibility to ensure that planet Earth can continue to be enjoyed by people in succeeding generations.

If there is one positive thing which can come out of the COVID-19 pandemic, it may be that populations in Western countries as a whole may start to realise that the economic systems we depend on are not resilient, and that when environmental factors start to challenge the underlying assumptions on which they operate everyday life stops operating in the easy way that has come to be expected.

The technological and resulting social developments of the last 70 years have been the result of organised economic activity driven by a wide range of organisations—private sector businesses developing technologies for profit, public sector organisations providing public goods, and various governmental and non-governmental entities working towards developing and monitoring frameworks which aim to protect societies from problems caused by these developments.

But many public and private sector organisations are starting to recognise connections between what they do and the growing challenges in social and environmental matters and are considering what they can do to operate more sustainably. An increasing number of businesses see sustainability as their core purpose, existing to develop renewable energy systems, exploring ways to remove plastic waste from the oceans, or developing synthetic alternatives to meat, for example. Many businesses are embracing sustainability as an incentive to change existing business practices, although others feel obliged to operate more sustainably as a result of increasing regulatory pressures or customer demand. In some cases, pressures for sustainability may come from the organisation's workforce itself. For some businesses, sustainability presents an existential threat: what will oil companies do when we are no longer allowed to burn fossil fuels?

Whatever the motivation, a common factor in all these organisations is recognising the need for change, or more precisely, adaptation to acquire a better fit within a new environment. Adaptation requires learning, learning to see how the business landscape is changing, learning why this is so, learning how to design, implement and evaluate strategies for adaptation. And of course, organisations are essentially groups of people, so what organisations learn to do is a result of what their people learn.

The aim of this book is to draw together two primary strands of thinking, first about sustainability and what this means and implies, and second about learning within organisations. Given the complexity of the discourse around sustainability, the content here is perhaps superficial but is presented as a starter in the subject for those who wish to develop an understanding of the basics. It is also hoped that this coverage provides a synthesis of the various dimensions within sustainability that are often discussed separately and helps to explain the complexity and interconnected nature of social and environmental sustainability. I then use systems thinking concepts and tools to tie these strands together, both as a way of sense-making and as a tool to help develop an appropriate learning strategy.

The coverage on learning is more detailed, as currently little has been written to help people working in the learning and development field address sustainability. There are many books about learning in organisations, how to design training, how to be a better trainer, how to facilitate learning, and so on, but the focus of much of this literature is often on how to promote learning within organisations operating within a frame of reference established by the political and economic systems which have contributed to the Great Acceleration. As I, along with many other far better qualified and more informed writers have suggested, the big question is whether we can ensure the sustainability of human existence by continuing with these norms, or if we need to change completely our way of thinking about the world and what we value about our existence. This is a major challenge at governmental level, as shown by the difficulties democracies currently face in addressing environmental concerns in a way which does not create a significant populist backlash. The challenge will be little different within organisations, where managers may have to think long and hard about implementing sustainability-oriented practices which threaten actual or potential job security. As these tensions show, a transition to sustainability is only partly a technical problem—as the iceberg metaphor tells us, most of the iceberg is hidden below water level, and with learning about sustainability the biggest challenges are dealing with what lies hidden in people's heads, their values, their philosophies of existence and their moral compass.

What I have to say about developing a learning strategy may seem somewhat different from other discussions about how to do this. For one thing systems thinking has not been used in this subject before to any great extent. Second, it draws on some ideas which do not seem to be explored very much in Human Resource Development (HRD) practice, primarily because learning about sustainability is significantly different from learning about a new product, service or process: it concerns an existential issue, existential to both organisations and humanity. One key idea is that our reality is actually a social construction, a proposal of the two American-Austrian sociologists Peter Berger and Thomas Luckmann in the 1960s. This means that our understanding of the world around us is shaped by social factors—which we can change if we wish. Another key idea comes from the work of the German critical philosopher Jürgen Habermas, whose theory of communicative action gave me both a framework which helped me to understand how different approaches to learning within organisations acknowledge (or not) the needs and interests of employees as members of a wider community and also contributed to some fundamentally important developments within systems thinking.

These alternative ideas seemed important because addressing sustainability means that we need to question the underlying assumptions on which current organisational practices, our societies and economies are based. As Thomas Kuhn saw it, we must embrace a paradigm shift. This has implications for HRD, which must also move to a new paradigm about learning and development, as its old methods may no longer be relevant in the coming world. In Kuhn's words:

> The transition from a paradigm in crisis to a new one from which a new tradition of normal science can emerge is far from a cumulative process, one achieved by an articulation or extension of the old paradigm. Rather it is a reconstruction of the field from new fundamentals, a reconstruction that changes some of the field's most elementary theoretical generalisations as well as many of its paradigm methods and applications. During the transition period there will be a large but never complete

overlap between the problems that can be solved by the old and by the new paradigm. But there will also be a decisive difference in the modes of solution.[4]

Modes of solutions for facilitating learning about sustainability-focused practice may therefore be significantly different than what we are used to at the moment. Of course, facilitating some learning may be relatively straightforward: learning how to operate in a way which reduces waste and pollution makes sense within existing ways of looking at business. But other aspects may be more problematic, particularly where learning has to challenge attitudes antagonistic to sustainability, for example where people are sceptical about the existence of climate change, or the relevance of the work they do to abstract concepts such as social equity. For these reasons, I spend some time in this book thinking about social factors which can influence learning, recognising that most of the learning we do is through our interactions with other people, and that how we see ourselves as social beings in our various communities, both inside and outside the workplace, has an important influence on how well we react to learning opportunities and change our behaviour.

Who is this book for?

I wrote this book with two particular groups of people in mind. The first group are those involved in general learning and development activities within and for organisations, for example, HRD professionals. I include myself in this group, as someone who has been commissioned to develop learning programmes on subjects as wide ranging as using new computer systems to process unemployment benefit payments through to how to survive being taken hostage by terrorist groups, with programmes on climate change and afforestation along the way (to give me some credibility in the subject of this book). If you are in this group you may have a good understanding of how to promote learning but may want to learn more about sustainability. For you, the initial chapters on sustainability, political economy and how organisations address sustainability issues will be of particular interest. However, because organisational sustainability requires a more or less dramatic change in the philosophy and value system of organisations and the people who work in them, you may find that you need to adopt more radical pedagogical ideas than you have worked with before, and so may find the sections on critical and transformative learning of value.

The second group of people who may be interested in this book are sustainability professionals who are engaged by organisations to help them implement sustainability strategies. For you, the chapters that may be of most interest are those which deal with facilitating learning within organisations. The chapters on sustainability and the political economy of sustainability may contain material with which you are more familiar, but there may be content with which you disagree. That is quite possible and even valuable: as is explained in the sections on critical learning, exploring areas of disagreement is fundamentally important to helping people review their mental models about how the world works. (The critical reader may see this as a sly, consultant's trick to provide excuses for unintentional errors—that may be true as well.)

How is the book structured?

There are broadly two parts to this book (Figure I.1). Chapters 1–4 explore sustainability itself. Chapter 1 provides a background to the development of the sustainability concept and outlines key themes which it embraces. As is discussed in Chapter 1, a central issue within the sustainability debate is the role of the economic system and how it has contributed to our current world. It is therefore useful to examine political economy as it relates to sustainability in more detail, and this is covered in Chapter 3. Chapter 4 then considers sustainability as it applies to organisational practice. Sitting within this first half of the book is Chapter 2, which introduces the subject of systems thinking, relevant within both discussions about sustainability and as a way of helping to develop learning strategies.

Chapters 5–11 focus on learning. The first four of these chapters look at four different aspects of a learning strategy, essentially explaining how to carry out a sustainability-focused learning (SFL) needs assessment. This is followed by a chapter on how to use this information to write a strategy. The book concludes with a chapter on how to evaluate the effectiveness of the strategy, and then a final chapter reflecting on key ideas that have emerged.

The book is therefore highly interdisciplinary, drawing on research in many different disciplines as well as from practical experience. This raises some problems of terminology, and I have tried where possible to point out where different disciplines use different languages to discuss the same subject. For example, the idea of a socially constructed reality leads to alternative names such as frames of reference, mental models and worldview, which are all somewhat similar. I offer my apologies for mistakes which have gone undetected.

Let us briefly look at each chapter in more detail. Chapter 1 looks at sustainability itself, starting with a historical review of how the modern concept of sustainability has developed, culminating in the Sustainable Development Goals (SDGs) of 2015. This leads on to an examination of the challenge of defining sustainability. While the 1987 World Commission on Environment and Development provided an initial definition of sustainability to which many people refer, things become much more complicated when people seek to define it in terms of specific areas of interest, meaning that there are dozens of other, not necessarily consistent, definitions. The contemporary discourse around sustainability has led to an idea that there are three dimensions to sustainability, environmental, social and economic, as represented, for example, by the so-called "triple bottom line". However, this conception is in itself problematic for various reasons:

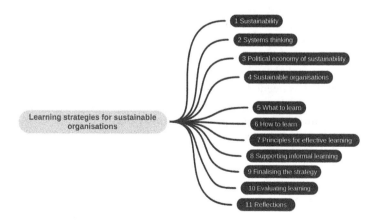

Figure I.1 Chapters in the book.

for example, there are many different explanations about what each of the three dimensions actually embraces, and also that the three-dimensional concept is not based on any actual model of sustainability (which has led to some suggestions that these dimensions are more a reductionist convenience to suit narrowly-defined academic disciplines). Each of these dimensions is examined in the context of the SDGs, in particular the relevance they have to organisational practice.

Chapter 2 introduces the key principles of systems thinking. What are the reasons for this? First, in general terms, systems thinking provides a useful perspective for looking at organisational behaviour and how learning takes place, but second, the United Nations' SDGs and the associated Education for Sustainable Development have identified systems thinking as a key competency for people to help them learn about sustainability. So as systems thinking may be unfamiliar to some readers, basic principles are introduced early in the book and these are then applied in subsequent chapters.

This chapter starts by explaining what I mean by a "system", and introduces the powerful idea of being able to look at any situation and considering it as a system in order to see what new understandings that may bring. It examines the three key principles of systems thinking, understanding the importance of interrelationships, appreciating multiple perspectives about a situation, and recognising the importance of boundary judgements (decisions about what is or is not significant) that are made regarding the situation being considered. The discussion of multiple perspectives allows us to look at different worldviews about sustainability, in particular the distinction between anthropocentric and ecocentric perspectives and the various refinements that there can be within these. This examination of perspectives also looks at an important, underpinning idea that systems thinking draws on, that our understanding of the reality within which we live is "socially constructed", that it is shaped by our lived experience—being aware of this creates up the possibility that we can think about situations from different perspectives and through different filters. The fundamental importance of these concepts throughout the book is highlighted through some "key ideas" boxes.

Systems thinking makes a heavy reliance on diagrams, simple illustrations of what we and others perceive to be happening in a situation of interest. How to use diagrams is explained through considering a case study, the story of Sheffield City Council's tree maintenance activities between 2014 and 2018. The chapter then considers some other relevant issues, such as purpose, the distinction between closed and open systems, the importance of being able to see sustainability as an example of a wicked problem, and the potential for new understandings created by complexity theory. Systems thinkers use diagrams to help with thinking (as a heuristic device), and it is therefore important to point out that they are often incomplete or inaccurate—and that there is actually value in these deficiencies. To remind readers of the reflective origins and purpose of these diagrams, I have used hand-drawn diagrams throughout, a technique which also shows how little artistic ability is needed to be a systems thinking diagrammer.

This chapter concludes by looking at three different systems thinking tools. The first of these is system dynamics, important in this context partly because of its centrality within one of the key early texts on sustainability, *The Limits to Growth*,[5] and partly because the causal flow diagrams on which it relies can often provide a useful heuristic for thinking about situations of interest. The second tool is the Viable System Model (VSM), a cybernetic way of looking at organisational behaviour and which is of particular value here because it provides a way of identifying what topics may need to be addressed in a sustainability-focused learning strategy. Third, we look at Critical

Systems Heuristics (CSH), a tool developed primarily to explore boundary judgements being made within a systems thinking investigation. CSH is of primary importance in this book because I am going to conceive of an SFL strategy as a system, and as such will need to make boundary judgements about what learning is important, what learning methodologies may or may not be significant, and what pedagogical principles could or should be deployed. Such a comprehensive examination also makes it a central tool within the evaluation of subsequent learning.

A key idea in systems thinking is that a system exists in an environment which influences the behaviour of the system, so it is important to look carefully at the environment within which organisations operate, which is determined primarily by factors of political economy. Chapter 3 considers two perspectives on political economy: neoclassical (and in its more recent incarnation, neoliberal) economics as a system of political economy which has had a profound influence on the progress of the Great Acceleration; and sustainability economics, which embraces a range of ideas including the Green New Deal in its various guises, the debate between proponents of sustainable growth and steady-state economics, and ideas such as the circular economy and doughnut economics.

Having explored the environment provided by the political economy, Chapter 4 looks at how organisations are responding to pressures to operate more sustainably. This starts by examining organisations as systems and briefly describes the history of the concept of organisational sustainability. It then considers what benefits organisations may derive from operating more sustainably, and this leads to an examination of the drivers for implementing sustainability strategies. This analysis draws on several different fields of organisational theory, as each provides a different perspective which helps us to identify organisational learning requirements. Having introduced the idea of the three dimensions of sustainability in Chapter 1, we can now look at how these are relevant in an organisational setting. Environmental sustainability is perhaps the easiest to consider and is by some way the dimension of sustainability which has received the most attention in research and other writing. Social and economic sustainability present, in certain ways, more difficulties for organisations. Economic sustainability is often reduced to simple profitability, and social sustainability raises potentially problematic issues about working practices, power relationships and social equity. The chapter concludes by looking at strategies that organisations can use to move towards more sustainable practice and how progress can be assessed. This provides an opportunity to look at the relevance of the study of organisational learning in the context of sustainability and introduces the valuable concepts of single and double loop learning. This enables us to present a simple level model of organisational sustainability that we can use as an input to the development of a learning strategy.

Chapter 5 starts the process of looking at how to develop an SFL strategy. The first step is to reflect on boundary judgements that are often made about learning strategies, judgements that often have their roots in an organisational culture shaped by the prevailing political economy. This chapter points out the importance of going beyond the usual technical focus of formal learning within organisations and the importance of including critical perspectives. To this end, this chapter shows how the boundary judgement questions of CSH (introduced in Chapter 2) can help us to reflect on what assumptions we may be (justifiably or erroneously) making at an initial stage.

The chapter continues by explaining that we can look at a learning strategy as having three components, such as the content of the learning, the mechanisms that will be deployed and the pedagogical principles that will be required. Chapter 5 focuses on identifying content, and to do this uses the VSM introduced in Chapter 2. Here the three-level model of organisational sustainability proposed in Chapter 4 helps us to see what differences there may be across organisations with different levels of engagement with sustainability.

In Chapter 6, we move on to looking at what learning mechanisms may be of relevance in an SFL strategy. Institutional learning governance structures such as HRD departments often restrict their interest to formal, directed learning activity such as training, but a systemic lens shows that organisational learning happens through many different modalities such as informal, incidental and self-directed, amongst others, which may flourish in the absence of any support or formal governance. Regardless of what learning mechanism operates, the quality of SFL may be affected by a wide range of factors, ranging from the contested understanding about what sustainability is, through the nature of the organisation's general and learning-specific culture, through group dynamic factors such as social capital and the learning transfer climate, down to the individual level where personal attributes, social identity and faith systems may be important.

Chapter 7 continues the process of assessing learning needs by thinking about pedagogical principles which may be important. As discussed previously, learning how to operate more sustainably goes beyond developing the technical skills of the workforce, and may involve helping people to reflect on what values sustainable practice represents, and what impact this may have on individuals and their personal value framework and sense of social identity. To do this this chapter looks at some key ideas in adult learning, such as andragogy, transformative learning and critical thinking. This chapter also looks at how these might be integrated into formal learning activities.

Chapter 8 concludes the process of assessing learning needs by looking at how support can be provided to encourage informal learning, using methods such as action learning, games and simulations, communities of practice and after-event reviews. We also look at how Human Resource Management can play a part in strengthening the learning culture for sustainability within an organisation.

The shortest chapter in the book, Chapter 9 draws on the framework of boundary judgement questions developed in Chapters 5–8 to create a checklist which can be used to inform the writing of a formal SFL strategy.

Concluding the learning and development cycle, Chapter 10 looks at the challenges involved in evaluating SFL activities. Starting from a critique of existing processes for evaluating training which are primarily focused on internal consequences and often ignore the external and possibly unintended consequences of learning activities, this chapter considers ways in which systems thinking can enhance evaluation and also serve to continue the process of learning about sustainability. Overall, the process of evaluation is based on CSH and the boundary judgements developed in previous chapters.

As a final chapter, Chapter 11 is about reflection and considers this at two levels. First, it reflects on key subjects from the book: the three dimensions of sustainability, the use of Habermas' theory of communicative action in thinking about ways in which learning happens, the value of recognising our everyday reality as socially constructed and how we have used systems thinking. Second, it looks at the importance of reflection itself in the process of learning, pointing out its central role in experiential concepts of learning and in making the shift from single to double loop learning. It also notes how reflection is often overlooked in performative approaches to learning.

Time for reflection

Throughout this book, I have included "Time for reflection" boxes.

In these boxes, you will find questions asking you to reflect on what you have just read, to compare it with your experience, or to see whether or not you agree with what I have written.

The idea of these is to encourage reflection as a way of helping you make sense of the subject.

Notes

1 Will Steffen et al., 'The Trajectory of the Anthropocene: The Great Acceleration', *The Anthropocene Review* 2, no. 1 (2015): 81–98.
2 IPCC, 'Climate Change Widespread, Rapid, and Intensifying', 2021, https://www.ipcc.ch/2021/08/09/ar6-wg1-20210809-pr/.
3 Richard Kock, 'Drivers of Disease Emergence and Spread: Is Wildlife to Blame?', *Onderstepoort Journal of Veterinary Research* 81, no. 2 (2014): 1–4; Katherine F. Smith et al., 'Global Rise in Human Infectious Disease Outbreaks', Journal of The Royal Society Interface 11, no. 101 (2014): 5.
4 Thomas Kuhn, *The Structure of Scientific Revolutions* (Chicago: University of Chicago Press, 1962), 85.
5 Donella H. Meadows et al., *The Limits to Growth* (London: Potomac Associates, 1972).

1 Sustainability

Development of a concept

When the last tree has been cut down,
the last fish caught,
the last river poisoned,
only then will we realize that one cannot eat money.

Saying attributed to native American culture

1.1 What this chapter covers

The aim of this chapter is to provide a grounding into what sustainability means and how the idea has emerged (Figure 1.1). It starts by tracing the history of the sustainability concept, looking at its origins in concerns about economic development in post-colonial countries which led to the engagement of the United Nations system, and parallel concerns in the scientific and environmentalist communities. It then looks at the problems which have been found in trying to define what sustainability might mean, and examines the three dimensions of sustainability, environmental, social and economic.

1.2 How a modern understanding of sustainability emerged

We start the story of how a modern understanding of sustainability emerged around the time of the Reformation in England. It is 1533. Henry VIII, King of England, is worried. He is worried about the long-term future of the nation's hemp crop. He is not interested in hemp's mood-altering properties that could take his mind off the problems of producing a male heir to the throne. He is worried because hemp is a vitally important raw material in ship construction, for ropes and sails, and England needs to build

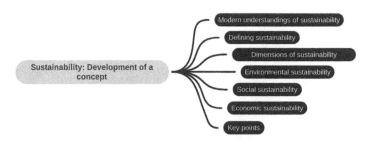

Figure 1.1 Map of Chapter 1.

DOI: 10.4324/9781003218296-2

a navy so that it can defend itself against the threatening maritime states of France and Spain. So he passes a law to make hemp cultivation a legal requirement: farmers will have to set aside about 1/10 hectare for growing flax or hemp; otherwise, they would be subject to a large fine.[1]

We do not know if the discussions at court used the word "sustainability", but this is what the issue at question is: ensuring that future generations of English people would be safe. This story shows that sustainability has a long history (and it also shows that English Europhobia goes back many centuries, but that is for another book). Concerns about sustainability of course go back to the beginning of humanity's existence: hunter-gatherers moved from one place to another as game became harder to find; early agricultural communities moved onwards as they exhausted one area of land; settled communities looked for ways to keep the land on which they depended for existence fertile.

Figure 1.2 shows a timeline for key developments in the sustainability discourse.

As time progressed the 18th century saw concerns in Germany about maintaining sustainable forestry yields to support the silver-smelting industry[2] and discussions by moral philosophers such as Adam Smith and John Stuart Mill about whether the economic changes they could see in their worlds might have negative implications for the fabric of society.[3] Writing *Capital* in the late 19th century, Karl Marx discussed the importance of protecting the natural environment for future generations:

> Even an entire society, a nation, or all simultaneously existing societies taken together, are not owners of the earth, they are simply its possessors, its beneficiaries,

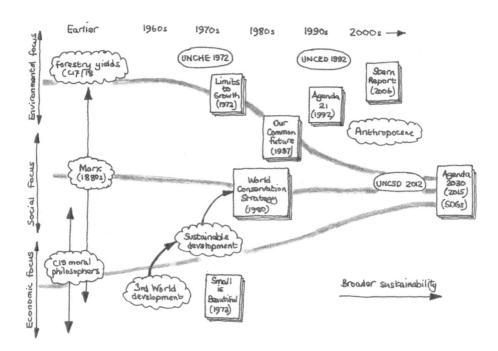

Figure 1.2 Timeline showing the development of the concept of sustainability.

and have to bequeath it in an improved state to succeeding generations as *boni patres familias* [good heads of the household].[4]

Marx was also keenly interested in soil fertility and wrote about the impact of the English industrial revolution on the long-term future of agricultural land. He recognised that moving people from an agricultural life into industrial employment would lead to people forgetting the importance of circulating natural waste back into the soil to enrich it:

> Capitalist production, by collecting the population in great centres, and causing an ever increasing preponderance of town population, on the one hand concentrates the historical motive-power of society; on the other hand, it disturbs the circulation of matter between man and the soil, i.e., prevents the return to the soil of its elements consumed by man in the form of food and clothing; it therefore violates the conditions necessary to lasting fertility of the soil.[5]

Present-day Marxist writers translate "circulation of matter" as the "metabolic rift", "... the material estrangement of human beings in capitalist society from the natural conditions of their existence".[6]

In more recent times, an interest in sustainability issues emerged in the 1960s, stimulated by such events as the impact of photographs of planet Earth taken during the Apollo programme and of environmentally aware publications such as Rachel Carson's 1961 *Silent Spring*.[7] This was also the period of decolonisation, and as the 1960s and 1970s progressed, there came increasing concerns about the social and economic development of what was then called "the Third World". As industrialisation spread around the world the negative environmental impacts that this created became more significant, and out of this discourse, the phrase "sustainable development" emerged.

Awareness of environmental degradation was also growing in the developed world. The problem of acid rain falling on Scandinavia in the 1960s caused by industrial pollution from the United Kingdom proved to be an important spark in the United Nations' engagement in sustainability.[8] The acid rain crisis prompted the Swedish government to introduce a resolution to the United Nations' General Assembly in 1968 calling for a conference on environmental matters, and the resulting 1972 United Nations Conference on the Human Environment (UNCHE) in Stockholm was the first international conference focusing on the environment. It led to the creation of the United Nations Environment Programme (UNEP) and initiated political processes which ultimately led to the establishment of the World Commission on Environment and Development (WCED) (also known as the Brundtland Commission). In 1987, the WCED published the report *Our Common Future*, a particularly significant moment in the evolution of the sustainability concept as it provided what is often seen as the basic definition of sustainability: sustainable development is "development that meets the needs of the present without compromising the ability of future generations to meet their own needs".[9]

The 1992 United Nations Conference on Environment and Development (UNCED) in Rio de Janeiro, popularly known as the "Earth Summit", led to the publication of *Agenda 21*, which was an attempt at establishing a framework for global sustainable development. It led to the development of international standard ISO 14001 covering sustainable development which requires organisations to develop and implement management systems that continually reduce environmental impacts.[10] Twenty years after

UNCED, the United Nations Conference on Sustainable Development (UNCSD), or Rio+20, was held, again in Rio de Janeiro. An outcome of Rio+20 was a decision to convene a working group which eventually published *Agenda 2030*,[11] which defined the Sustainable Development Goals (SDGs).

There are 17 SDGs (Figure 1.3), the first 16 of which address sectoral issues and the final one looks at partnerships needed to enable achievement of the other goals. Within the SDGs, there is a clear attempt to address the range of social, economic and environmental issues associated with the development and to highlight the interlinkages between sectors and issues. Each goal is broken down into a number of targets, which both help to make tackling the goals less daunting and create flexibility so that countries can adapt them to their particular context.[12] They also make it a little easier to see connections between the sectoral goals, which is useful as the official presentation of the SDGs provides little discussion about their systemic interactions.[13]

The SDGs have been well received and praised for making a significant step forward in addressing both social and environmental aspects of sustainability, and for, albeit in a limited way, recognising the complex interactions between these dimensions. However, in the words of one major review of the SDGs, while "ambitious and aspirational", they are "... necessary but not sufficient to lead humanity towards long-term sustainable development".[14] One reason offered for this is that they do not challenge the power structures and systems of political economy which have contributed to the damaging global dynamics which operate in the early 21st century: for example, they still focus on the importance of economic growth (Goal 8) as a means for achieving the goals.[15] In that respect, they have been described as representing a contemporary, institutional interpretation of sustainable development, based on a somewhat unquestioning acceptance of contemporary neoliberal political economy.[16] There is a more detailed discussion about neoclassical and neoliberal perspectives on sustainability and economic growth in Chapter 3, Section 3.3.2.

As well as this history of sustainability in the intergovernmental system, there is another timeline involving concerned practitioners and academics. In 1972, *The Ecologist* magazine dedicated a whole issue to its *Blueprint for Survival* manifesto, a strategy for a sustainable society (in fact, one of the earliest uses of the term in this context) which

Figure 1.3 The 17 Sustainable Development Goals.

would cause minimum disruption to ecological processes, conserve materials and energy, enable a stable population, and create "… a social system in which the individual can enjoy, rather than feel restricted by, the first three conditions".[17] It also offered, 50 years before the COVID-19 pandemic, the prescient warning that:

> Not only is it increasingly difficult to control the vectors of disease, but it is more than probable that urban populations are being insidiously weakened by overall pollution levels… At the same time international mobility speeds the spread of disease. With this background… could easily provoke a series of epidemics—and we cannot say with confidence that we would be able to cope with them.[18]

This period also saw the publication of Ernst Schumacher's influential *Small Is Beautiful*, which drew on ideas from Buddhism and the writings of Gandhi to question the pursuit of material prosperity, the dehumanisation of modern industrial work, and to propose "production by the masses" through appropriate uses of technology rather than by mass production.[19]

In 1970, Hasan Ozbekhan, a member of the Club of Rome, a group of former heads of state, senior United Nations officials and other professionals, wrote a paper entitled *The Predicament of Mankind*,[20] which identified, as an "illustrative" list, 49 "continuous critical problems" faced by humanity. These ranged from "Explosive population growth with consequent escalation of social, economic, and other problems", through to "Insufficient understanding of Continuous Critical Problems, of their nature, their interactions and of the future consequences both they and current solutions to them are generating".[21]

The paper served as an invitation for consultancy groups to develop a "dynamic computerised model" which could explore the implications of the continuous critical problems over time. The successful proposal was submitted by Jay Forrester at the Massachusetts Institute of Technology (MIT), and the subsequent research led to the publication of *The Limits to Growth* in 1972. The MIT project combined the mathematical modelling technique of systems dynamics[22] with nascent computer technology to develop a sophisticated model of how they perceived the world's economy and its associated environments to operate, and after several iterations arrived at what they called the World3 model.[23] They entered assumptions about how the economy operated into World3 and ran it so that it predicted how different aspects of the economy would behave until the year 2100.

World3 was designed to produce graphs showing the output levels of eight variables over the period from 1900 to 2100. The variables were population, industrial output per capita, food per capita, pollution (compared to 1970 levels) and non-renewable resources (as a fraction of 1900 reserves), birth rates, death rates and level of services (health and education). Perhaps the most illuminating output from the model comes from the so-called "standard run", where input variables are based on human values and the functioning of the population-capital system as it was viewed in the 1970s. The results were not encouraging for the future of humanity—"The basic behavior mode of the world system is exponential growth of population and capital, followed by collapse".[24] There would be a collapse in industrial output by about 2030 because natural resources would have been depleted by that stage. Prior to that an increasing amount of capital resources would have been expended on increasingly expensive resource extraction, leading to little availability for food production or future growth. The global population would continue to rise until the middle of the 21st century, at which point it would start to drop dramatically because of food shortages. The model was run with different input variables, such as assuming greater resource availability, new technological developments and birth control measures severely reducing population growth. One model (Stabilised World Model II) predicted some stability but this relied on applying these restrictions by 1975. Delaying introduction to 2000 led to another collapse scenario, albeit less dramatic than in the standard run.

The phenomenon of slow growth followed by sudden collapse is not a new observation: the Roman writer Seneca observed that "… increases are of sluggish growth, but the way to ruin is rapid".[25] The American anthropologist and historian Joseph Tainter noted that this trajectory may be seen in the history of many earlier civilisations.[26] As they became more sophisticated, the complexity of keeping society together required more and more investment in resources such as administration, defence and education, but as time went by the marginal rate of return for this investment deteriorated until it became too expensive (as also predicted by World3). At this point, societies started to fracture as people became disaffected, and just small disturbances could trigger a sudden collapse. Tainter notes that this experience accords with cyclical understandings of time, as in Hinduism and Buddhism, but that it does not suit the linear expectations of creation-based monotheistic societies at all. He therefore stresses the importance of understanding the history of civilisations, echoing the Spanish philosopher George Santayana's famous aphorism: "Those who cannot remember the past are condemned to repeat it".[27]

Time for reflection

What are your thoughts about humanity's current trajectory? Where do you think we might be on the World3 projection?

What aspects of Tainter's ideas about complexity, if any, can you see emerging in our current reality?

The Limits to Growth was hugely influential with environmentally concerned groups, but economists and industrial lobbies who felt threatened by its projections quickly reacted with a sustained campaign of agnotology. This was similar to what had happened to Rachel Carson and her writing a decade earlier about the dangers of DDT, and, years later, to how the tobacco industry ridiculed health concerns by the anti-smoking lobby and to how in the early 21st century the fossil fuel industry supports a climate change denial lobby.[28]

However, as data has continued to be gathered in the early 21st century and concern about environmental degradation has started to strengthen, interest in *The Limits to Growth* has revived. A number of studies comparing its predictions with current data have reported close correlations with *The Limits to Growth* standard run in a number of the variables, in particular, population, birth and death rates and industrial output.[29] Levels of food supplies and non-renewable resources are slightly higher than predicted and pollution slightly less. Although correlations vary, the differences are not great, and the trends shown by contemporary data are in line with *The Limits to Growth* predictions, leading to a conclusion that:

> Based simply on the comparison of observed data and the LtG scenarios presented above, and given the significantly better alignment with the standard run scenario than the other two scenarios, it would appear that the global economy and population is on the cusp of collapse.[30]

One clear weakness in the World3 model is that it failed to anticipate the importance of greenhouse gas emissions and their impact on the climate. However, whether this casts doubt on the validity of the World3 model or that the model simply presents a more positive view of the future than seems to be reality has not yet been established.

A more fundamental critique of *The Limits to Growth* was made by Alexander Christakis,[31] one of the original members of the Club of Rome. His criticism was based on research that he subsequently conducted into the 49 continuous critical problems and their interrelationships. In this research, he used a computer-based process for analysing dialogue to identify potential connections between the critical problems and found that the problem which seemed to be a root cause of all the other problems was CCP-18, "Growing irrelevance of traditional values and continuing failure to involve new value systems". Christakis noted that the World3 modelling process had failed to incorporate in any way the values driving the dynamics observed in the technical model, almost as if the values which drive the modern technological world are so subconsciously ingrained that they were invisible. This is an interesting observation because it shows how important bringing these values to the surface is when trying to effect any sustainability-related changes. This will be a key issue in later chapters looking at sustainability-focused learning.

While *The Limits to Growth* provided a look forward at what might happen, the dramatic graphs[32] illustrating what has come to be known as the "Great Acceleration"[33] provide a historical record of what has actually happened. Figure 1.4 shows just one of these graphs, that for primary energy use. Using data about a variety of measures of human existence starting in 1750 and continuing through to the present day, the team collecting Great Acceleration data show how there has been a dramatic increase in many of these measures since about 1950. These measures include such things as various forms of consumption, exploitation of ocean fisheries, atmospheric CO_2 levels and biodiversity, to name just a few.

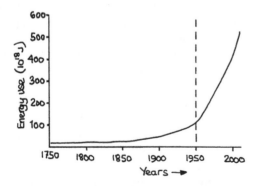

Figure 1.4 Great Acceleration graph showing primary energy use.

Another emerging theme is the increasing reference to human activity creating a new geological era, the "Anthropocene", a name coined by the stratigraphers Eugene Stoermer and Paul Crutzen.[34] There is some debate as to when the Anthropocene started, but Crutzen suggested that an appropriate date would be at the start of the British industrial revolution, specifically 1784 with the invention of the steam engine,[35] a date which aligns well with Marx's observation of the opening of the metabolic rift. An alternative suggested year is 1950, which comes from the discussions about the Great Acceleration mentioned previously,[36] and that the first atomic bomb explosions in 1945 deposited layers of previously unknown radioactive isotopes around the world, layers which will be noted by stratigraphers of the next millennium (if, of course, humanity still exists).

To summarise, there is extensive scientific evidence to suggest that human activity, particularly over the last 70 years, has caused significant and perhaps irreparable damage to the planet on which we live. We may even have been responsible for triggering what is being called the sixth mass extinction in the history of our planet.[37] Although we have not yet reached the time of planetary collapse predicted in *The Limits to Growth*, mapping contemporary evidence against its predictions shows alarming levels of correlation.[38] For example, global economic growth has slowed considerably in the last decade compared to the end of the 20th century, and the growing importance of such things as shale gas extraction and deep-sea mining for mineral extraction shows that the decades of easy access to resources may be coming to an end.[39]

However, despite intergovernmental agreements such as the 2015 Paris Agreement, the emergence of radical groups such as Extinction Rebellion and increasing media acknowledgement of a climate emergency, progress on real action remains frustratingly slow to those engaged with the subject. Perhaps the decades of material progress enjoyed by populations in Western countries have turned people into passive consumers not willing to reflect on the possibility that this may not be able to continue. Perhaps the existential nature of the dangers inherent within climate change is too difficult for people to contemplate.

A well-funded climate change denial movement has also inhibited change and has served to politicise environmental activism so that it has become associated with left-wing politics, a phenomenon noted particularly in the United Kingdom and the United States.[40] This also aligns with developing attitudes to science in general, where in the United States there is evidence that there is growing scepticism about science generally, particularly amongst people who may be described as "educated conservatives".[41]

What might change the low levels of public concern about environmental degradation? One interesting line of thought is provided by the German sociologist Ulrich Beck, who suggested that the "industrial society" of the 19th and early 20th centuries, where science developed ways to transcend nature and improve society, has been replaced by the "risk society", where the challenges we face are now largely created by scientific progress itself.[42] Environmental crises caused by climate change and the increasing numbers of zoonotic diseases associated with environmental degradation (such as COVID-19 in 2020) may be seen as examples of this.[43] Beck, reflecting that there is no "...storming of the Bastille because of the environmental destruction threatening mankind",[44] suggests that the discussion about sustainability remains expert and elitist, and that in order to develop a "cosmopolitan solidarity" within society there needs to be greater awareness about the interrelationship between social inequality and climate change.

Beck also considers how globalisation has changed the balance of power between states and corporations, commenting that transnational corporations increasingly operate like "private quasi-states" that have no democratic legitimacy and so do not have any necessary commitment to communities that they serve,[45] an important point for reflection in the context of this book. At some point, Beck speculates, an environmental crisis of sufficient proportion could precipitate an "enforced enlightenment", where the winners in capitalism would communicate and cooperate with losers (such as environmentalists), leading to a radical change in existing social and economic structures.[46]

Box 1.1

I would say that there has recently been a shift in people's mindsets, and this may be to do with the pandemic, where people are thinking more about how they operate in society, about the value of others, about people more at risk in society. So people have started to think about a broader agenda which does tie in with more general awareness about climate change.

Natalie Wilkinson, NG Bailey

As the quotation in Box 1.1 suggests, during 2020 and 2021, the COVID-19 pandemic provided a catalyst for such discussions to start to emerge, with increasing levels of media discussion about "building back better" and the need for a "green recovery".[47] As part of this movement, there is increasing use of the word "regenerative" to suggest that there is a need to improve or strengthen the world that we have, rather than to just sustain it at its current levels of degradation.

1.3 Defining sustainability

We can now move on to develop a better understanding about what sustainability means. The WCED explanation of sustainability (stated earlier) is the most commonly quoted definition, but it creates what is commonly known as a "contested concept", a term elucidated by Walter Gallie in the 1950s.[48] As this is a term which comes up quite a lot in this book, it is worth discussing this briefly, as at the outset of any learning activity about sustainability it would be essential to discuss what the term means. According to Gallie, a contested concept has four characteristics: that as a whole it signifies some valued achievement, that this achievement must be internally complex, that explanation of its value requires some discussion of its internal features, but that what constitutes value may change over time or according to the worldview of interested parties. Using this lens on sustainability, we can see that it is indeed a valued achievement, that achieving sustainability is a complex undertaking, that explaining the value of sustainability requires considerable discussion (of which this book is but one tiny part), and that ideas about sustainability continue to develop, not necessarily harmoniously.

What does that mean for us? The WCED definition of sustainability is useful but its generality makes it open to many interpretations. Complications start when people seek to define it more precisely in order to further their own arguments, and by 2007 there were already more than 300 different definitions circulating in the academic world.[49] For example, sustainability may be viewed by different actors as persistence, resilience, avoiding damage or degradation, or respecting the environment[50]—but alternatively, it could just mean stasis.[51] In the business world, sustainability is used to describe an organisation's ability to stay profitable over an extended period. Sustainability is also contested because it is dynamic, with what it requires constantly changing as background conditions change; and largely indefinite, being abstract and long-term.[52] Perceptions of environmental value are also often very different: it is valuable because it provides essential raw materials; the environment has intrinsic value so it should be protected; or it has cultural value so its degradation impoverishes society. Differing intergenerational and intragenerational perspectives also affect people's understanding about value.[53]

Further confusion arises when there is talk about "sustainable development", because "development" is also a contested concept. In one area of discussion it refers to the economic development of low-income countries, but in others, it is used to discuss some sort of change in the nature of economic activity, and in this context, it often becomes synonymous with "growth".[54] However, dictionary definitions distinguish between the two quite clearly: growth refers to an increase in size, whereas development concerns expansion and advancement. Using these definitions, sustainable development should refer to a desirable enhancement of economic activity which allocates resources towards producing products or services which are more sustainable, for example, bicycles rather than cars.[55] On the other hand, sustainable growth refers to a more general idea that economic activity can continue to expand in size: this is also a highly contested concept and is explored in more detail in Section 3.3.2. The concept of sustainable development is therefore "… something of an intellectual quagmire of contested uncertainty".[56]

Time for reflection

Before reading this part of the chapter, what was your understanding of sustainability?
   Has this changed at all?
   How do you think the contested nature of the concept may affect attempts to help people learn about sustainability?

1.4 The dimensions of sustainability

The contested nature of sustainability emerges in its full glory when we consider what are often referred to as the "three pillars" of sustainability, economic, social and environmental. At first sight, these seem to be useful conceptualisations to help us develop a better understanding of sustainability, but when we consider them in more detail we realise the complexities that they create. So where does the idea of the three pillars come from? One analysis of the intergovernmental and academic literature[57] suggests that the first significant reference to the three dimensions came in the 1980 International Union for the Conservation of Nature's (IUCN) *World Conservation Strategy*, a report addressing then-emerging concerns about economic development and its impact on nature. The report observes, "Unless ecological considerations influence the development process along with social and economic considerations… the prospects of avoiding ecological harm and of making the best use of living resources are dim".[58]

Subsequent intergovernmental publications have continued the reification of the three-dimensional construct. For example, in 1992, *Agenda 21* stated that governmental decision-making should "... achieve the progressive integration of economic, social and environmental issues in the pursuit of development that is economically efficient, socially equitable and responsible and environmentally sound".[59] The ILO's guidelines on a just transition to sustainable economies defines sustainable development as having "three dimensions—economic, social and environmental—which are interrelated, of equal importance and must be addressed together".[60]

As the discourse based on the three-dimensional construct has developed, so has the number of ways in which it may be presented as a visual metaphor. This includes representation as intersecting or nested circles, as a three-legged stool or as three pillars, the latter being commonly used in United Nations literature. However, metaphors conceal as well as reveal. Bounded circles imply a clarity about what each contains (which does not exist), stool legs and pillars suggest that each could stand on its own, whereas without environmental sustainability there can be no economy or society.[61] A more recent metaphor is that of the three dimensions being an ongoing, interleaved, triple helix,[62] an interesting representation because this introduces the time dimension, that as time progresses the strands weave in and out of each other, interacting and affecting each other.

The three-dimensional understanding of sustainability seems to have emerged somewhat by chance and not through any specific theoretical framework, although each of the three dimensions is clearly recognisable in, for example, *The Limits to Growth* World3 system dynamics model. It is surprising that even though the discourse around sustainability constantly refers to the interconnections between social, environmental and economic factors, that the most popular metaphors for sustainability have such reductionist qualities. Such metaphors may be convenient for academic research with each dimension fitting neatly into a discrete field of study, but this does not necessarily help with understanding sustainability as a holistic concept.

With these concerns in mind, we can continue by looking at the dimensions in more detail.

1.5 Environmental sustainability

So much has been written about environmental sustainability that it can be difficult to pull it all together into some meaningful narrative. This section highlights a few of the most significant publications of the past two decades.

Based on a comprehensive review of multiple independent studies, the 2019 UNEP report *Global Environment Outlook GEO-6* says that the following risks are well established:

- Climate change "... poses a serious challenge to future economic development", and "... poses risks to human societies through impacts on food, and water security..., and on human security, health, livelihoods and infrastructure".[63]
- Resource depletion, "... the grades of most mined ores are in gradual decline, meaning that the most easily and economically refined ores have already been exploited".[64]
- Biodiversity "... is being eroded by land-use change, direct exploitation, climate change, pollution and invasive alien species".[65]
- Pollution is "... a major source of damage to the health of the planet (well established), human health (well established), equity (well established) and economic sustainability (established but incomplete)."[66] There are estimates "...that 80% of

all people who live in cities and 97% of urban residents in low-income and middle-income countries are exposed to air that does not meet WHO air quality guidelines. In the absence of major intervention, the air pollution death toll is projected to double by 2050".[67]

GEO-6 draws heavily on a hugely influential paper from 2009 written by Johan Rockström and others from the Stockholm Resilience Centre.[68] This paper introduced the idea of "planetary boundaries", safe levels below which interconnected "earth-system processes" should be operating (Figure 1.5). These processes are climate change, biodiversity loss, the nitrogen and phosphorus cycles, stratospheric ozone depletion, ocean acidification, global freshwater use, change in land use, atmospheric aerosol loading and chemical pollution. If levels in these systems are exceeded, they have the potential to trigger unexpected changes in interconnected subsystems, which because of their nonlinear nature could potentially have catastrophic consequences for human life.

Rockström's team concluded that by 2009, three of the planetary boundaries—climate change, the rate of biodiversity loss and interference with the nitrogen cycle—had already been crossed, and that the boundaries for global freshwater use, change in land use, ocean acidification and the phosphorus cycle were being approached. A 2015 update claimed that the boundary for changes in land use was also then close to being breached.[69]

The planetary boundaries concept presents nine distinct boundaries, but of course these are all intimately connected and mutually interdependent in different ways. What these complex relationships in practice do has been described as providing "ecosystem

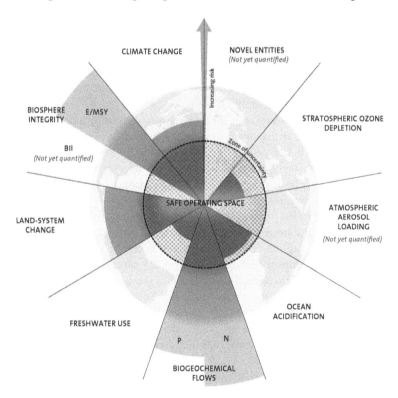

Figure 1.5 The planetary boundaries (2015 update). (Credit: J. Lokrantz/Azote based on Steffen et al. 2015.)

services", a concept developed by the Millennium Ecosystem Assessment project in the early 2000s. Building on the idea of an ecosystem as a "dynamic complex of plant, animal, and microorganism communities and the non-living environment interacting as a functional unit",[70] ecosystem services describe the benefits that these bring to humanity. Four services have been suggested:

- provisioning services such as food, water and timber
- regulating services that affect climate, water, disease and waste
- cultural services which provide recreational, spiritual and aesthetic benefits
- supporting services, including soil formation, photosynthesis and nutrient cycling.

These operate at multiple levels, so for example at a local level forested areas provide services regulating the run-off of rain—when trees are removed, as they are for creating grouse shooting moors, heavy rain pours down hillsides and floods urban settlements.[71] At a global level, the climate of North America and north-west Europe in particular is regulated by the Gulf Stream, or more technically, the Atlantic Meridional Overturning Circulation (AMOC), but as climate change appears to be slowing its flow considerably, it may in the lifetime of my grandchildren stop completely, with unpredictable and perhaps disastrous consequences for the climate of the United Kingdom.[72]

An important concept in environmental sustainability is carrying capacity, which may be defined as the maximum population of a particular species that can exist indefinitely in a particular situation. The term has been used in animal husbandry for a long time, for example in considering how many sheep or cattle can graze on a particular piece of land, and this setting was explored by Garrett Hardin[73] in 1968 in a significant paper entitled *The tragedy of the commons*. Hardin's paper considered how common grazing land was used: each individual farmer would benefit by increasing the number of their animals grazing the land, so numbers would increase until the carrying capacity of the common grazing was exceeded, at which point everyone would start to suffer. It is not hard to see how this analysis can apply on a global scale.

Avoiding the tragedy of the commons is the major socio-environmental question of the current day. Answers to the question inevitably are shaped by worldviews. For example, Hardin's own personal beliefs led him to state that the solution was to restrict the "freedom to breed",[74] a position which has made the paper understandably controversial. Another example comes from Bali, where rice, the staple crop, is grown in a series of paddy fields which cascade down from the mountainous centre of the island to the coast. Regulating the flow of water as rainfall comes and goes is therefore crucial, but this is managed effectively through the *subak* system, where priests and farmers along the length of a watercourse cooperate to regulate the flow of water to ensure that everyone's fields receive adequate water. An attempt to introduce a technical solution to replace the *subak* system based on the principles of the Green Revolution in the late 1970s led to a collapse of rice production and great suffering. As with Christakis' observations on the failure of *The Limits to Growth* to take value systems into consideration, this development project overlooked the fundamental value of altruism which drives Balinese agriculture.[75]

The SDGs provide a useful way to bring together a coherent summary of what environmental sustainability means. Although the SDGs have been presented in a way which deliberately integrates economic, social and environmental concerns, it is possible to identify individual goal targets which have a strong environmental perspective. Table 1.1 represents my interpretation of which of the SDGs may be seen as pertaining to environmental sustainability.

Table 1.1 Environmental sustainability targets in the SDGs

SDG	Target related to environmental sustainability
2 End hunger	2.3 Double agricultural productivity.
	2.4 Ensure sustainable and resilient food production systems.
	2.5 Maintain genetic diversity of agricultural resources.
3 Ensure healthy lives	3.9 Reduce exposure to hazardous chemicals and pollution.
6 Sustainable water management and sanitation	6.1 Access to safe and affordable drinking water.
	6.2 Adequate and equitable sanitation.
	6.3 Improved water quality.
	6.4 Improved efficiency of water usage.
	6.5 Integrated water resource management.
	6.6 Protection of water-related ecosystems.
7 Access to sustainable energy	7.1 Access to energy services.
	7.2 Increase renewable energy supplies.
	7.3 Improve energy efficiency.
8 Sustainable economic growth	8.4 Decouple economic growth from environmental degradation.
9 Sustainable industrialisation	9.4 Environmentally sound technologies and industrial processes.
11 Sustainable human settlements	11.6 Reduce the environmental impact of cities.
12 Sustainable consumption and production	12.2 Sustainable management and use of natural resources.
	12.3 Reduce global food waste.
	12.4 Environmentally sound management of waste.
	12.5 Reduce waste generation.
	12.8 Ensure access to information about sustainable lifestyles.
13 Combating climate change	13.1 Strengthen adaptive capacity to climate change.
	13.2 Integrate climate change measures international policies.
	13.3 Improve education and institutional capacity on climate change mitigation and adaptation.
14 Sustainable use of oceans	14.1 Prevent and reduce marine pollution.
	14.2 Manage marine and coastal ecosystems.
	14.3 Minimise ocean acidification.
	14.4 End overfishing.
	14.5 Establish protected coastal and marine areas.
15 Sustainable use of terrestrial ecosystems	15.1 Conserve and restore terrestrial and inland freshwater ecosystems.
	15.2 Implement sustainable management of forests.
	15.3 Combat desertification.
	15.4 Conserve mountain ecosystems.
	15.5 Reduce degradation of natural habitats.
	15.7 End poaching and trafficking of protected species.
	15.8 Prevent introduction of alien species.
	15.9 Integrate ecosystem and biodiversity values into national and local planning.

Notes:
- Goals and target text adapted from Agenda 2030.[89] For a more complete understanding of the goals and targets, you are referred to https://sdgs.un.org/2030agenda.
- The SDGs have been structured in a way to avoid a social–environmental–economic categorisation; hence, distinctions are not necessarily completely obvious.
- Several targets have been classified under two different headings, because they cannot be clearly defined as being associated with one particular dimension of sustainability.

Time for reflection

Having read through this summary of issues related to environmental sustainability, what areas are particularly relevant to you, either for your organisation or in your community?

Think about the planetary boundaries concept. What impact might your organisation's activities have on any of these?

1.6 Social sustainability

If I were to walk down the street and ask the first person I met to explain what "environmental sustainability" meant to them, they would probably offer a meaningful explanation, perhaps about climate change or pollution of the oceans. But if I were to ask them to talk about "social sustainability", I am not so sure that they would be able to provide such an explanation. In another way of looking at this, David Attenborough has over the last few years been involved in many influential documentaries about the sustainability of life on Earth and has most definitely made people around the world aware of the problems of marine pollution and how deforestation makes it much harder for animals to find places to live. But what might the response be to documentaries about gentrification forcing poor people out of a neighbourhood where they have lived for years? Sympathy perhaps, indifference possibly, but also with some thought that this is a positive sign of increasing affluence in an area. Here we have a way of looking at the difference between environmental and social sustainability over what is essentially the same problem—enforced homelessness. It suggests that the difficulty with social sustainability is that it elicits feelings derived from a political perspective which are not necessarily present when people think about environmental sustainability.

As discussed previously in this chapter, the sustainability discourse emerged out of concerns about sustainable social and economic development in less developed countries in the 1960s (concerns that are still relevant). Here the debate about equity is still central: for most people around the world, meeting basic needs is a priority and it may be impossible to invest the time and money on activities designed to protect the natural environment, such as being selective about what crops to grow or animals to eat, how to use solar technology or build better quality housing. This continuing pressure from lower-income countries may be seen in the SDGs, where a significant number of goals and targets address social sustainability concerns.

But away from the United Nations arena, as the sustainability discourse developed it became more strongly influenced by affluent, Western countries where social concerns were less pressing (and perhaps inconvenient to discuss), and issues of environmental sustainability came to dominate. Maintaining the focus on environmental issues, what may be described as a "narrow" interpretation of sustainability,[76] makes it possible to avoid the elephant in the room of domestic social inequity, which, were it to be discussed more openly could lead to mounting disquiet about the philosophies of political economy which have dominated the West for the last 30 years.

The overall result of this lack of attention to social issues is that an understanding of social sustainability is constrained by a lack of a consistent theoretical framework[77] which can cut across political prejudice, and that much of the discussion about social sustainability is "… somewhat chaotic and sometimes contradictory or confusing".[78]

As the discourse around social sustainability has developed, there has been an ever-increasing awareness that definitions are based on different perspectives, representing alternative viewpoints on politics, culture, economics and history, amongst others. However, despite the lack of a clear, agreed definition, three core principles have emerged,[79] that social sustainability addresses:

- social equity, such as access to services and opportunities, empowerment, and the ability of institutions to adapt to social equity needs
- social cohesion, how individuals and communities connect with each other, and
- meeting basic needs such as nutrition, housing, education, health, employment and other human rights.[80]

Unlike the scientific basis of the concerns surrounding environmental sustainability, claims about social sustainability tend to be highly contested and different from one location to the next. So, for example, claiming that the United Kingdom of 2021 is characterised by low social equity, questionable social cohesion and highly unequal access to basic needs is a description that some, but not all readers will agree with. One attempt to provide a more quantifiable picture of social sustainability comes from Robert Putnam, an American sociologist who has been particularly concerned with civic engagement, and the degree to which people take part in shared, social activities such as voluntary work, membership of clubs, and other aspects of what might be called "citizenship". He analysed how the use of particular words and phrases changed between 1880 and 2020 and concluded that from the 1920s to the 1960s there was an increasing emphasis in published materials on what he calls "We" rather than "I", after which the trend reversed, and the emphasis shifted towards "I".

So why did things change in the 1960s? Putnam's analysis, although based on developments in the United States, may provide lessons for other advanced, Western societies. The post-war baby boom meant that there was an unusually high proportion of young people becoming socially active during the decade, the social and cultural norms forged during the Depression and the Second World War were being questioned, the Vietnam War was causing massive unrest, political assassinations and the civil rights movement caused enormous uncertainty, and so on. All of these factors made people question old assumptions, and they started to look inwards for answers, and the 1970s became "the me decade". George Monbiot's analysis of the alienation that has developed in modern Western societies in more recent times highlights the consequences of increased car ownership, so that people increasingly travel alone, live further away from family and friends, and create levels of traffic which function as barriers to drive communities apart. Increasing reliance on multichannel television, the internet and social media also all reinforce the sense of individualism and isolation.[81] Arguably much of this has been encouraged by and provides fertile ground for neoliberal economics which started to develop momentum in the United Kingdom and the United States in the 1970s—the significance of this for sustainability is considered in more detail in Chapter 3.

As in the previous section, Table 1.2 lists the SDG goals and targets that I see to be of particular relevance here.

Table 1.2 Social sustainability targets in the SDGs

SDG	Target related to social sustainability
1 End poverty	1.3 Implement social protection systems.
	1.4 Ensure equal rights to economic resources.
	1.5 Build resilience of poor and vulnerable people.
2 End hunger	2.1 End hunger and ensure sufficient access to food for all.
	2.2 End all forms of malnutrition.
3 Ensure healthy lives	3.1 Reduce global maternal mortality ratio.
	3.2 End preventable deaths of newborns and young children.
	3.3 End communicable disease epidemics.
	3.4 Reduce premature mortality from non-communicable diseases.
	3.5 Strengthen prevention and treatment of substance abuse.
	3.6 Halve global deaths from road accidents.
	3.7 Ensure universal access to sexual and reproductive health care services.
	3.8 Achieve universal healthcare coverage.
4 Inclusive and equitable education and lifelong learning	4.1 Ensure all girls and boys complete secondary education.
	4.2 Ensure equal access to early childhood development.
	4.3 Ensure equal access to all for vocational and tertiary education.
	4.4 Increase numbers of youth and adults with technical and vocational skills.
	4.5 Eliminate gender disparities in education.
	4.6 Ensure literacy and numeracy for all ages.
	4.7 Ensure all people are able to promote sustainable development.
5 Achieve gender equality	5.1 End discrimination against women and girls.
	5.2 Eliminate violence against all women and girls.
	5.3 End harmful practices against children and women.
	5.4 Recognise and value unpaid care.
	5.5 Ensure opportunities and participation for women in leadership and decision-making in all sectors.
	5.6 Ensure universal access to sexual and reproductive health rights.
8 Sustainable economic growth	8.7 Eradicate forced labour and modern slavery.
	8.8 Protect labour rights.
10 Reduce inequality	10.2 Promote social, economic and political inclusion of all people.
	10.3 Eliminate discriminatory laws, policies and practices.
	10.7 Facilitate orderly, safe and responsible migration.
11 Sustainable human settlements	11.1 Ensure access to all for safe and affordable housing.
	11.2 Provide access to safe, affordable and sustainable transport systems.
	11.3 Enhance inclusive and sustainable urbanisation.
	11.4 Strengthen efforts to protect and safeguard cultural and natural heritage.
	11.5 Reduce deaths and numbers affected by natural disasters.
13 Combating climate change	13.3 Improve education and institutional capacity on climate change mitigation and adaptation.
16 Promote peaceful and inclusive societies for sustainable development	16.1 Reduce all forms of violence.
	16.2 End abuse and all forms of violence against children.
	16.3 Promote the rule of law for all.
	16.4 Reduce illicit financial and arms flows.
	16.5 Reduce corruption and bribery.
	16.6 Develop effective, accountable and transparent institutions.
	16.7 Ensure responsive representative decision-making at all levels.
	16.8 Strengthen the participation of developing countries in global governance.
	16.9 Provide legal identity for all.
	16.10 Ensure access to information about fundamental freedoms.

Time for reflection

How has your understanding of the term "social sustainability" been developed by this explanation?

The political nature of social sustainability has been mentioned: what issues do you think are particularly important in your society, and to what degree are these accepted or contested by others you know?

Of course, as we continue to develop a more comprehensive picture of what social sustainability might mean, its potential interactions with environmental sustainability become clearer, and these are not necessarily mutually constructive. Indeed, as the pressure for implementing environmental sustainability measures grows, the challenges to maintaining aspects of how people live which are seen as important for ensuring social sustainability increase: for example, if social sustainability is taken to include maintaining the freedom to travel as currently enjoyed, this may conflict with the environmental sustainability requirement to reduce pollution and energy consumption. On the other hand, if people's basic needs are being met they are better able to take action to help with environmental sustainability, such as through improving the thermal insulation of their property or using low energy consumption appliances. This highlights the importance of developing an understanding of the social psychology of how people see their relationship with the environment, so that environmental sustainability policies work *with*, rather than in competition with social sustainability demands. This complex relationship is looked at in more detail in Chapter 2, where the concept of a "socio-environmental system" is discussed.

1.7 Economic sustainability

The previous section explained how social sustainability is a contested concept, and this progression towards less clarity continues with economic sustainability. On the face of it, the idea is simple—it is about keeping the economy working for the benefit of future generations. However, as academics like to say, we have a problem with ontology. Environmental sustainability explores actions needed to sustain the environment (which I can see, touch and smell), and social sustainability explores actions for sustaining society, again something that exists physically. But can I see or touch "the economy"? Not really. It exists, but as a conceptual construct. What I do see are people working, businesses making things, shops selling stuff and so on. In other words, the economy manifests itself as an activity, and it is not "a thing" that can be preserved or protected as it is. Furthermore, this activity determines how society functions, and so economics cannot be separated from society and hence social sustainability. The general acceptance of a three-dimensional construct for sustainability may therefore complicate rather than clarify.

This was a problem Karl Polanyi, the Hungarian economic anthropologist uncovered when trying to describe what "the economy" was in pre-industrial societies, where he found that it was often hidden away in discreet localised, interpersonal resource exchanges, such as barter or truck.[82] This shows us that human existence is essentially about an interaction with the natural environment: we grow food to eat, we extract minerals with which to make things, we return what we do not use to the environment. The economy is simply a mechanism which has been invented to facilitate this interaction.

We therefore need to clarify what we mean by economic sustainability: is it about sustaining the economy as it is for future generations, or is it about developing an economy that sustains society and the environment?

Very often the first question is assumed—how can we organise society and use the environment to keep our present economic system working? This is definitely the question that mainstream economists seek to answer in the institutional literature produced by organisations such as the OECD and the United Nations. Globally, capitalism of some form is the economic belief system which prevails and which delimits what ideas can be legitimately discussed.[83] Conventional discussions about economic sustainability therefore draw heavily on the importance of "the maintenance of capital", that the amount of capital (whatever that may be) remains constant as time passes.[84] From this perspective, social activity and use of the natural environment should be organised in a way so that sufficient capital exists in the system to keep everything moving smoothly.

In capitalist thinking, capital is generally seen as having monetary value, and as thinking about the other two dimensions of sustainability has developed, contemporary economists have become interested in thinking about how these can be quantified in terms of capital. We have, therefore, amongst others, human capital, a concept discussed in more detail in Chapter 5 with regard to learning, social capital, an indication of how strongly connected a network of people may be, and natural capital, a value attached to the natural environment.

Two problems then arise. First, how can these be quantified in a way which allows comparison and aggregation? An example of the difficulty of doing this is in the debate about the "social cost of carbon" (SCC). This is an estimate of the damage caused by burning each additional ton of carbon, in terms of its effect on agriculture, sea-level rise, ocean acidification, human health and so on. The limited scientific understanding of the exact mechanisms through which burning carbon affects the social and natural environments means that there are many different ideas about how this should be calculated, and the algorithm chosen reflects a political worldview. For example, while the UK government's *Dasgupta Review*[85] explains that its value has been estimated at anywhere between $15 and $200 per tonne, the journalist Robert Devine notes that during the United States' Trump Administration, the official SCC was defined as $1![86]

Second, much economic theory is based on an assumption about substitutability of resources, that if one resource becomes too expensive another can be substituted. However, as the ecological economist Herman Daly notes, it is simply not possible to substitute freely between financial, human, social and natural capital, particularly in the light of the finite quality of natural capital.[87]

Let us return to the second question—should economic sustainability actually be about developing an economy that sustains society and the environment? Historically, only as societies moved away from subsistence farming and fewer people were involved in processing raw materials (Marx's metabolic rift) did the abstract concept of money become more significant. So the economy is actually a social technology, a shared, socially constructed understanding that once we exchange coins or banknotes or wave plastic cards over electronic boxes an exchange of resources becomes possible.

The economy therefore exists more as an idea than as an object—which means we could change it radically by just thinking about what we want it to achieve. So from this perspective what we really mean by "economic sustainability" is how the design of this social technology can facilitate either or (preferably) both social and environmental sustainability. Our current social technology sees economics as "the science which studies human behaviour as a relationship between ends and scarce means which have alternative uses".[88] But what is "scarce"? This definition means that we put a price on products that we buy to eat, on the mineral resources that we use to make something, and on labour that is needed, but attach no price to the space within the environment where we dump waste products, as rivers historically seemed like infinitely deep places within which we could pour industrial waste and the sky an infinitely large space where carbon dioxide would dissipate. Empirically, those may have been reasonable assumptions up until 100 years ago, even if they would have always had an ethically dubious quality.

Asking that second question therefore opens up the possibility of thinking about how "the economy" should be redesigned to create more social and environmental sustainability. This whole issue of the social technology of the economy is explored in more detail in Chapter 3.

So, for now putting aside this fundamental question about what economic sustainability actually means, what subjects might it actually embrace? As previously, the SDGs provide a basic list of what is relevant (Table 1.3).

Table 1.3 Economic sustainability targets in the SDGs

SDG	Target related to economic sustainability
1 End poverty	1.1 Eradicate extreme poverty everywhere.
	1.2 Reduce the proportion of people living in poverty.
5 Achieve gender equality	5.4 Recognise and value unpaid care and domestic work.
8 Sustainable economic growth	8.1 Sustain per capita economic growth.
	8.2 Achieve economic productivity.
	8.3 Promote job creation and business development policies.
	8.5 Achieve full and productive employment and decent work for all.
	8.6 Reduce the proportion of youth not in employment or education.
	8.9 Devise policies to promote sustainable tourism.
	8.10 Strengthen the ability of financial institutions to serve all people.
9 Sustainable industrialisation	9.1 Develop infrastructure to support economic development and human well-being.
	9.2 Promote sustainable industrialisation.
	9.3 Improve access for small-scale enterprises to financial services.
	9.5 Enhance scientific research.
12 Sustainable consumption and production	12.1 Implement the Framework of Programmes on Sustainable Consumption and Production Patterns.
	12.6 Encourage business to adopt sustainable practices and report on progress.
14 Sustainable use of oceans	14.6 Prohibit certain forms of fisheries subsidies.
	14.7 Increase economic benefits to small island developing states.
16 Promote peaceful and inclusive societies	16.4 Reduce illicit financial and arms flows.
17 Strengthen the Global Partnership for Sustainable Development	17.1 Strengthen domestic resource mobilisation.
	17.2 Implement official development assistance commitments.
	17.3 Mobilise additional financial resources for developing countries.
	17.4 Assist developing countries to attain long-term debt sustainability.
	17.5 Implement investment promotion regimes for least developed countries.

My decision about including an SDG target in this table rather than in the tables for social and environmental sustainability was based on if it contained an explicit or implicit reference to finance. In many cases, the financial reference is closely linked to some social or environmental goal, which supports the idea that "the economy" is essentially a socially engineered system to ensure that people have enough food, shelter and healthcare provision to maintain a functioning social system.

1.8 Key points in this chapter

The concept of sustainability has emerged during the last half-century, and ideas about what it is and how we can work towards it are a major focus of international organisations like the United Nations and the OECD (Figure 1.6). However, while ensuring environmental sustainability is an existential requirement for humanity, too often the interrelationship between the environment and society is overlooked, perhaps because social sustainability raises inconvenient questions about power structures in society and how countries are governed.

The three-dimensional conceptualisation of sustainability recognises this complexity, but thinking about ways in which the relationship between social and environmental issues can be addressed is too often impeded by what we understand about economic sustainability.

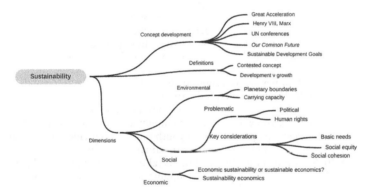

Figure 1.6 Key points covered in this chapter.

Time for reflection

What are your thoughts about the three dimensions of sustainability? The discussion about economic sustainability challenged some ideas about how the world works—what are your thoughts on that?

What about the relationship between social and environmental sustainability? How can you see this relationship playing out in your world?

1.9 Further reading

Our common future, the World Commission on Environment and Development, Oxford University Press, 1987: the seminal text on sustainable development as it is currently understood.

The limits to growth, Donella H Meadows et al, Pan Books, 1972: to develop a deeper understanding of how system dynamics was used to make projections about humanity in the 21st century.

There is no Planet B: A handbook for the make or break years, Mike Berners-Lee, Cambridge University Press, 2019. A powerful exploration of the changes needed to move towards greater environmental sustainability.

Notes

1. James McClure, 'Henry VIII's Reign Was a Golden Age for Hemp', *Civilized*, 2020, https://www.civilized.life/articles/henry-viii-england-hemp/.
2. George Julnes, 'Evaluating Sustainability: Controversies, Challenges, and Opportunities', *New Directions for Evaluation* 2019, no. 162 (2019): 15.
3. Ben Purvis, Yong Mao, and Darren Robinson, 'Three Pillars of Sustainability: In Search of Conceptual Origins', *Sustainability Science* 14, no. 3 (2019): 681–95.
4. Karl Marx, *Capital: A Critical Analysis of Capitalist Production*, vol. III (New York: Vintage, 1981), 911.
5. Karl Marx, *Capital: A Critical Analysis of Capitalist Production*, vol. II (London: George Allen & Unwin, 1887), 513.
6. John Bellamy Foster, 'Marx's Theory of Metabolic Rift: Classical Foundations for Environmental Sociology', *American Journal of Sociology* 105, no. 2 (1999): 383.
7. Anne E. Egelston, *Sustainable Development: A History* (Springer Science & Business Media, 2012).
8. Egelston.
9. WCED, *Our Common Future* (Oxford University Press, 1987), 24.
10. Pratima Bansal, 'The Corporate Challenges of Sustainable Development', *Academy of Management Perspectives* 16, no. 2 (2002): 122–31.
11. United Nations, 'Transforming Our World: The 2030 Agenda for Sustainable Development' (New York: United Nations, 2015), https://sdgs.un.org/2030agenda.
12. Frank Biermann, Norichika Kanie, and Rakhyun E. Kim, 'Global Governance by Goal-Setting: The Novel Approach of the UN Sustainable Development Goals', *Current Opinion in Environmental Sustainability* 26 (2017): 26–31.
13. Mark Stafford-Smith et al., 'Integration: The Key to Implementing the Sustainable Development Goals', *Sustainability Science* 12, no. 6 (2017): 911–19.
14. IIASA, 'Transformations to Achieve the Sustainable Development Goals: Report Prepared by The World in 2050 Initiative', TWI2050 (Laxenburg, Austria: International Institute for Applied Systems Analysis, 2018), 5.
15. Nina Eisenmenger et al., 'The Sustainable Development Goals Prioritize Economic Growth over Sustainable Resource Use: A Critical Reflection on the SDGs from a Socio-Ecological Perspective', *Sustainability Science* 15 (2020): 1101–10; Keith R. Skene, 'No Goal Is an Island: The Implications of Systems Theory for the Sustainable Development Goals', *Environment, Development and Sustainability*, no. 23 October (2021): 9993–10012.
16. Lynley Tulloch and David Neilson, 'The Neoliberalisation of Sustainability', *Citizenship, Social and Economics Education* 13, no. 1 (2014): 26–38.
17. The Ecologist, 'A Blueprint for Survival', *The Ecologist*, 1972, 8.
18. The Ecologist, 5.
19. E.F. Schumacher, *Small Is Beautiful: A Study of Economics as If People Mattered* (London: Abacus, 1973).
20. Hasan Ozbekhan, 'The Predicament of Mankind' (Club of Rome, 1970).
21. Ozbekhan.
22. The principles of system dynamics are discussed in more detail in Chapter 2.

23 An interactive version of the World3 model is available at https://insightmaker.com/insight/1954/The-World3-Model-Classic-World-Simulation.
24 Donella H. Meadows et al., *The Limits to Growth* (London: Potomac Associates, 1972), 142.
25 As quoted by Tim Jackson and Robin Webster, 'Limits Revisited: A Review of the Limits to Growth Debate' (All-Party Parliamentary Group on Limits to Growth, 2016), 17.
26 Joseph A. Tainter, 'Sustainability of Complex Societies', *Futures* 27, no. 4 (1995): 397–407.
27 Wikipedia, 'George Santayana', in *Wikipedia*, 2021, https://en.wikipedia.org/w/index.php?title=George_Santayana&oldid=1001208319.
28 John Cook et al., 'America Misled: How the Fossil Fuel Industry Deliberately Misled Americans about Climate Change', *Fairfax, VA: George Mason University Center for Climate Change Communication*. https://www.Climatechangecommunication.Org/America-Misled, 2019.
29 Jackson and Webster, 'Limits Revisited'; Graham M. Turner, 'On the Cusp of Global Collapse? Updated Comparison of the Limits to Growth with Historical Data', *GAIA - Ecological Perspectives for Science and Society* 21, no. 2 (2012): 116–24.
30 Turner, 'On the Cusp of Global Collapse?', 120.
31 Alexander N. Christakis, 'A Retrospective Structural Inquiry of the Predicament of Humankind', in *Rescuing the Enlightenment from Itself*, ed. John P. van Gigch and Janet MacIntyre-Mills, vol. 1 (Springer, 2006), 93–122.
32 For example, see New Scientist, 'Special Report: The Facts about Overconsumption', *New Scientist*, 2008, https://www.newscientist.com/article/dn14950-special-report-the-facts-about-overconsumption/.
33 Will Steffen et al., 'The Trajectory of the Anthropocene: The Great Acceleration', *The Anthropocene Review* 2, no. 1 (2015): 81–98.
34 P.J. Crutzen and E.F. Stoermer, 'The "Anthropocene"', *IGBP Newsletter* 41 (2000): 17–18.
35 Steffen et al., 'The Trajectory of the Anthropocene'.
36 Steffen et al.
37 Anthony D. Barnosky et al., 'Has the Earth's Sixth Mass Extinction Already Arrived?', *Nature* 471, no. 7336 (2011): 51–57; Corey J.A. Bradshaw et al., 'Underestimating the Challenges of Avoiding a Ghastly Future', *Frontiers in Conservation Science* 1 (2021): 9.
38 Graham M. Turner, 'A Comparison of The Limits to Growth with 30 Years of Reality', *Global Environmental Change* 18, no. 3 (2008): 397–411; Turner, 'On the Cusp of Global Collapse?'; Jackson and Webster, 'Limits Revisited'.
39 Jackson and Webster, 'Limits Revisited', 15.
40 S. Fisher, R. Fitzgerald, and W. Poortinga, *British Social Attitudes 35: Climate Change: Social Divisions in Beliefs and Behaviour* (London: National Centre for Social Research, 2018); Lawrence C. Hamilton, 'Public Awareness of the Scientific Consensus on Climate', *Sage Open* 1 11, no. October–December (2016): 1–11.
41 Gordon Gauchat, 'Politicization of Science in the Public Sphere: A Study of Public Trust in the United States, 1974 to 2010', *American Sociological Review* 77, no. 2 (2012): 167–87.
42 Ulrich Beck, 'From Industrial Society to the Risk Society: Questions of Survival, Social Structure and Ecological Enlightenment', *Theory, Culture & Society* 9, no. 1 (1992): 97–123.
43 Ulrich Beck, 'Reframing Power in the Globalized World', *Organization Studies* 29, no. 5 (2008): 793–804; Ulrich Beck, 'Climate for Change, or How to Create a Green Modernity?', *Theory, Culture & Society* 27, no. 2–3 (2010): 254–66; Katherine F. Smith et al., 'Global Rise in Human Infectious Disease Outbreaks', *Journal of The Royal Society Interface* 11, no. 101 (2014): 1–6.
44 Beck, 'Climate for Change, or How to Create a Green Modernity?', 254.
45 Beck, 'Reframing Power in the Globalized World', 798.
46 Shih-wei Hsu, 'Alternative Knowledge Management', in *Handbook of Research on Knowledge Management*, ed. Anders Örtenblad (Cheltenham: Edward Elgar Publishing, 2014), 424–39.
47 Malcolm Bull, 'Coronavirus Is Our Chance to Completely Rethink What the Economy Is For', *The Guardian*, 2020, sec. Opinion, https://www.theguardian.com/commentisfree/2020/may/31/coronavirus-economy-change-pandemic; B. Latour, 'Imaginer les gestes-barrières contre le retour à la production d'avant-crise', *AOC Media - Analyse Opinion Critique* (blog), 2020, https://aoc.media/opinion/2020/03/29/imaginer-les-gestes-barrieres-contre-le-retour-a-la-production-davant-crise/; L. Krebel et al., *Building a Green Stimulus for COVID-19: A Recovery Plan for a Greener, Fairer Future* (London: New Economics Foundation, 2020).

48 Walter Bryce Gallie, 'Essentially Contested Concepts', *Proceedings of the Aristotelian Society*, 56 (JSTOR, 1956), 167–98.
49 Martin Geissdoerfer et al., 'The Circular Economy – A New Sustainability Paradigm?', *Journal of Cleaner Production* 143 (2017): 758.
50 Jules N. Pretty, 'Participatory Learning for Sustainable Agriculture', *World Development* 23, no. 8 (1995): 1247–63.
51 Güler Aras and David Crowther, 'Corporate Sustainability Reporting: A Study in Disingenuity?', *Journal of Business Ethics* 87, no. 1 (2009): 279.
52 Justin M. Mog, 'Struggling with Sustainability—a Comparative Framework for Evaluating Sustainable Development Programs', *World Development* 32, no. 12 (2004): 2139.
53 F. Gale, *The Political Economy of Sustainability* (Cheltenham: Edward Elgar Publishing Ltd, 2018).
54 Robert Goodland and Herman Daly, 'Environmental Sustainability: Universal and Non-Negotiable', *Ecological Applications* 6, no. 4 (1996): 1002–17.
55 Herman Daly, 'A Further Critique of Growth Economics', *Ecological Economics* 88 (2013): 20–24.
56 Mog, 'Struggling with Sustainability—a Comparative Framework for Evaluating Sustainable Development Programs', 2140.
57 Purvis, Mao, and Robinson, 'Three Pillars of Sustainability'.
58 IUCN, 'World Conservation Strategy: Living Resource Conservation for Sustainable Development' (International Union for the Conservation of Nature and Natural Resources, 1980), 37.
59 UNSD, 'Agenda 21' (United Nations Sustainable Development, 1992), para. 8.4.
60 ILO, *Guidelines for a Just Transition towards Environmentally Sustainable Economies and Societies All* (Geneva: International Labour Organization, 2015), 4.
61 Neil K. Dawe and Kenneth L. Ryan, 'The Faulty Three-Legged-Stool Model of Sustainable Development', *Conservation Biology* 17, no. 5 (2003): 1458–60.
62 Massimo Scalia et al., 'Governance for Sustainability: A Triple-Helix Model', *Sustainability Science* 13, no. 5 (2018): 1235–44.
63 P. Ekins, J. Gupta, and P. Boileau, eds., *Global Environment Outlook GEO-6: Healthy Planet, Healthy People* (Cambridge: Cambridge University Press, 2019), 22.
64 Ekins, Gupta, and Boileau, 92.
65 Ekins, Gupta, and Boileau, 142.
66 Ekins, Gupta, and Boileau, 76.
67 Christiana Figueres, Philip J. Landrigan, and Richard Fuller, 'Tackling Air Pollution, Climate Change, and NCDs: Time to Pull Together', *The Lancet* 392 (2018): 1502.
68 Johan Rockström et al., 'Planetary Boundaries: Exploring the Safe Operating Space for Humanity', *Nature* 461, no. 24 September (2009): 472–75.
69 Will Steffen et al., 'Planetary Boundaries: Guiding Human Development on a Changing Planet', *Science* 347, no. 6223 (2015): 736–47.
70 Millennium Ecosystem Assessment Board, 'Ecosystems and Human Well-Being: Synthesis' (Washington, DC: Millennium Ecosystem Assessment, 2005), v.
71 George Monbiot, 'This Flood Was Not Only Foretold—It Was Publicly Subsidised', *The Guardian*, 29 December 2015, http://www.theguardian.com/commentisfree/2015/dec/29/deluge-farmers-flood-grouse-moor-drain-land.
72 L. Caesar et al., 'Current Atlantic Meridional Overturning Circulation Weakest in Last Millennium', *Nature Geoscience* 14, no. 3 (2021): 118–20, https://doi.org/10.1038/s41561-021-00699-z.
73 Garrett Hardin, 'The Tragedy of the Commons', *Science* 162, no. 3859 (1968): 1243–48.
74 Hardin, 1248.
75 Ben Ramalingam, *Aid on the Edge of Chaos: Rethinking International Cooperation in a Complex World* (Oxford: Oxford University Press, 2013), 239–43.
76 Michael Jacobs, 'Sustainable Development as a Contested Concept', in *Fairness and Futurity: Essays on Environmental Sustainability and Social Justice*, ed. A. Dobson (Oxford University Press, 1999), 36.
77 Merlina Missimer, Karl-Henrik Robèrt, and Göran Broman, 'A Strategic Approach to Social Sustainability—Part 1: Exploring the Social System', *Journal of Cleaner Production* 140 (2017): 32–41.

78 Vallance, Perkins, and Dixon, 'What Is Social Sustainability?', 345.
79 Chris Landorf, 'Evaluating Social Sustainability in Historic Urban Environments', *International Journal of Heritage Studies* 17, no. 5 (2011): 463–77; Andrea Colantonio, 'Social Sustainability: A Review and Critique of Traditional versus Emerging Themes and Assessment Methods', in *Second International Conference on Whole Life Urban Sustainability and Its Assessment: Conference Proceedings* (Loughborough University, 2009), 865–85.
80 Landorf, 'Evaluating Social Sustainability in Historic Urban Environments', 472.
81 George Monbiot, *Out of the Wreckage: A New Politics for an Age of Crisis* (London: Verso Books, 2017).
82 Karl Polanyi, *The Great Transformation* (Farrar & Rinehart, 1944).
83 Tulloch and Neilson, 'The Neoliberalisation of Sustainability'.
84 Goodland and Daly, 'Environmental Sustainability'.
85 Partha Dasgupta, 'The Economics of Biodiversity: The Dasgupta Review' (London: HM Treasury, 2021), 155.
86 Robert S. Devine, *The Sustainable Economy: The Hidden Costs of Climate Change and the Path to a Prosperous Future* (New York: Anchor Books, 2020), 49.
87 Daly, 'A Further Critique of Growth Economics'.
88 Lionel Robbins, 1932, quoted in Ha-Joon Chang, *Economics: The User's Guide* (London: Pelican, 2014).
89 United Nations, 'Transforming Our World: The 2030 Agenda for Sustainable Development'.

2 Systems thinking, complexity and sustainability

2.1 What this chapter covers

The aim of this chapter is to provide a basic grounding in some key principles of systems thinking, enough so that you can see how relevant they are to sustainability and to understand how systems thinking can be used in sustainability-focused organisational learning. Figure 2.1 summarises what it covers.

The chapter starts with an explanation about what a system is, how we think about systems and why this is important in this book. To illustrate this, we then look at a case study of an environmental issue which had social implications in order to show how some simple systems thinking ideas can help to shine light on such a situation.

We follow this by looking at some key principles about systems thinking, how a system may be interpreted in terms of the interrelationships between its elements, the different perspectives that there may be about the system, and boundary judgements which influence how we see the system. It is then important to think about purpose, what the system is doing.

These are then followed by three important considerations about system behaviour: the difference between closed and open systems, and the implications this has for sustainability; the concept of a wicked problem or mess and how this relates to systems thinking; and complexity theory, a set of ideas closely related to systems thinking.

Figure 2.1 Map of Chapter 2.

DOI: 10.4324/9781003218296-3

Finally, we consider three systems thinking "tools", methods which have been developed drawing on the principles of systems thinking. The first is system dynamics, the method used in *The Limits to Growth*; the second, the Viable System Model, is a method which is particularly useful for understanding how organisations operate; and the third is Critical Systems Heuristics (CSH), a tool which we can use to help plan or evaluate in a way which creates a more holistic result.

Key point

Throughout this chapter, you will see boxes like this, indicating key points that will be referenced throughout the rest of the book. This should help you appreciate the importance of each important idea as we come to it.

2.2 What is systems thinking?

René Descartes' 1637 *Discourse on Method* is sometimes regarded as one of the most significant texts in Western philosophical writing. The turbulence of the Reformation had destroyed the conviction that the purpose of humanity was to serve God, which enabled Descartes to propose that the universe in which we exist was "... composed of purposeless particles each pursuing its course mindless of others".[1] Mind and matter were completely different and separate entities, and what a human being was could be understood in machine terms, reducible to the sum of its parts. This way of thinking proved extremely effective in scientific research and in technological development, and Cartesian thinking, as it is now called, dominates the way we are taught to think about all aspects of our lives.

Systems thinking turns Cartesian thinking on its head: rather than trying to understand a whole by looking at individual parts, we try to understand parts by looking at the whole.

Systems thinking is of importance for several reasons. Martin Reynolds and Sue Holwell suggest three general reasons why systems thinking can help any practitioner[2]:

- It can help to make sense of the relationships between different elements in a situation and provide a more holistic understanding.
- It can draw out different and perhaps contrasting perspectives on a given situation. It can therefore contribute to a more pluralist resolution.
- It can help us to explore and reconcile power relationships and potential sources of conflict in a situation.

Sustainability can only really be understood by using a systemic perspective that seeks to be more holistic by exploring the interconnections between relevant issues. This is recognised in research that has been done into how sustainable development can be covered in education. Education for Sustainable Development (ESD) was introduced in *Agenda 21* as an essential focus for learning about sustainability, within the educational system, training and for general public awareness.³ Subsequent research into what ESD should cover concluded that a key component was systems thinking, variously defined as:

> the ability to recognize and understand relationships, to analyse complex systems, to perceive the ways in which systems are embedded within different domains and different scales, and to deal with uncertainty.⁴

And:

> the ability to collectively analyze complex systems across different domains (society, environment, economy, etc.) and across different scales (local to global), thereby considering cascading effects, inertia, feedback loops and other systemic features related to sustainability issues and sustainability problem-solving frameworks.⁵

We look again at systems thinking as an important competency for understanding sustainability in Section 5.6.3.

So what is a "system"? A starting point is that a system is "A collection of entities... that are seen by someone... as interacting together... to do something".⁶ Within this definition an entity could be anything discrete, a physical object or even an idea. It is relatively easy to conceive of physical objects as being entities within a system: for example, a system to write a book would include such things as research materials, a computer, a printer and an author. As these interact, a book emerges. This could be called an "engineered" system, because it has been deliberately created to achieve something. Physical objects may also be seen to exist in a "natural" system, such as the environment, where plants and animals interact.

We also have "systematic" and "systemic". The Oxford English Dictionary defines "systematic" as "done or acting according to a fixed plan or system; methodical", and this implies a certain linearity of working. Elements in an engineered system, for example, one which processes transactions in a bank, would work systematically, and I work systematically (mostly) when developing a new training programme. "Systemic" has a quite different meaning, defined as "of or relating to a system as a whole". Working systemically means seeing things within the context of a whole, so, for example, a term which was often seen in the media during discussion of Black Lives Matter during 2020 was "systemic racism", an observation that policies and practices operating across society sustained racism. Systems thinking practitioners make much greater use of the word systemic than of systematic, although each has its place.

So far in this introduction to systems thinking I may have created an idea that systems are clearly observable "things", and that I can clearly describe how they operate. This is sometimes called first-order systems thinking, where I am acting as an observer, describing the system from outside, and in everyday conversation this is how we usually think of systems. However, the true power of systems thinking comes when we can abstract ourselves from reality and develop the ability to look at any particular situation we are interested in and think about it *as if it were a system*. By doing this, we are actually placing ourselves within the system rather than being a detached observer, and our thinking about the system changes what it apparently is and does. For example, we might seek to understand Human Resource Development better by thinking about it as "a system to promote learning within the organisation", or as "a system to ensure standardised behaviour". What insights can I gather by reflecting on these different purposes?

38 Key principles of systems thinking

Second-order systems thinking turns what we are looking at, a *situation* of interest, into the conceptual construct of a *system* of interest. Contemporary writing on systems thinking suggests that whenever we practice systems thinking we are always working with a conceptual construct.[7] Such second-order systems thinking is immensely powerful because with it we can apply systems thinking principles to any situation to improve our understanding of what seems to be happening. This abstraction is not necessarily an easy thing for newcomers to systems thinking to grasp, but hopefully things will become clearer through subsequent chapters.

This is perhaps the key distinction between systems thinking and what is often referred to in many standard management theory texts as "systems theory". Systems theory narratives tend to draw primarily on the application of basic principles of transformation and feedback to organisational practice, that a particular real-world situation is actually a system. "Systems thinking", on the other hand, refers to the alternative perspective of considering a situation as a conceptually constructed system.

Key point

The distinction between first- and second-order systems thinking is very useful when thinking about evaluating sustainability-focused learning (Chapter 10).

The definition of a system given above contains four words which need to be examined further: interaction, someone, collection and do. The first three relate to three principles which are of fundamental importance in understanding systems thinking, a trinity of factors described as the active endeavours of understanding interrelationships between relevant entities, engaging with multiple perspectives on the situation of interest, and reflecting on boundary judgements made.[8] The fourth word alludes to an observation that all systems have a purpose. We will look at each of these terms, but it will be useful to do this by reference to a case study.

2.3 Case study: the Sheffield tree maintenance story

This case study looks at a real example of how societal and environmental issues interacted and shows how a systems thinking perspective can help us to develop new insights. Martin Reynolds and Sue Holwell note that systems thinking can help us "see the wood for the trees",[9] and this is particularly relevant in this case study.

Our situation of interest is one which propelled my own city of Sheffield to (temporary) international fame in 2018.[10] The citizens of Sheffield are proud of the claim that their city has apparently more trees than any other city in Western Europe, about 5 million in fact. Of these, about 36,000 lined the streets within the city. Sadly, by the early 2000s, Sheffield's streets were in a sorry state, with potholed roads and uneven pavements due to decades of underinvestment in maintenance. So in 2012, Sheffield City Council and the national government's Department for Transport agreed a contract with a private company, which we can call XYZ plc, for various highway maintenance activities. This included both resurfacing roads and maintaining roadside trees by removing old and diseased trees, and replacing with saplings old trees which were breaking up pavements and creating hazards.

Initially, things went smoothly. In many areas, people were happy to have trees removed, as they were thought to be interfering with television reception and resin dripped onto cars. However, around 2014 stories started to circulate that the contractors were not just removing old and diseased trees, but were simply clearing whole streets because it was cheaper. Matters came to a head in 2016 when XYZ announced that they were going to remove trees in an area in the southwest of the city, an area with a high concentration of middle-class, environmentally aware and well-educated residents. Residents along one particular street mobilised and staged demonstrations to stop the tree removals. To avoid the protests and get on with their work, XYZ decided to start operations at about 5 o'clock one morning, but residents were woken by the noise and rushed out of their houses to stop the contractors. The police were called, and two elderly women were arrested for obstructing the workers. At this point, the story moved beyond the local and became of international interest.[11]

How can we use systems thinking to explore this situation? The first thing to do is to get some idea about who is involved and what their relationships are, and a useful way to do that is through graphical representations. As Peter Checkland, one of the key figures in contemporary systems thinking, noted "… human affairs reveal a rich moving pageant of relationships, and pictures are a better means for recording relationships and connections than is linear prose".[12] As we shall see, drawing pictures is a very important part of applied systems thinking.[13]

The first drawing that I created was a "rich picture" (Figure 2.2). As you can see, this draws on my highly developed artistic talents—an important point to note because people are often reluctant to draw pictures because they "can't draw". Being able to draw is not important for a rich picture. I started by drawing two trees outside a house, then someone with a chainsaw, and then added other actors and how they related to each other: Sheffield City Council giving a contract to the plc, the police arresting protesters and the media watching. This process immediately started me thinking about who is involved, how they are related and so on. The rich picture creation process done with a group of interested people is a valuable exercise in its own right.

Figure 2.2 Rich picture for the Sheffield tree maintenance story.

40 *Key principles of systems thinking*

Figure 2.3 was the next graphical step: this is a system map and helps us to identify the significant actors in a situation of interest. It also creates our system of interest, which comprises the contractor XYZ, the Department of Transport and Sheffield City Council. These actors interacted, for example, through conversations and meetings where decisions were made about areas of the city where tree felling would take place and which particular trees would be felled. From my perspective and understanding of what happened, residents had only limited involvement in these discussions, so I decided to place them in the "environment" of the system, the "environment", comprising those elements "that affect the system, but are not controlled by it".[14] To make my decision clear I drew a line around the three actors in the system.

However, as the story developed and started to attract media interest, it became necessary to add the media to the system map, again placing them in the environment because they were not involved in the decision-making processes (Figure 2.4).

Then I needed to consider the police. Are they in the environment or are they in the system? My conclusion was that they were part of the system as they took an active part in making sure that the tree felling could take place, so this is represented by Figure 2.5.

After the tree felling story went global, the city council started to realise that consultations with local residents were important, and so they started to involve neighbourhood

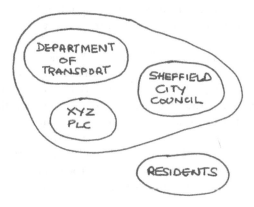

Figure 2.3 The system for managing Sheffield's trees.

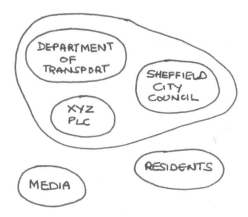

Figure 2.4 The updated system map with the media.

groups and associated independent tree experts in the decision-making process. So my final system map moves the residents into the system and removes the police because they were no longer necessary (Figure 2.6).

The decisions about where to draw the line separating the system from the environment were crucial: in systems thinking terminology this is about making boundary judgements. Boundary judgements have the potential to open up powerful conversations about assumptions being made by the various entities. What does this situation have to say about local democracy? Decisions were made by elected councillors, but should further local consultation have been made before tree felling action started? What does this have to say about the way council services in the United Kingdom have been privatised over the last few decades? As the row escalated, the city council refused to explain how decisions were being made about tree felling because this was a matter of "commercial confidentiality". How does what happened fit in with the council's professed recognition of a "climate emergency",[15] the global need to plant more trees to increase carbon capture, and the enaction of local democracy?

Let us pause to think about how I had used the diagrams. They had helped me to think about who was involved and how they were connected, but as I thought more about the story I decided to talk to someone who had been closely involved in what had actually happened. I used my diagrams to explain how I understood what had happened and then listened to their thoughts. As a result, we put together a more balanced explanation. On

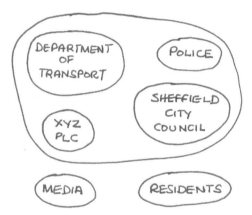

Figure 2.5 Updated system map with the police.

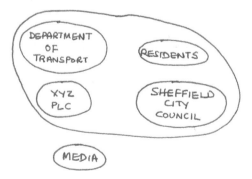

Figure 2.6 Updated system map with residents in the system.

reflection, I should have involved them right from the very beginning and we could have collaborated on developing the rich picture and system maps. We could have invited other people as well, people who were on the streets protesting, police, the contractor, the media. Each would have their own thoughts based on their own particular perspective. The rich picture and system map would have provided a focus around which we could have discussed our limited understandings and worked towards a shared, agreed version of the truth.

This story shows how systems thinking is not just about systems that we can see clearly. How tree maintenance was happening in Sheffield was not an obvious system, but by looking at it as if it were a system we were able to use a set of ideas which created a wider range of possible understandings about what was going on and to help us understand what possible actions could be taken here and in similar situations in the future.

The story also illustrates how social and environmental issues interact and create what has been called a socio-environmental system (SES).[16] The SES concept proposes that how and where people live is a result of a dynamic interaction with the natural environment. From this perspective, the economy is the mechanism which contributes to how this relationship works. The impact of Hurricane Katrina on New Orleans in 2005 has been examined as an example of an SES.[17] The central area of the city which was the worst affected by the inundation of the flood defences had a largely African-American population, and their relative poverty had contributed to a lack of attention being paid to maintaining the flood defences. Poverty also meant that these residents found it much harder to evacuate when the storm hit, meaning that they were disproportionately affected. A similar phenomenon was seen during the COVID-19 pandemic as it affected the United Kingdom, where poorer communities living in lower quality housing where they could not maintain safe social distances at home or being in employment where they could not work from home, suffered higher infection and death rates than did more affluent communities.[18]

Notice the different patterns of influence in the stories: for New Orleans, the environmental disaster had an impact on society, whereas in Sheffield society had an impact on the environment. The tree maintenance programme ran into problems when XYZ started chopping down trees in a part of the city heavily populated by what might be described as wealthier, more environmentally conscious residents, who were better able to mobilise themselves and the media than might have been possible in poorer parts of the city, a stark contrast to the New Orleans example.

Social conditions are intimately connected with the way an economy is designed. In the Sheffield story, tree maintenance, which historically would have been a public authority responsibility, has, because of the United Kingdom's neoliberal economic policies since the 1980s, been contracted out to a private sector organisation. According to neoclassical economic thinking, XYZ plc should prioritise self-interest, so any decision to clear cut streets rather than spend time assessing arboreal health may seem perfectly rational. As the Friedman Doctrine says, private sector companies have no social responsibility other than to increase profits for their shareholders.[19] This shows that an SES actually plays out within a social–environment–economy nexus.

Systems thinking such as this helps us to think through the potential behaviour of an SES. Depending on how society, the environment and the economy interact will affect the system's:

- resilience, how it will react to shock
- adaptability, what it will do as a reaction to external influences, and

Key principles of systems thinking 43

- transformability, how elements and relationships within the SES can be changed to make it more resilient and adaptable.[20]

Before moving on it would be useful to explain how the tree maintenance story came to a conclusion. As a result of the bad publicity the city received, tree maintenance activities were suspended and the city council entered into discussions with local action groups and the Woodland Trust about what to do next. The outcome was the Sheffield Street Tree Strategy, now seen as a positive blueprint for tree maintenance activities around the entire United Kingdom, and which has informed new national legislation. What we see here is the systems property of nonlinearity, that a small action (elderly women being arrested in the early hours for trying to protect a few trees) led to unpredictable major consequences. One might say that mighty oaks from little acorns grow ...

Time for reflection

Think about a situation you have experienced or know something about where an SES has been shocked, perhaps through the COVID-19 pandemic or a natural disaster.

How resilient was the system? Did it react smoothly or was there chaos and confusion?

How did it react to the shock? What happened as a reaction?

As a result of the shock, has the system transformed itself or been transformed in any way?

2.4 Interrelationships

Having used this case study to show how we can think about systems and represent them diagrammatically, we can carry on and look at the three core principles of systems thinking, interrelationships, perspectives and boundaries.

Firstly, interrelationships. A primary requirement within a system is that its entities are interrelated, in other words, that they interact with each other. There are several different ways in which interactions can be seen. One is through influence, that one entity can exert pressure on another, for example, through having greater knowledge, more status, or through a contractual relationship. We can show a pattern of influences in a system using an influence diagram.

Figure 2.7 shows an influence diagram that represents my perspective on the Sheffield tree management system. Again, I developed this diagram by thinking about the relationships between the various entities and what seemed to be happening in the story. Involving people with experience of the story would have again generated much discussion and perhaps new understandings about the relationships involved.

Influence diagrams have certain conventions. A line should have an arrow indicating the direction of influence. Where influence works both ways there should be two lines. The thickness of a line indicates the strength of influence.

So how have I interpreted the events in terms of influence? The city council exerted considerable influence over XYZ to get the tree felling done, and having signed a

44 *Key principles of systems thinking*

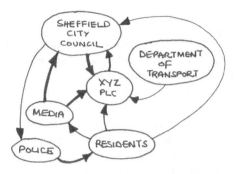

Figure 2.7 Influence diagram for the tree management system.

contract, XYZ's ability to influence the council was limited. The residents exerted some influence over the XYZ workers through their demonstration and resistance, and this was perhaps a greater level of influence than they felt they had over the city council. The city council was able to influence the police to take action against the residents, and this created considerable influence on what residents were able to do. Eventually, it was the publicity created by the stories in the media which put pressure on the city council to consult more effectively with residents, and of course, XYZ did not want to attract the level of negative publicity that was building, nationally and internationally.

You can see that the influence diagram provides an effective way of capturing this somewhat dense textual explanation. Often what is more important than the final diagram is the process of drawing it, as this encourages more holistic thinking about what is actually going on in a situation. This is particularly important when done as a group activity with interested parties, as the process can help to bring limited and partial individual understandings to the surface, making discussions about assumptions possible. For example, what influence did the Department of Transport have over the city council? The diagram does not show any, but that may be more a representation of my limited understanding of the situation. This would encourage me to investigate further.

The final result can provide a very useful way of presenting a summary of what the systems thinker's perspective is of the situation.

Key point

I use influence diagrams in Chapter 3 to explain possible impacts of neoliberal political economy, and in Chapter 10 as a tool to improve understanding in the evaluation process.

System maps are used in:

- Chapter 3 to explain fundamental differences between neoclassical economics and sustainability economics;
- Chapter 4 to illustrate the idea of an organisation as an open system; and
- Chapter 10, again to help understanding during evaluation.

Key principles of systems thinking 45

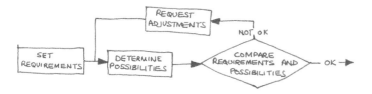

Figure 2.8 Contractual negotiations as a feedback loop.

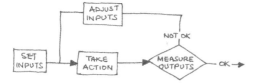

Figure 2.9 Basic feedback loop.

Of course, influence can work both ways, as shown in Figure 2.7. Sheffield City Council may have contractual influence over XYZ, but as the ones with the labour force, knowledge and equipment they can exert influence over the council about what actually gets done. The process of negotiating a contract may therefore be conceptualised in terms of feedback, as shown in Figure 2.8.

Feedback is another fundamental idea in systems thinking. More generally, it can be represented in a basic feedback loop diagram as in Figure 2.9.

Feedback is everywhere. When I take action by cycling up a hill, one output is my heartbeat. If that gets too fast, I slow down my rate of pedalling so that it falls back to a safer level. Climate change is an example of feedback on a global scale. When human action produces levels of greenhouse gases which are unacceptably high, we should adjust the levels of these actions so that the level falls back to what we think is safe.

Feedback underpins the study of cybernetics and is also central to system dynamics, both of which are considered in more detail later.

2.5 Perspectives

The second principle about systems thinking is that of engaging with multiple perspectives. Engaging with multiple perspectives is also something that is very important in facilitating learning, as if new knowledge does not readily find a way of engaging with a learner's understanding of the world it is less likely to take hold. This applies particularly to learning about sustainability, as this subject touches on deeply held values and fundamental understandings about the world. It is therefore worthwhile looking more closely at how individual perspectives develop and what implications this has for what knowledge is seen as important and even legitimate.

The idea that we can look at a situation of interest and think about it as if it were a system in order to understand it better is based on the idea of social constructionism, that the understanding of how the world around us works is not the same for everyone.

46 *Key principles of systems thinking*

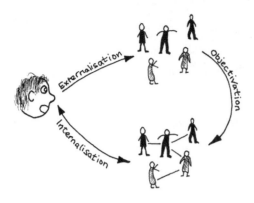

Figure 2.10 The social construction of knowledge.

Writing in the 1960s, Peter Berger and Thomas Luckmann[21] argued that every individual's understanding about how the world around them works is based on what they see and how they interpret what is happening. This process is shown in Figure 2.10.

Human activity is habitualised, in that we tend to behave in predictable patterns because this makes life much easier and allows us to take part in a wider range of activities. Habitualisation creates institutions which determine that women do this, men do that, these people are family, those people cannot be trusted, these values are important in our lives, and so on. A baby looks at the world around them (in Berger and Luckmann's language, they externalise), sees these behaviours in practice and objectivates them into a particular framework. They then internalise these institutionalisations as part of their own way of thinking and behaving. As the individual grows, they contribute to how their community operates and this will have an impact on its objectivation. Similarly, internalisation creates an individual's sense of identity, and they project this back into their objectified world so that they become accepted as part of their particular community. This concept of social identity will become important in later chapters when we look at factors influencing what people are prepared to learn.

Within this institutionalised world there will be knowledge which is deemed to be legitimate, and hence knowledge which is illegitimate. Subscribing to illegitimate knowledge will be discouraged:

> … any radical deviance from the institutional order appears as a departure from reality. Such deviation may be designated as moral depravity, mental disease, or just plain ignorance.[22]

The process described so far is what Berger and Luckmann call "primary socialisation", how an infant becomes part of its community. As the infant matures to adulthood s/he starts to enter different communities (for example, at work) and this constitutes a different framework which leads to a "secondary socialisation". Different frameworks will legitimate different sets of knowledge, and this can be problematic as these will be seen as artificial. Pedagogues in later life, whether they are teachers, university lecturers or organisational trainers, need to be aware that a primary internalised reality will always be in the way of new internalisations, and so they must adopt appropriate techniques to facilitate learning:

> The more these techniques make subjectively plausible a continuity between the original and the new elements of knowledge, the more readily they acquire the accent of reality.[23]

Social constructionism tells us that the perspectives that people hold about the world and about what such things as sustainability mean are determined by their life stories and experiences. In systems thinking, this lens through which the world is seen is referred to as a worldview (sometimes using the German word *Weltanschauung*). Worldview is a concept which seems clear enough but becomes more complex when you try to define exactly what it encompasses. A useful framework suggested for this may be that a worldview is an amalgam of an individual's understanding of five interrelated areas[24]:

- Belief about the nature of being (ontology), how did our world come about, what is its relation to "the divine"?
- What is knowledge, how do we know what is real and what knowledge is legitimate?
- What is a good life? What are moral, ethical and aesthetic values?
- What is the position and purpose of human beings in the universe?
- How should society be organised and how should societal problems be addressed?

These ideas become particularly important when thinking about how people respond to learning about sustainability, a subject discussed in more detail in Chapter 6.

These understandings underpin a number of different worldviews about sustainability which usefully define particular perspectives. Probably the most commonly used term is anthropocentric, which means that the person sees the natural environment as external to humankind, and as a resource to be managed.[25] Related to this is ecomodernism[26] (or technocentrism), which is a perspective associated with traditional economic models and which believes that technological advances and market-based strategies regarding resource usage will lead to sustainable use of the natural environment. *The Ecomodernist Manifesto*,[27] a 2015 declaration published by an international group of academics, provides a good example of what holders of this perspective believe. Ecofeminism[28] sees a root cause of environmental damage as being a male-centred way of perceiving and structuring the world, and ecosocialism sees capitalism as having created a "metabolic rift"[29] between humanity and nature which can only be remedied through collective control and common ownership of means of production.[30]

What is generally seen as the opposite to anthropocentricism is ecocentrism. This perspective is based on a belief "… that ecosystems have inherent worth for maintaining planetary homeostasis and all life".[31] Extensions of the ecocentric perspective include deep ecology,[32] which prioritises the natural environment over the social environment, and theoecocentrism, which proposes that individual belief and thought processes, sometimes through religion or spirituality, have a key role to play in promoting sustainability.[33] Deep sustainability[34] seeks to address root causes of sustainability through the development of a "learning society" which would help individuals to rethink their concept of "self", while ecoconsciousness[35] encourages a deeper understanding of interdependent existence within an ecosystem.

48 *Key principles of systems thinking*

Key point

Social constructionism can be used to explain how we think about the economy as something unchangeable (as in Chapter 1), and I refer to it again in:

- Chapter 3, in talking about political economy and the hegemony of capitalist thinking
- Chapter 4, in reviewing how individuals and organisations may change their value frameworks by "reconstructing" their reality
- Chapter 5, suggesting the importance of training as a social construction
- Chapter 6, where what knowledge is seen to be legitimate is influenced by constructed realities
- Chapter 7, where social construction is a fundamental part of transformative learning and critical thinking.

It is also useful as a way of understanding the distinction between unitarist and pluralist ways of looking at management, discussed several times in Chapters 5, 6, 7 and 9.

2.6 Boundary judgements

Social constructionism implies that we each create our own particular understanding of the world we see around us. This means that as we go about our daily lives we constantly make decisions about what is or is not important, what something means and does not mean, and so on based on our own unique understanding. In systems thinking these are called boundary judgements.

The question of what boundary judgements are made in any systemic enquiry was addressed in the 1970s by Charles West Churchman,[36] and his ideas were refined by Werner Ulrich[37] in developing CSH, a tool for questioning boundary judgements which will be discussed in more detail below (Section 2.13), and which forms a basic structure for developing our learning strategy (in later chapters). Ulrich[38] proposed 12 questions which highlight boundary judgements made about a system:

1. Who benefits from the system?
2. What is the purpose of the system?
3. What is the measure of success of the system?
4. Who makes decisions about the system?
5. What system resources and constraints does the decision-maker control?
6. What conditions of the system's operation are outside of the control of the decision-maker?
7. Who is involved in the design of the system?
8. What expertise (knowledge and experience) is needed to design the system?
9. What guarantees of success do the sources of expertise offer?

Key principles of systems thinking 49

10 Who will represent people that are affected by but not involved in the system?
11 What opportunity do people affected by the system have to avoid its effects?
12 What is the worldview underlying the design of the system?

This list clearly shows the potential minefield involved in boundary judgements. Just for Question 1 and the Sheffield tree management system, who does benefit? Sheffield City Council, which has fewer trees to worry about? XYZ plc, who profit from the contract? The residents of Sheffield, who will have fewer tree roots in the pavements to trip over?

Note Question 12 about the underlying worldview. An anthropocentric worldview would see the trees as being a problem to be managed, whereas an ecocentric worldview might see them as an aspect of nature that should be respected and that urban planning should be based around them, not the other way. The answers to all the previous 11 questions will be influenced by the underlying worldviews held by those providing the answers, but people can often find it hard to articulate what their worldview is.

We have now looked at the three core principles of systems thinking, interrelationships, perspectives and boundary judgements. It is important to realise that these form a nexus (Figure 2.11): interrelationships have an impact on perspectives and are in turn influenced by perspectives; perspectives shape boundary judgements; and boundary judgements will have an impact on interrelationships. As is commonly observed, everything is connected.

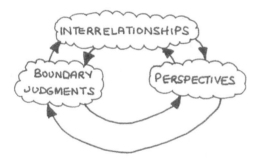

Figure 2.11 The interrelationships, perspectives and boundary judgements nexus.

Key point

Boundary judgements are a fundamentally important subject throughout this book. We will use a structured way of making boundary judgements in order to develop and evaluate a sustainability-focused learning strategy.

2.7 Purpose

The fourth keyword in the definition of a system was about "doing" something, and Question 2 in Ulrich's boundary judgements checklist was "What is the purpose of the system?" Purpose is something which needs to be considered carefully because we immediately run into a problem of semantics. There is a growing interest in business about "purpose", a somewhat nebulous concept which may best be expressed by describing *why* we are doing what we do. This meaning of the term can be seen as an example of what Chris Argyris and Donald Schön would call an "espoused theory",[39] discussed in more detail in Chapter 4.

Argyris and Schön contrasted an espoused theory with "theory-in-use", what happens in reality. Here it is useful to think about Sir Stafford Beer's observation: "The purpose of a system is what it does"[40] (systems thinkers call it POSIWID). On its own, this may seem rather cryptic, but it makes more sense when we consider the words that followed this statement:

> [purpose] stands for a bald fact, which makes a better starting point in seeking understanding than the familiar attributions of good intentions, prejudices about expectations, moral judgements, or sheer ignorance of circumstances.

Beer's observation cuts to the chase, because what an organisation actually does is usually multifaceted, and it is in the conflict between these facets that the challenges arise. For example, an organisation's purpose might be to improve standards of environmental protection but it also needs to generate profits to benefit shareholders—how is the balance between these two purposes managed? This distinction is useful because it is in exploring the gap between espoused theory and theory-in-practice that effective learning can happen.

In our case study, the espoused purpose of the Sheffield tree management system was to control disease and make roads and pavements safer, in Beer's terms, "moral judgements". However, from some perspectives the "bald facts" were that its purpose was to cut down trees. Confronting the dialectic between the moral judgements and bald facts about purpose actually opened up a conversation about what the system's purpose or purposes was or should have been and led to a positive and successful outcome.

Questions about purpose become highly relevant when we think about organisational sustainability, particularly for private sector organisations reliant on public investment. The traditional concept of an investor as someone interested in developing a business is being increasingly challenged by the greater significance of investment by fund managers whose primary interest is in short-term profitability and higher share prices. Charles Handy comments that "… to turn shareholders' needs to a purpose is to be guilty of a logical confusion, to mistake a necessary condition for a sufficient one".[41] In other words, the purpose of an organisation should be to provide a product or a service, not to increase shareholder value, but in an aggressive capitalist economy, this distinction may be lost.

This is even more relevant for hybrid organisations which are based around providing a socially or environmentally valuable function, but which need to maintain profitability. Interesting research by Mary Ann Glynn[42] at the Atlanta Symphony Orchestra showed that a musicians' strike in 1996 was caused by a conflict of identity when musicians, for whom success was measured by artistic creativity and excellence, came into

Key principles of systems thinking 51

conflict with the Orchestra's management, who prioritised financial profitability. Such tensions are also apparent when public services are contracted out to private sector organisations, where the public good of maintaining a healthy tree population in a city becomes balanced against the profit-seeking imperatives of a public limited company. Life is much easier for organisations which can subscribe without feelings of guilt to the Friedman Doctrine.

Time for reflection

This may prove to be a challenging question. What is the purpose of your organisation? In Beer's terms, think about the "bald facts", "moral judgements" or "good intentions". What different purposes can you identify?

Your answers to these questions will suggest how radical any transformation in your organisation to improve sustainability may need to be, and this will have a bearing on how to facilitate sustainability-focused learning.

2.8 Closed and open systems

It may seem surprising to introduce the Second Law of Thermodynamics into a book about organisational learning, but its implications are of fundamental importance in understanding sustainability. The Second Law states that heat always moves from a hotter body to a cooler body: when I put a hot cup of tea on my desk as I am writing it cools down, and in the process warms up my office. However long I wait, the heat in my office will not flow back into the teacup. In broader terms, the energy has become disordered: from being located in one small place it has dissipated throughout a larger area. This concept of increasing disorder is called entropy. The tendency of entropy is always to increase (to become more disordered), and this can only be reversed by providing energy, which I could do for my cup of tea by using a heat pump to extract energy from the air to put back into the teacup, but, of course, that requires an external source of energy.

What is the significance of this for organisational sustainability? Figure 2.12 is a form of system map which shows how an organisation functions. It provides products and

Figure 2.12 Organisation as an open system.

services to a market and in return receives financial returns. It uses the financial returns to buy the resources and energy it needs from the outside world (its environment). If it were not able to buy resources and energy it would stop functioning, and because it relies on these inputs to keep it going, the organisation system is described as open. Relating this to the Second Law of Thermodynamics, by absorbing energy from outside it has managed to keep entropy low. If no resources or energy were available, the organisation's entropy would increase, activities would slowly wind down as it used up any reserves that it had and eventually it would collapse and fall apart. This resonates with the work of Joseph Tainter[43] (see Chapter 1) who observed that as societies become more complex they require more energy to maintain complexity, but as the complexity increases the cost of the energy increases disproportionately and eventually the society cannot justify this expenditure and collapses.

The relevance for sustainability starts to become clear. Planet Earth has finite reserves of fossil fuel and natural resources, and so this means that as time progresses the entropy on the planet will increase. This may be mitigated by the use of renewable technologies such as photovoltaic cells and wind power, which effectively opens the system a little. However, to exploit these technologies we need raw materials such as lithium and rare earth elements which are finite, so the openness may be illusory. So while individual organisations can see themselves as open systems, when you consider together the organisations in the entire world, overall they operate as a closed system.

Key point

The concept of closed and open systems is important in:

- Chapter 3, to understand arguments about the impossibility of continuous economic growth
- Chapter 4, where organisations may be seen as open systems.

2.9 Wicked problems

The Sheffield tree management case study shows how difficult it is to plan and implement a programme such as tree management when there are so many conflicting perspectives and expectations. In systems thinking language, this is known as a complex situation. Again, to clarify some terminology, complex situations are problematic in many ways more than those which are just complicated: for example, docking a space shuttle with the International Space Station relies on highly complicated but predictable mathematics and technology, and if everything is done correctly, the docking will be successful.

However, situations which involve the vagaries of human behaviour will be complex—unexpected things will happen and plans may go awry. Situations such as these have been described as "wicked problems" by Horst Rittel and Melvin Webber.[44] Most problems we have to deal with in organisations have some degree of wickedness, and this certainly applies to facilitating sustainability-focused learning. So how do we recognise a wicked problem? Let us look at the 10 characteristics of a wicked problem that Rittel and Webber suggest.

1. **Wicked problems cannot be fully defined**. How does an organisation operate sustainably? As Chapter 1 showed, there are many different dimensions to perspectives about what sustainability means, and so it is impossible to develop a strategy or plan which will enable an organisation to be perfectly sustainable in the eyes of everyone.
2. **Wicked problems have no stopping rule**. How does an organisation know when to stop, when is it sustainable? Although work progresses on developing measures of sustainability, the impossibility of precisely defining or measuring sustainability means that all measures will be uncertain. Also, as time goes by and the challenges present in the world evolve, the requirements for sustainability will also change. Organisational sustainability will therefore be an ongoing and never-ending challenge.
3. **Solutions to a wicked problem are not true or false**. Whatever strategies an organisation adopts to improve its sustainability, and whatever sustainability-focused learning you support, there will always be something that could be improved. There will never be a satisfying "clunk" as the docking latches engage. Whatever we do to improve sustainability can only make things better or worse.
4. **There is no ultimate test for a solution**. While a sustainability strategy may mean that certain indicators for sustainability are achieved, there is no guarantee that this will continue to be the case in the next week, month or year.
5. **Every attempt changes the situation**. If the space shuttle misses the ISS at the first attempt, it can try again as if starting from scratch. However, if you implement a training programme aimed at supporting your organisation's sustainability strategy and it is unsuccessful, you will have changed people's perceptions about sustainability in some way. If you try again, you will have to try something different.
6. **There is no defined set of possible solutions to a wicked problem**. There are an infinite number of ways in which you can seek to strengthen learning about sustainability in an organisation, through using different learning strategies, targeting different people, and so on. Deciding on the best strategy to adopt is therefore a complex matter.
7. **Every wicked problem is unique**. Every organisation and every department within an organisation will have a different relationship to sustainability, and so what the best strategy is for learning will also be different everywhere. "Off-the-shelf" training packages and "sheep dip" learning strategies may work for some, but will probably not work for all.
8. **Every wicked problem is the symptom of another problem**. At the organisational scale, organisations must exist within an institutional environment which probably encourages unsustainable behaviour: for example, if greenhouse gas emissions are not regulated, any single organisation which takes action to control their own emissions, will be at a disadvantage commercially. Within organisations, each separate function will have some qualities of wickedness which impact on other functions. Resolving these problematic interactions requires high-level organisational redesign, so it is always easier to look for problems at a lower level (which is one reason why training is always recommended as a solution).

54 *Key principles of systems thinking*

9. **There are multiple ways to explain why a wicked problem exists**. Sustainability is a contested concept and everyone may understand it differently, based on their own worldview or what they can see as actions they can take.
10. **Who implements a solution has no right to be wrong**. Implementing any form of learning activity within an organisation is always fraught with problems, and you as a learning facilitator will be held responsible for strategies which do not work. (Of course, if it works, probably no one will thank you!)

Rittel and Webber's 1973 conception of a wicked problem has to some degree been reinvented for the early 21st century by the idea of VUCA, volatility, uncertainty, complexity, ambiguity. Neologised to describe the characteristics of a military operation, VUCA has now been adopted by the business world to summarise factors facing contemporary organisations.[45] In a VUCA world, there is:

- Volatility—instability and unpredictability in terms of, for example, what may happen socially (the early morning attempts to chop down trees led to the arrest of elderly women which resulted in international interest and a public relations crisis)
- Uncertainty—about whether any given event is meaningful (for example, what are the long-term implications of the 2020 Black Lives Matters protests for an organisation?)
- Complexity—interconnected elements (the different priorities for Sheffield City Council, central government and local residents)
- Ambiguity—uncertainty about cause and effect, what *will* happen as an organisation adopts a sustainability strategy?

Why is it important to understand the characteristics of a wicked problem or a VUCA environment? To paraphrase an old saying, if everything you see is a nail, all you need is a hammer. With a rational, Cartesian mindset, all problems are amenable to a scientific approach and hence a solution where everything is resolved, but it is morally wrong to treat a wicked problem as a tame one simply to make strategy development easier. For example, one strategy that is often used to try and make a change is to set a target as a simple measure of success. This generally leads to people focusing on achieving the target at the priority of other aspects of performance, so that, overall, things get worse.[46] Examples of this appear in the news most days: at the time of writing a crisis in the UK dentistry service was attributed in part to government target setting which rewarded treating patients quickly. This resulted in a preference for quick treatments such as extraction rather than remedial work which protected patients' long-term oral health, a more systemically desirable outcome.[47] If we treat a situation as a wicked problem we can use different and potentially more useful, sense-making tools such as systems thinking and hence develop more effective responses.[48]

What wicked problems may we come across in this book? The Sheffield tree management situation is clearly a perfect example of a wicked problem. For example, it was a strategy designed in response to external pressures of cost-cutting and privatisation, but which was seemingly at odds with the global need for afforestation; different people had different ideas about how tree management should have been carried out; when the tree felling happened in one particular residential area the entire situation changed.

Facilitating learning in response to any organisational problem has many wicked characteristics: different people will define the problem in different ways, any single

Key principles of systems thinking 55

problem in an organisation is invariably connected to other problems, implementing poorly designed training can make the situation worse, there are many different ways to try and improve the situation, and so on. Unfortunately, there is a strong tendency in the learning and development profession to conceptualise situations where learning seems to be required as tame problems, as sufficiently well-defined and bounded to make it possible to think that learning is a "solution" which will make things right as long as we develop clear learning objectives, design specific training programmes, and conduct evaluations based on the original objectives.

And of course, organisational sustainability is a major wicked problem: how do we define sustainability, how do we know when our organisation is operating sustainably, how every organisation works towards sustainability will be unique, and so on.

Time for reflection

Training programmes are often intended to "solve" problems that are actually wicked problems.

Look back over the characteristics of a wicked problem, and see how this explanation fits situations in your organisation for which training is seen as a response.

2.10 Complexity theory

To a certain extent, complexity theory sits rather awkwardly in this chapter on systems thinking because its relationship to the type of systems thinking described previously is contested. Writing from the perspective of a "traditional" systems thinker, Michael Jackson summarises concerns raised about complexity theory[49]: that it says nothing new, that what complexity theory presents can be explained from earlier systems thinking ideas; that its origins in the physical sciences do not necessarily mean that it can be used in the less deterministic arena of human behaviour. On the other hand, Ralph Stacey, a key proponent of complexity theory in management, sees it as quite distinct from systems thinking, arguing that traditional concepts are too wedded to linear relationships and a search for stability.[50] Nevertheless, complexity theory has proved beguiling and is perhaps seen as a somewhat "sexier" subject than systems thinking, even though it may be essentially the same thing.

Further arguments exist about how to decide if a particular situation is an example of a complex system, arguments which we may dissolve by simply going back to the idea of thinking about a situation "as if it is a system". If we do this, we can think about any system of interest as complex and see how that helps with sense-making. A complex system has a number of characteristics[51]:

- It has a large number of elements.
- The elements interact, physically or through transferring information.
- Elements influence and are influenced by others in the system.
- Interactions are nonlinear, in that small interactions can have large effects and vice versa.

56 Key principles of systems thinking

- Interactions are generally short range, to immediate neighbours in the system.
- Interactions can create feedback, directly or indirectly.
- It is usually an open system, interacting with its environment.
- Being an open system, it can control the level of entropy and operate at a level some way away from an equilibrium state, which is where increasing levels of entropy would cause interactions to cease.
- It has a history, so what has happened before contributes to what is happening at any particular instant.
- Each element in the system is only aware of what is happening in its immediate vicinity.

In a human complex system, each element is an individual who behaves according to their own set of rules. These rules will draw on a number of sources, such as personal and social identities which prioritise certain assumptions, norms, beliefs and values, and mental models about how their particular world operates. These will have developed as a result of prior individual or group learning (as from Berger and Luckmann's social constructionism). As each individual goes about their daily activities, interacting with others in their immediate network, an overall system behaviour emerges which cannot be predicted by reductively examining the behaviour of each individual: this is the principle of emergent behaviour, a fundamentally important concept in both conventional systems thinking and complexity theory. Such a system may be known as a complex adaptive system (CAS).

Time for reflection

Think back to the Sheffield tree maintenance story. See if you can relate each of these characteristics to what happened, and think about how seeing the situation as a CAS creates new insights for you.

Complex adaptive systems may also be seen as self-organising, in that they "... develop or change internal structures spontaneously and adaptively in order to cope with, or manipulate, their environment".[52] This is an important point to reflect on, as it shows that they develop their own sense of purpose, and that any attempts from outside to influence what a CAS is doing need to recognise this ongoing dynamic. External pressures to enforce change will simply lead to new rules emerging so that the organisation shifts to a new dynamic configuration. Because of nonlinearity, this shift may be small or large, and even relatively small pressures for change can lead to significant reactions.

A particular challenge with human complex systems is that each individual learns from experience, so the rules which they follow in interacting within their network will constantly be changing, meaning that the network's overall behaviour will also change. In principle, this should mean that the performance of the network and individuals becomes more robust, more reliable or better able to deal with changes and unexpected developments in their environment,[53] but this depends on the freedom that individuals have to change the rules by which they operate. If their context means that they are not able to adapt based on their experience, the emergent behaviour may no longer be appropriate to the demands of the external environment. On the other hand, if they are given carte blanche to learn and adapt freely, the emergent system behaviour may diverge significantly into something quite unexpected. This is the complexity theory concept of the "attractor", that there are different dynamically stable ways in which the complex system can operate, and that a small change within the system can flip its overall behaviour from one attractor to another. Hence the metaphor about a butterfly flapping its wings in the Amazon rainforest triggering an Atlantic storm.

In an organisational context, each team or department will have rules that create stable, predictable behaviour which maintains the overall organisational identity of the system, but which does not react to changing environmental circumstances. At the other extreme, individuals will create their own rules which allow them to respond effectively to the environment but deviate from the organisational rules. Stacey calls these "legitimate" and "shadow" systems.[54] Somewhere in the middle is a "sweet spot", or in complexity language, the "edge of chaos", at which point the CAS is stable enough to maintain a coherent identity yet be dynamic enough to be spontaneous and adaptive. The adaptation of rules within a CAS which allows it to adapt effectively to changing environmental conditions may be seen as contributing to the development of a collective intelligence.[55]

There are lessons here for learning strategies. Organisations traditionally see learning as happening through formal, training activities, which are designed to transmit an understanding of the legitimate system rules. If the design and delivery of the training do not make it possible for people to question or challenge these legitimate system rules from the perspective of how they relate to the actual operational environment, then these people may find it difficult to implement the requirements of the training. On the other hand, informal learning, where people regularly and routinely discuss ongoing problems, leads to the development of workarounds or informal practices, the shadow system. This may be ideal for responding to the variety of everyday life but may lead to inconsistent and potentially even illegal behaviour. An ideal learning strategy, therefore, should be one that seeks to find the edge of chaos, which communicates the requirements of the legitimate system but listens to and adapts to relevant demands from the shadow system. How this might happen is explored in more detail in later chapters.

A CAS is also dependent on its history. Learning and development practices in organisations are often heavily influenced by what has been done in the past—certain training methods were used, particular people were involved, informal learning was not seen as significant, and so on. This learning and development saga contributes to a (possibly unrecognised) set of rules which participants in the learning and development CAS employ and which constitute the legitimate system. Development of a sustainability-focused learning strategy provides an opportunity to reflect on how the shadow system of informal learning can be integrated into the wider workplace CAS in order to make learning more flexible and responsive to the challenges of sustainability.

The butterfly metaphor means that we can never be really sure what the consequences will be of any change we make to a CAS. In a team, just one new person starting can have a dramatic, nonlinear effect on how the team behaves. People charged with strategic planning know this only too well, and this is why scenario planning has

58 Key principles of systems thinking

become a valuable technique for developing organisational strategies. Here, the focus is on thinking about what different probable futures there are and making sure that actions being taken move the organisation in a desirable direction. The mental flip is to think about a vision of the future, and then as the behaviour of your CAS emerges, to monitor, tweak and adjust its internal rules so that the system moves in the direction of the vision. A belief in organisations as self-organising leads us to the idea of adaptive management, that management is an iterative process where we constantly adjust decisions that we make so that we move towards our desired vision, learning as we go. This idea underlies the Framework for Strategic Sustainable Development (FSSD), a strategic approach to implementing an organisational sustainability strategy, discussed in more detail in Chapter 4.

Key point

Complexity is important in:

- Chapter 4, where complexity theory helps to understand how an organisation may progress towards sustainability.
- Chapters 6, 7 and 8, where the concept of the edge of chaos helps to understand the need to balance formal and informal learning.
- Chapter 10, where it illustrates the limitations of conventional approaches to learning evaluation.

Time for reflection

What is the saga of learning and development in your organisation?
   What are the "rules" about what you do and do not do?
   How do the legitimate and shadow knowledge systems interact and deal with variety?

2.11 System dynamics

The concluding sections in this chapter look at a number of systems thinking "tools" which draw on the core concepts of the systems thinking methodology as described in the previous sections.

The first tool to look at is system dynamics (SD). We look at this first not because it is the most useful for our purposes in this book, but for two other reasons. Firstly, it is the systems thinking tool that was employed in *The Limits to Growth*, and so occupies an important place in the history of sustainability; and secondly, SD is what systems thinking *is* in probably the most widely read and influential management textbook covering systems thinking, Peter Senge's 1990 *The Fifth Discipline*.

The basic principle in SD is that a change in the level of some element of a system has an effect on other elements which also change, and the resulting sequence of effects directly or indirectly feeds back to the original element, creating a feedback loop. As the number of interconnected elements increases, the number of possible interrelationships increases dramatically, so it was only with the advent of the early electronic computers that SD started to become a powerful tool for understanding system behaviour.

The Limits to Growth is the classic example of this early use of SD. Figure 2.13 is a feedback loop from the World3 model which we can use to explain the principles of SD.

Here called a causal flow diagram, it is drawn using certain (not always consistent) conventions. Each of the four elements is a level of something, so that it can go up or down. It is generally easiest to state levels in a positive way where relevant (for example, increases rather than contractions) as this makes it easier to understand what the diagram is saying. Each of the elements is connected by a single-headed arrow indicating the direction of impact. Each of the connections is given a "+" or a "–", where:

- "+" indicates a positive relationship, so as the first element increases, the second element also increases, and vice versa
- "–" indicates an inverse relationship, so that as the first element increases, the second element decreases, and vice versa.

What does this diagram suggest? As the population increases, the food available per capita will decrease (inverse relationship). This will mean that mortality increases (inverse), and this will mean that the number of deaths per year also increases (positive). But as the number of deaths increases the population will start to decrease (inverse). This loop therefore suggests that populations will stabilise because of food availability. This is the classic Malthusian trap and is an example of a balancing (or stabilising) loop, indicated by the scales symbol inserted in the middle of the loop. Of course, this is only a small part of the story about population dynamics, and on its own, while

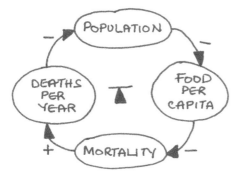

Figure 2.13 Causal flow diagram for population and food per capita (based on Meadows et al, 1972, p. 99).

logically correct, is not particularly useful as a descriptor of a real-world situation. This was one of the reasons why classical economists ridiculed *The Limits to Growth*'s predictions—if particular loops are isolated or values held constant the model can seem banal or simplistic.

Figure 2.14 introduces more complexity. Examining the left-hand, Fertility, loop first, as population increases, the services which can be provided per capita decrease, education and family planning decreases and fertility will increase. The number of births per year goes up and the population continues to increase. This is a reinforcing loop (shown by the spiral) which means that the situation will continue to develop in whichever direction it is currently going in, so that if the population were decreasing, the factors in the loop would continue to put pressure on the population to continue to decrease. Next, looking at the Mortality loop, as the provision of services decreases, health services decrease, mortality rises, deaths per year rise and the population will decrease, leading to an increase in services per capita. So this loop is, as before, a balancing loop. Note that a quick way of working out if a loop is reinforcing or balancing is to count the number of inverse relationships: in a reinforcing loop there will be zero or an even number, and in a balancing loop there will be an odd number.

This now raises the question as to what happens overall? This will depend on the interaction of two factors. Firstly, there is the strength of the relationships in the loop. If services per capita do decrease and the impacts in the fertility loop are stronger overall than those in the mortality loop, then the population will probably continue to rise, but this would be mitigated by the mortality loop. But also time will have an impact: the relative speed at which these factors change will influence the rate of growth.

This introduces the issue of quantitative measures, and this is where computer technology helped SD to explore more complex interactions. By adjusting the variables in each loop, this model of reality can provide different predictions of what will happen over time. If we look at each loop we can identify elements which can be adjusted more easily or where there would be a greater effect, and these become possible "points of leverage", places in the causal flow loops which could be particularly effective at causing desirable change. For example, if the quality of education and family planning were strengthened so that it had a marked impact on fertility, the fertility loop could reverse and the population could start to decrease. This is what is projected to happen over the coming century, with improved female education contributing to low fertility rates and a stabilisation of the world population at about 11 billion people (Figure 2.15).

Figure 2.14 Causal flow diagram showing the impact of services (adapted from Meadows et al, 1972, p. 101).

Key principles of systems thinking   61

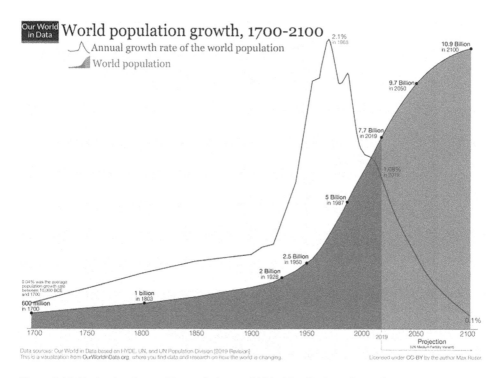

Figure 2.15 Projection in world population to 2100. (Credit: Max Roser.)

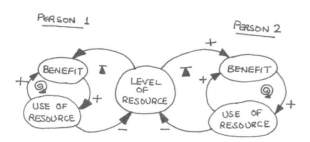

Figure 2.16 Causal flow loop for the tragedy of the commons.

As noted previously, *The Fifth Discipline* drew considerable attention to SD as a way of using systems thinking to improve management practices. In it, Senge identified a number of "archetypes", basic patterns of causal flow loops which he said could be seen in operation in organisations. One of these was the "tragedy of the commons", a reference to the Garrett Hardin[56] paper discussed in Chapter 1.

Figure 2.16 shows how the dynamics Hardin described can be represented as an SD archetype. Each person uses a shared resource and derives benefit, so they continue to do this (reinforcing loops). However, this means that the level of the shared resource (the commons) falls. If there is no intervention in the system, the level will reach a value where it is no longer of any benefit to either and can no longer be used.

62 Key principles of systems thinking

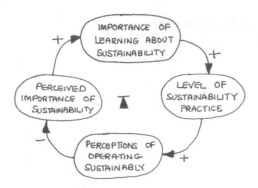

Figure 2.17 Causal flow loop for the importance of learning about sustainability.

SD was originally designed as a way to develop quantitative models of a situation of interest. However, it can also be used in a qualitative mode for developing an understanding of a situation where variables are not particularly easy to quantify. Used in this way they can help to provide some insight into how a particular situation might unfold over time.

For example, Figure 2.17 suggests what might happen when a strategy for sustainability-focused learning is introduced. Initially, sustainability is seen as important, so people will feel that learning about sustainability is more important. This will contribute to higher levels of sustainability-focused practices so that people will feel that the organisation is operating sustainably. However, this could then mean that sustainability is seen to be less important. This would mean that there is a balancing loop, and that it is difficult to maintain interest over time in learning about sustainability. Of course, this may not be the case as other factors need to be considered, and strategies could be implemented to maintain perceptions of importance. So the value of sketching out a loop of this sort is in helping to identify what might happen and what can be done to achieve the desired effect.

Time for reflection

You should now have an idea about how to draw causal flow diagrams.

Try drawing a few to get the hang of how they work and see whether you develop any new insights about a situation.

One idea is to think back to the references to Joseph Tainter's suggestion that societies collapse as it becomes too expensive to maintain their complexity (Sections 1.2 and 2.8). How might you represent those dynamics in a causal flow diagram?

Another possibility is a dynamic noticed by Chris Argyris relating to the professional development of experts—why are they sometimes reluctant to learn?

You will find some suggested (but not necessarily definitive) answers to these at the end of this chapter.

2.12 The Viable System Model

The Viable System Model (VSM) developed by Sir Stafford Beer[57] is a management cybernetics tool which can be used to explore how organisations operate. Like SD, cybernetics is based on feedback, but the key difference is that in cybernetics the feedback is used to implement some form of control, as was shown in Figure 2.9.

VSM is not the easiest tool to understand, but people who are experienced in using it claim that it is the most powerful tool they know of for developing an understanding of what is actually happening in an organisation. The challenge in understanding may be because usually when we ask someone how their organisation works they usually look for an organisational structure chart. This shows what different departments, divisions, and so on the organisation has, but says nothing about *how* the organisation works, how these different elements interact with each other. The strength of VSM is that it ignores structure and focuses on how information flows through the organisation.

The underlying principle in VSM is that of managing "variety". Variety is a concept developed by Ross Ashby,[58] who defined it as the number of distinct elements in a situation of interest. He also proposed the Law of Requisite Variety, which states that in order to control a system, the controller of the system must be able to match the variety presented by the system.

We can explain what this means by thinking about someone working in a call centre. Every day they receive dozens of calls from customers, most of whom may have "standard" problems, but some will have a unusual problem. If the call handler is to offer a good service, they must be able to deal with both standard and unusual problems: in other words, they must be able to match the variety that the customers in their system are presenting. If the handler can only deal with standard problems, they will have to refer unusual problems to someone else so that the requisite variety can be provided. Immediately we see an implication for organisational learning—that the learning provided must be able to ensure requisite variety. Can this be done by a single training course? Perhaps not, so call handlers may talk among themselves about how to deal with the unusual problems that come up from time to time, unconsciously developing requisite variety. Here we can see an obvious parallel with the edge of chaos concept discussed in Section 2.10.

Beer developed VSM by thinking through what needed to happen in organisational practice to make sure that requisite variety was achieved at as low a level in the organisation as possible. So, for example, it would be preferable for call handlers to be able to deal with unusual problems rather than refer them upwards to senior management. Figure 2.18 shows the model that Beer proposed for ensuring an efficient management of variety through an organisation.

The model proposes five interacting systems (Table 2.1) which should be functioning effectively at all levels in the organisation. If they are, the organisation should be, in VSM terms, viable.

System 1 is usually described as the set of primary activities in the organisation, activities that provide an exchange of value with the environment, while the other systems are support activities needed to make sure that System 1 operates effectively. What these activities are will depend on the organisation's business, but as an example might include production, sales and customer dispatch. What is a primary activity in one organisation might be a support activity in another: Patrick Hoverstadt offers the example of accounting, which would be a primary activity for an accountancy firm but

64 Key principles of systems thinking

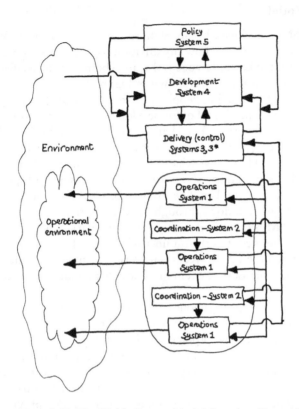

Figure 2.18 The Viable System Model (based on Beer, 1979).

Table 2.1 VSM systems

VSM system	Function
1	Operations, providing value to the environment.
2	Coordination of System 1 activities.
3	Delivery, managing delivery.
3★	Monitoring, providing feedback on delivery.
4	Development, gathering information from the environment.
5	Policy, maintaining identity.

a secondary activity in a building company.[59] A test for a primary activity is to think about whether it could be "sold off" as a separate business.

System 2 coordinates System 1 activities. So, for example, production, sales and dispatch need to be coordinated so that the right number of products are manufactured to suit the level of sales, and that dispatch is able to send these off to the customer efficiently.

System 3 manages the delivery of Systems 1 and 2, so this would conventionally be seen as the activity of line management. This would involve providing the necessary resources (materials and information) for these two systems to function.

System 3★ (usually called '3 star') is the reporting or performance monitoring system, the reverse of System 3. In VSM terminology this is sometimes known as the algedonic system. Through this system, Systems 1 and 2 provide feedback on how well they are performing or if they are having problems, so that System 3 can take appropriate action.

System 4 makes sure that what is happening fits in with the requirements of the environment. This will therefore include such things as seeing what changes are happening in the marketplace, considering new technological developments, communicating with customers, managing change processes, and so on.

System 5 is where the identity of the organisation is held. It needs to define the organisation's values and make sure they are implemented (governance) and to coordinate activities of Systems 3 and 4 to make this happen.

So far we have talked about the model as it relates to an organisation as a whole. For small organisations this may be satisfactory, and I can, for example, analyse my own one-person consultancy practice from a VSM perspective. However, as organisations grow they find the need to change their organisational structure to suit what they do, for example, they may set up regional or market sector divisions. These are responses to environmental variety, and each of these divisions needs to be able to manage its own environmental variety so that it does not have to pass this variety up to the parent company (as with the call handler example). So each organisational level, whether it be division, department, business unit, team, whatever, needs to be viable, and the systems in Figure 2.18 must all be present and functional. This ability of VSM to work at different levels in an organisation is described as recursion.

There is another aspect of recursion to consider. In the call handler example, a call handler is in System 1, as they provide value to their customer. If they are to be able to control the variety that they have to deal with, they must have the autonomy to do this, but to have autonomy they must themselves be viable. This means that every System 1 must be a viable system in its own right, which means that if we look inside System 1 activities we must be able to see Figure 2.18 in action again.

It is probably at this point that newcomers to VSM put their heads in their hands, as this recursive quality can be very difficult to understand. It is helpful to remember that VSM is a model of activity, not a structure, which is why it can be applied successively at different levels of organisational activity. Fortunately, the aim of this book is not to produce VSM consultants, but to show you how VSM can be used to identify what learning may be needed in an organisation to support sustainability-focused learning, so it will be sufficient to have a basic understanding.

VSM as it is normally applied focuses on how these systems need to operate and interact so that the organisation remains viable and successful in a conventional business sense. However, it is possible to apply the principles of VSM to organisational sustainability in order to develop some ideas about how well the system is operating from a sustainability perspective. Markus Schwaninger's work on VSM and sustainability suggests how this may be done.[60]

System 1 conventionally looks at the "positive" value exchanged with the environment. However, delivering a service or product may have negative value implications that are normally overlooked as externalities, for example, pollution, greenhouse gas emission or destructive social consequences. Conventionally the service or product is provided in exchange for a financial value, but if the service or product has a negative impact on the environment then logic dictates that the financial transfers should work in the other direction. So a key question to ask for System 1 is what negative value is this primary activity delivering to the environment?

The sustainability responsibility of System 2 is to coordinate System 1 activities so that negative exchange values are minimised. Convening "sustainability circles" with representatives from different primary activities could provide a way of developing a shared sustainability consciousness. System 2 activities are particularly important during periods of organisational change, such as might be experienced in a shift towards sustainable practice.

System 3 must operate in a way to make sure that Systems 1 and 2 are operating in a sustainability-conscious way, and System 3★ reports on audits into the social and natural environmental impacts of the primary activities.

System 4 monitors the environment, looking to see what negative impact the organisation is having on the environment and gathering information about relevant drivers for sustainability, such as regulation, customer pressure, potential economic benefits for sustainable practice, and so on.

Everything that happens internally as part of Systems 2, 3, 3★ and 4 needs to happen in a way which is socially and environmentally sustainable, and making sure that this happens is the responsibility of System 5. System 5 needs to embody what Schwaninger calls the organisation's "ecological ethos" and will establish and maintain the organisation's sustainability-related ethical climate and associated values. These should be embodied in some form of sustainability vision statement.

Although getting to grips with VSM and understanding how it operates is not easy, it does provide a very useful way of looking at what information flows through an organisation and how this is done. As such it can provide a very useful tool to use in an analysis of what learning strategies may be needed in an organisation to support sustainability. We use VSM in Chapter 5 in order to draw up an outline specification for what content needs to be covered in a sustainability-focused learning strategy. This practical application of the tool will help to make its principles clearer.

2.13 Critical Systems Heuristics

The final tool discussed in this chapter is CSH. Reference has already been made to CSH in Section 2.6 which looked at boundary judgements. One of the criticisms which was made of systems thinking in its early years was that it did not offer a way of looking at the implications of power in a given situation of interest. Power is manifested by decisions about what is done and not done, what is important and not important, and so on, which are essentially boundary judgements. This question of what is valid in any particular situation of interest lies at the heart of the "theory of communicative action" proposed by the German critical philosopher Jürgen Habermas.[61] According to Habermas, clear and open discussion is needed if we are to be confident about the truth and sincerity of other people's claims. Integrating this with other systems ideas developed by Charles West Churchman, the Swiss systems thinker Werner Ulrich[62] developed CSH as a systematic approach to help question these judgements.

The approach is based around the 12 questions listed in Section 2.6. In CSH Ulrich divides these questions into four sets of issues: motivational factors involved in the system of interest, power within the system, knowledge required by the system, and the legitimacy of the system in the eyes of people affected by it. Within each category, Ulrich identifies three categories for examination: the stakeholders relevant in each category, the concerns that these stakeholders would have, and the key problems associated with resolving the concern; crudely speaking, who, what and why. Table 2.2 shows how these categories and questions are structured.[63]

Let us consider the design of a training programme as an example of a system of interest. Although we can address the questions in any order, a fundamentally important question is Q12, what is the worldview for the system? One answer to this might be that training is an effective way to achieve the required purpose, a questionable assumption, as will be discussed in more detail in Chapter 5. Worldview influences subsequent questioning, but it is often easiest to continue with purpose. What is the purpose of the programme? We generally answer that question by specifying aims and objectives. Then we must agree some quality criteria—what is the measure of improvement relevant to the programme? Then we could specify the client, who takes part in the programme? And so we continue for the other questions. Each answer we make is a boundary judgement, which means a decision about what is in the programme and what is not, what successes are relevant and what are not, and so on. You can see the highly political and sometimes somewhat arbitrary decision-making processes that often go on with little significant research or reflection, and how certain questions may never be asked at all.

CSH can be used in different modes which have been described as ideal mapping, empirical and normative.[64] Ideal mapping uses CSH as a planning tool to map out what we should do in a system of interest to make sure that we are as aware as possible of the boundary judgements that we are making. This mode is used in Chapters 5 to 9 where we use it to map out the structure of a sustainability-focused learning and development strategy.

In empirical mode, we look at a system of interest as it is happening or has happened and identify answers as we see them. Then, in normative mode, we look at the system more critically and ask what the answers *ought* to be. Empirical and normative modes are sometimes employed simultaneously if we are trying to evaluate an activity. In the context of a training programme evaluation we might ask questions such as:

- Who provided the subject matter knowledge, what subject matter knowledge did they provide and what guarantees were provided that this was the relevant knowledge (empirical mode), and
- Who *should have* provided the subject matter knowledge, what subject matter knowledge should have been provided and what guarantees should have been sought to give assurance that this was the relevant knowledge (normative mode).

Table 2.2 Boundary categories within CSH

		Stakeholders (who)	Stakeholder concerns (what)	Key problems (why)
The involved	Sources of motivation	Client	Purpose	Measure of improvement
	Sources of power	Decision-maker	Resources	Decision environment
	Sources of knowledge	Expert	Expertise	Guarantee of expertise
The affected	Sources of legitimation	Witness	Emancipation	Worldview underlying system

The answers to the two sets of questions might be the same, but if not the difference has the potential to open up questioning about why this is the case. For example:

- Was it due to power relationships—was the expert knowledge provided by a senior manager who could not be challenged?
- Was this issue adequately considered in the learning needs assessment?

The use of CSH to evaluate learning programmes is examined in more detail in Chapter 10.

2.14 Key points in this chapter

Systems thinking presents a counterpoint to Cartesian thinking: rather than trying to understand how the whole works by looking at the parts, we seek to understand how parts work by looking at the whole (Figure 2.19). It offers a way to help us make more sense of a situation, draw out alternative perspectives, and explore the implication of power relationships.

Drawing simple diagrams, such as system maps and influence diagrams, is an easy way to start to use systems thinking principles. As you do this you will start to understand the interrelationships working in a system which may create feedback, the multiple perspectives that exist about a situation, and the boundary judgements that must inevitably be made. Not all systems are obviously systems, but we can always try to imagine that something is a system and ascribe to it a purpose. This is a very important and powerful way of improving understanding about what is or may be, or should be, happening.

When considering sustainability, a very important concept is the distinction between open and closed systems. This is of particular importance in sustainability economics (see Chapter 3), as current economic systems treat industrial activity as an open system, whereas Planet Earth is effectively a closed system. The problem here is entropy.

Most human activity situations can be regarded as wicked problems. These have a number of characteristics, including being hard to define, lacking any clear end point

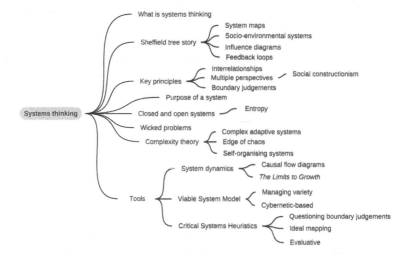

Figure 2.19 Key points in this chapter.

and being closely connected with other wicked problems. Recognising that a situation is wicked opens the mind to a different range of ways forward, and systems thinking can provide a powerful tool for doing this.

It can sometimes be helpful to think about situations, including those in organisations, as complex adaptive systems. These will behave in a particular way, but small changes inside the system can lead to radical changes in overall behaviour. In an organisational setting, it is important to remember the tension between legitimate and shadow systems, and the desirability of operating at the edge of chaos to ensure consistency and flexibility.

Systems thinking offers a number of tools which can be used to explore situations of interest. These include SD, which relies on causal flow diagrams and can help to clarify how a situation might unfold, VSM, which is useful for diagnosing what is happening or should happen within an organisation, and CSH, which is designed to help show what boundary judgements are, should or could be made in a particular system of interest.

2.15 Further reading

Systems Approaches to Management, Michael Jackson, 2000, an excellent summary to key ideas in systems thinking and how they relate to management in organisations. It is particularly useful as a guide to the many philosophical arguments that go on within the systems thinking community.

Complexity and Creativity in Organizations, 1996, and *Strategic Management and Organisational Dynamics*, 2011, both by Ralph Stacey, are reference textbooks about management and complexity theory.

Aid on the Edge of Chaos, 2013, Ben Ramalingam, how complexity applies to international development, but with useful sections on adaptive management and systemic learning.

The Fractal Organization, Patrick Hoverstadt, 2008, an accessible guide to using VSM.

Systems Approaches to Making Change: A Practical Guide, Martin Reynolds and Sue Holwell, 2010, a course reader for the Open University MSc course in systems thinking, so an excellent introduction to the principles and tools discussed in this chapter.

The Open University also provides a free basic course on systems thinking, available through OpenLearn at: https://www.open.edu/openlearn/science-maths-technology/computing-ict/systems-thinking-and-practice/content-section-0?active-tab=description-tab

2.16 Possible answers to reflection questions

Here are some possible answers to the reflection question in Section 2.11. These may not be the same as your thoughts, but that does not mean you are wrong! The important thing is to compare these different ideas and see what learning emerges. We will all have a different perspective on how these situations might unfold.

2.16.1 Collapse of complex societies

Figure 2.20 is a possible representation of Tainter's description of why complex societies fail. Increasing complexity increases the cost of services, but the marginal return on the investment in such costs goes down, leading to less investment being made in such

70 Key principles of systems thinking

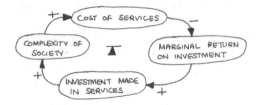

Figure 2.20 Causal flow diagram for the collapse of complex societies.

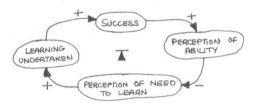

Figure 2.21 Causal flow diagram for the professional development of experts.

services. This will consequently lead to a reduction in complexity. This loop suggests that complexity will reach a level and then stabilise, but of course it simplifies matters considerably. People who are used to ever-increasing sophistication may grow restless if they feel that their lives have stagnated, so we could elaborate on the diagram by adding another loop about social unrest.

You can think more about the implications of a stagnation in social complexity and develop the diagram and see what learning you can derive from it.

2.16.2 Professional development of experts

In 1991 the organisational learning expert Chris Argyris wrote a paper reflecting on the challenges of persuading clever people in organisations to learn.[65] His conclusion, represented by Figure 2.21, was that as people become more successful the perception they have of their own ability increases, and that this means that they see less need to learn anything, and so enrol for fewer courses, read fewer books, and so on. Unfortunately, this can lead to a deterioration in their position in the organisation, especially if there are others who do not share that perception!

You may also want to think about how such factors as innovation and likelihood of promotion could be included in this causal flow diagram.

Notes

1 Kenan Malik, *The Quest for a Moral Compass: A Global History of Ethics* (London: Atlantic Books, 2014), 180.
2 Martin Reynolds and Sue Holwell, 'Chapter 1: Introducing Systems Approaches', in *Systems Approaches to Managing Change: A Practical Guide*, ed. Reynolds M. and S. Holwell, 2nd ed. (London: Open University and Springer, 2020), 17–18.
3 UNSD, 'Agenda 21' (United Nations Sustainable Development, 1992), para. 36.1–36.3.
4 M. Rieckman, 'Learning to Transform the World: Key Competencies in ESD', in *Issues and Trends in Education for Sustainable Development*, ed. A. Leicht, J. Heiss, and Won Jung Byun (Paris: UNESCO, 2018), 44.

5 Arnim Wiek, Lauren Withycombe, and Charles L. Redman, 'Key Competencies in Sustainability: A Reference Framework for Academic Program Development', *Sustainability Science* 6, no. 2 (2011): 207.
6 R. M. Morris, 'Thinking about Systems for Sustainable Lifestyles', *Environmental Scientist* 18, no. 1 (2009): 16.
7 Reynolds and Holwell, 'Chapter 1: Introducing Systems Approaches', 8.
8 Martin Reynolds, '(Breaking) The Iron Triangle of Evaluation', *IDS Bulletin* 46, no. 1 (2015): 71–86.
9 Reynolds and Holwell, 'Chapter 1: Introducing Systems Approaches', 8.
10 For a more detailed account of this story, see: https://en.wikipedia.org/wiki/Sheffield_tree_felling_protests.
11 Ellie Violet Bramley, 'For the Chop: The Battle to Save Sheffield's Trees', *The Guardian*, 25 February 2018, http://www.theguardian.com/uk-news/2018/feb/25/for-the-chop-the-battle-to-save-sheffields-trees.
12 P. Checkland and J. Scholes, *Soft Systems Methodology in Action* (Chichester: John Wiley & Sons Ltd, 1991), 45.
13 There is an excellent guide to the basics of diagramming for systems thinking at: http://systems.open.ac.uk/materials/T552/.
14 R. Carter et al., *Systems, Management and Change* (London: Harper & Row Ltd, 1984), 111.
15 Sheffield City Council, 'Sheffield Responds to the Climate Emergency', accessed 24 February 2021, https://www.sheffield.gov.uk/home/your-city-council/climate-emergency-response.
16 Ellen Scully-Russ, 'The Contours of Green Human Resource Development', *Advances in Developing Human Resources* 17, no. 4 (2015): 411–25; Brian Walker et al., 'Resilience, Adaptability and Transformability in Social–Ecological Systems', *Ecology and Society* 9, no. 2 (2004).
17 Chester W. Hartman, Gregory Squires, and Gregory D. Squires, *There Is No Such Thing as a Natural Disaster: Race, Class, and Hurricane Katrina* (New York: Routledge, 2006).
18 For example, BBC, 'Coronavirus Exposes Inequalities, First Minister Says', *BBC News*, 31 May 2020, https://www.bbc.com/news/uk-wales-politics-52866523.
19 Milton Friedman, 'A Friedman Doctrine – The Social Responsibility of Business Is to Increase Its Profits', *The New York Times*, 1970, 13 September edition.
20 Walker et al., 'Resilience, Adaptability and Transformability in Social–Ecological Systems'.
21 Peter L. Berger and Thomas Luckmann, *The Social Construction of Reality: A Treatise in the Sociology of Knowledge* (London: Penguin Books, 1991).
22 Berger and Luckmann, 82.
23 Berger and Luckmann, 163.
24 Annick Hedlund-de Witt, 'Exploring Worldviews and Their Relationships to Sustainable Lifestyles: Towards a New Conceptual and Methodological Approach', *Ecological Economics* 84 (2012): 74–83.
25 Angela Espinosa and Jon Walker, *A Complexity Approach to Sustainability: Theory and Application* (Singapore: Imperial College Press, 2011), 16.
26 Ellen Scully-Russ, 'Human Resource Development and Sustainability: Beyond Sustainable Organisations', *Human Resource Development International* 15, no. 4 (2012): 399–415.
27 John Asafu-Adjaye et al., 'An Ecomodernist Manifesto', 2015, www.ecomodernism.org.
28 Val Plumwood, *Feminism and the Mastery of Nature* (London: Routledge, 2003).
29 John Bellamy Foster, 'Marx's Theory of Metabolic Rift: Classical Foundations for Environmental Sociology', *American Journal of Sociology* 105, no. 2 (1999): 366–405; Karl Marx, *Capital: A Critical Analysis of Capitalist Production*, vol. II (London: George Allen & Unwin, 1887), 514.
30 Desta Mebratu, 'Sustainability and Sustainable Development: Historical and Conceptual Review', *Environmental Impact Assessment Review* 18, no. 6 (1998): 493–520.
31 Helen Borland and Adam Lindgreen, 'Sustainability, Epistemology, Ecocentric Business, and Marketing Strategy: Ideology, Reality, and Vision', *Journal of Business Ethics* 117, no. 1 (2013): 176.
32 Arne Naess, 'The Deep Ecological Movement: Some Philosophical Aspects', *Philosophical Inquiry* 8 (1986): 10–31.
33 Espinosa and Walker, *A Complexity Approach to Sustainability*, 17.
34 John Foster, 'Sustainability, Higher Education and the Learning Society', *Environmental Education Research* 8, no. 1 (2002): 35–41.

35 Edmund O'Sullivan and Marilyn M. Taylor, *Learning toward an Ecological Consciousness: Selected Transformative Practices* (New York: Palgrave MacMillan, 2004).
36 Charles West Churchman, *The Systems Approach and Its Enemies* (New York: Basic Books, 1979).
37 Werner Ulrich, *Critical Heuristics of Social Planning: A New Approach to Practical Philosophy* (New York: John Wiley & Sons, 1983); Werner Ulrich, 'Critical Heuristics of Social Systems Design', *European Journal of Operational Research* 31, no. 3 (1987): 276–83.
38 Ulrich, 'Critical Heuristics of Social Systems Design'.
39 C. Argyris and D. A. Schön, *Organizational Learning: A Theory of Action Perspective* (Reading, MA: Addison-Wesley Publishing, 1978).
40 Stafford Beer, 'What Is Cybernetics?', *Kybernetes: The International Journal of Systems & Cybernetics* 33, no. 3–4 (2004): 7.
41 Charles Handy, 'What Is a Business For?', *Harvard Business Review* 80, no. 12 (2002): 50.
42 Mary Ann Glynn, 'When Cymbals Become Symbols: Conflict over Organizational Identity within a Symphony Orchestra', *Organization Science* 11, no. 3 (2000): 285–98.
43 Joseph A. Tainter, 'Sustainability of Complex Societies', *Futures* 27, no. 4 (1995): 397–407.
44 Horst W.J. Rittel and Melvin M Webber, 'Dilemmas in a General Theory of Planning', *Policy Sciences* 4, no. 2 (1973): 155–69.
45 Nathan Bennett and G. James Lemoine, 'What a Difference a Word Makes: Understanding Threats to Performance in a VUCA World', *Business Horizons* 57, no. 3 (2014): 311–17.
46 For an excellent dissection of the United Kingdom's target setting culture, read John Seddon, *Systems Thinking in the Public Sector* (Axminster: Triarchy Press, 2008).
47 James Tapper, 'Patients Struggling to Get NHS Dental Care across England, Says Watchdog', *The Guardian*, 6 February 2021, http://www.theguardian.com/society/2021/feb/06/patients-struggling-to-get-nhs-dental-care-across-england-says-watchdog.
48 Raymond L. Ison, Kevin B. Collins, and Philip J. Wallis, 'Institutionalising Social Learning: Towards Systemic and Adaptive Governance', *Environmental Science & Policy* 53 (2015): 105–17.
49 M. Jackson, *Systems Approaches to Management* (New York: Kluwer Academic, 2000), 201.
50 Ralph D. Stacey, *Strategic Management and Organisational Dynamics: The Challenge of Complexity*, 6th edition (Prentice Hall: Financial Times, 2011), 235–36.
51 Cilliers P., *Complexity & Post-Modernism: Understanding Complex Systems* (London, Routledge, 1998), 3–5.
52 Paul Cilliers, *Complexity and Postmodernism: Understanding Complex Systems* (London: Routledge, 2002), 90.
53 Elena Antonacopoulou and Ricardo Chiva, 'The Social Complexity of Organizational Learning: The Dynamics of Learning and Organising', *Management Learning* 38, no. 3 (2007): 277–95.
54 Ralph D. Stacey, *Complexity and Creativity in Organizations* (San Francisco, CA: Berrett-Koehler Publishers, 1996).
55 Laurie E. Paarlberg and Wolfgang Bielefeld, 'Complexity Science—An Alternative Framework for Understanding Strategic Management in Public Serving Organisations', *International Public Management Journal* 12, no. 2 (2009): 236–60.
56 Garrett Hardin, 'The Tragedy of the Commons', *Science* 162, no. 3859 (1968): 1243–48.
57 Stafford Beer, *The Brain of the Firm* (London: Allen Lane: The Penguin Press, 1972); Stafford Beer, *The Heart of Enterprise* (Chichester: John Wiley & Sons, 1979).
58 W. R. Ashby, *An Introduction to Cybernetics* (London: Chapman & Hall, 1956).
59 Patrick Hoverstadt, *The Fractal Organization: Creating Sustainable Organizations with the Viable System Model* (Chichester: John Wiley & Sons, 2011), 97.
60 Markus Schwaninger, 'Organizing for Sustainability: A Cybernetic Concept for Sustainable Renewal', *Kybernetes* 44, no. 6/7 (2015): 935–54.
61 Jürgen Habermas, *The Theory of Communicative Action*, trans. Thomas McCarthy, vol. 1: Reason and the realization of society, 2 vols (Boston: Beacon Press, 1981); Jürgen Habermas, *The Theory of Communicative Action*, trans. Thomas McCarthy, vol. 2: *Lifeworld and System: A Critique of Functionalist Reason*, 2 vols (London: Heinemann Educational Books, 1984).
62 Ulrich, *Critical Heuristics of Social Planning*; Ulrich, 'Critical Heuristics of Social Systems Design'.

63 W. Ulrich and Reynolds M., 'Chapter 6: Critical Systems Heuristics: The Idea and Practice of Boundary Critique', in *Systems Approaches to Managing Change: A Practical Guide*, ed. Reynolds M. and S. Holwell (London: Open University and Springer, 2020), 256.
64 Ulrich and Reynolds, 287.
65 Chris Argyris, 'Teaching Smart People How to Learn', *Harvard Business Review* 69, no. 3 (1991): 99–109.

3 The political economy of sustainability

3.1 What this chapter covers

This chapter provides an introduction to the political economy of sustainability. Figure 3.1 shows how it is organized.

Economics has been described as the study of how scarce resources are allocated. At a basic level, it might be seen as how people use resources from the natural environment, for example, how they buy and sell food, how they acquire materials needed to construct shelters, and so on. Early societies would have conducted this allocation through a process of exchange, deciding how much wheat was worth how much timber perhaps, but in modern societies, we have money as a medium of exchange. How an economy works is therefore a social technology, an artefact created to meet particular needs. As such, if it does not meet our needs, we can change it.

The aim of this chapter is to provide a basic explanation about two ways in which this social technology works: first, the status quo of capitalism, and second, alternatives which can be considered under the heading of "sustainability economics". Such an overview is useful, as when we look at organisational sustainability in Chapter 4, we will need to understand how the political economy landscape within which an organisation operates has an impact on its adaptation to sustainability.

3.2 Capitalism

The global economic system that we recognise today started to emerge in the late 19th century, as new scientific and technological developments increased the scale of industrial activity and led to calls for a stronger theoretical understanding of how economies worked. The result was what we now call neoclassical economics, characterised by an emphasis on the role of the market in determining prices and an interest in developing mathematical models of how the economy worked. This also led to the dropping of the

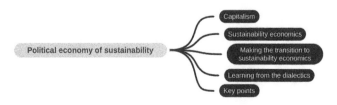

Figure 3.1 Map of Chapter 3.

DOI: 10.4324/9781003218296-4

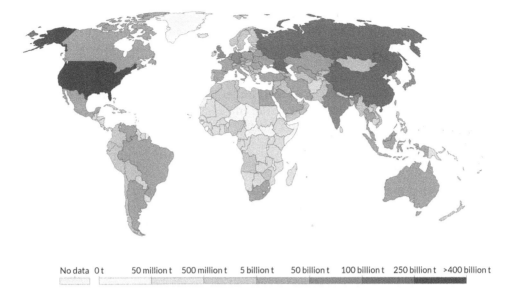

Figure 3.2 CO_2 emissions by world region (Source: Ourworldindata.org).

word "political" from the study of what had been called "political economy", as it was felt that the discipline was now becoming a science.

The start of the Great Acceleration (and arguably the Anthropocene) in 1950 marks the point at which the role of capitalist economics in changing global ecosystems becomes particularly significant. This can be seen in Figure 3.2, a map which shows cumulative CO_2 emissions from 1750 to 2019. The capitalist economies of Western Europe and North America have made by far the biggest contributions, and that in recent decades they have been joined by the state-controlled capitalism of China. Although climate change deniers challenge the causality, there is a strong correlation between capitalism and the massive increases of CO_2 in the atmosphere and its consequent implications for environmental sustainability. It is therefore interesting to reflect on Max Weber's prescient closing comments in his 1905 analysis of the Protestant ethic:

> [T]he modern economic order ... is now bound to the technical and economic conditions of machine production which to-day determine the lives of all the individuals who are born into this mechanism, not only those directly concerned with economic acquisition, with irresistible force. Perhaps it will also determine them until the last ton of fossilized coal is burnt.[1]

While living standards and economic freedoms in North America and Western Europe grew, the political repression in the so-called "Iron Curtain" countries prompted a group of economists led by Friedrich Hayek to start meeting in the Swiss village of Mont Pèlerin to discuss what they saw as the threats to social and economic freedom imposed by the collectivism and repression in the Communist countries. The ideas of the Mont Pèlerin Society as it came to be known, caught the attention of Margaret Thatcher in the late 1970s, and she decided that this was the way forward for the British economy: there would be no alternative. The Reagan administration in the United

States also saw great value in the ideas, and what we now know as neoliberalism became established as the orthodox form of neoclassical economics in two of the world's most important economies, the United States and the United Kingdom. It has also become accepted as orthodoxy to a greater or lesser degree in economies around the world as commercial globalisation developed.

What are the key characteristics of neoliberal economics and what implications do these have for sustainability? We can consider five particular aspects: its focus on the market as the perfect decision-maker, the emphasis on financial efficiency, financialisation, intellectual property issues and ethics.

3.2.1 Primacy of the market

In neoliberal thinking the marketplace is the perfect processor of information, always leading to the optimum decision, and that any attempts to interfere with the working of the marketplace will result in a sub-optimal outcome. This applies to everything—education, health and all issues concerned with the environment can be improved by market-based decisions. Even me as an individual, who:

> is not just an employee or student, but also simultaneously a product to be sold, a walking advertisement, a manager of her résumé, a biographer of her rationales, and an entrepreneur of possibilities.... She is all at once the business, the raw material, the product, the clientele, and the customer of her own life.[2]

Philip Mirowski describes this as "everyday neoliberalism". Everyday neoliberalism and the meritocracy of the late 20th century proved good bedfellows: if you take your opportunities and market yourself, you will be a success. However, this also means that being marginalised in society is your fault, you have not worked hard enough or recognised the demands of the market.

Market primacy has implications for both social and economic sustainability. For social sustainability and the need to address basic needs, social equity and social cohesion perspectives, the market means that societal basic needs such as education and health are marketised, trades unions are suppressed and employment laws are designed on the basis that the market will make the best decisions.

As regards social equity, neoliberalism claims a trickle-down effect, that as the tide of wealth rises, everyone's boats will rise with the tide—inequality is not important because everybody gets richer. This belief draws on what is known as the "Kuznets curve" (Figure 3.3), a model derived from a 1955 paper by Simon Kuznets.[3]

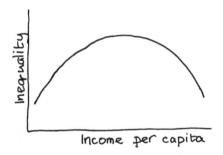

Figure 3.3 Representation of the Kuznets curve.

The political economy of sustainability 77

Although Kuznets himself never drew this diagram, others have drawn it based on his conclusions, and over time it has become reified as "what happens", perhaps because it offers a strong justification for pursuing neoliberal economic policies. However, it is generally overlooked that most of Kuznets' paper discusses the weaknesses in available data and the unreliability of his conclusions, and more recent research tends to conclude that it is not valid, and that inequality increases in line with average income per capita.[4] Less clearly articulated by neoliberal economists is that inequality is necessary: the better off can use their wealth to create new opportunities for those less well off, who are in turn inspired to work harder.

A lack of social equity also has an impact on social cohesion. Wilkinson and Pickett[5] assert that the main problem caused by inequality is the damaging effect of comparisons people make with other, better-off people. These comparisons have a profound impact on each individual's sense of self-esteem and well-being, and this contributes to a range of social problems which affect levels of trust, mental illness, life expectancy, infant mortality, obesity, children's educational performance, teenage births, homicides, imprisonment rates and social mobility.[6] From this line of thinking the success of neoliberalism in making individuals look at themselves as products to be sold may ultimately have a negative effect on social sustainability.

Figure 3.4 is an influence diagram which tries to show the logic of this argument. Neoliberalism promotes the importance of seeing oneself as a commodity, and this necessarily means that we compare ourselves against others. But what this comparison shows will be influenced by our perceptions of inequality, so that if we feel we are lower than most other people in society our level of self-esteem and well-being will fall. This may also be influenced by social media, a technological development which has been enthusiastically embraced by neoliberalism as a tool for increasing self-commodification. As individual levels of well-being deteriorate, social sustainability indicators will also suffer.

As regards environmental sustainability, neoliberal economists make similar claims for the beneficial effects of the market economy on environmental sustainability. Early research[7] claimed that there was an Environmental Kuznets Curve, as shown in Figure 3.5.

However, as with the original Kuznets curve, further research has shown its limitations, in that the relationship between environmental degradation and income per capita depends very much on factors such as the industries being considered, the nature of degradation examined and local variables related to regulation.[8]

Market-based decisions should mean that environmental pressures drive the market to take actions which maintain the environment in a condition that actors in the

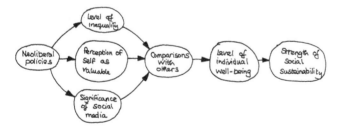

Figure 3.4 Influence diagram showing the possible impact of neoliberal policies on social sustainability.

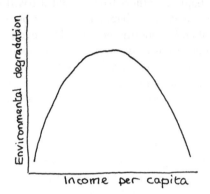

Figure 3.5 The Environmental Kuznets Curve.

market desire, an ecomodernist perspective. This would mean that market solutions will minimise environmental degradation, using, for example, carbon trading schemes for offsetting carbon emissions,[9] or private sector development of new geoengineering technologies such as carbon capture.[10] However, in the early 21st century, the gathering pace of environmental degradation raises the question as to whether this can happen quickly enough: as reported in the 2007 *Stern Review*, the potential scale of long-term damage done to the global natural environment through neoliberal policies "… must be regarded as market failure on the greatest scale the world has seen".[11]

A number of different factors have contributed to this market failure. First, in the neoliberal economy the degree to which an organisation responds to market signals is measured by its share price, and this is determined to a significant extent by financial profitability. This means that commercial organisations are forced to take a short-term perspective on their activities in order to satisfy shareholders, the Friedman Doctrine. The short-term focus on profitability means that commercial organisations are reluctant to invest in research and development to produce innovations which could contribute to environmental improvements which would only prove profitable in the long term.[12]

The focus on the short term rather than the long term also leads to the emphasis in neoliberal economics on high rates of economic discounting. As markets tend to take a short-term view of transactions, the neoliberal perspective assumes a higher discount rate which reduces the projected future cost of environmental damage, making it more rational to delay making investments related to environmental sustainability.[13] A major criticism of *The Stern Review* made by neoliberal economists concerned Stern's recommendation that discounting rates for environmental costs should be low (around 1–1.5% per annum, implying that long-term costs would be high): the influential American economist William Nordhaus, advocated a rate of 4–4.5% per annum, implying a much less problematic future, a position which Thomas Piketty describes as "opportunely consistent with the U.S. strategy of unrestricted carbon emissions".[14]

Minimising the cost of social and environmental impacts is also achieved by classifying such costs as externalities, "a consequence of an economic activity which affects other parties without this being reflected in market prices".[15] In formal economic theory, quality of the natural environment is a public good, which is a particular example of an externality: people can enjoy a public good without paying for it and one person's enjoyment does not preclude the enjoyment of another person. Neoliberal economics treats the impact of commercial activity on the natural environment as an externality because as a public good the cost of the impact is not included in the market calculations of price. However, while this might have been empirically (if not ethically) justifiable in earlier times, the assumption that the environment is not scarce and therefore not relevant to economic calculations may no longer be valid.

3.2.2 Financial efficiency or resilience

Market-based decisions emphasise financial efficiency. However, as discussed in Section 2.3, if a socio-environmental system is to remain effective over a period of time it must have two qualities: firstly, it must be efficient so that it can remain organised with a minimum expenditure of effort and energy; and secondly, it must be resilient so that it can respond to and survive external disturbances. These two qualities are constantly in tension: resilience requires redundancy, extra mechanisms or subsystems which can be called on when needed, but these will require investment for maintenance and so will reduce efficiency. A robust socio-environmental system must therefore allow for this trade-off between the two qualities.

Neoliberal efficiency reduces resilience, so we see problems such as the 2007 financial crisis where the neoliberal economy was completely unable to find solutions: massive government interventions were necessary to restore some measure of stability (so that neoliberalism could return in due course, of course!). The COVID-19 pandemic also illustrated the inability of neoliberal economics to create a society resilient enough to cope with massive disruptions without government support.

3.2.3 Intellectual property protection

Neoliberalism emphasises the primacy of private enterprise, and this is by its very nature competitive, with organisations striving to achieve an advantage over competitors. An important way in which they can do this is by creating intellectual property which they then protect to justify the investment made for its creation. A neoliberal perspective emphasises the importance of strengthening intellectual property rights, and studies have shown that during the last 30 years the scope of what may be protected has increased significantly: intellectual property can now cover human beings, computer code and even business practices.[16] The problem when developing new technologies aimed at protecting environmental sustainability is that the payback period may be long and uncertain, so it is therefore possible that the dissemination of technologies which could contribute to the mitigation of long-term environmental damage could be hampered by intellectual property issues.[17]

3.2.4 Financialisation

Early in the history of capitalism people invented interest-bearing debt. Originally the idea was that as a lender you would give someone money, they would make something with it and return to you a share of their profit as interest. In the neoliberal world, this goes one stage further, where you buy money itself in the hope that its value will increase, such as through currency trading or the use of specialised "financial instruments", essentially bundles of other people's debts. This is called financialisation, and its effectiveness at making profit has meant that it now may be more attractive to buy and

80 *The political economy of sustainability*

sell money than to invest in actual job-creating commercial activities. The combined effects of the privatisation of finance and financialisation mean that it has become less likely that investments are made in long-term public good projects aimed at social or environmental sustainability.[18]

3.2.5 Ethics and neoliberalism

To the neoliberal mind ethical considerations about caring for future generations are not seen as significant for two reasons.[19] Firstly, because people make economic decisions based on self-interest, we need not consider the preferences of those unborn because they do not interact with the market, and secondly, because the price determined by the market takes consideration of all available information, ethical considerations will already be factored in.

3.2.6 Neoliberal economics as a system

Based on this explanation of neoliberal economics and what they mean for business, I can construct a diagram to capture my understanding of these ideas (Figure 3.6). This is something of a hybrid diagram, being a combination of a system map and an influence diagram, and I have done this because it helps my understanding of neoliberal economics *as a system*. My understanding sees organisations and the market as forming a system with the other elements being in the environment. I have presented the market as a cloud to illustrate its nebulous quality. Financial institutions provide investment capital to help the organisation to operate, but also speculate by investing in the market. The organisation extracts resources from both the social and natural environments. The state has a minimal but vital role in ensuring that a status quo of light regulation is maintained.

Figure 3.6 also illustrates the importance of what economists call the "factors of production", traditionally seen as labour, capital and natural resources. The organisation in this diagram draws in each of these to develop its products and services. Neoclassical

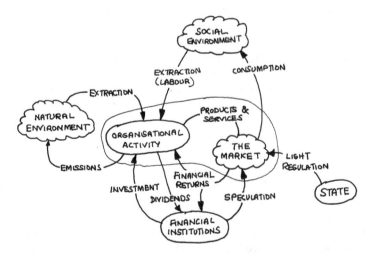

Figure 3.6 System map and influences in the neoliberal economic system.

economics places a great deal of importance on the idea of "substitutability", which states that as the supply of one factor becomes too expensive, we can substitute to another one: for example, if labour becomes too expensive, we use capital to develop technology which reduces the need for labour, or if one resource becomes too expensive we switch to another. However, as the ecological economist Herman Daly has pointed out, a fundamental flaw in this argument is that substitutability can only work up to a certain point: if, for example, if natural resources run out you cannot substitute by using more labour.[20]

It is important to note that this system map presents the organisation and the market as an open system—both the organisation and the market are able to import energy from the environment in order to maintain a low level of entropy (a concept discussed in Section 2.8). As we shall see in the following section, this is a real problem in neoliberal thinking—Planet Earth and its organisations are not open systems, and this has major implications.

In Chapter 2, we talked about espoused purpose and POSIWID, the idea that the purpose of a system is what it does. Neoliberal political economy espouses a way forward to a sustainable future through ecomodernist strategies, but POSIWID suggests that, on the basis of the evidence of the last 40 years, this will not happen. It is therefore no surprise that positions on how to deal with social and environmental sustainability are politically polarised. Social justice has always been closely associated with a left-wing political perspective, but in recent years environmental sustainability has also become political, with right-wing scepticism about action on climate change planning.

Time for reflection

What do you think about this analysis of Western industrial capitalism? It is written from my own perspective as a non-economist and as someone who questions whether neoliberalism can provide an answer to issues of social and environmental sustainability.

You do not have to agree with my observations—in fact, most good learning comes from not agreeing with a position, and then reflecting on relative merits of the different arguments.

3.3 Sustainability economics

3.3.1 The development of sustainability economics

One of my favourite films is *Star Trek: First Contact*. For those readers unlucky enough to have not yet seen it, the plot concerns the malevolent Borg (catchphrase: "Resistance is futile") travelling back in time from the 24th century to the middle of the 21st century to assimilate the human race, closely pursued by Captain Jean-Luc Picard's USS Enterprise starship. Leaving aside the potential allegorical connections between the Borg and neoliberal economists, in one scene Lily Sloane, one of the 21st-century characters follows Picard through the bowels of the Enterprise as they seek to destroy the Borg Queen. She asks Picard how much he earns for being captain of such an enormous vessel and is astonished when he replies that acquiring wealth is no longer the driving force in people's lives, and that 24th-century people work to better humanity.

If *Star Trek* is to be believed, it would seem that at some point in the next three centuries humanity realises that economics is a social construction, and that it does not inevitably mean that human endeavour is focused on the need to acquire piles of money—there may be higher justifications for existence. Sustainability economics is a starting point for this and seeks to move our contemporary acceptance of capitalism on to a level which may actually make it possible for humanity to survive until the 24th century.

What is sustainability economics? For many years "environmental economists" have grappled with the challenges of accounting for environmental externalities, for example, assessing the costs of pollution or the financial benefits which might accrue from a particular area of land, which is a discipline fitting nicely into the mathematical world of neoclassical economics. Interest started to develop in how economics related to social and environmental affairs in the 1970s, perhaps being best represented by Ernst Schumacher's *Small Is Beautiful*. This field then became known as ecological economics as it sought to integrate elements of ecology, thermodynamics, ethics and other considerations into economic analysis. More recently the term "sustainability economics" has emerged as a way of bringing together ecological and social concerns.[21] Four attributes for sustainability economics have been proposed: a focus on the relationship between humans and nature; orientation towards a long term and uncertain future; the importance of intergenerational and intragenerational justice; and a concern for non-wastefulness in allocating natural goods and services and human-made substitutes.[22]

This section will look at some of the key ideas in contemporary sustainability economics. First, we will look at what I have called the growth problem. A major concern in sustainability economics is challenging the conventional assumption that economies must grow in order to survive, but if not, what can or should happen in the future. We will then go on to look at some specific ideas which have been put forward for economic systems which can support a sustainable relationship between humanity and the natural environment.

3.3.2 The growth problem

At some point during most months in my adult lifetime, I have heard or read the words "Last month the economy grew by…". If it grew I felt a sense of relief, and if it contracted a sense of mild panic developed. Why? For most of that time, I had no real idea what "the economy growing" meant, but non-growth seemed to pose some sort of existential threat to me and my loved ones. What was actually growing (or not) was the country's Gross Domestic Product (GDP), defined on the United Kingdom government website as a measure of "… of the total value of all the goods made, and services provided, during a specific period of time".[23]

Although knowing how the United Kingdom's GDP is progressing is now a fundamental part of my life, it has not always been so. The then newly-established Organisation for Economic Co-operation and Development (OECD) declared growth to be the object of all economic policy in 1961,[24] and the United Kingdom adopted it as official policy in 1962 with the creation of what was then called the National Economic

Development Council.[25] Growth is a logical outcome and a functional requirement of a capitalist economy.[26] With capitalism being based on the idea of interest-bearing debt so that commercial activity increases investment, the idea of economic growth seems quite sensible, and is, on the face of it, a good thing.

Problems start to emerge when we look at the detail. What are the goods made and the services provided? Many things are obvious: anyone buying this book will have contributed to the GDP, but so also will someone who buys a bag of cocaine or solicits the services of a sex worker—in 2014 the Financial Times reported that the United Kingdom's GDP was boosted by £10 billion when its Office for National Statistics (ONS) updated how it calculated GDP to include these activities.[27] We are familiar with hearing how much the City of London contributes to the national GDP, but a lesser-known fact is that people in London consume twice as much cocaine as in any other European city,[28] a statistic that adds a new dimension to the understanding that London contributes disproportionately to the British economy. GDP also grows when bad things happen: for example, the Deepwater Horizon oil spill in 2010 contributed $65 billion to the GDP of the United States.[29] This example also illustrates a fundamental weakness in GDP: a significant contribution to GDP comes from the destruction of a country's natural capital which cannot be replaced. This is rather like me increasing my own personal GDP by selling my house and spending my pension pot on having fun—sooner or later the music stops.

As with all targets, trying to meet the requirements for GDP is an incentive for undesirable activities: travelling long distances for a daily commute increases GDP while damaging family life and increasing greenhouse gas emissions; cutting down a forest to sell the timber increases GDP while destroying biodiversity. It is also telling that while GDP measures illegal drug consumption it does not pay any attention at all to the enormous amount of unpaid work which goes on in most economies, such as caring and domestic maintenance, the great majority of which is carried out by women.

Another problem with GDP itself is that it does not necessarily tell us directly what is happening in the economy with such things as employment. For a start, it is a national figure and conceals regional disparities. There is also little evidence that a growing GDP has a significant impact on health or happiness. Angus Deaton points out that once a certain level of national income has been achieved so that epidemiological death is largely eliminated, health and life expectancy is not increased by more wealth.[30] The increasing amount of research into measurements of national happiness in recent decades has consistently shown that increases in GDP have virtually no impact on how satisfied people are with their lives.[31]

A more fundamental problem with GDP and the whole concept of growth is illustrated by the simple graph in Figure 3.7. This illustrates a question which is never discussed in bland announcements about "last month's economic growth", which is "What happens next?" When the objective of economic activity is constant growth, we are talking about exponential increases. For example, if the economy grows at 2% every year, it will double every 35 years, which means twice as many goods produced, services sold, cocaine snorted, trees chopped down and sex workers solicited. And doubling again after another 35 years, and so on. So where does it end? To infinity and beyond? The mindless monthly recital of last month's GDP increase prevents public discussion about what it might mean if it stops growing.

Which it must, as predicted by the Second Law of Thermodynamics, as explained in Section 2.8. As Kenneth Boulding[32] put it in the 1960s, we live on Spaceship Earth,

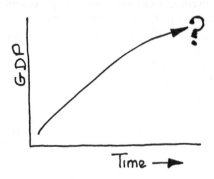

Figure 3.7 The future of economic growth.

a closed thermodynamic system with finite physical resources and to a large extent finite sources of energy. Because of this, the entropy of Spaceship Earth will slowly increase until all life on the planet ceases. Certain natural processes can help to keep entropy low, such as photosynthesis by green vegetable matter, but the massive scale of deforestation we currently see means that this natural regulation mechanism is slowly being eliminated. The development of solar technology opens up some possibilities for less finite sources of energy, but the manufacture of the necessary equipment requires energy and natural resources in itself, and as the ecological economist Nicholas Georgescu-Roegen[33] explained, the energy required to produce such technology must be subtracted from the energy that it produces in order to see if it is worthwhile. The same equation applies to deep-sea mining, shale gas extraction, gathering minerals from asteroids, and all of the other advanced technologies that ecomodernists claim will save humanity. Recycling used materials only delay the inevitable: recycling requires energy and the loss of some material so that even here entropy inexorably grows.

So continual growth is impossible, and the sooner the economics profession acknowledges this, the sooner alternative development strategies can be considered. Unfortunately, because the growth of GDP is the official measure of economic health even though what it means is little understood, it has acquired a somewhat unjustified and arguably misleading position of importance. For one thing, it excludes the possibility of discussing questions such as: "Do we have enough?" What could be more meaningful as an indicator of social and environmental sustainability would be measures that relate more directly to people's lived experience, such as indicators of happiness or well-being.[34] For example, in 2019, it was reported that a trend towards falling life expectancies had been observed in the United Kingdom[35]—could monthly updates on how many more years one could expect to live have a salutary effect on how people organise their lives and perceive how they are being managed? Such measures of progress might help us to see, as Ernst Schumacher put it:

> the hollowness and fundamental unsatisfactoriness of a life devoted primarily to the pursuit of material ends, to the neglect of the spiritual… man's [sic] needs are infinite and infinitude can be achieved only in the spiritual realm, never in the material.[36]

Although there are significant problems associated with the concept of growth, its central importance in Western industrial capitalism means that it is an integral part of some sustainable economy proposals, in particular the Green New Deal conceptualisations offered by the OECD and United Nations (see Section 3.3.3), and Sustainable Development Goal (SDG 8). The OECD define green growth as "… fostering economic growth and development while ensuring that natural assets continue to provide the resources and environmental services on which our well-being relies".[37] It is seen as essential as a way to finance the investments needed to move to a green economy. This, however, rests on an assumption that growth will generate the investments needed to protect the environment at a faster rate than environmental degradation will have a negative effect on economic activity, and this is by no means assured. Many studies show that the factor of climate change alone may have a significant negative impact on economic activity.[38]

An alternative to the constant growth model is the "steady-state economy", an idea associated with Herman Daly,[39] although it is not a new concept—in the middle of the 19th century, John Stuart Mill wrote about a "stationary state of population and capital", which he argued would create possibilities for "all kinds of mental culture, and moral and social progress".[40] A steady-state economy would hover around an optimal level and activity would focus on outputs that contribute to sustainable social and natural environments.[41] However, there are problems with the idea. Firstly, what is the optimal level, and how can an economy be organised so that it hovers indefinitely around it? Secondly, as resource degradation inevitably occurs, societies will need to adapt, and doing this while maintaining a steady state of economic activity would be difficult. The steady-state economy also does not escape the entropy problem, although it may delay the onset of its more catastrophic implications.

Going even further, there are advocates of "degrowth" economics, which would imply society adapting to a very different lifestyle, based on different visions of prosperity and much less reliance on material wealth and consumption.[42]

It is suggested that within a capitalist system so dependent on constant growth, both steady-state and degrowth policies would almost certainly lead to massive unemployment, reductions in living standards and probable social conflict.[43] Of course, this is what the legitimated knowledge within the socially constructed reality of capitalism predicts: we are constantly exhorted to spend and consume, assured that this will bring us happiness, when in reality decades of research shows that wealth does not bring happiness. The flip side is what happens if our material circumstances deteriorate if we have less? Again, a large body of research conducted globally and over decades suggests that we would not necessarily collapse into depression and disintegrate as a society. Humanity seems to have what Adam Smith called a "natural and usual state of tranquillity",[44] a level of contentment which is to some extent inherited, and to which we gravitate whatever our level of material wealth. This may explain why the capitalist economy has decided that we all need to be constantly bombarded by inferences about our inadequacies and advertisements for products and services which would resolve these. Buddhist teachings that our suffering is caused by our attachment to these worldly concerns find no place in this consumer world.

3.3.3 The Green New Deal(s)

The original "New Deal" was the programme of public investment which helped pull the American economy out of the aftermath of the Great Crash of 1929. The phrase was used again in January 2007 when the New York Times columnist Thomas Friedman,[45] reflecting on the impact of climate change, wrote about the need for a "Green New Deal" to respond to the looming climate emergency. The challenge was picked up by a group of environmental economists and politicians in the United Kingdom, and in 2008 the New Economics Foundation published *A Green New Deal*.[46] The United Nations Environment Programme (UNEP) published its own proposals for such a programme in 2009,[47] followed by the OECD in 2011.[48] Perhaps the greatest publicity the idea received was in 2019 when Alexandria Ocasia-Cortez and Ed Markey submitted a congressional resolution for an American Green New Deal.[49]

Although there are differences in emphasis in these different articulations of a Green New Deal, there are three main areas of similarity[50]:

- Decoupling, the act of disconnecting economies from the use of carbon-based fuels is of central importance.
- Government intervention in infrastructure building is essential as a way of creating new "green jobs".
- Taxation regimes must be redesigned so that they promote environmentally friendly economic activities.

The differences in the proposals largely reflect the nature of the organisation publishing them: the emphasis in the UNEP report is very much on environmental issues, and the OECD focuses on job creation through green policies. Both emphasise the need for economic growth to fund changes. While UNEP and the OECD may be seen as "establishment" perspectives, the New Economics Foundation (NEF) Green New Deal is quite different, representing the opinions of more left-wing economists and environmentalists. They attach considerably more importance to reforms to the global economic system, and they also stress the importance of social justice rather than simply creating jobs. Ann Pettifor, one of the original NEF report authors, elucidates the key principles of their version of the Green New Deal:[51]

- A steady-state economy, respecting the nine planetary boundaries and adopting the principles of the circular economy, reducing, reusing and recycling.
- Limited needs, not limited wants, focusing on satisfying essential human needs.
- Self-sufficiency, promoting the ideas that societies can look after themselves while ensuring that public rather than private wealth is developed.
- Mixed-market economy, ensuring an optimal mix of private and public sector activities, with the state supporting large-scale transformative projects implemented at a local level by entrepreneurs.
- Labour-intensive economy, utilising a "carbon army" of workers to implement the transformation to the new economy.
- Monetary and fiscal coordination, better governmental control over interest rates, money supply and spending, and taxation to support a green economy.
- Abandon delusions of infinite expansion.

The American Resolution is similar, and has five major goals:

- Net-zero greenhouse gas emissions.
- Millions of high-wage jobs.
- Investment in infrastructure and industry.
- Clean air and water, climate and community resilience.
- Justice and equity by stopping oppression.

3.3.4 The circular economy

The idea of the "circular economy" emerged during the 1980s as a reaction against the linear extract-produce-use-dump model of industrial activity which had been largely unchanged for centuries. The circular paradigm aims to be restorative or regenerative by following practices which minimise energy usage and improve how products are designed so that objects last longer and can be maintained, repaired or refurbished easily, and that at the end of their life they can be recycled. The ideas of the circular economy clearly have a part to play in sustainability, and this is recognised by institutions such as the European Commission and UNEP, who have both published reports and developed strategies relating to the implementation of circular principles.[52]

Circular economy ideas focus primarily on environmental sustainability by seeking to reduce resource and energy consumption. Proponents claim that there are also benefits to social sustainability, through, for example changing people's attitudes to material possessions ("the sharing economy"), increasing employment opportunities through repair and recycling activities, and strengthening social capital through shared participation, although these benefits tend to be emergent rather than specific intentions.[53]

However, the circular economy can only ever be just part of a sustainability solution. First, the Second Law of Thermodynamics and entropy, as discussed previously, shows that it is impossible to reuse and recycle everything—there is always some degradation and loss of material and energy.[54] The energy required in implementing recycling schemes may also be considerable and perhaps even unjustifiable.[55] Following circular economy principles may also "lock in" old, environmentally problematic technologies or materials and reduce the opportunities for developing new products which are, in the longer term, more sustainable. Thinking about sustainability as a wicked problem composed of ill-defined and multiple, interlocking sub-problems (Section 2.9) helps us to realise that minimising waste materials from one industrial process through implementing circular economy principles may stop the supply of essential raw materials for other processes, forcing them to extract virgin materials rather than process waste. Transitions to circular economy principles therefore need to take into consideration the wider, complex nature of production and emission chains involved.[56]

It is also important to think about the social benefits which accrue from existing patterns of production and consumption and how these could be affected by a circular economy approach: for example, studies have shown how providing and consuming certain types of food has an important role in many societies, and adopting a circular economy approach to controlling food supplies could be socially problematic.[57] Finally, a deeper criticism of the circular economy is that it may be seen as a strategy which fits within an existing exploitative, economic system and does nothing to change the fundamental principles by which industrial production operates (particularly if it draws an emphasis away from reducing energy consumption[58]), and so functions as a form of greenwashing.

3.3.5 Doughnut economics

Kate Raworth's concept of doughnut economics[59] presents a vision of the ends for a sustainable world rather than focusing on the means of economic activity without an end goal other than a vaguely conceived prosperity as with neoclassical economics. The big attraction of this approach is that we then know what we are aiming for, whereas our current capitalist economics simply says that the economy must constantly grow and we can make sustainability happen.

88 *The political economy of sustainability*

Figure 3.8 illustrates the (American) doughnut concept. The ring of the doughnut is the "safe and just space for humanity", enabled by an economy which is regenerative (meaning that resources are used carefully, recycled and reused as much as possible) and distributive (by changing patterns of land ownership, how currency is used, increasing employee ownership of their places of work, changing the discriminatory tax treatment of human and robot labour, and opening up practices which restrict the creation and dissemination of intellectual property). For example, Raworth suggests that instead of rewarding the possession of currency through interest, a negative charge (or demurrage) could be applied regularly to keep the currency active, encouraging money to be used and redistributed rather than treated as a commodity.[60]

The space inside the doughnut provides the "social foundation" and identifies 12 basic requirements for human existence to which all should have access, these representing a synthesis of social factors in the Sustainable Development Goals and the Universal Declaration of Human Rights.

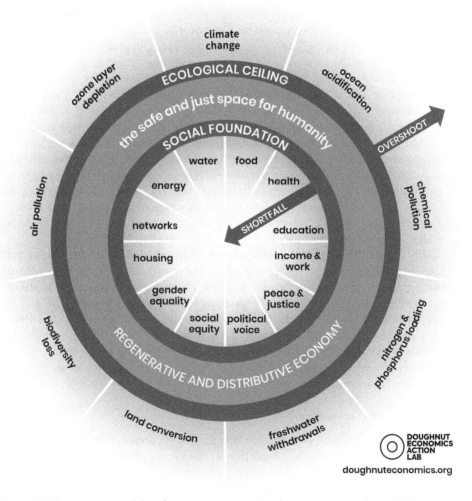

Figure 3.8 The structure of doughnut economics. (Credit: Kate Raworth and Christian Guthier.)

Finally, the space outside the doughnut represents Rockström et al's nine planetary boundaries[61] which we must respect. Transgressing any of these represents an overshoot (and, as noted in Section 1.5, four of these have already been overshot).

Thinking back to the discussion about complex adaptive systems in Section 2.10, the unpredictable nature of how such systems behave means that the best strategy to adopt is focusing on achieving a vision, and then monitoring, tweaking and adapting depending on the behaviours you see emerging from your system. Raworth suggests that economic management should move from a "machinebrain" to a "gardenbrain" mode of thinking, to "... get stuck in, nurturing, selecting, repotting, grafting, pruning and weeding the plants as they grow and mature".[62] In an organisational learning setting that means moving away from fixed objective-based learning and training programmes and adopting a more adaptive approach to learning: understanding learners and their value systems and motivations, introducing new ideas, reflecting on how these are accepted (or not), reviewing, refining and consolidating, all the time holding on to a vision of what it means for your organisation to operate as part of a regenerative and distributive economy.

Doughnut economics provides a vision for the future, but it does not necessarily provide a roadmap for dealing with the social and political obstacles that must be overcome to achieve it. It says little about how value systems which may be inimical to the vision can be changed—while wealth is fetishised in the West as the ultimate desirability, even though there is substantial evidence to suggest that ever-increasing wealth does not contribute to ever-increasing happiness, the acceptance of the principles of doughnut economics will always be difficult.

3.4 Making the transition to sustainability economics

The previous sections have described radically different systems of political economy. Capitalism represents a tried and tested system which has undisputedly brought material benefits to people around the world (if not equally) but has also significantly contributed directly and indirectly to the social and environmental problems that we face in the early 21st century, and in its present form is not sustainable. The various ideas put forward for sustainability economics represent more or less radical approaches to moving forward. Although these potential ways forward differ considerably, there are a number of common features about the economic system which they may seek to create, and Figure 3.9 is an attempt at a graphical summary.

We can compare this to the system map in Figure 3.6. A key difference here is the dashed line representing a system boundary enclosing everything except solar energy. This illustrates that sustainability economics recognises that organisational activity and human existence take place in an essentially closed system. Prior to the development of solar energy technology, it was completely closed, but we now have the possibility to capture solar energy directly to produce heat and electricity rather than rely on it to enable the growth of plant and animal life which could then be exploited. Nevertheless, natural resources are still finite. There is increasing interest in deep-sea mining, but this would come at huge financial cost and would inevitably cause massive levels of environmental damage. Asteroid mining remains science-fiction and again would require financial investment and sources of energy at literally astronomic levels.

The new model sees a very different role for the state. In the neoliberal system, the state exists primarily to make sure that neoliberal economics rolls on undisturbed,

90 The political economy of sustainability

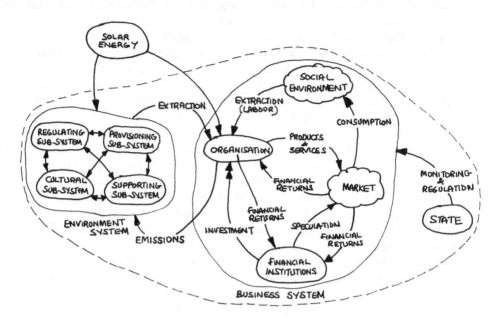

Figure 3.9 Organisation system maps in a sustainable economy.

with the market taking care of all problems that come along. But as we have seen with the 2008 financial crash and the COVID-19 pandemic, it generates a global economic system with no resilience which in times of crisis requires state rescue. While ecomodernists would argue that the market will create technological solutions that will save humanity, the evidence that this will happen is not reassuring, to say the least.

Figure 3.9 also attempts to show the importance of ecosystem services in the natural environment. As discussed in Chapter 1, ecosystem services are fundamentally important for the existence of all life but are completely ignored and taken for granted in conventional economic accounting. So what would it cost if we were to try and do it ourselves, to do all of the necessary provisioning, regulating, supporting and cultural servicing that the natural environment currently does for free? Well, according to a team led by the ecological economist Robert Costanza, about $125 trillion.[63] To put that in perspective, the total GDP of every country in the world in 2011 was $75 trillion.[64] Clearly we cannot afford to do it ourselves, so protecting our free ecosystem services should be an absolute priority.

3.5 Learning from the dialectics

This chapter has tried to summarise two very different perspectives on the political economy of social and environmental sustainability. Neoclassical and neoliberal political economies stress the importance of the market, and assert that this will stimulate the development of geo-technologies and lead to "market-based instruments" which will ensure the necessary social stability and environmental protection. On the other hand, the various Green New Deal proposals and ideas such as the circular economy and doughnut economics remain somewhat abstract and lack a clear, practical roadmap.

This may seem to present a major problem for supporting organisational learning which can contribute to sustainable organisational practice. However, the contrasts, disjunctions and contradictions between these perspectives present us with a dialectic, a set of opposing ideas which can form the basis for learning. According to the critical pedagogue Henry Giroux, the principle of the dialectic can:

> ... help people analyse the world in which they live, to become aware of the constraints that prevent them from changing that world, and, finally to help them collectively struggle to transform that world.[65]

What are the constraints? Perhaps neoliberalism's greatest strength has been its ability to insinuate its ideas into every aspect of our lives, as in the idea of "everyday neoliberalism" discussed earlier. As this has happened our ability to think of the world working in a different way has been shut down. Political scientists describe this as hegemony, where, as in Berger and Luckmann's social constructionism, a dominant group defines what knowledge is legitimate. One of the most influential writers about hegemony was the Italian Marxist Antonio Gramsci.[66] Theorising about revolution, Gramsci distinguished between a war of manoeuvre (violent struggle) and a war of position, the subtle, ongoing delimiting of thought which makes even thinking about resistance futile. For a war of position:

> ... an unprecedented concentration of hegemony is necessary, and hence a more "interventionist" government, which will take the offensive more openly against the oppositionists and organise permanently the "impossibility" of internal disintegration—with controls of every kind, political, administrative, etc., reinforcement of the hegemonic "positions" of the dominant group, etc.[67]

We can see this as having happened in the field of political economy. Until the turn of the 20th century, the study of reconciling ends and scarce means was known as "political economy", but then in an attempt to position the discipline on an equal footing with the physical sciences and convince people that its studies were rational, predictable and objective rather than being based on subjective political and ethical opinion, the professional bodies representing political economists dropped the word "political".[68] Seeing economics as a science makes it possible to designate certain knowledge as legitimate and to reject other knowledge, in much the same way as physical scientists can dismiss the ideas of those who believe the Earth to be flat or that the sun revolves around the Earth. Neoclassical thinking dominates in this scientific view, and other perspectives find no place. This is seen in the curricula for economics undergraduates in many Western countries where there is no room for alternative ways of thinking about economics.[69] Universities, where new generations of the most influential people in society are educated for their lives ahead, have been particular agents for changing the definitions of acceptable knowledge. University research seems to be becoming increasingly focused on subjects of commercial importance to the exclusion of subjects which may contribute to a public good, and university teaching has become focused on producing individuals ready to take an unquestioning place in the neoliberal society.[70]

There is a certain irony that a movement whose original purpose in the Mont Pèlerin Society was to protect freedom of thought should now be deciding what understanding of economics is legitimate. Mainstream economists may try very hard to portray their profession as a science, but ultimately economics is about politics and ethics, and those of us with a responsibility for facilitating any form of learning across society have a moral responsibility to confront this hegemonic thinking about how the economy should work. In the words of Ha-Joon Chang:

> Once we learn that different economic theories say different things partly because they are based on different ethical and political values, we will have the confidence to discuss economics for what it really is—a political argument—and not a 'science' in which there is clear right and wrong.[71]

What needs to change for this to happen? The biggest challenge is probably what is generally described as the "political will" for change. Current systems of political economy bring big benefits to a small number of people, and they exert considerable influence and pressure on national and global decision-makers. George Monbiot suggests that this hegemony continues because it tells a story that people can understand, that over-mighty states have crushed freedom, and that through free markets ordinary people can prosper and triumph over their oppressors.[72] As of yet, no credible alternative narrative has emerged which can persuade a critical mass of people to review how they value their lives to the extent that they will reject the current political and economic paradigm.

For this to happen there may need to be some major crisis which triggers an "enforced enlightenment", as Ulrich Beck has suggested (see Section 1.2). Ann Pettifor suggests that this could happen through another major economic collapse, but this time one from which neoliberalism does not rise from the ashes.[73] The COVID-19 pandemic, itself almost certainly caused by environmental degradation and spread by unquestioned globalisation, has triggered discussions about the dialectic between our pre-pandemic lives and the possibilities for "building back better", and how we may be able to create societies which are more just and respect environmental boundaries. For example, we need to reflect on questions such as:

- When people were confined to their homes, levels of air pollution dropped, making skies clearer and healthier. Should we prioritise policies which make clean air normal?
- Lockdown and homeworking meant that people spend more time with family than in the workplace. How important should that be?

If (when?) the enforced enlightenment happens, organisations need to be prepared.

Time for reflection

What thoughts do you have about a transition from conventional to sustainability economics?

Is it possible or desirable?

What benefits or disadvantages do you think it might bring to you, your family, or the organisation where you work?

Did your experience of the COVID-19 pandemic make you think differently about how the economy and society work?

3.6 Key points in this chapter

Figure 3.10 summarises the key points in this chapter.

The system of political economy which has had the greatest impact on social and environmental sustainability is capitalism. Although capitalism has been implemented in different ways throughout the years, neoclassical economics and its neoliberal derivative have been the most influential schools of thought powering the Great Acceleration.

Neoclassical economics understands that all economic decisions are made by "the market", and interference by outside organisations such as government or trades unions needs to be prevented. Social and environmental impacts which are not part of the market transaction are seen as externalities and do not need to be considered in pricing considerations.

Neoliberalism sees inequality as important as a way to encourage greater participation, and that inequality will disappear as societies become richer. Investment in measures to prevent or mitigate climate change needs to be discounted at a higher rate because the benefits to future generations are unknown. Neoliberalism places considerable emphasis on protecting intellectual property, which could make it harder for environmentally effective technologies to be disseminated at scale. Ethical discussions are not necessary in a neoliberal economy because ethical considerations are factored into the market price.

The emphasis that neoliberalism places on economic efficiency is at the expense of resilience, and experience in the 2008 financial crash and 2020 COVID-19 pandemic shows that state intervention is essential when the market is disrupted.

Sustainability economics challenges the concept of indefinite growth due to the finite nature of global resources. Some form of steady-state economics may be necessary. The Green New Deal refers to several proposals which have been made in recent years advocating investment in technologies which contribute to environmental sustainability, and legislative and tax changes to promote green employment and a reduction in inequality.

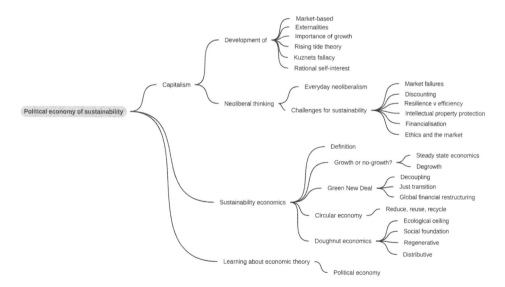

Figure 3.10 Key points in this chapter.

Doughnut economics is a proposal for how societies could operate, based on people existing in a safe and just space respecting an ecological ceiling determined by planetary boundaries and maintaining a socially just foundation. It recommends a circular economy approach where possible.

The possibility of transition from the status quo to a political economy favouring social and economic sustainability seems problematic and may only occur in the event of a major financial or environmental catastrophe, sufficient to make a significant change in public opinion.

3.7 Further reading

The three reports outlining initial ideas about the Green New Deal are all available online:

- NEF *A Green New Deal*, https://neweconomics.org/about/our-missions/green-new-deal
- UNEP *A Global Green New Deal*, https://sustainabledevelopment.un.org/
- OECD *Towards Green Growth*, https://www.oecd.org/greengrowth/48012345.pdf

The Case for the Green New Deal, Ann Pettifor, Verso, 2019: an elaboration and update of the NEF 2008 GND by one of the original authors.
Economics: The User's Guide, Ha-Joon Chang, Pelican, 2014: an excellent, readable guide to the different schools of economics that have been significant over the centuries.
Doughnut Economics, Kate Raworth, Chelsea Green Publishing, 2017.
The Sustainable Economy, Robert S. Devine, Anchor Books, 2020: a journalistic account of the relationship between conventional economics and the environment, focusing on recent developments in the United States.

Notes

1 Max Weber, *The Protestant Ethic and the Spirit of Capitalism* (New York: Charles Scribner's Sons, 1958), 181.
2 Philip Mirowski, *Never Let a Serious Crisis Go to Waste: How Neoliberalism Survived the Financial Meltdown* (London: Verso Books, 2013), 108.
3 Simon Kuznets, 'Economic Growth and Income Inequality', *The American Economic Review* 45, no. 1 (1955): 1–28.
4 Thomas Piketty, *Capital in the Twenty-First Century* (Cambridge, MA: Harvard University Press, 2017).
5 R. Wilkinson and K. Pickett, *The Spirit Level: Why Equality Is Better for Everyone* (London: Penguin Books, 2010), 36–45.
6 Wilkinson and Pickett, 19.
7 Gene M. Grossman and Alan B. Krueger, 'Environmental Impacts of a North American Free Trade Agreement' (National Bureau of Economic Research, 1991).
8 For example, Hidemichi Fujii and Shunsuke Managi, 'Which Industry Is Greener? An Empirical Study of Nine Industries in OECD Countries', *Energy Policy* 57 (2013): 381–88; Mariano Torras and James K. Boyce, 'Income, Inequality, and Pollution: A Reassessment of the Environmental Kuznets Curve', *Ecological Economics* 25, no. 2 (1998): 147–60; Elizabeth A. Stanton, 'The Tragedy of Maldistribution: Climate, Sustainability, and Equity', *Sustainability* 4, no. 3 (2012): 394–411.
9 William D. Nordhaus, *A Question of Balance: Weighing the Options on Global Warming Policies* (New Haven, CT: Yale University Press, 2008).
10 Martin Bohle, 'Handling of Human-Geosphere Intersections', *Geosciences* 6, no. 1 (2016): 3.

11 Nicholas Stern, *The Economics of Climate Change: The Stern Review* (Cambridge: Cambridge University Press, 2007), 27.
12 Stern, 399.
13 Frank Ackerman, 'Climate Economics in Four Easy Pieces', *Development* 51, no. 3 (2008): 325–31; Ari Rabl, 'Discounting of Long Term Costs: What Would Future Generations Prefer Us to Do?', *Ecological Economics* 17 (1996): 137–45.
14 Piketty, *Capital in the Twenty-First Century*, 741.
15 OED, ed., *Concise Oxford English Dictionary* (Oxford: Oxford University Press, 2002).
16 Rebecca Lave, Philip Mirowski, and Samuel Randalls, 'Introduction: STS and Neoliberal Science', *Social Studies of Science* 40, no. 5 (2010): 659–75.
17 Stern, *The Economics of Climate Change*, 566.
18 Ann Pettifor, *The Case for the Green New Deal* (London: Verso, 2019).
19 Julie A. Nelson, 'Ethics and the Economist: What Climate Change Demands of Us', *Ecological Economics* 85 (2013): 145–54.
20 Herman Daly, 'A Further Critique of Growth Economics', *Ecological Economics* 88 (2013): 20–24.
21 Stefan Baumgärtner and Martin Quaas, 'What Is Sustainability Economics?', *Ecological Economics* 69, no. 3 (2010): 445–50.
22 Baumgärtner and Quaas, 446.
23 HM Treasury, 'Gross Domestic Product (GDP): What It Means and Why It Matters', GOV.UK, accessed 16 February 2021, https://www.gov.uk/government/news/gross-domestic-product-gdp-what-it-means-and-why-it-matters.
24 Pettifor, *Green New Deal*, 108.
25 Edward J. Mishan, *The Costs of Economic Growth* (Harmondsworth, England: Pelican Books, 1969), 27.
26 David Barmes and Fran Boait, 'The Tragedy of Growth' (London: PostitiveMoney, 2020).
27 Sarah O'Connor, 'Drugs and Prostitution Add £10bn to UK Economy', *Financial Times*, 29 May 2014, https://www.ft.com/content/65704ba0-e730-11e3-88be-00144feabdc0.
28 Ross Lydall, 'Londoners Snort 23kg of Cocaine a Day... Twice as Much as Any Other European City', *Evening Standard*, 10 October 2019, https://www.standard.co.uk/news/london/londoners-snort-23kg-of-cocaine-a-day-twice-as-much-as-any-other-european-city-a4258421.html.
29 Ron Bousso, 'BP Deepwater Horizon Costs Balloon to $65 Billion', *Reuters*, 16 January 2018, https://www.reuters.com/article/uk-bp-deepwaterhorizon-idUKKBN1F50O6.
30 A. Deaton, *The Great Escape: Health, Wealth, and the Origins of Inequality* (Princeton, NJ: Princeton University Press, 2013), 37.
31 R. Skidelsky and E. Skidelsky, *How Much Is Enough? Money and the Good Life* (London: Penguin Books, 2013), 102–3.
32 Kenneth Boulding, 'The Economics of the Coming Spaceship Earth', in *Environmental Quality in a Growing Economy* (Sixth RFF Forum on Environmental Quality, Washington, DC: Johns Hopkins Press, 1966).
33 Nicholas Georgescu-Roegen, 'Energy and Economic Myths', *Southern Economic Journal* 41, no. 3, 1975, 347–81.
34 Barmes and Boait, 'The Tragedy of Growth'.
35 Patrick Collinson, 'Life Expectancy Falls by Six Months in Biggest Drop in UK Forecasts', *The Guardian*, 7 March 2019, http://www.theguardian.com/society/2019/mar/07/life-expectancy-slumps-by-five-months.
36 E.F. Schumacher, *Small Is Beautiful: A Study of Economics as If People Mattered* (London: Abacus, 1973), 31.
37 OECD, 'Towards Green Growth' (Paris: OECD Publishing, 2011), 9.
38 Robert S. Devine, *The Sustainable Economy: The Hidden Costs of Climate Change and the Path to a Prosperous Future* (New York: Anchor Books, 2020), 209–13.
39 Robert Goodland and Herman Daly, 'Environmental Sustainability: Universal and Non-Negotiable', *Ecological Applications* 6, no. 4 (1996): 1002–17.
40 John Stuart Mill, *Principles of Political Economy*, ed. J.M. Robson, vol. II–III (Toronto: University of Toronto Press, 1965), quoted in Tim Jackson and Robin Webster, 'Limits Revisited: A Review of the Limits to Growth Debate' (All-Party Parliamentary Group on Limits

to Growth, 2016); Nicholas Georgescu-Roegen, 'Energy and Economic Myths', *Southern Economic Journal* 41, no. 3 (1975): 347–81.
41 H. Daly, 'How to Move to a Steady-State Economy from a Failed-Growth Economy', *Pacific Ecologist* 19, Winter/Spring (2010): 21–25; W. Rees, 'Denying Herman Daly: Why Conventional Economists Will Not Embrace the Daly Vision', in *Beyond Uneconomic Growth*, ed. J. Farley and D. Malghan, Advances in Ecological Economics (Cheltenham: Edward Elgar Publishing, 2016).
42 Christine Bauhardt, 'Solutions to the Crisis? The Green New Deal, Degrowth, and the Solidarity Economy: Alternatives to the Capitalist Growth Economy from an Ecofeminist Economics Perspective', *Ecological Economics* 102 (2014): 60–68; Jackson and Webster, 'Limits Revisited'; Robert Pollin, 'De-Growth vs a Green New Deal', *New Left Review*, no. 112 (2018): 5–25.
43 Barmes and Boait, 'The Tragedy of Growth'; Pollin, 'De-Growth vs a Green New Deal'.
44 Adam Smith, The Theory of Moral Sentiments (Kinaid and Bell, 1759), quoted in Jonathan Haidt, The Happiness Hypothesis: Putting Ancient Wisdom and Philosophy to the Test of Modern Science (Random House, 2006), 86.
45 Thomas L. Friedman, 'Opinion | A Warning From the Garden', *The New York Times*, 19 January 2007, sec. Opinion, https://www.nytimes.com/2007/01/19/opinion/19friedman.html.
46 Green New Deal Group, 'A Green New Deal' (London: New Economics Foundation, 2008).
47 Edward B. Barbier, 'Rethinking the Economic Recovery: A Global Green New Deal' (United Nations Environment Programme, 2009).
48 OECD, 'Towards Green Growth'.
49 Sunrise Movement, 'What Is the Green New Deal?', Sunrise Movement, accessed 17 February 2021, https://issuu.com/sunrisemvmt/docs/gndres.
50 Emil Urhammer and Inge Røpke, 'Macroeconomic Narratives in a World of Crises: An Analysis of Stories about Solving the System Crisis', *Ecological Economics* 96 (2013): 62–70.
51 Pettifor, *Green New Deal*.
52 European Commission, 'Closing the Loop – An EU Action Plan for the Circular Economy' (European Commission, 2015); European Commission, 'New Circular Economy Strategy - Environment - European Commission', accessed 22 February 2021, https://ec.europa.eu/environment/circular-economy/index_en.htm; UNEP, 'Circularity', UNEP - UN Environment Programme, 10 November 2019, http://www.unep.org/circularity.
53 Martin Geissdoerfer et al., 'The Circular Economy – A New Sustainability Paradigm?', *Journal of Cleaner Production* 143 (2017): 757–68.
54 Georgescu-Roegen, 'Energy and Economic Myths'.
55 Keith R. Skene, 'No Goal Is an Island: The Implications of Systems Theory for the Sustainable Development Goals', *Environment, Development and Sustainability*, October (2020).
56 Jouni Korhonen, Antero Honkasalo, and Jyri Seppälä, 'Circular Economy: The Concept and Its Limitations', *Ecological Economics* 143 (2018): 37–46.
57 Josephine Mylan, Helen Holmes, and Jessica Paddock, 'Re-Introducing Consumption to the "Circular Economy": A Sociotechnical Analysis of Domestic Food Provisioning', *Sustainability* 8, no. 8 (2016): 794.
58 Keith Ronald Skene, 'Circles, Spirals, Pyramids and Cubes: Why the Circular Economy Cannot Work', *Sustainability Science* 13, no. 2 (2018): 479–92.
59 Kate Raworth, *Doughnut Economics: Seven Ways to Think like a 21st-Century Economist* (Hartford, VT: Chelsea Green Publishing, 2017).
60 Raworth, 274.
61 Johan Rockström et al., 'Planetary Boundaries: Exploring the Safe Operating Space for Humanity', *Nature* 461, no. 24 September (2009): 472–75.
62 Raworth, *Doughnut Economics*, 158.
63 Robert Costanza et al., 'Changes in the Global Value of Ecosystem Services', *Global Environmental Change* 26 (2014): 152–58.
64 Devine, *The Sustainable Economy: The Hidden Costs of Climate Change and the Path to a Prosperous Future*, 83.
65 H.A. Giroux, *Ideology, Culture and the Process of Schooling* (London: The Falmer Press, 1981), 116.

66 A. Gramsci, *Selections from the Prison Notebooks of Antonio Gramsci*, trans. Q. Hoare and G. Nowell Smith (London: Lawrence & Wishart, 1971).
67 Gramsci, 238–39.
68 Ha-Joon Chang, *Economics: The User's Guide* (London: Pelican, 2014), 120; Joe Earle, Cahal Moran, and Zach Ward-Perkins, *The Econocracy: On the Perils of Leaving Economics to the Experts* (London: Penguin Books, 2017), 95.
69 Earle, Moran, and Ward-Perkins, *The Econocracy: On the Perils of Leaving Economics to the Experts*.
70 Lave, Mirowski, and Randalls, 'Introduction'.
71 Chang, *Economics: The User's Guide*, 164.
72 George Monbiot, *Out of the Wreckage: A New Politics for an Age of Crisis* (London: Verso Books, 2017).
73 Pettifor, *Green New Deal*.

4 The sustainable organisation

4.1 What this chapter covers

Figure 4.1 shows what this chapter covers. The chapter represents an attempt to pull together different ideas relating to organisational sustainability, in order to develop a coherent picture which may serve as some form of framework for a sustainability-focused learning and development strategy. It does not intend to be a complete guide to what a sustainable organisation is or how it progresses towards sustainability—that is something for other books.

It tries to provide answers to three basic questions:

- Why is operating sustainability important to an organisation?
- What factors need to be considered in a sustainability strategy?
- What factors need to be included in a strategy for learning about sustainability?

4.2 What is a sustainable organisation?

The first thing to do is to try and explain what we mean by a "sustainable organisation". Unfortunately, as might be expected from the discussion in Chapter 1 about the contested understanding of sustainability, this will not be straightforward.

First, what is an "organisation"? Texts on management and organisational behaviour contain many different definitions of "an organisation". Our starting point will be a definition provided by Richard Scott that organisations are relatively highly formalised "collectivities oriented to the pursuit of relatively specific goals" and which are "purposeful" in the sense that the activities and interactions of participants are coordinated".[1] Within this definition, we can include anything from more or less formal

Figure 4.1 Map of Chapter 4.

DOI: 10.4324/9781003218296-5

community groups through to transnational corporations with turnovers greater than many nation-states. What I am thinking about in writing this book is a legally established entity which harnesses the collective power of individuals to provide a product or service to societies that it serves. This might include public sector organisations, such as local, national or international government agencies, the not-for-profit non-governmental or charity sector, or private sector organisations.

While organisations are legal entities, the word "organisation" is also used as a *metaphor* for describing how a collection of individuals collaborate. It is convenient to talk about organisations doing this and doing that, but this conceals the fact that it is always individuals making decisions and taking actions. Nevertheless, as with any system, the coordinated, collective behaviour of individuals leads to an emergent identity and pattern of behaviour which can stay clearly defined for decades: Rolls-Royce and General Motors are organisations with clear identities even though the people who started the businesses more than 100 years ago and their original employees are no longer there. So while it is often useful to use the term "organisation" as shorthand, it is important to remember that we are always talking about individuals, whose decisions are shaped by values which draw on both an organisational and an external social identity.

The importance of capitalism in Western economies means that most thinking about how organisations operate is centred around private sector, profit-seeking, organisations, and this is certainly the focus in research about how organisations should approach sustainability. As such, this writing often uses other terms such as "businesses", "corporations" or "firms" to describe organisations, but this runs the risk of limiting the relevance of whatever it discusses to the private sector. This may sometimes be relevant, but often lessons for the private sector are relevant to non-profit-seeking organisations as well—even public sector bodies may be disbanded if they are not seen as delivering the services for which public money or charitable donations are paying. For this reason, the ideas presented in this book should be of relevance to all organisations, however they are constituted.

Much writing about organisations draws on the idea that they may be seen as systems, although the understanding of what a "system" is may vary considerably and be somewhat different to the working definition offered in Chapter 2. Richard Scott distinguishes between rational, natural and open conceptualisations of organisations as systems.[2] Rational systems are exemplified by Weber's idea of the bureaucratic organisation and Taylor's scientific management, where the emphasis is on structure. Natural systems approaches focus on internal behaviours aimed at ensuring the survival of the organisation, and these are exemplified by the human relations and social systems schools of thinking. Scott observes that what these have in common is that they see organisations as closed systems, in that they do not pay too much attention to the interactions that the organisation will have with its environment. Such perspectives reflect boundary judgements which minimise the importance of the environment within which the organisational system operates and could be seen as illustrating an assumption of domination over nature as discussed in previous chapters. Rational and natural systems approaches dominated organisational thinking until the 1950s, and this may go some way to explaining why concerns about the relevance of social and environmental issues to organisational practice is a relatively new phenomenon.

In contrast, open systems approaches see organisations as, well, open systems, and emphasise process, paying much closer attention to interactions with their operational environments.

100 *The sustainable organisation*

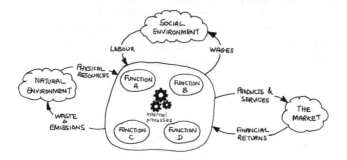

Figure 4.2 An organisation as an open system.

In a seminal work on organisations as open systems, Daniel Katz and Robert Kahn[3] proposed nine characteristics of an organisation as an open system. Figure 4.2 helps to illustrate these characteristics:

- Importation of energy. Energy in its most general sense (for example, physical resources, labour, information) is drawn into the system.
- Throughput. Processes within the organisation transform the energy inputted into products or services.
- Output. The product or service is output to the (systemic) environment—in economic terms, the marketplace. For not-for-profit organisations, the outputs are products or services which provide some public good, for which the organisation is rewarded by receiving money from other sources so that it can continue the transformation process.
- Cycle of events. Financial returns from the outputs make it possible for the input to be repeated so that the throughput can continue.
- Negative entropy. Constant absorption of energy makes it possible for the organisation to maintain its structural integrity (reducing its entropy).
- Feedback mechanisms throughout the system provide negative feedback which allows for error correction. Without negative feedback, the system will absorb too much or too little energy and cease to function.
- Dynamic homeostasis. Feedback will ensure that the organisation operates at a steady level of activity. This is not a true, motionless equilibrium, but one where activity fluctuates around an optimum level.
- Differentiation. Feedback and optimisation will lead to differentiation of functions so that structure varies according to levels of activity.
- Equifinality. The same output state can be achieved in many different ways.

From a sustainability perspective, the important thing to note here is the maintenance of negative entropy. Only open systems can control entropy. As discussed in Chapter 2, if any of the inputs is stopped, entropy will increase and the organisation will cease to function. Most open systems theorising about how organisations operate only considers the relationship of organisations with their marketplace. Human resource theory sometimes looks at the relationship with the social environment, but it is only within the last

25 years that serious attention has been given to how organisations interact with their *natural* environment, an attention that has arisen because this relationship is in serious danger of breaking down.

While seeing an individual organisation as an open system was historically a reasonable assumption, as economic activity has increased through the course of the Great Acceleration the explosion in the numbers and scale of organisations means that such an assumption is no longer reliable. What organisations are collectively doing is having a massive impact on the natural environment, to a degree where the exchange of resources and waste as shown in Figure 4.2 may no longer continue to function, at which point the social environment may also no longer be able to function effectively. The natural environment, Spaceship Earth, is essentially a closed system as regards natural resources, and this means that eventually, every organisation may have to face the reality that they are also in effect a closed system, and that the Grim Reaper of entropy will come calling.

This leads to a working definition of the sustainable organisation, albeit somewhat abstract:

> A sustainable organisation is one which manages its relationships with the social and natural environments in order to maintain low levels of internal and external entropy.

The aim of this chapter is therefore to consider the role of organisations in furthering environmental and social sustainability, while maintaining their own economic sustainability, or viability.

4.3 The emergence of an organisational sustainability concept

So how has this organisational responsiveness to the dangers of an unsustainable future emerged? Figure 4.3 highlights the key developments. The first glimmerings in the corporate world of an awareness about responsibilities other than making a profit seem to have emerged in the 1920s, the early stages of Robert Putnam's "We" period (see Chapter 1, Section 1.6), with discussion developing about what was then called corporate philanthropy. This introduced ideas about corporate codes of conduct, the importance of community service and the role of corporate managers as public trustees. This awareness strengthened and the idea of Corporate Social Responsibility (CSR)

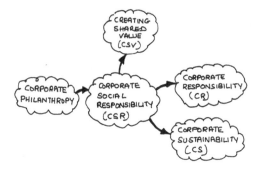

Figure 4.3 The development of the organisational sustainability concept.

emerged in the 1960s and has attracted a wide range of explanations and definitions. For example, Archie Carroll, one of the leading writers about the subject, suggests that "The CSR firm should strive to make a profit, obey the law, be ethical, and be a good corporate citizen".[4]

CSR can be both internal or external. Internal CSR refers to how an organisation treats its employees, and much of the research about internal CSR sits within the field of human resource management (HRM), leading to concepts such as "green" or "sustainable" HRM. As such, internal CSR focuses primarily on social aspects of sustainability. External CSR refers to activities aimed at external stakeholders, and this may be socially oriented, through work with communities relevant to the organisation, or with an environmental focus.

It is not difficult to find information about organisational CSR practice—an internet search can easily locate annual reports. What is noticeable is that these reports are increasingly being called "sustainability reports", illustrating how the traditional idea of CSR has been replaced by organisational sustainability.

CSR is a process improvement or philanthropic activity which is a relatively simple way for an organisation to claim that it is having a more sustainable impact on its social and natural environments. However, in the absence of any agreement about what exactly CSR is and hence how it can be evaluated in any way, it may be used as a way to divert attention from other activities which have a negative impact, a process sometimes known as "greenwashing".

The "Social" in CSR is significant: up until the 1990s the idea that organisations had responsibilities to anything other than owners or investors was largely limited to social implications—theories of organisational behaviour rarely considered the environment. However, after the 1987 publication of *Our Common Future* interest started to grow in what was starting to become known as "corporate sustainability" (CS) (corporate because the literature is largely focused on the implications of sustainability on maintaining organisational profitability). This led to a move away from the term CSR to CR, just Corporate Responsibility. Also emerging since about 2010 has been the idea of Creating Shared Value (CSV), discussed in more detail below.

So in the 2020s, we find a variety of terms being used to describe related ideas. Although terms such as CR and CSV have reasonably well understood and agreed definitions, the same cannot be said for organisational sustainability. One result of this is that there is a considerable blurring of the concepts in the extensive literature looking at the subject. It also contributes to the greenwashing problem—any organisational contribution to a social or environmental situation may be described as organisational sustainability.

The contested nature of sustainability means that there are many definitions of organisational sustainability; however, a starting point is:

> Corporate sustainability refers to a systematic business approach and strategy that takes into consideration the long-term social and environmental impact of all economically motivated behaviors of a firm in the interest of consumers, employees, and owners or shareholders.[5]

What does organisational sustainability look like in practice? An enormous range of activities can be considered as seeking to address organisational sustainability, but broadly, these can be considered as philanthropy, business practice or product-related.[6]

Table 4.1 Examples of activities furthering organisational sustainability

	Examples of organisational sustainability activities		
Philanthropy	Donations of cash Product donations	Employees volunteering Public service announcements	Charity events Collections from customers
Business practices	Reducing pollution levels Fair trade	Recycling Observing sustainability standards programmes	Advertising policies Following sector codes of practice
Product-related	Energy-efficient designs Product quality	Organic products Restrictions on controversial products	Selection of product ingredients

Time for reflection

What do you think about this categorisation and listing of activities to support organisational sustainability?

What activities do you currently take which are aimed towards social or environmental sustainability? How do they fit into this categorisation?

Does the categorisation suggest any new possibilities for you? What might these be?

4.4 What drives organisations towards sustainability?

There are many reasons why organisations decide to pursue a sustainability strategy, some proactive in order to achieve something, and some reactive as a response to some form of pressure, although distinguishing between these two is not always easy. An alternative way of looking at this is that drivers may be instrumental (aimed at achieving something), relational (aimed at improving relationships), or moral (satisfying ethical considerations).[7] Each of these brings benefits, and most organisations will respond to a combination of them, but how they are prioritised will be different for every organisation.

In order to explore these drivers more carefully, we will look through the lenses of various "theories of the firm" that are used by economists and organisational theorists. In this context "theories" are not actually completely theoretical: most organisational theory is based on observation about how real organisations behave and there is an ongoing dialectical relationship between theory and practice: as managers seek to apply what they learn from theory, they change organisational practice, consequently influencing new theory. Organisational theory only really started to pay attention to how social or environmental problems might affect how an organisation operated in the 1990s, and in this section, we will look at how contemporary research is addressing sustainability concerns.

4.4.1 Stockholder theory

Stockholder theory focuses on the relationship of an organisation with its market and pays little attention to other factors. We might therefore represent this as Figure 4.4, where social and natural environments play no part.

According to the theory, the organisation does what is necessary to maximise returns to its stockholders through the market value of the business. Driven by this perspective, there has been much research looking at the instrumental, financial implications of organisational sustainability-type activities. The results of this research are not particularly consistent, mainly because there are so many ways in which organisations seek to operate sustainably and levels at which this can be done. However, there is a reasonable amount of evidence that there is a positive connection, that organisations with a strong ethical commitment do seem to be rewarded by improved financial returns and hence show greater stability.[8]

Curiously, as noted by one of the most influential writers on the subject, Marc Orlitzky, this both refutes and supports the claims of neoclassical economists regarding the purpose of an organisation (for example as in the Friedman Doctrine). It refutes it by showing that a commitment to social good is actually beneficial to shareholders, but supports it by showing that the market recognises the value of socially and environmentally beneficial practice, and therefore that government or institutional regulation is unnecessary.[9]

However, while there is much research interest in identifying the benefits of sustainable practice to organisations, there is something of a gap in assessing the benefits of sustainability activities to apparent beneficiaries. Does this reflect an underlying assumption that sustainability is about helping the organisation rather than the targets of benevolence?[10]

Critics of stockholder theory see it as promoting a short-term outlook and ignoring externalities and negative impacts on society and the environment, and attracts the particular ire of business ethicists, who have described it using phrases such as "an outmoded relic" and "corporate Neanderthalism".[11] These perceptions may be strengthened by the increasing importance of paying senior executives with stock options, opportunities to buy shares in the organisation. A problem with this is that executives may want to realise the benefits of this as quickly as possible and so implement measures to stimulate a short-term increase in share value, realise their profits, and then move on to another organisation before problems set in. Another more recent trend is the increasing importance of institutional investment, in the form of hedge funds, private equity investment and pension funds which seek short-term returns on investment.

However, it needs to be acknowledged that stockholder theory is simply concerned with an organisation doing what its investors want, and it does not attempt to address the organisation's ethical position regarding social and environmental sustainability. It therefore does not preclude investment in organisations pursuing sustainability if this is seen to be a good investment decision, and socially responsible investing is increasingly important: for example, in the United States, the value of such investments grew by 325% between 1995 and 2011.[12]

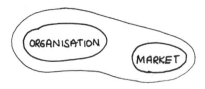

Figure 4.4 System map for stockholder theory.

4.4.2 Social contract theory

Social contract theory derives from principles developed by Jean-Jacques Rousseau in the 1760s, that rulers and their subjects maintain a stable relationship where the subjects remain acquiescent as long as the ruler provides protection in terms of maintaining peace and providing essential services. Social contract theory therefore, although having pragmatic roots, implies that organisations need to operate according to an accepted ethical code so that their customers stay as customers. This perspective suggests both relational and moral drivers for sustainable practice.

When applied to organisational practice, social contract ideas are sometimes described as "corporate citizenship". This has become increasingly recognised in recent years as globalisation has seen the growing significance of transnational corporations who, through the internet, can operate across international boundaries and so may see themselves as not limited by national legal jurisdictions or local moral standards. As a specific example, during the COVID-19 pandemic Amazon arguably was transformed from a shopping website into a public utility as a provider of essential services, and yet it uses its international reach to minimise national tax liabilities and has been criticised for its restrictive labour practices.[13] As well as being monitored by the media, organisations are increasingly being held to account for their part of the social contract bargaining by independent organisations such as NGOs, social movements, and even investment companies who see the strategic importance of sustainability.[14] Thinking about organisational practice from a social contract perspective also highlights the importance of human rights issues, such as how it may discriminate against people on the basis of gender, age, race, or other factors.

The psychological contract between an organisation and its employees is an example of a social contract, and breaches of such a contract can create internal pressures. For example, in 2018, 3,000 employees signed a letter to Sundar Pichai, the CEO of Google, and apparently over a dozen employees subsequently resigned in protest at the organisation's involvement in Project Maven, a project integrating facial recognition systems into military drones—as a result, Google abandoned its involvement.[15]

So-called "social enterprises" may be seen as working to support a social contract by delivering some form of social good—with a loose definition of "social", this might have both social or environmental aims. Such organisations can be constituted to generate a fair profit or be non-profit organisations. Public sector organisations, such as local, regional, national or international government bodies, should also be dedicated towards maintaining social contracts relevant to the community that they serve.

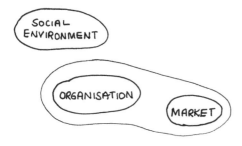

Figure 4.5 System map for a social contract view of organisations.

Social contract theory allows us to develop our system map by including the social environment in the organisation's systemic environment (Figure 4.5).

4.4.3 Institutional theory

The theory of the firm which has perhaps proved most useful in understanding organisational sustainability is institutional theory. Although institutional theory developed in the 1970s, only in the late 1990s did researchers start to look at how it could contribute to understanding organisational sustainability.[16]

Institutional theory is concerned with the relationship between organisations and their "institutional landscape", in systems thinking terminology, the environment within which they operate. It is also an important basic concept in organisational learning, discussed below.

Institutions are:

> … the humanly devised constraints that structure human interaction. They are made up of formal constraints (e.g., rules, laws, constitutions), informal constraints (e.g., norms of behavior, conventions, self-imposed codes of conduct), and their enforcement characteristics. Together they define the incentive structure of societies and specifically economies.[17]

People in a capitalist society rely on transactions for survival, and transactions are much easier to complete if you play by the rules of the game as set by the institutions. Societal norms and values within the landscape will have a profound effect on which institutions are strong or weak. As Douglass North, the Nobel prize-winning economist commented (perhaps with the state-approved activities of 16th-century English sea captains in mind), "if the institutional framework rewards piracy then piratical organizations will come into existence".[18] So players in the capitalist game organise themselves in a way which suits the institutional landscape, but of course, as they evolve they will start to influence the landscape themselves by introducing enhancements to make the game even more successful for themselves. However, by the same logic, if the landscape changes to reward sustainable behaviour, organisations will find it financially attractive to invest in sustainable practice. The Sustainable Development Goals (SDGs) have added such a sustainability-focused element to the institutional landscape.

We can look at this process of adaptation as an example of learning: as the landscape changes an organisation learns how to behave differently so that it can remain viable. This perspective on organisational behaviour and change is captured within the study of organisational learning, a discipline upon which we will draw extensively in succeeding chapters.

Of course, as organisations change what they do they also change the landscape, so there is a dynamic relationship between the two. We can view this relationship as a spiral dynamic,[19] illustrated in Figure 4.6. Landscape 1 drives organisational behaviour 1, which creates Landscape 2, and the organisation learns to adapt to behaviour 2, and the process continues.

However, what organisations do is not the only factor influencing the institutional landscape. Figure 4.7 suggests a more complex set of relationships, bringing in society,

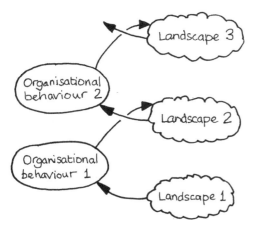

Figure 4.6 Institutional theory as a spiral dynamic.

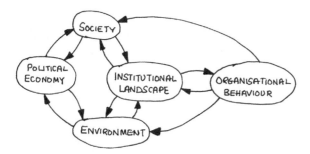

Figure 4.7 Feedback processes influencing the institutional landscape.

the environment and political economy. For example, the political economy bubble contains not only national economic policies but also geopolitical considerations, such as political relations with sometimes repressive regimes in major oil producing countries and deciding how to manage the globally important but environmentally damaging aviation industry.[20] Such complexity recognises the potential implications of Ulrich Beck's risk society concept (Chapter 1, Section 1.2) which lurks in the background: that societal or environmental conditions may degrade to a point where an enforced enlightenment could trigger potentially massive changes in what is seen as legitimate within an institutional landscape. For example, in May 2021 the environmental group Friends of the Earth persuaded Dutch courts that the oil company Royal Dutch Shell was legally obliged by the Paris climate agreement to cut carbon emissions by 45% by 2030.[21] Recent changes in legislation regarding the fulfilment of public sector construction projects in the United Kingdom now make it mandatory to fulfil social value commitments, as illustrated in the quotation in Box 4.1. The four variables of organisational behaviour, society, political economy and the environment now interact in a number of feedback loops which will all have an impact on the characteristics of the institutional landscape.

> **Box 4.1**
>
> The most significant change I have seen in the last 12 months is the addition of financial penalties for not achieving social value key performance indicators. So, for example, if somebody in the construction sector has agreed to take on 25 apprentices through the course of a hospital building project, there is now a contractual mechanism where they can be penalised if they don't deliver on that. So for the first time something that was considered voluntary and a nice to have is now legally binding.
>
> Natalie Wilkinson, NG Bailey

Constraining this evolutionary perspective on institutional change is the idea of institutional isomorphism.[22] According to this, different organisations working in the same fields will experience powerful forces acting on them which make them all start to behave similarly. This happens in three ways. First, coercive isomorphism would occur as a result of pressures to conform and to work within legitimate frames of understanding. Second, mimetic isomorphism would happen as organisations copied each other in how they dealt with uncertainty. Third, there will be normative isomorphism which happens as the field of work becomes more professionalised, with people working in the field having been educated following the same curricula and having developed the same institutional mindset. This reduces the variety of ideas that circulate in an organisational field and can clearly have a negative impact on sustainability-related innovation. The problems caused by this hegemonic thinking in changing mindsets about neoliberal economic policies as a result of limited ways of thinking were discussed in Chapter 3, Section 3.5.

Spiralling evolution or stagnation? The concepts of spiral dynamics and institutional isomorphism pull in different directions, one suggesting steady progress and the other stasis. In reality, there will probably always be sufficient variety within any organisational field to stimulate some form of overall evolution, but it is important for individual organisations to reflect on the degree to which they are "stuck", captured by the three forces of isomorphism. Normative isomorphism is the pressure of most interest to learning and development practice, and points to the importance of adopting critical approaches within learning and development strategies.

We can now update our system map to include the natural environment to show how this influences the institutional landscape (Figure 4.8).

A study by John Campbell[23] suggested a number of features of institutional landscapes which would have an effect on stimulating interest in sustainability strategies. For profit-seeking organisations, their relative strength in their particular landscape is crucial: too much or too little competition may make embracing sustainability seem too risky, which may also be the case if their particular sector is also weak. The influential business strategy theorist Michael Porter proposed what is known as the "Porter hypothesis", that environmental regulation stimulates organisational innovation, creating the possibility for a competitive advantage.[24] State regulation in the landscape is very important, particularly if this is based on negotiation and consensus. A perception that regulations will be enforced should create a culture of self-regulation. As well as state regulation, it is important that there is independent monitoring by social movement organisations,

Figure 4.8 System map including social and natural environments.

institutional investors and the media. Key journals and networking events relevant to the sector should promote the importance of sustainability. Organisational membership of trade and employer associations and a willingness to engage in dialogue with trades unions, community groups and other stakeholders helps to strengthen a sustainability culture.

When the institutional landscape exists within a neoliberal political economy it would be expected that state regulation will be minimal and that other institutions which interfere with the functioning of the market, such as trades unions may also be weak. Some studies do show that while the effects of the Porter hypothesis are correct and regulation stimulates innovation improving productivity, the overall effect of regulation on business performance is often negative.[25]

4.4.4 Stakeholder theory

Stakeholder theory proposes that organisations have duties to not only the owners and investors of a business, but to employees, customers, communities within which the organisation operates, and others.[26] It is often used in discussions about business ethics, where it helps to raise important questions about broader moral responsibilities that an organisation has.

It is however criticised as a theory to help organisations make decisions about what they should do on the practical grounds that it is in reality difficult to define precisely just who are stakeholders, how to consult them all effectively, and how to make decisions which maximises every stakeholder's satisfaction.[27] For example, it may be argued that the environment itself is a stakeholder, so how is this drawn into consultations?

Stakeholder theory does draw attention to two particular groups of people who can have a profound impact on how successful an organisation is, customers and employees.

First, as public awareness of issues related to social and environmental sustainability grows, people may seek to satisfy their sense of civic duty by purchasing products or services from organisations they see as operating ethically. It has also been noted that people often perceive products and services from organisations they see as operating ethically as being of better quality.[28] Natalie Wilkinson's observation about her own organisation (Box 4.2) shows how younger people entering the workforce are also changing things: Millennials and Generation Z have grown up in a technologically connected world, are much more aware of both environmental crises and the interconnectedness of people around the world and hence may be more attracted to products and services from organisations with a strong ethical profile.[29]

> **Box 4.2**
>
> We have the rise of a new population, Generation Z, who are now coming through into the workplace and starting to disrupt it, starting to challenge people who have been in roles for a long time, saying 'Why don't we do this, why are you doing that?' They're bringing new ideas to the table.
>
> Natalie Wilkinson, NG Bailey

Employees are also important stakeholders. We have already referred to the Project Maven example of employees challenging organisational activities which were seen to be unacceptable ethically, but positive behaviour can also bring benefits: as Fozia Parveen suggests in Box 4.3, a strong social or environmental ethical commitment can be a strong draw for high-quality potential employees, as well as having a positive impact on employee behaviour and their commitment to the organisation.[30]

> **Box 4.3**
>
> The younger generation want to work for companies that are thinking about sustainability, so if we want to attract the best talent we've got to make sure that we are complying with what's required. We then have to think about how to retain them, because they are our future."
>
> Fozia Parveen, ISG Ltd

4.4.5 The resource-based view

The final theory of the firm to explore here is the resource-based view (RBV) which is primarily related to instrumental drivers for sustainability. RBV is fundamentally different from the theories we have looked at so far: while these have all considered how an organisation relates to the world outside, RBV is concerned with the internal dynamics of the organisation. Its central argument is that an organisation can achieve a competitive advantage through the development of its internal resources, its ability to design, produce, procure, deliver and so on better than its competitors. The most important contributor to this is the knowledge and skill of its employees. This can contribute to a competitive advantage because how people operate in an organisation is complex, making it difficult for competitors to understand what works well and hence replicate it. RBV is particularly useful from a learning and development perspective, as it guides us towards how resources need to be strengthened.

RBV started to emerge as a distinct theory of the firm in the 1970s, but it was not until Stuart Hart put forward a theory about a natural-resource-based view of the firm in 1995[31] that RBV started to address sustainability. Hart's argument was that an organisation's ability to address environmental issues would become increasingly important as a way of developing a competitive advantage. He identified three areas where organisations should seek to strengthen their capability, in pollution prevention, product stewardship (adopting sustainability principles throughout procurement chains and product life cycles), and sustainable development (applying the principles of pollution prevention, product stewardship and using clean technology to promote social and economic development in low-income countries).[32] Focusing on these three areas would mean that an organisation should strengthen its human resources so that they are better able to innovate and have the knowledge and skills that will become increasingly relevant in the future. It might also be expected that people working in organisations with this greater environmental focus would develop an appropriate framework of values which would support this.

4.4.6 Lessons from theories

What might all this mean? Figure 4.9 is an attempt to pull together these different theories and identify what implications for learning and development may be. In the left-hand "Perspective" column are the first four theories considered and the drivers for sustainability that they imply. On the right-hand "Learning opportunities" side is the RBV, and proposals for what resources need to be strengthened to address these drivers. Broadly speaking, these are related to developing a values framework which is in line with social and environmental sustainability, strengthening the ability to innovate, to think about how an organisation needs to operate in a new sustainability paradigm, and to expand the boundaries about how decision-making about sustainability-related issues happens.

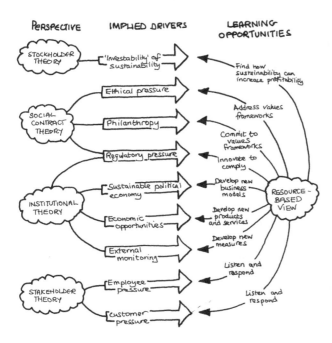

Figure 4.9 Drivers for sustainability and learning implications of theories of the firm.

Time for reflection

What other lessons might you be able to draw from this reflection on organisational theory?

What drivers for sustainability are relevant to your own organisation, and what implications do these have for strengthening resources?

4.5 Three dimensions of organisational sustainability

In Chapter 1, we saw how sustainability has been conceptualised as having three dimensions, environmental, social and economic. Thinking about organisational sustainability has followed a similar trajectory, in more recent years taking a broader perspective seeking to integrate both environmental and social concerns.

Working at the more micro level of organisations brings the dynamic tensions between the three dimensions into a greater focus so that it becomes somewhat easier to see the trade-offs which develop when prioritising one dimension over the others.

Figure 4.10 illustrates these interrelated tensions and shows how they are influenced by the landscape of the political economy. We might see an example in the Sheffield tree maintenance story (Chapter 2), where there was a tension between the environmental sustainability of protecting trees, the social sustainability of maintaining a pleasant neighbourhood for living in, and the economic sustainability of a private sector company.

4.5.1 Economic sustainability

In this chapter we look first at economic sustainability because how an organisation relates to its economic landscape is an existential question: if it cannot remain viable as an organisation then it cannot contribute to environmental or social sustainability. This

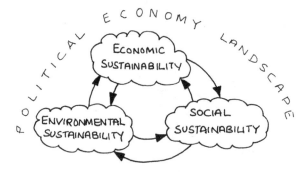

Figure 4.10 Tensions between economic, social and environmental sustainability in a political economy landscape.

applies to all types of organisations, whether they are profit-seeking, not-for-profit or public sector.

The discourse around economic sustainability as relevant to organisational practice seems to interpret the term in two different ways, one emphasising internal considerations and the other external. The internal view of organisational economic sustainability is probably the most commonly explored, as it draws on the business literature's idea of sustainability, that it is about keeping the business going: in that sense, what we are really talking about is organisational *viability*. For example, one definition states that:

> Economically sustainable companies guarantee at any time cashflow sufficient to ensure liquidity while producing a persistent above average return to their shareholders.[33]

This definition does highlight the importance of finance, that all organisations need to be able to generate sufficient cash flow to enable them to maintain the throughput that forms the basis of what they do. However, cash flow on its own is not enough to keep an organisation viable. It is also important to make sure that as cash flows through the organisation it maintains its levels of capital and does not consume them in order to keep the money rolling. In the context of sustainability, that means that the organisation must protect its sources of both natural capital (environmental resources and sinks) and social capital, which comprises the human capital of its employees, manifested in skills, motivation and commitment, and societal capital, the capital represented by such things as healthcare, education and public infrastructure. At the organisational level therefore, as at the global level, the three dimensions are intimately connected.

So, as discussed earlier in Section 4.4.3, what decisions an organisation makes about prioritising or balancing contributions to sustainability will be influenced by what the landscape deems as desirable. A neoliberal political economy where externalities remain as externalities and discounting rates are high creates a landscape where the pressure is on organisations to strongly prioritise profit over social and environmental sustainability considerations, whereas if the dominant political economy were oriented towards sustainable economics, the situation would be quite different, and different decisions would seem legitimate. Social values influence what business decisions are seen as acceptable: as the quotation in Box 4.4 highlights, racism may legitimate decisions which contribute to financial viability, but which run completely counter to principles of social sustainability.

Box 4.4

In the United States the reality of racism means that there are sacrificial communities. Powerful people decide a plant has to be built, and you can build it there because those people see it as a disposable community.

Gail Francis, RE-AMP

This raises a question about what constitutes a fair profit. Profit serves legitimate purposes: it provides the owner of a business with a return which rewards the risk they have taken, it provides capital which can be reinvested in developing the business, and it can serve to attract further investment. However, generating and maximising profit may become the primary role purpose of what the organisation does, and this may be more problematic. How is the profit used? If those taking profit from the organisation use it in unsustainable ways, then sustainable practices in the organisation start to look somewhat hypocritical.

The external perspective on organisational economic sustainability is when we consider how organisations can contribute to maintaining the economies within which they operate. In broad terms what this means may be shown by those SDG targets which have an economic sustainability focus, as suggested in Table 1.3 in Chapter 1. Some specific examples are also useful. Consider a pharmaceutical company manufacturing a drug which has valuable therapeutic properties, but which is highly addictive. Although its primary use is beneficial, it can be traded within and reinforces the illicit drug market, destroys individuals' relationships and creates significant social problems. In the absence of strong action to rectify the harm done, what this organisation is doing has a negative impact on economic sustainability because of the financial costs that society must bear in dealing with the effects of addiction, money that could be used in more productive ways. There is also of course a negative impact on social sustainability in this scenario.

As an alternative consider the example of Danish pharmaceutical company Novo Nordisk, which among other things, manufactures drugs used to treat diabetes.[34] It makes a profit on these drugs, but there are indirect financial impacts as well. People whose diabetes is controlled place fewer demands on the health service, saving money, and they are better able to contribute to the national economy, increasing national wealth.

A further complication is that an organisation which seeks to produce more environmentally sustainable products and finds ways to do this more efficiently may reduce the cost of them to the consumers, with the unfortunate effect that it leads to greater consumption, a phenomenon known to economists as the "Jevons paradox". An example is that increasing the fuel efficiency of cars encourages people to drive more and to buy new cars more frequently as they strive to become ever more environmentally friendly.

These issues illustrate that thinking about the wider economic impact of what an organisation does is not a trivial matter and requires much thinking about what boundaries to draw. In economic language, we have to look at externalities and think about whether they should be more like "internalities". Tools are available to do this, such as Life-Cycle Assessment (LCA), as defined within the ISO 14000 series of international standards.

This is also recognised in the concept of "social value" expressed in terms of a Social Return on Investment, a methodology which helps to quantify the social benefits of infrastructure developments.[35] Social value has a legal status in the United Kingdom as a consequence of the Public Services (Social Value) Act 2012—private and public sector organisations working on public infrastructure projects are required to be able to demonstrate that they contribute to the well-being and resilience of individuals, communities and society affected by what they are doing. Fozia Parveen, Head of Social Value for the global construction specialist company ISG describes one aspect of what this might mean in Box 4.5.

> **Box 4.5**
>
> What we are trying to do is look at different kinds of measures and data capture for social value. So for example, how many people on our sites are from various differing backgrounds; i.e ex-offenders, Black or Asian minority groups, young people, care leavers, any with disabilities?
>
> Fozia Parveen, ISG Ltd

One subject that highlights both conceptions of economic sustainability is the concept of CSV. This was developed by leading management theorists Michael Porter and Mark Kramer who propose that organisations should seek to "create shared value" by re-conceiving products and markets, redefining productivity in the value chain, and enabling "local cluster development". This means identifying partner organisations, and then collaborating to open new markets for products and services which meet a social need as well as generate profits. Kramer further developed the CSV idea by explaining how organisations work in an "ecosystem" of markets, suppliers and distributors, affected by government policies and cultural norms. CSV then relies on the principles of "collective impact":

> the idea that social problems arise from and persist because of a complex combination of actions and omissions by players in all sectors—and therefore can be solved only by the coordinated efforts of those players, from businesses to government agencies, charitable organizations, and members of affected populations.[36]

Implementing collective impact requires a common agenda, a shared measurement system, mutually reinforcing activities, constant communication and dedicated support from independent organisations. Business strategies should mesh with public priorities, drawing on aims such as those within the UN's SDGs.

Proponents of CSV attempt to draw a clear line between it and CSR: they claim, for example, that much CSR may be seen as philanthropy, whereas CSV is about increasing economic and social value[37]; CSR places social needs at the periphery of organisational practice, whereas CSV places them at the core[38]; CSV elevates social need to a strategic level whereas CSR addresses disconnected activities.[39]

However, it is also argued that CSV has merely re-presented CSR in a language which appeals to managers of large corporations.[40] CSR and CSV may address different areas of social needs: because a primary objective in CSV is to generate profit,[41] a CSV strategy may mean that an organisation is reluctant to address "... really thorny CSR issues, such as human rights or bribery and corruption".[42]

While CSV has attracted a considerable amount of interest in the business world, its real significance for sustainability has been the subject of some debate. CSV stresses the potential for "win-win" situations, but the emphasis tends to be on financial success which may be at the expense of achieving social goals where these are in tension: here CSV may be seen as a more sophisticated attempt at greenwashing. An example of this is where Western corporations integrate suppliers in low-income countries into their supply chains: this provides jobs, meeting a social need, but if these jobs are in so-called sweatshop conditions which are dangerous and unhealthy, is the social outcome positive?[43]

It is also argued that CSV pays little attention to more systemic aspects of corporate activity such as tax avoidance and lobbying for less regulation, and although Kramer's later article addresses the concept of the CSV ecosystem and the relationship of corporations with government, the ethics of the unequal power distribution between large multinational corporations and cluster partners, particularly those in low-income countries, is not addressed. Porter and Kramer acknowledge that CSV presumes compliance with the law and ethical standards, but critics point out that a concept aimed at restoring trust in capitalism should arguably integrate a moral framework rather than just assume it.[44]

Finally, with its focus on economic viability and social issues, CSV does not explicitly address environmental sustainability.

In conclusion, CSV seems to be a potentially attractive model to large corporations seeking to operate in a more ethically yet still financially viable manner. However, by not addressing in sufficient detail how to resolve complex social and environmental issues it may still be seen as a "business as usual" approach to sustainable practice.

4.5.2 Environmental sustainability

What can organisations do to further environmental sustainability? The first answer to this question is to look at the SDG targets related to environmental sustainability (Table 1.1 in Chapter 1) and think about how these relate to what your organisation does.

In Chapter 2, Section 2.5, we looked at the issue of perspectives and identified two polarities of thought about sustainability as anthropocentric and ecocentric. This distinction continues through to organisational sustainability, where the anthropocentric perspective is often described as "technocentric" or ecomodernist. Based on an Enlightenment belief in the power of science and technology, this view proposes that organisations can contribute to sustainability through the development of new technologies which reduce environmental degradation, use materials more efficiently, can capture greenhouse gases, and so on.[45] Some examples being discussed are spraying saltwater into the Arctic sky in order to create a layer of white crystals which will reflect heat back into space,[46] and depositing large quantities of iron into the ocean to stimulate the ability of phytoplankton to absorb carbon dioxide from the atmosphere.[47] Interesting though these ideas may be, there are numerous examples where scientific research has been used to justify technical interventions in natural ecosystems, but which have had disastrous unintended and unforeseen consequences (for example, google "Australian cane toad").

Contrasting with the techno-rationality of ecomodernism, ecocentrism rejects the concept of human dominion over nature and advocates developing harmonious relationships with the natural environment and organisational missions which prioritise long-term, global sustainability. Existing measures of organisational performance such as profit need to be enhanced by measures of contribution to environmental protection and degradation.

Advocates of ecocentric management identify a number of key principles: environmental integrity, product stewardship and using raw materials more efficiently or effectively.[48] Environmental integrity means operating in a way which respects the carrying and regenerative capacities of the atmosphere and does not erode land, air and water resources. This requires effective waste and energy management systems. Product stewardship focuses on product design, and advocates a "cradle-to-grave" philosophy, requiring such things as avoiding planned obsolescence, making repair and maintenance easier, and planning for eventual disposal or recycling.[49]

Improved use of raw materials may be through circular economy principles, reducing, reusing and recycling. It has been suggested that the most widely adopted ecocentric principle is reducing raw material usage, sometimes described as "eco-efficiency". However, an emphasis on eco-efficiency may be seen as "... a necessary, but not sufficient, prerequisite for full sustainable development",[50] and that focusing on it may lead (or enable) organisations to overlook other, perhaps more challenging, strategies for better environmental sustainability such as, for example, cradle-to-cradle "eco-effectiveness",[51] where production is a closed loop activity and the resting place of one product provides the raw material for a new product.

An economy which emphasises environmental sustainability has the potential to create significant numbers of what are often described as "green jobs". The International Labour Organization (ILO) claims this is going to have an impact in several different ways: there will be structural changes in the labour market, meaning that some occupations will disappear, new ones will emerge, and that there will be a significant need for retraining; and even within occupations which remain, there will be new knowledge and skill requirements.[52] Related to this, the ILO promotes the concept of a "just transition", national economic policies and organisational strategies which:

> foster a competitive, low-carbon, environmentally sustainable economy and patterns of sustainable consumption and production, and contribute to the fight against climate change.[53]

Recent criticism of organisational approaches to environmental sustainability has been a perceived failure to connect with the scientific literature about planetary boundaries. Focusing:

> ... on corporate behaviour in isolation from ecologically material impacts risks creating an unbalanced picture of progress, one that decouples social and organizational efforts for sustainability ... from the on-the-ground, in-the-air, and through-the-water material impacts of collective corporate and consumer activity.[54]

Research into organisational approaches to environmental sustainability tends to focus on single issues relevant to a particular sector rather than addressing the more complex issue about how organisational practice may impact on the interrelated constraints of planetary boundaries. The siloed nature of academic research and more practitioner-oriented literature means that there is often little crossover from journals like *Nature* to those read by corporate executives, so that many senior managers may be unaware of the planetary boundaries concept.

An important exercise for every organisation should therefore be to reflect on how its activities impact on the nine boundaries, as illustrated in Figure 4.11, where I have added a "profile line" to show how this graphic might provide an aid for reflection on organisational environmental sustainability.

118 *The sustainable organisation*

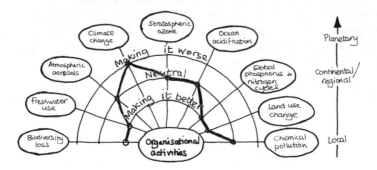

Figure 4.11 Querying the impact of organisational activities on planetary boundaries.

Note: The profile line shows how you might use this diagram to reflect on your own organisation. For each boundary, assess your level of impact for each boundary and circle that point on the scale. Join the dots to create your planetary boundary profile.

Time for reflection

Think about the nine planetary boundaries. What impact do you think your organisation's activities have on each of these?

You might want to draw your own organisation's profile as in Figure 4.11. The smaller the better! It will be interesting to reflect on how difficult it is to decide what impact your organisation's activities have on each of these boundaries.

What implications might this have for your approach to improving your environmental sustainability?

4.5.3 Social sustainability

As the providers of most employment within society, organisations have a huge part to play in how well society functions, and hence its sustainability. However, as we saw in Chapter 1, what social sustainability means is a subject of much political debate. As with the other dimensions of sustainability, the SDG targets provide an important starting point for thinking about what the implications will be for organisations (see Table 1.2 in Chapter 1 for those relating to social sustainability).

In a careful examination of what social sustainability means for organisational practice, the American academic John Campbell suggested[55] that, depending on one's perspective, it might mean providing a decent living wage, or not damaging a local community, or that an organisation behaves in a way that is approved of by stakeholders, or …—the difficulty becomes apparent. He suggested a more workable definition may be to think about a minimum behavioural standard, that organisations should not knowingly do anything to harm stakeholders, and that if harm is done, it should be rectified. This resonates with Mary Anderson's "do no harm" principle, a cornerstone of humanitarian aid programmes.[56] We can translate Anderson's observations about the effect of humanitarian aid into organisational practice—what an organisation does can:

- be subverted for undesirable purposes
- reinforce negative socio-economic dynamics
- have an impact on social relationships
- have a negative impact on local, community issues.

Historically, there is a long tradition of organisations working towards social sustainability. For example, a number of 18th- and 19th-century industries were established by Quaker families, who had a strong belief in taking care of employees and improving communities (a tradition continued by the Quaker community to this day). The Catholic Social Tradition requires that business owners see their business as a community, and that they should be concerned with the growth and development of employees.[57]

What these historical examples also show is that organisational strategies for social sustainability may operate in two different ways: one internally, where the focus is on employee welfare, and the other externally, where the organisation has a responsibility to the outside community (corporate citizenship). External social sustainability is arguably easier for an organisation to be involved in, as it has the potential for providing good public relations and also does not necessarily affect what happens inside the organisation. Internal social sustainability is potentially much more complex with implications for everything from organisational structures to its working culture.

Some issues have both external and internal implications, for example automation. Many factors are driving increasing levels of automation in the workplace. The increasing power of artificial intelligence (AI) and machine learning (ML) is opening up many new possibilities for replacing people, rather than just in manufacturing. Another is the paradox that, in the United Kingdom at least, when a human being does a job an organisation pays a tax on this, whereas when a machine does the same job, the organisation can claim tax relief on the cost. This helps to make automation cost-effective, but other factors including reliability, increased precision, the ability to work 24/7, and so on are also important. Concerns about automation go back to the early days of the Industrial Revolution with the 19th-century Luddites for example, but the contemporary concern is that the expanding use of AI and ML threatens a much wider range of jobs, professional as well as manual.

Exploring the wider implications of modern forms of automation goes beyond the scope of this book, and research into what it might mean is still in its infancy, but in brief, it may have implications for external social sustainability in that fewer people could be needed in the workforce meaning higher levels of unemployment, greater income inequality, and lower levels of engagement with society for example. Meaningful employment is a vitally important part of socialisation, and societies where fewer people are working and communicating the values inculcated by regular, ongoing employment, may become less coherent and stable.[58] Fewer people working also means fewer people able to buy the products or services of what an organisation does.

Regarding internal social sustainability, automation may remove much of what makes work meaningful to an individual through reducing or eliminating what offers someone satisfaction in their work, and perceptions of increasing levels of automation may increase levels of anxiety over concerns about job security. Of course, technology does not have to lead to such consequences. Automation to increase mass production is a consequence of a profit-driven system, and it is possible to think differently: technology could be used to increase job satisfaction, to promote even higher quality artisanal production. AI and ML could be used in a way which made such work more satisfying while at the same time increasing its environmental sustainability.[59] There really is a choice.

External social sustainability was a traditional focus of what was originally called CSR. For example, in a report aimed at senior executives in the United States, the business research organisation Conference Board provided a comprehensive list of what CSR activities typically included (extracts from which are shown in Table 4.1).[60] They identified philanthropy (external donations and activities), five product-related activities (more related to environmental sustainability), and 31 business practices, of which 26 had an external focus.

We can now move on to think about internal social sustainability, using the themes discussed previously, social equity, social cohesion and meeting basic needs.

Meeting basic needs is perhaps the most straightforward of the three. Drawing on a framework developed by Chris Landorf,[61] the organisation needs to make sure that its employees:

- have access to adequate sources of nutrition while they are at work
- work in appropriate conditions, such as being warm, dry, safely constructed, etc
- receive the training necessary for them to be able to carry out their work responsibilities, and have access to other learning opportunities which can further their employment progression
- can work free from concerns about disease or injury
- have terms of employment which provide appropriate levels of job security
- are safe in their work and protected from crime.

There is no space here to explore these in detail, but it would be useful to look briefly at some of these requirements. For example, job security is severely compromised by the development of the "gig economy", characterised by individuals selling their labour using technology platforms.[62] Such work may be locally delivered, such as through food delivery or providing transport services, or remote, through data inputting or computer programming. Typically, gig workers are classified as self-employed, so employing organisations have minimal employer responsibilities, such as no sick pay or holiday entitlement, and the workers are not, in principle, constrained to a specific workplace or working hours. As such, the gig economy is a perfect example of everyday neoliberalism, where each individual markets themselves, probably free from the market distortions of labour regulations and unionisation. The internet may facilitate this development:

> Before the Internet, it would be really difficult to find someone, sit them down for ten minutes and get them to work for you, and then fire them after those ten minutes. But with technology, you can actually find them, pay them the tiny amount of money, and then get rid of them when you don't need them any more.[63]

Although attractive to many people, evidence is emerging about the potential negative consequences of gig working. Low hourly rates mean that people may have to work long, irregular, unsociable hours alone to earn enough to live on, leading to problems of social isolation and associated health problems. Decisions about how work is allocated may be made using algorithms, so an individual does not have a manager to discuss things with. There is often little opportunity for professional development or access to training within such forms of employment. Some forms of gig work may expose individuals to danger where, because of their employment status, they are not protected by health and safety legislation. There have also been stories of where gig workers are unwittingly used to carry out illegal activities, such as drug deliveries.[64]

Similar arguments also apply to offshoring, the practice of transferring work to countries where labour costs are lower. It is often the case that labour regulations in such countries are weaker than in European or North American countries, making it possible to deny responsibility for socially unsustainable practices. This also applies to environmental sustainability, so for example, the United Kingdom government can claim to have reduced greenhouse gas emissions when this has been achieved in part by an increasing reliance on technology imported from countries where labour regulations allow lower wages and conditions of employment that would be unacceptable domestically.[65]

The COVID-19 pandemic drew considerable attention to possibilities for more flexible working practices. For many people, it made it possible to "work from home" connecting to office IT systems remotely. This has various potential implications for internal social and also environmental sustainability. It reduces the amount of time spent commuting and means that families can spend more time together. Less commuting by private car reduces greenhouse gas emissions and leads to improved air quality. There are also arguments for shorter working weeks, such as, for example, by introducing three-day weekends. Again, there are arguments for and against in terms of sustainability: it could enable families to spend more time together, and for individuals to develop personal pursuits which provide personal satisfaction, but within a consumption-driven economic culture, it could simply release more time for pursuing environmentally unsustainable activities. It could also discriminate against socially and economically disadvantaged groups, who could not afford to work fewer hours or who do not have the capability to embrace new opportunities, and hence it may have a negative effect on wider social sustainability.[66]

However, working from home may have a negative effect on the second theme of social sustainability, social cohesion within a workplace. Not physically meeting colleagues may have a negative effect on the social capital within an organisation, reducing the amount of informal learning which might otherwise happen. Remote working makes it harder for a workforce to meet to discuss human resource issues if these arise. Working from home also transfers work from a legally regulated office space to a home environment, making it possible that working conditions will be poorer. For example, in early 2021 there were media reports about junior banking staff coming under pressure to work extremely long hours that may not have been possible had they been working in an office.[67] The need to protect confidential data also led to reports about employers installing technology which could monitor people's behaviour in their own private residences.[68]

Social capital is related to the sense of identification that employees feel about the organisation and its identity, in this context as regards its sustainability ethos. The potential tensions between organisational and personal social identity and implications for learning are discussed in more detail in Chapter 6.

Participation is another factor contributing to social cohesion within an organisation. How do employees think they participate in decision-making within the organisation, and what sense of autonomy do they feel? In Chapter 2, we looked at the workplace as a complex adaptive system, where the legitimate system pushing conformity and compliance is in tension with the shadow system, representing local attempts to respond to operational variety. Autonomy allows people to do this effectively, but this needs to be balanced against the need for organisational coherence, to operate at the point of the edge of chaos. This can all be helped by opportunities for informal learning, for work teams to be able to manage their own activities and set their own goals as appropriate.

The third theme is social equity. The aspect of this which has probably been most carefully investigated is about how organisational practices discriminate between men and women. Such research has only really become significant since the 1990s and is still struggling to become fully integrated into mainstream organisational theorising. In a similar way to how theories of the firm have historically failed to consider the relationship of organisations with the natural environment, they have also failed to acknowledge differences between the behaviours and values of men and women, and have, according to feminist thinking, assumed a dominant, male perspective. Early important writers on organisational theory such as Max Weber and Frederick Taylor (obviously men) lived at a time when society was highly gendered and it may not have even occurred to them that women could occupy senior positions in organisations. It was not until 1979 that a significant management text considering gender issues appeared, with Rosabeth Moss Kanter's *Men and Women of the Corporation*.[69]

One of the earliest analyses of how organisations are structured was Max Weber's early 20th-century examination of bureaucracies. Weber described how bureaucracies are based around roles which are discharged according to "calculable rules" without regard to the characteristics of the role-holders.[70] Many, if not most, contemporary large organisations still work on the same basis, in that they function through having particular roles with specific responsibilities that can, in principle, be filled by anyone. The priority for an organisation is therefore to fill the role with whoever can fulfil those responsibilities most effectively. In an influential paper in 1990, Joan Acker[71] drew attention to the ongoing importance of hierarchical, bureaucratic thinking in organisational design, observing that this favoured members of society who had minimal external responsibilities, essentially men. Bureaucratic structures also make it easier to justify pay differentials by claiming that they are based on the requirements of a role, even though that role may not effectively be open to all members of society.[72] This structural inequity also extends to organisational infrastructure: for example, Caroline Criado Perez describes the often inadequate provision of female toilets in office buildings, and how "progressive" organisations may provide gyms and other recreational facilities for employees but rarely offer on-site childcare services.[73]

Institutional isomorphism may also play a role. In a male-dominated institutional landscape, each individual organisation will feel subtle pressure to also be represented by men rather than women.[74] Normative isomorphism encourages a conformist way of behaving and thinking: the difficulty that women have in progressing to more senior levels within an organisation may be related to older, more confident women challenging male-oriented dominant ways of thinking.[75]

The bureaucratic system could therefore be regarded as "gendered", discriminating against women who would have to break their commitment to the organisation for child-rearing, and who could well be expected by prevailing societal norms to take on other caring responsibilities.

Weber's analysis of organisational structure emerged at the same time as mass production was starting to become significant, and this was heavily influenced by the scientific management ideas of people like Frederick Taylor, who proposed a number of key principles; these included that a manager had responsibility for planning and thinking about work organisation, work design should be based on scientific principles and be defined precisely and that workers should be monitored to make sure that these procedures are followed.[76] Classical management theory developed from these perspectives, emphasising unity of command, a clear single line of authority, appropriate levels of specialisation, respect for authority and the pre-eminence of line (rather than support) functions.[77]

However, a significant body of research has developed suggesting that men and women do not equally prioritise hierarchical thinking in this way. Although her work has proved controversial, Carol Gilligan's assertion[78] that respecting hierarchies and following rules is based on a male sense of morality while women prioritise decision-making based on relationship maintenance has been shown to have a strong empirical justification.[79] Studies into how the structure of new organisations differs between those created by men or women do show that women-driven organisations do tend to adopt a more web-like than hierarchical structure, and that role responsibilities take greater account of individuals and their particular situation.[80] Some researchers have also shown a positive relationship between the number of women on boards of directors and engagement with CSR,[81] and that a significant majority of organisations achieving B Corp status (see Section 4.7) are owned by women.[82]

Richard Scott describes the redefinition of boundaries whereby external values come to challenge the role-focused nature of a bureaucratic structure as "de-bureaucratisation".[83] Figure 4.12 is a way of illustrating this, with values represented by a more female way of thinking penetrating the organisational system.

This gendering of organisational structure and systems is a subtle way in which male hegemony in organisational life is maintained, but it is also important to reflect on how such hidden assumptions also may discriminate against other groups, for example on the basis of age, race, social class, disability or sexuality.[84]

The aim of this section has been to look briefly at some of the different ways in which organisational practices may have an impact on social sustainability. One important point to remember is that however these issues are addressed, two perspectives on what is done are important. It is not only the responsibility of the organisation to take whatever actions are necessary to try and deliver internal social sustainability, but employees themselves must confirm that these actions have been successful. It is, in fact, one of the criticisms of how organisational sustainability strategies are evaluated that employees' perspectives are often not considered.[85]

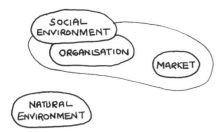

Figure 4.12 The de-bureaucratisation of the organisation.

What the section also perhaps highlights is that external strategies showing social responsibility may be valuable for public relations purposes and be relatively painless, but to deliver internal social responsibility may be much more complex and difficult to achieve, potentially presenting as it does existential questions about how the organisation functions. However, taking internal social sustainability seriously does represent a willingness to "walk the talk", and be authentic about such responsibilities.

Time for reflection

What are your reactions to this discussion about social sustainability?

Dealing with internal social sustainability potentially presents a major issue for organisations who wish to operate, and be seen as operating, sustainably.

How do you think your organisation could be seen from this critical perspective?

What might you like to change?

4.6 Levels of organisational sustainability

The degree to which organisations approach sustainability varies from not recognising it as an issue to consider through to seeing social and/or environmental sustainability as their purpose, achieved through a particular competence. In this section, we will try to make some sense of this situation in a way which contributes towards thinking about sustainability-focused learning.

4.6.1 Levels of learning

In this section, we will draw upon organisational learning ideas to think about how organisations adapt differently to their sustainability landscape. The systems thinking thread which runs through this book draws us to the work of Chris Argyris and Donald Schön. Together and individually they developed a number of ideas which have proven to be extremely influential in helping us to understand how organisations change (or not). The first aspect of their work which we will look at is about how organisational behaviour is shaped by "theories of action".[86] At an individual level, this is a frame of understanding that a person holds about what they need to do in order to achieve a specific outcome. There are two forms of this theory of action. Firstly, there is an "espoused theory", which is the theory of action which people claim they follow: for example, someone might say, "I think it is very important that we do what we can to minimise carbon dioxide emissions". Secondly, there is the "theory-in-use", which is what people actually do: for example, the same person might also say, "I drive to work because it is more convenient than catching public transport". People not recognising that there is a difference between what they think and what they do is a common cause of difficulties when they need to adapt to new situations.

In an organisational setting, the organisation's theory-in-use is created as individual theories-in-use are integrated into public maps (for example, standard operating procedures and organisational charts) and become established as what the organisation does. The same distinction between espoused theory and theory-in-use also applies at organisational level. For example, during one consultancy assignment, I was asked to travel from the United Kingdom to Geneva. The organisation I was working for had a policy on sustainability which encouraged employees to minimise energy consumption. However, when I asked for permission to travel by train from the United Kingdom to Geneva, I was told that this was against travel policy, and that I needed to fly. The espoused theory of reducing carbon dioxide emissions had not yet forced a change on the theory-in-use of business travel.

What happens when an individual comes across a situation where their theory-in-use does not seem to work? Consider Figure 4.13. The individual takes action based on an existing set of assumptions and checks the consequences. If the check passes and the theory-in-use is confirmed, no problem. However, if this check fails they may recognise that they need to do something different in order for things to work. For example, when I asked the administrator in the organisation I was visiting about travelling by train, they thought about it and then said that I could do that but only claim for the cost of the airfare. Argyris and Schön call this single loop learning: a new strategy has been developed but the underlying norms and assumptions remain unchanged.

Now think about what we see in Figure 4.14. Suppose instead that the administrator had gone back to the organisation's public map about business travel, and had said that existing procedures needed to be changed, that the norms and assumptions that they embodied were no longer relevant in the contemporary business world. They would rewrite the business travel procedures so that train travel would become a new norm. This would be double loop learning.

The distinction between single and double loop learning in this example is relatively clear, but Argyris and Schön point out that in the messy world of reality there is not necessarily a clear distinction between the two, rather a spectrum of possibilities. In Chapter 7, we look closely at the ideas of critical and transformative learning and will see strong parallels between these and double loop learning.

Because single loop learning is adequate for most everyday experiences, individuals are socialised (as Berger and Luckmann pointed out) to not question norms and assumptions but just amend strategies if a change is needed.[87] Argyris called the tendency to avoid questioning assumptions and stick to single loop learning as Model I behaviour,

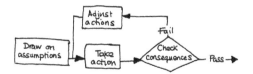

Figure 4.13 Single loop learning.

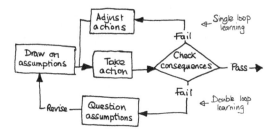

Figure 4.14 Single and double loop learning.

and when seen at organisational level he described it as Organisation I (or O-I) behaviour. On the other hand, when individuals or organisations *are* prepared to discuss assumptions, consider different perspectives, base action on complete and valid information and share power and move to double loop learning, this could be seen as Model II (or O-II at the organisational level) behaviour. He saw that the problem of keeping to O-I behaviour led to negative dynamics within group work settings, with defensive behaviours predominating. However, O-II behaviour:

> ...should decrease dysfunctional group dynamics because the competitive win/lose, low-trust, low-risk-taking processes are replaced by cooperative, enquiry-oriented, high-trust and high-risk-taking dynamics. Finally, dysfunctional norms and games of deception should decrease, as well as the need for camouflage, camouflage of the camouflage, and the defensive activities described [previously].[88]

If an organisation can continue to function effectively by simply adjusting assumptions and strategies, then single loop learning is adequate. However, in the complex, dynamic and turbulent environments associated with sustainability, it may not be adequate and a shift to double loop learning is essential. Effective organisational learning therefore depends on individuals being able to recognise the tensions between the situation they are facing and how best to respond, incorporating both single and double loop learning as appropriate. Shifting from single to double loop learning may not be easy, as it places great demands on resources of time, human capital and emotional energy.

The importance of being able to engage in double loop learning when following a sustainability strategy should be clear. One of the recurring challenges identified in this book so far has been that acceptance of sustainability is driven by personal values, and only through the process of double loop learning can these be questioned and, as necessary, be influenced.

4.6.2 Levels of learning and organisational sustainability

Referring to this idea of single and double loop learning, we can look at different levels of commitment to sustainability as being the result of different levels of reflection on assumptions about sustainability and organisational practice. For example, what is the underlying assumption about the primacy of profitability? What assumptions are made about the organisation's impact on the environment? What assumptions are made about employment practices? Are economic and social sustainability seen only as internal (or external) issues only? And so on.

Progress towards strengthening organisational sustainability means that an ever-increasing number of underlying assumptions and associated beliefs and values need to be examined. Organisations are therefore going to exist on a spectrum of possibilities, but to make the situation more manageable when it comes to planning a sustainability-focused learning strategy we will simplify things with a model.

Figure 4.15 is an attempt to create a simple three-level model of organisational sustainability practice which can help us to work towards a learning and development strategy. It refers to the single and double loop learning concept and also draws on a distinction between exploitation and exploration.[89] Exploitation describes a strategy where an organisation sticks with what it already knows, and simply refines processes and procedures in order to comply with external pressures. On the other hand, with an exploration strategy, an organisation looks for new ways of doing things, experimenting and innovating. Exploitation uses single loop learning and is a safe strategy, at least

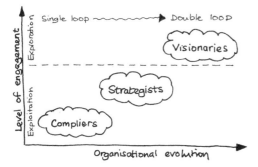

Figure 4.15 Levels of engagement in organisational sustainability.

in the short term. It incurs minimal organisational risk, but may trap the organisation in sub-optimal behaviour and reduce its ability to innovate and adapt as the landscape continues to change. Exploration strategies require double loop learning, questioning assumptions, and therefore have the greatest potential to contribute to social and environmental sustainability, but are not without risk.

What are the three levels? At the lowest level of engagement with sustainability, organisations may be described as compliers. Assumptions are not questioned, and the focus is on keeping the business going and adopting the minimum number of sustainability-related strategies needed to satisfy stakeholders, regulatory requirements and pressures to conform from the institutional landscape. This is probably the most likely initial strategy for large commercial corporations, not necessarily because senior managers do not want to adopt more sustainability strategies, but because the isomorphist pressures of their particular institutional landscapes tend to be greater, and juggernaut-like as they are, major change is much more difficult.[90]

At higher levels of engagement with the idea of sustainability, the organisation may embrace sustainability as a business strategy. More double loop learning happens, as people in the organisation start to question assumptions underpinning the organisation's existence. Organisations still want to keep their existing business going and underlying assumptions about profit maximisation may remain, but they see operating sustainably as demonstrating values that they wish to follow and being a basis for developing a competitive advantage in their particular sector. Box 4.6 shows how this works for ISG in the construction sector.

Box 4.6

Our policies ensure clients realise that ISG is really thinking about sustainability. It's very powerful, especially when it comes to getting new business. Clients are asking more and more about Social Value and Sustainability, and they want to work for businesses who are considering all these elements. ISG has a number of core values, one being "Always Care" which really embeds our thinking around this agenda. As a construction company, we hope we can lead the way for others to follow suit.

Fozia Parveen, ISG Ltd

Michael Porter suggested that organisations can follow three different strategies to develop and maintain a competitive advantage[91]: to be the least cost, to differentiate themselves from competitors, or to find a niche within which to operate. These could be manifested by:

- developing environmentally friendly products and services, utilising circular economy principles, minimising resource usage and waste emission (least cost)
- promoting social and environmental aspects of products and services, such as through certification schemes such as Fairtrade or FSC (Forest Stewardship Council), or through emphasising environmentally friendly packaging (differentiation)
- identifying small sectors of the economy where there is a steady market amongst knowledgeable customers for sustainability-produced products or services—for example, bakers and sandwich chains offering vegan fillings in takeaway products (niche strategy).

With this level of engagement change towards sustainable practice is slow and incremental and is characterised by a continuous improvement mentality. Such strategies have been criticised as necessary but not sufficient to be truly effective, and that in reality they "… represent anti-sustainability and act merely to slow down the eventual death and destruction of resources and habitats".[92]

Visionary organisations are fully engaged with the idea of sustainability and use double loop learning extensively to question assumptions and think about how to transform what they do. These are organisations where promoting social or environmental sustainability (or both) is why they do what they do, and for whom profit generation is to some extent about ensuring that they remain viable for this purpose rather than as an end in itself. Existing organisations may work through each of the levels, while new organisations may clearly position themselves at this level.

One area of interest for such organisations is in what has become called the "base of the pyramid",[93] the poorest in the world and the poorest in individual societies. This is also the province of the social enterprise, organisations which have been brought into being in order to further some social or environmental aim, while at the same time seeking to make sure that they can cover their operational costs.

Visionary strategies represent a very different approach. There is now an emphasis on eco-effectiveness and cradle-to-cradle processes rather than the cradle-to-grave perspective of eco-efficiency. From a social sustainability perspective, the emphasis on domination and control is replaced by harmony with nature and participative approaches to decision-making—in Carol Gilligan's terms, replacing a male morality by one which is more female in origin.[94] Rather than an emphasis on competition with other organisations in the same institutional landscape, collaboration is encouraged as a way of normalising sustainability-related behaviours.

Frederic Laloux's concept of the "teal organisation" may be seen as visionary in terms of internal social sustainability.[95] It provides a radical counterpoint to the Weberian bureaucracy: for example, organisations operate through self-organising teams with no formal authority structure; training focuses on organisational culture and the relationship between individual and organisational purpose; people rotate through the organisation so that they have a clear understanding about how all aspects work; performance appraisals are conducted with peers; there is complete transparency of information across the organisation; values are regularly discussed; and there is an emphasis on the organisation as a community. The emphasis in the teal organisation is very much on social sustainability, and although Laloux does not address environmental sustainability in great detail, he does point out the importance of organisational practice addressing the environmental concerns of its employees. He says that employees need to ask themselves the question, "What is the right thing to do?" and from that question decide what is feasible.

To summarise, complier organisations practice social and environmental sustainability because it is a regulatory requirement, strategist organisations see sustainability as a way of maintaining or improving viability, and visionary organisations are those who see viability as a way of improving social and environmental sustainability. Of course, this is a highly reductive and simplistic model, but as the statistician George Box once famously stated, "All models are wrong but some are useful".[96] In reality, organisations may be found along a continuous spectrum of the three levels, and even within the same organisation there may be variations. However, I hope that this particular model may provide a useful starting point in developing a learning strategy.

Time for reflection

Where do you think your organisation is within this model?

What characteristics can you identify in order to make this assessment?

In what direction is it moving?

4.6.3 Evolution towards sustainability

Figure 4.15 does not necessarily imply an inevitable progression through increasing levels of engagement to sustainability, although organisational Darwinism might suggest that this is to some degree inevitable. What might be the challenges along the way?

The internal dynamics involved in such a process of change may well be complex and politically challenging. For example, even in the face of strong institutional pressures to operate more sustainably, internal factions may resist change. Organisational size may also be problematic: larger organisations may be interested in principle in sustainability and be able to invest more into relevant research and development, but find it more difficult to make large-scale changes due to the infrastructural changes and numbers of people involved.[97]

In addition to these strategic concerns are fundamental issues about employee engagement with sustainability, and this drives to the heart of this book and what it seeks to achieve. Although the decision to adopt a sustainability strategy will probably (although not necessarily) be driven by senior management, its success will very much depend on how it engages with the diversity of opinions within the organisation and how individuals participate in the change process. For example, a sustainability strategy which is driven by senior management without employee engagement may be viewed rather sceptically.

Perhaps inevitably, evolution through levels of engagement will create all manner of tensions within an organisation—it will present challenges to existing cultures of power, how decisions are made, what the organisation's identity is, and so on. While potentially difficult, the dialectics that these create open up great possibilities for learning, particularly the double loop learning described earlier.

The Framework for Strategic Sustainable Development (FSSD)[98] looks at how to navigate this change process from a complex adaptive system perspective. Recognising the inherent unpredictability of a self-organising system, the FSSD relies on backcasting where the organisation defines its own vision of sustainability and then through a series of constantly monitored small steps seek to make progress in moving towards this vision.

Complexity implies certain structural characteristics. First, there must be a diversity of opinion and experience within the organisation, so that different ideas can be explored as the system adapts. Second, participants within the system must be able to recognise how things are changing and adapt appropriately so that progress towards the sustainability vision is maintained: in other words, the actors in the system must learn so that the system as a whole can learn. Thirdly, there must be trust within the system: without trust, a negative, destructive pattern can develop within the system. One of the qualities of a complex adaptive system (as described in Chapter 2, Section 2.10) is that its individual elements only have limited knowledge and only interact with elements in their vicinity. In a social system, this means that people must feel confident that everyone within the entire system is committed and can be relied upon. Finally, there must be a shared understanding about what the organisation is seeking to achieve, or in terms that have been used elsewhere, what the *purpose* of the organisation is. Both trust and shared understanding are elements in the concept of social capital, also discussed elsewhere in this book.

4.6.4 Implications for managing

How can we pull together this multitude of ideas into something that might be able to contribute to a learning and development strategy? Drawing on ideas presented in this chapter,[99] Table 4.2 tries to provide a useful comparison of the differences in implied managerial style between the three levels.

Table 4.2 Implications for management across different strategies for sustainability

Aspect of management	Complier	Strategist	Visionary
Goals	Growth and profit maximisation Compliance with regulation	Identification of competitive advantage through sustainability Profit-focused but attention to social and environmental performance Taking account of SDGs	Strong contribution to social and environmental sustainability Quality of life of all stakeholders considered
Values	Anthropocentric, male-dominated Competitive	Meritocratic, but structural discrimination remains Recognition of validity of alternative values	Ecocentric, integrating feminist values Unity of social and environmental issues Altruistic Collaborative
Products	Focus on function, style and price	Design incorporates minimal resource usage, waste and pollution Product life-cycle stewardship	Minimal life-cycle costs, environmentally friendly Focus on satisfying needs rather than wants

Production	Energy and resource intensive	Eco-efficient, socio-efficient	Low energy, minimal emissions Eco-effective, socio-effective
Organisation	Hierarchical, top-down, centralised	Flatter but still hierarchical	Non-hierarchical, networked, participative decision-making
Environment	Domination over nature	Struggling to balance domination with harmony	Harmony with nature
Vision of the future	Short-term	Balancing short-term viability with longer-term issues	Regenerative, restorative

Of course, in a crude, reductionist three stage model, it is impossible to capture the subtlety as factors change from one level to another; however, this simple categorisation may help to provide some food for thought about what the managerial implications will be of embracing organisational sustainability.

4.7 Assessing progress towards organisational sustainability

Douglas Adams' *The Hitchhiker's Guide to the Galaxy* was almost required reading for geeky types of my generation. In one of its more famous passages, the computer Deep Thought spends many years thinking about the answer to the "Great Question" about life, the universe and everything, and works out that it is "42".[100] There are similarities with assessing progress towards sustainability, as being able to describe progress towards sustainability with a 42-like answer is equally unlikely.

First, a fundamental problem is that both sustainability and organisational sustainability are contested concepts, meaning that there are many different ideas about what constitutes value for each. Organisational sustainability can be viewed from the three different dimensions of environmental, social and economic sustainability, but while there are obvious connections between the dimensions, there are no models which draw together and capture the complexity of their interrelationships. This is further complicated by the various possible perspectives: does an organisation self-assess, is an external body involved, or should the organisation's external stakeholders express an opinion? This is a classic example of the challenge of making boundary judgements.

Second, how can we predict what happens in the future? The core idea of sustainability is about protecting future generations, but how can we be sure that anything we do today will be the right thing to do? At best, we can move forward with a reasonable degree of confidence, particularly where there are quantifiable measures we can use, for example, the level of carbon dioxide in the atmosphere or another planetary boundary. However, in terms of social sustainability, what is the best way to organise how societies work?

The third problem is one common to all attempts to assess organisational effectiveness: what do we examine? There are three possible ways of making judgements about how well an organisation is performing: we can consider either what the organisation is doing (activities), what it achieves (outcomes), or how it goes about what it is doing (structure).[101] Each has limitations. If we assess activities, how can we be confident that these are the right activities to protect future generations? Reporting on activities completed does not necessarily say anything about activities planned. Outcome reporting is complicated by the tension between quantitative and qualitative data, particularly where outcomes are not easily amenable to representation as a "42". Reporting that the organisation has a Chief Sustainability Officer and has defined standard operating procedures and codes of practice does not say anything about how effective these structural features are.

A further issue to consider is where sustainability strategies become absorbed by a target-driven culture so that sustainability is measured by achieving goals. This is a particular problem if goals are to some extent arbitrary so that when they are achieved the organisation can claim to be sustainable. However, a common theme in the literature about measuring organisational sustainability is that it should be seen as a process, not an endpoint, be driven by a vision, and be open to the constant development of new understandings and new interpretations, in which case a target-driven approach is inappropriate.

Despite, or perhaps because of, these challenges, the assessment of organisational sustainability is a rich field of research. Probably the best-known idea is the "triple bottom line" (TBL or 3BL), attributed to John Elkington.[102] However, perhaps because of its ubiquity, there is a considerable amount of ambiguity over what it means. The term is sometimes used in a conceptual way, referring in general terms to the need for organisations to take into account each of the three dimensions of sustainability. In Elkington's more focused concept, it is used to describe the actual "bottom line", the realities of an organisation's activities, and relies on an idea that it is possible to represent social and environmental sustainability achievements in the same objective, quantifiable manner as can the organisation's economic sustainability (its viability). In this sense, it appeals to the same managerial logic that embraced Kaplan and Norton's "balanced scorecard"[103] in the early 1990s.

It is in the detail of how this is done that the problems appear. The economic dimension appears easiest as money is quantifiable, but we then come back to the question of whether we consider internal or external organisational economic sustainability: is it simply adequate profit (financial viability), or should it embrace the wider economic implications of what the organisation does (as in the earlier discussions about pharmaceutical companies)? Environmental accounting is more problematic although there are well-developed ways of calculating environmental impacts. For example, there are obvious costs, for monitoring emissions, for operating licences and permits, for insurance for using hazardous substances, paying fines, and so on. Techniques such as life-cycle analysis and environmental impact assessments also provide ways of estimating the financial costs of organisational activities, so that the often-ignored externalities of neo-classical economics are taken into account.

Probably the biggest difficulties come with quantifying social sustainability. There are techniques available for assessing social impacts of what an organisation does, but it can be difficult to gather reliable data from these because of factors such as the time that it can take for social impacts to unfold and the problems of identifying clear cause and effect chains and quantifying "impact" because of a lack of baseline data. Measuring internal social sustainability is also highly problematic. Earlier we considered these in terms of meeting basic needs, social cohesion and social equity, but how do these manifest themselves in a quantifiable way? The concept of social capital suggests itself as one possibility, but how is this measured? Recent developments in the technique of social network analysis may offer some ways of generating quantitative information about social factors such as creativity, trust, social bonding within work groups and bridging across groups,[104] but the development of these techniques is still in its infancy.

As has been mentioned several times before, there are no models which link the interrelationships between the three dimensions of sustainability, so a simple presentation of three figures runs a significant risk of being meaningless as a way of representing an organisation's actual engagement with sustainability. So even if reliable, quantitative information can be presented for each bottom line, what does it mean in totality? If economic sustainability is x, environmental sustainability is y, and social sustainability is z, then what is the relationship:

$$f(x,y,z) = 42?$$

In reality, a profit-seeking organisation must always prioritise its own economic sustainability in order to ensure viability: the need for such organisations to prioritise profit is something about which both Karl Marx and Milton Friedman would agree.[105]

The ambiguities and uncertainties of incorporating social and environmental sustainability in this equation mean that TBL reporting can always leave organisations open to accusations of greenwashing, particularly when it is self-reported. Also, as organisational reporting is historic, it says nothing about the present or future, so that we can look at a company's 2019 sustainability report but know nothing about what happened in 2020. John Elkington himself reflected in 2018 that while widely accepted, the TBL had so far failed to produce a systemic change in the way organisations operate and deal with sustainability, and that profit was still the most important element. Perhaps its success as a way of merely *suggesting* organisational sustainability has made it harder for more rigorous, reliable methodologies to be developed?

Nevertheless, as a metaphor for an integrative assessment of an organisation's progress towards sustainable practice, the TBL idea has been influential. We can consider two different applications of the principle, the Global Reporting Initiative (GRI) and the B Corp movement.

The GRI[106] was launched in 2000 as a set of standards covering economic, social and environmental concerns. They were developed by a collaborative effort involving business, government, labour associations and academia, and are presented as a public good, free to download and regularly updated. Organisations review the standards and their performance against them and then write a report following a standard approach. The 2020 standards[107] contain 34 measures which include economic performance, market presence, indirect economic impacts and procurement practices (economic sustainability); material and energy usage, water and effluents, biodiversity consequences (environmental sustainability); employment practice, labour relations, health and safety, training and education, diversity and equal opportunities (social sustainability).

The comprehensive nature of the standards has been criticised as a potential weakness, in that the standards do not clearly distinguish between assessments of structure or outcomes, nor do they help organisations to understand the interrelationships between different indicators.[108] It is also suggested that the standards emphasise the activity of working towards sustainability rather than looking at what is actually achieved.[109]

The other significant TBL-inspired sustainability initiative is the B Corp movement.[110] The idea originated from legislation in some US states which created the "Benefit Corporation", a legal status which eased the legal requirement on a private company to maximise shareholder value. The status of "Community Interest Company" (CIC)[111] in the United Kingdom is somewhat similar. Being a B Corp does not mean having a different legal status but is rather a form of branding, as a way of showing that the organisation upholds certain sustainability-related values. To become a B Corp an organisation completes an assessment of their social and environmental impact, this is reviewed by assessors in B Lab, and if the organisation meets a minimum score, they can describe themselves as a B Corp. The assessment looks at organisational governance, its mission, ethics and transparency; the impact the organisation has on its workers through remuneration, benefits and opportunities for development; the impact the organisation has on communities in which it has a part; its impact on the natural environment; and whether the products or services the organisation offers provide a benefit to customers or contribute to social or environmental concerns.[112]

A major challenge for the B Corp movement seems to be scalability. Research suggests that the great majority of B Corps are small organisations,[113] but the comparative novelty of the standard makes it hard to identify whether this is a structural issue or due to the comparatively slow speed at which large organisations can move in embracing sustainability. The experience of multinational food manufacturer Danone, which had several subsidiaries accredited as a B Corp and was pursuing a policy of social and environmental responsibility, but then had to release their CEO due to investor pressure[114] suggests that structural issues may be significant.

These are just some of the ways in which organisational sustainability may be assessed. It is important to remember the SDG targets (Tables 1.1, 1.2 and 1.3 in Chapter 1), which although high level can contribute to an organisational vision of what its own sustainable practice should be. There are many other more focused assessment schemes, often serving particular purposes. For example, there is the MSCI ACWI Sustainable Impact Index[115] rating system used by ethical investors, and the stock market focused Dow Jones Sustainability Index and the FTSE4GOOD Index. The United Nations Global Compact[116] provides a register of organisations committed to follow 10 principles relating to human rights, labour practices and environmental sustainability. There is also the idea of the "ecological footprint", which seeks to relate organisational practice to the Earth's carrying capacity. ISO 14000 provides a set of standards against which organisations can assess their environmental sustainability performance.

In summary, providing measures about achievements in sustainability has attracted much interest, even though the methods used to provide meaningful measures still need much development. Nevertheless, there is enough consistency between the various ideas that have been developed for us to be able to draw some conclusions about what may be useful in sustainability-focused learning activities. This will be developed further in Chapter 5.

Time for reflection

How does your organisation assess its performance towards social and environmental sustainability?

Do you use TBL reporting? If so, how do you balance economic, social and environmental sustainability measures?

What are the strengths and weaknesses in your assessment regime?

How does the assessment process contribute to learning and development strategies?

4.8 Key points in this chapter

Figure 4.16 summarises the key points from this chapter.

Organisations may be viewed as open systems which need to work carefully with their social and natural environments in order to maintain low levels of entropy in order to remain viable.

Organisational sustainability as a concept has developed since early ideas about corporate philanthropy, and embraces ideas such as CSR and CSV. A range of theories about how organisations operate may be used to understand why organisations are increasingly interested in operating sustainably, and these include being attractive to investors, ethical and regulatory pressures changes in the institutional landscape due to more economic incentives, and pressures from employees and customers.

For organisational economic and social sustainability, there are both internal and external considerations, whereas for environmental sustainability, considerations are external (Table 4.3).

The SDGs provide high-level suggestions about what organisations may need to focus on to strengthen sustainable practice.

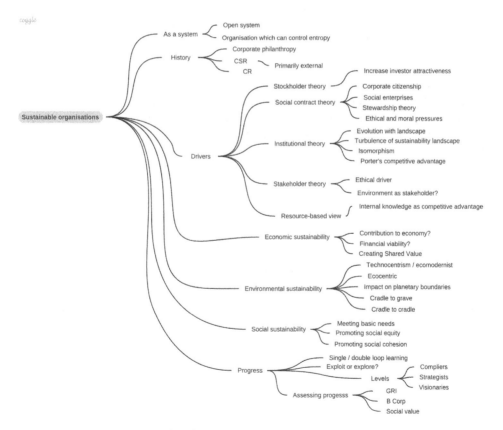

Figure 4.16 Key points in this chapter.

Table 4.3 Internal and external considerations of the sustainability dimensions

	Economic sustainability	Social sustainability	Environmental sustainability
Internal considerations	Financial viability	Internal organisational practices	
External considerations	Impact on the wider economy	Impact on society	Impact on the natural environment

For an organisation, economic sustainability may be seen as ensuring that it remains financially viable, but may also mean considering the impact that the organisation's activities have on the wider economy within which it works.

Anthropocentric perspectives on environmental sustainability suggest that new opportunities for organisations may arise from the need to develop technologies to prevent or reverse the effects of environmental degradation. Ecocentric perspectives emphasise the need to respect environmental integrity, practice product stewardship and use raw materials efficiently. Organisations should pay close attention to the planetary boundaries concept and reflect on the degree to which they are contributing to breaches in these.

Social sustainability addresses the need to ensure basic needs are met and that the organisation's activities contribute to social equity and social cohesion. Organisations need to address social sustainability both externally and internally. Working towards internal social sustainability means reflecting on such things as working practices and sources of structural inequity which may discriminate against particular groups of people.

A transition towards more sustainable practice requires moving from single loop to double loop learning, where assumptions are questioned and new norms and values adopted. Depending on the degree of double loop learning that an organisation embraces, its progress towards sustainability may be seen as compliers, strategists or visionaries.

There are a variety of ways in which progress towards sustainability may be assessed, but all are complex and have limitations.

Notes

1 W. Richard Scott, *Organizations: Rational, Natural, and Open Systems*, 3rd ed. (Englewood Cliffs, NJ: Prentice-Hall, 1992), 23.
2 Scott, *Organizations: Rational, Natural, and Open Systems*.
3 Daniel Katz and Robert L Kahn, *The Social Psychology of Organizations* (New York: John Wiley & Sons, 1966).
4 Archie B. Carroll, 'Corporate Social Responsibility: Evolution of a Definitional Construct', *Business & Society* 38, no. 3 (1999): 289.
5 Manfred Max Bergman, Zinette Bergman, and Lena Berger, 'An Empirical Exploration, Typology, and Definition of Corporate Sustainability', *Sustainability* 9, no. 5 (2017): 10.
6 John Peloza and Jingzhi Shang, *'Sustainability and Customer Value', Sustainability Matters: Why and How Corporate Boards Should Become Involved* (New York: The Conference Board, 2011).
7 Ruth V. Aguilera et al., 'Putting the S Back in Corporate Social Responsibility: A Multilevel Theory of Social Change in Organizations', *Academy of Management Review* 32, no. 3 (2007): 836–63.

8 For example, see Marc Orlitzky, Frank L. Schmidt, and Sara L. Rynes, 'Corporate Social and Financial Performance: A Meta-Analysis', *Organization Studies* 24, no. 3 (2003): 403–41.
9 Orlitzky, Schmidt, and Rynes, 424.
10 Peter Lund-Thomsen, 'Corporate Social Responsibility: Towards a New Dialogue?', in *Social Learning towards a Sustainable World: Principles, Perspectives, and Praxis*, ed. Arjen E.J. Wals (The Netherlands: Wageningen Academic Publishers, 2007), 297–312.
11 John Hasnas, 'The Normative Theories of Business Ethics: A Guide for the Perplexed', *Business Ethics Quarterly* 19, no. 8 (1998): 10.
12 Stefan Ambec and Paul Lanoie, 'The Strategic Importance of Environmental Sustainability', in *Managing Human Resources for Environmental Sustainability*, ed. S.E. Jackson et al. (Chichester: John Wiley & Sons Ltd, 2012), 27.
13 Wendy Liu, 'Coronavirus Has Made Amazon a Public Utility—so We Should Treat It like One', *The Guardian*, 2020, sec. Opinion, https://www.theguardian.com/commentisfree/2020/apr/17/amazon-coronavirus-public-utility-workers.
14 John L. Campbell, 'Why Would Corporations Behave in Socially Responsible Ways? An Institutional Theory of Corporate Social Responsibility', *Academy of Management Review* 32, no. 3 (2007): 946–67.
15 Sean Hollister, 'Nearly a Dozen Google Employees Have Reportedly Quit in Protest', *CNET*, 2018, https://www.cnet.com/news/google-project-maven-drone-protect-resign/.
16 P. Deveraux Jennings and Paul A. Zandbergen, 'Ecologically Sustainable Organizations: An Institutional Approach', *Academy of Management Review* 20, no. 4 (1995): 1015–52.
17 Douglass C. North, 'Economic Performance through Time', *The American Economic Review* 84, no. 3 (1994): 360.
18 North, 361.
19 Jean Garner Stead and W. Edward Stead, 'The Coevolution of Sustainable Strategic Management in the Global Marketplace', *Organization & Environment* 26, no. 2 (2013): 162–83.
20 Tim Newton, 'Organizations and the Natural Environment', in *The Oxford Handbook of Critical Management Studies*, ed. Mats Alvesson, T. Bridgman, and Hugh Willmott (Oxford University Press, 2011), 125–43.
21 Daniel Boffey, 'Court Orders Royal Dutch Shell to Cut Carbon Emissions by 45% by 2030', *The Guardian*, 26 May 2021, http://www.theguardian.com/business/2021/may/26/court-orders-royal-dutch-shell-to-cut-carbon-emissions-by-45-by-2030.
22 Paul J. DiMaggio and Walter W. Powell, 'The Iron Cage Revisited: Institutional Isomorphism and Collective Rationality in Organizational Fields', *American Sociological Review* 48, no. 2 (1983): 147–60.
23 Campbell, 'Why Would Corporations Behave in Socially Responsible Ways?'
24 Michael Porter and Claas Van der Linde, 'Green and Competitive: Ending the Stalemate', *Harvard Business Review* 73, no. 5 (1995): 120–33.
25 Ambec and Lanoie, 'The Strategic Importance of Environmental Sustainability'.
26 R. Edward Freeman, *Strategic Management: A Stakeholder Approach* (Boston, MA: Pitman Publishing, 1984).
27 Hasnas, 'The Normative Theories of Business Ethics'; Rodrigo Lozano, Angela Carpenter, and Donald Huisingh, 'A Review of "Theories of the Firm" and Their Contributions to Corporate Sustainability', *Journal of Cleaner Production* 106 (2015): 430–42.
28 Alexander Chernev and Sean Blair, 'Doing Well by Doing Good: The Benevolent Halo of Corporate Social Responsibility', *Journal of Consumer Research* 41, no. 6 (2015): 1412–25.
29 Corey Seemiller and Meghan Grace, *Generation Z: A Century in the Making* (London: Routledge, 2018).
30 Chitra B. Bhattacharya, Sankar Sen, and Daniel Korschun, 'Using Corporate Social Responsibility to Win the War for Talent', *MIT Sloan Management Review* 49, no. 2 (2008): 36–44; Stephen Brammer, Andrew Millington, and Bruce Rayton, 'The Contribution of Corporate Social Responsibility to Organizational Commitment', *The International Journal of Human Resource Management* 18, no. 10 (2007): 1701–19.
31 Stuart L. Hart, 'A Natural-Resource-Based View of the Firm', *Academy of Management Review* 20, no. 4 (1995): 986–1014.
32 Stuart L. Hart and Glen Dowell, 'Invited Editorial: A Natural-Resource-Based View of the Firm: Fifteen Years After', *Journal of Management* 37, no. 5 (2011): 1464–79.

33 Thomas Dyllick and Kai Hockerts, 'Beyond the Business Case for Corporate Sustainability', *Business Strategy and the Environment* 11, no. 2 (2002): 133.
34 V. Jennings, 'Addressing the Economic Bottom Line', in *The Triple Bottom Line: Does It All Add Up?*, ed. Adrian Henriques and Julie Richardson (London: Routledge, 2013).
35 SROI Network, 'A Guide to Social Return on Investment' (Liverpool: Social Value Network, 2012), https://socialvalueuk.org/wp-content/uploads/2016/03/The%20Guide%20to%20Social%20Return%20on%20Investment%202015.pdf.
36 Mark R. Kramer and Marc W. Pfitzer, 'The Ecosystem of Shared Value', *Harvard Business Review* 94, no. 10 (2016): 84.
37 Fernando G. Alberti and Federica Belfanti, 'Creating Shared Value and Clusters: The Case of an Italian Cluster Initiative in Food Waste Prevention', *Competitiveness Review: An International Business Journal* 29, no. 1 (2019): 41.
38 Michael Porter and M.R. Kramer, 'Creating Shared Value', *Harvard Business Review* 89, no. 1/2 (2011): 64.
39 Andrew Crane et al., 'Contesting the Value of the Shared Value Concept', *California Management Review* 56, no. 2 (2014): 133.
40 Crane et al., 132.
41 Regina Moczadlo, 'Creating Competitive Advantages—The European CSR-Strategy Compared with Porter's and Kramer's Shared Value Approach', *Ekonomski Vjesnik: Review of Contemporary Entrepreneurship, Business, and Economic Issues* 28, no. 1 (2015): 251.
42 Laura Corazza, Simone Domenico Scagnelli, and Chiara Mio, 'Simulacra and Sustainability Disclosure: Analysis of the Interpretative Models of Creating Shared Value', *Corporate Social Responsibility and Environmental Management* 24, no. 5 (2017): 416–17.
43 Gastón de los Reyes Jr, Markus Scholz, and N. Craig Smith, 'Beyond the "Win-Win" Creating Shared Value Requires Ethical Frameworks', *California Management Review* 59, no. 2 (2017): 142–67.
44 Crane et al., 'Contesting the Value of the Shared Value Concept'.
45 For example, see John Asafu-Adjaye et al., 'An Ecomodernist Manifesto', 2015, www.ecomodernism.org.
46 Elizabeth Kolbert, *Under a White Sky: The Nature of the Future* (London: The Bodley Head, 2021).
47 Alfred Wegener Institute for Polar and Marine Research, 'Iron Fertilization Of Oceans: A Real Option For Carbon Dioxide Reduction?', *ScienceDaily*, accessed 11 April 2021, https://www.sciencedaily.com/releases/2007/06/070608142214.htm.
48 Hart, 'A Natural-Resource-Based View of the Firm'; Paul Shrivastava, 'The Role of Corporations in Achieving Ecological Sustainability', *Academy of Management Review* 20, no. 4 (1995): 936–60.
49 Pratima Bansal, 'The Corporate Challenges of Sustainable Development', *Academy of Management Perspectives* 16, no. 2 (2002): 122–31; Pratima Bansal, 'Evolving Sustainably: A Longitudinal Study of Corporate Sustainable Development', *Strategic Management Journal* 26, no. 3 (2005): 197–218; Hart, 'A Natural-Resource-Based View of the Firm'; Hart and Dowell, 'Invited Editorial'.
50 Thomas N. Gladwin, Tara-Shelomith Krause, and James J. Kennelly, 'Beyond Eco-Efficiency: Towards Socially Sustainable Business', *Sustainable Development* 3, no. 1 (1995): 35.
51 William McDonough and Michael Braungart, *Cradle to Cradle: Remaking the Way We Make Things* (Albany, CA: North Point Press, 2010).
52 ILO, 'Promoting Decent Work in a Green Economy' (Geneva: International Labour Organization, 2010), 10.
53 ILO, 'Guidelines for a Just Transition towards Environmentally Sustainable Economies and Societies All' (Geneva: International Labour Organization, 2015), 4.
54 Gail Whiteman, Brian Walker, and Paolo Perego, 'Planetary Boundaries: Ecological Foundations for Corporate Sustainability', *Journal of Management Studies* 50, no. 2 (2013): 308.
55 Campbell, 'Why Would Corporations Behave in Socially Responsible Ways?'
56 Mary B. Anderson, *Do No Harm: How Aid Can Support Peace—or War* (Boulder, CO: Lynne Riener Publishers, 1999).
57 Jerry A. Carbo et al., *Social Sustainability for Business* (London: Routledge, 2017).

58 Daphne T. Greenwood, 'The Three Faces of Labor: Sustainability and the Next Wave of Automation', *Journal of Economic Issues* 53, no. 2 (2019): 378–84.
59 Ron Eglash et al., 'Automation for the Artisanal Economy: Enhancing the Economic and Environmental Sustainability of Crafting Professions with Human–Machine Collaboration', *AI & Society* 35, no. 3 (2020): 595–609.
60 Peloza and Shang, 'Sustainability and Customer Value', 54.
61 Chris Landorf, 'Evaluating Social Sustainability in Historic Urban Environments', *International Journal of Heritage Studies* 17, no. 5 (2011): 472.
62 Alex J. Wood et al., 'Good Gig, Bad Gig: Autonomy and Algorithmic Control in the Global Gig Economy', *Work, Employment and Society* 33, no. 1 (2019): 57.
63 Valerio De Stefano, 'The Rise of the "Just-in Time Workforce": On Demand Work, Crowdwork, and Labor Protection in the "Gig Economy"', *Comparative Labor Law and Policy Journal* 37, no. 3 (2016): 476.
64 Ursula Huws et al., 'Work in the European Gig Economy' (Brussels: Foundation for European Progressive Studies, 2017); Wood et al., 'Good Gig, Bad Gig'.
65 Fiona Harvey, 'Britain Merely "outsourcing" Carbon Emissions to China, Say MPs', the Guardian, 18 April 2012, http://www.theguardian.com/environment/2012/apr/18/britain-outsourcing-carbon-emissions-china.
66 P. Bottazzi, 'Work and Socio-Ecological Transitions: A Critical Review of Five Contrasting Approaches', *Sustainability* 11, no. 14 (2019): 3852.
67 Kalyeena Makortoff, 'Goldman Sachs' Junior Bankers Rebel over "18-Hour Shifts and Low Pay"', *The Guardian*, 24 March 2021, http://www.theguardian.com/business/2021/mar/24/goldman-sachs-junior-bankers-rebel-over-18-hour-shifts-and-low-pay.
68 Peter Walker, 'Call Centre Staff to Be Monitored via Webcam for Home-Working "Infractions"', *The Guardian*, 26 March 2021, http://www.theguardian.com/business/2021/mar/26/teleperformance-call-centre-staff-monitored-via-webcam-home-working-infractions.
69 Rosabeth M. Kanter, *Men and Women of the Corporation* (New York: Basic Books, 1979).
70 M. Weber, *Economy and Society*, vol. 3 (New York: Bedminster Press, 1968), 975.
71 Joan Acker, 'Hierarchies, Jobs, Bodies: A Theory of Gendered Organizations', *Gender & Society* 4, no. 2 (1990): 139–58.
72 Scott, *Organizations: Rational, Natural, and Open Systems*, 191.
73 Caroline Criado Perez, *Invisible Women: Exposing Data Bias in a World Designed for Men* (London: Penguin Random House, 2019).
74 Scott, *Organizations: Rational, Natural, and Open Systems*, 185–86.
75 Rachel Shabi, 'Women Reach 40 and Hit Their Stride ... Only to Be Cruelly Shoved aside at Work', *The Guardian*, 7 April 2021, http://www.theguardian.com/commentisfree/2021/apr/07/women-40-work-sidelined-sexist-standards.
76 F. Taylor, *Principles of Scientific Management* (New York: Harper & Row, 1911).
77 Gareth Morgan, *Images of Organization*, Updated Edition (Thousand Oaks, CA: Sage Publications, 2006), 19.
78 Carol Gilligan, *In a Different Voice: Psychological Theory and Women's Development* (Cambridge, MA: Harvard University Press, 1982).
79 For example, Barbara Bird and Candida Brush, 'A Gendered Perspective on Organizational Creation', *Entrepreneurship Theory and Practice* 26, no. 3 (2002): 41–65.
80 Bird and Brush, 51–52.
81 Lorenzo Ardito, Rosa Maria Dangelico, and Antonio Messeni Petruzzelli, 'The Link between Female Representation in the Boards of Directors and Corporate Social Responsibility: Evidence from B Corps', *Corporate Social Responsibility and Environmental Management* 28 (2021): 704–20.
82 Maretno Harjoto, Indrarini Laksmana, and Ya-wen Yang, 'Why Do Companies Obtain the B Corporation Certification?', *Social Responsibility Journal* 15, no. 5 (2019): 621–39.
83 Scott, *Organizations: Rational, Natural, and Open Systems*, 186.
84 Dana M. Britton and Laura Logan, 'Gendered Organizations: Progress and Prospects', *Sociology Compass* 2, no. 1 (2008): 107–21.
85 Eglė Staniškienė and Živilė Stankevičiūtė, 'Social Sustainability Measurement Framework: The Case of Employee Perspective in a CSR-Committed Organisation', *Journal of Cleaner Production* 188 (2018): 708–19.

86 C. Argyris and D. A. Schön, *Organizational Learning: A Theory of Action Perspective* (Reading, MA: Addison-Wesley Publishing, 1978).
87 Chris Argyris, *Reasoning, Learning, and Action: Individual and Organizational* (San Francisco, CA: Jossey-Bass, 1982).
88 Argyris, 106.
89 James G. March, 'Exploration and Exploitation in Organizational Learning', *Organization Science* 2, no. 1 (1991): 71–87.
90 F. Gale, *The Political Economy of Sustainability* (Cheltenham: Edward Elgar Publishing Ltd, 2018), 150.
91 Michael Porter, *Competitive Strategy* (New York: Free Press, 1980).
92 Helen Borland and Adam Lindgreen, 'Sustainability, Epistemology, Ecocentric Business, and Marketing Strategy: Ideology, Reality, and Vision', *Journal of Business Ethics* 117, no. 1 (2013): 179.
93 Hart and Dowell, 'Invited Editorial'.
94 Gilligan, *In a Different Voice*.
95 Frederic Laloux, *Reinventing Organizations: A Guide to Creating Organizations Inspired by the next Stage of Human Consciousness* (Millis, MA: Nelson Parker, 2014).
96 George EP Box, 'Robustness in the Strategy of Scientific Model Building', Technical summary report (Madison: University of Wisconsin-Madison, 1979).
97 Bernd Siebenhüner and Marlen Arnold, 'Organizational Learning to Manage Sustainable Development', *Business Strategy and the Environment* 16, no. 5 (2007): 339–53.
98 Göran Ingvar Broman and Karl-Henrik Robèrt, 'A Framework for Strategic Sustainable Development', *Journal of Cleaner Production* 140 (2017): 17–31.
99 In particular, Borland and Lindgreen, 'Sustainability, Epistemology, Ecocentric Business, and Marketing Strategy'; Paul Shrivastava, 'Ecocentric Management for a Risk Society', *Academy of Management Review* 20, no. 1 (1995): 118–37.
100 D. Adams, *The Hitchhiker's Guide to the Galaxy* (New York: Del Rey Books, 1979).
101 Scott, *Organizations: Rational, Natural, and Open Systems*.
102 John Elkington, *Cannibals with Forks: The Triple Bottom Line of Twenty-First Century Business* (Oxford: Capstone Publishing, 1997).
103 Robert S. Kaplan and David P. Norton, 'The Balanced Scorecard — Measures That Drive Performance', *Harvard Business Review*, no. January-February (1992): 71–79.
104 For example, A. MacGillivray, 'Social Capital at Work: A Manager's Guide', in *The Triple Bottom Line: Does It All Add Up?*, ed. Adrian Henriques and Julie Richardson (London: Routledge, 2013); A. Stephens, E. Lewis, and S. Reddy, 'Inclusive Systemic Evaluation for Gender Equality, Environments and Marginalized Voices' (New York: UN Women, 2018); J.P. Hatala, 'Social Network Analysis in Human Resource Development: A New Methodology', *Human Resource Development Review* 5, no. 1 (2006): 45–71.
105 Rob Gray and Markus Milne, 'Towards Reporting on the Triple Bottom Line: Mirages, Methods and Myths', in *The Triple Bottom Line: Does It All Add Up*, ed. Adrian Henriques and Julie Richardson (Routledge, 2004), 70–80.
106 https://www.globalreporting.org/.
107 GSSB, 'Consolidated Set of GRI Sustainability Reporting Standards 2020' (Global Sustainability Standards Board, 2020), https://www.globalreporting.org/standards/download-the-standards/.
108 Cory Searcy, 'Setting a Course in Corporate Sustainability Performance Measurement', *Measuring Business Excellence* 13, no. 3 (2009): 49–57; Raine Isaksson and Ulrich Steimle, 'What Does GRI-Reporting Tell Us about Corporate Sustainability?', *The TQM Journal* 21, no. 2 (2009): 168–81.
109 Peter A.C. Smith and Carol Sharicz, 'The Shift Needed for Sustainability', *The Learning Organization: An International Journal* 18, no. 1 (2011): 73–86.
110 https://bcorporation.net/.
111 https://www.gov.uk/government/organisations/office-of-the-regulator-of-community-interest-companies.
112 Elsa Diez-Busto, Lidia Sanchez-Ruiz, and Ana Fernandez-Laviada, 'The B Corp Movement: A Systematic Literature Review', *Sustainability* 13, no. 2508 (2021).

113 Harjoto, Laksmana, and Yang, 'Why Do Companies Obtain the B Corporation Certification?'; Wendy Stubbs, 'Characterising B Corps as a Sustainable Business Model: An Exploratory Study of B Corps in Australia', *Journal of Cleaner Production* 144 (2017): 299–312.
114 Katie Askew, 'Danone Jettisons Faber as Chairman and CEO: Will His Legacy of Sustainable Business Survive?', foodnavigator.com, 15 March 2021, https://www.foodnavigator.com/Article/2021/03/15/Danone-jettisons-Faber-as-Chairman-and-CEO-Will-his-legacy-of-sustainable-business-survive.
115 https://www.msci.com/msci-acwi-sustainable-impact-index.
116 https://www.unglobalcompact.org/.

5 Developing a learning strategy 1
What to learn

5.1 What does this part of the book cover?

In the first half of this book, we looked at the context driving the pressure for organisational adaptation—what sustainability means, what implications this may have for systems of political economy, and how organisations will need to adapt to these changing demands. In Chapter 4, we developed some outline ideas about what implications this would have for what actually happens inside an organisation—what may change in people's work, and what implications there might be for management.

As we move on to the second half of the book, the focus changes to developing a learning strategy. This covers seven chapters, illustrated in Figure 5.1.

Chapters 5–8 are presented as aspects of a learning needs assessment process. For convenience, we will look at these sequentially, but in reality, the needs assessment process should explore them in parallel, working iteratively towards writing the final learning strategy (Chapter 9).

Chapters 5–7 are structured following the three elements of a programme of learning suggested by the American educationalist Henry Giroux[1]: content, what someone needs to learn (Chapter 5); mechanisms, the practical arrangements whereby this learning can happen (which here we show as including both formal and informal possibilities) (Chapter 6); and principles, philosophies of learning which can make formal learning more effective

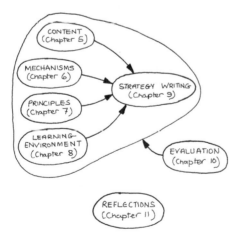

Figure 5.1 The structure of Chapters 5–11.

DOI: 10.4324/9781003218296-6

(Chapter 7). Chapter 8 looks at how informal learning can be supported and also looks at the environment within which learning will happen: this chapter also considers the role that human resource development (HRD) and human resource management (HRM) can play in supporting informal learning and strengthening the learning environment.

Chapter 10 considers the evaluation of how the entire learning system works, and, in conclusion, Chapter 11 is about reflection, reflection on key points covered in the book and reflection as a fundamental part of learning.

5.2 What this chapter covers

This chapter focuses on identifying the content for sustainability-focused learning (SFL). Figure 5.2 illustrates what it covers. It starts by critically examining the origins of HRD, and then introduces the subject of learning needs assessment and shows how systems thinking can contribute to the process, and continues by developing an initial map of what content might be included within a strategy for SFL, what we will refer to as SFL by just a full stop.

5.3 The emergence of training as a specialist activity

5.3.1 The historic roots of human resource development

As systems thinkers, the first thing we will do in this detailed look at the relationship between learning and organisational sustainability is to pause and reflect on some boundary judgements of relevance to an SFL strategy.

The first boundary judgement to make is about what I mean by "learning". I see learning as what happens when we change what we do in response to evolving demands from our outside world. In our context learning about sustainability addresses what knowledge, skills and attitudes people in organisations need to develop in order to support an adaptation to sustainable organisational practice.

One such boundary judgement is that learning happens through training, although in historical terms this is a comparatively recent idea. For centuries learning how to do a job relied largely on working with an expert who provided instruction and judged performance, and this continued until the middle of the 20th century: few organisations recognised "training" as a separate function, such that in 1946 only 29% of US corporations reported having a specific training function.[2]

The transition to what we know now started during World War II. In the United States, the sudden need to train large numbers of troops led military planners to ask the

Figure 5.2 Map of Chapter 5.

educational psychologists of the time to develop new, more systematic approaches to workplace learning, and, as a result, the "training expert" appeared.[3] The trend continued with the post-war economic boom leading to increasing levels of specialisation and the emergence of "management skills" as a new need, and consequently the social technology of the "training department" became reified.

As the concept of training as a specialist activity solidified, the idea of "human resources" (HR) started to appear in the United States. It is now widely established, particularly in the neoliberal-influenced United States and the United Kingdom, but less so in European countries where there has been a stronger social democratic tradition.[4] This divergence may in part be a result of the different histories of industrialisation in Europe and the United States: in the latter case, the rapid growth of the railway and oil industries in the late 19th century occurred at a time when central government was still limited, so the influence of corporate culture on society was much greater than in Europe, where industrialisation occurred in a context of well-established central governments and social cultures.[5]

This relative strength of corporate culture in the United States contributed to what is sometimes known as a unitarist philosophy about management, which means a belief that what is good for the organisation is good for the employee. This contrasts with a pluralist approach where employees, through trade unions or other forms of social structure, play a more significant role in organisational decision-making.[6] A unitarist philosophy may be seen in Strategic Human Resource Management (SHRM):

> ... an approach to making decisions on the intentions and plans of the organisation concerning the employment relationship and the organisation's recruitment, training, development, performance management, reward and employee relations strategies, policies and practices.[7]

SHRM means that HR policies are matched vertically to an explicit business strategy and horizontally to co-ordinate with other HR policies. It also leads to the learning and development role of HR, HRD, adopting a "performative" focus, where its primary aim is to improve organisational performance rather than to support any broader concept of employee development.[8]

5.3.2 Critical perspectives on HRD

We can now take a closer look at the implications of the HRD concept. To do this we will draw on the work of the German critical philosopher Jürgen Habermas (introduced briefly in Chapter 2). His theory of communicative action[9] proposed that in order to function effectively in the world individuals need to be capable in three distinct but connected areas of knowledge (as illustrated in Figure 5.3).

Technical (sometimes referred to as instrumental) knowledge is about knowing how to control our environment: in my personal life, this might be about how to cook an omelette, while in my working life this would be about how to do my job. Communicative (or practical) knowledge is about how we interact with other people and make judgements about what they say: for example, are they telling the truth, what are their intentions, how reliable are they, and so on. Emancipatory knowledge is about what we value in the world, our freedom and our sense of what is important in our lives. Together, communicative and emancipatory knowledge create what Habermas calls a

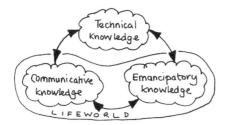

Figure 5.3 Habermas' conception of knowledge interests.

person's "lifeworld", a term which seeks to capture the somewhat undefinable nature of our individual existence.

Habermas was particularly concerned with how the technical interests of our working lives impinge on our lifeworld. From this perspective, performative learning prioritises the technical interest and minimises the emancipatory interests of learners, which, it is argued, leads to HRD "... disengaging with its roots in humanistic social science and its original concern for the well-being of individuals in organizations and for developing human potential"[10] and neglecting its responsibility for beneficence.[11] Ignoring the emancipatory interests of employees may damage their well-being and challenges the psychological contract that they expect.[12] SHRM may be seen as reducing employees to the same level as machinery, and as the economic historian Philip Mirowski puts it, serves to:

> ... deconstruct any special status for human labor, ... and reduces the human being to an arbitrary bundle of "investments", skill sets, temporary alliances ... and fungible body parts.[13]

A performative focus may not even be an effective long-term strategy: it may lead to learning becoming mechanistic and lacking critical reflection[14]; it can restrict the possibility of learning leading to innovation[15]; and may emphasise learning which concentrates on short-term market demands.[16]

As we will see, thinking about the tensions between technical, emancipatory and communicative interests can provide a useful way of thinking about how learning within organisations happens, particularly with regard to a subject such as sustainability which has such strong associations with moral and ethical frameworks. Ignoring emancipatory interests can lead to learning which fails to engage the interests of learners and does not allow clear communication between the organisation and the learner, which can lead to distrust.

This perspective on learning also resonates with ideas discussed previously. Complexity theory highlights the importance of balancing the legitimate and shadow systems, the latter here being represented by the lifeworld. SHRM may also be seen to represent hegemonic thinking, which we previously discussed in looking at the problems of looking at political economy from a different perspective (Chapter 3, Section 3.5), and to which we will return in Chapter 7 (Section 7.2.3) when we consider critical thinking.

We will therefore return to these ideas throughout the next few chapters as we look at how learning about sustainability may best be addressed. To help with this we will

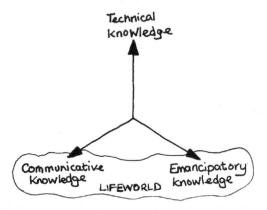

Figure 5.4 The Habermas learning space triangle.

use Figure 5.4, which can give us what we might call the "Habermas learning space". With this heuristic we can position different approaches to learning to show how they can contribute to each of the three dimensions.

Time for reflection

If you work in HRD, what do you think about this criticism? What do you accept, and what do you reject?

In your experience, what is the current trajectory of HRD in terms of becoming more environmentally and socially conscious?

5.4 Basic principles of identifying learning needs

Identifying the requirements for SFL will be (or at least should be) done through a learning needs assessment (LNA) process, also sometimes called learning or training needs analysis. In reality, there is often only lip service paid to analysing learning needs, and what learning subsequently takes place is often determined by organisational traditions or whatever those involved in learning and development are comfortable doing. This sorry state of affairs is confirmed by both practitioner and academic research.[17]

It is hard to imagine that many other parts of an organisation would be prepared to spend large amounts of money without carrying out a rigorous cost-benefit analysis of some sort, so why are LNAs done so infrequently? There are various reasons why this may be the case: that it takes too long and a solution is needed immediately; there is insufficient expertise to do it; senior management does not think it necessary; it is too expensive; there is no perceived value in doing it; senior managers are confident that training is the solution; or that decisions about learning strategies are made by people who know nothing about learning strategies.[18] Running a training programme may also be a convenient quick fix which avoids the need to question structural or cultural weaknesses within the organisation. The influential HRD academic Elwood Holton III has described this as resulting in HRD operating a "customer service model", responding somewhat unquestioningly to demands for training from senior management.[19] It is to be hoped that several of these problems may be alleviated by reading this book!

A thorough LNA process achieves a number of things. Most obviously, it identifies what needs to be learnt in order to implement change, but it also should identify what obstacles there may be in effecting change: these may range from relatively straightforward practical problems to do with changing processes or procedures, through to much less obvious and not necessarily rational political objections to change.[20] There is a more complete discussion about what these might be in Chapter 6. In this respect, it should also identify where structural issues are more problematic and learning is not a worthwhile strategy to pursue. It also provides a benchmark to help with subsequent evaluation activities, as no learning activities can be effectively evaluated if there is no idea about the starting conditions. In fact, the processes for an LNA and evaluation are similar in terms of the need to make sense of a situation of interest and understand how making changes may affect or have affected the situation.

However, it is important to remember that, referring to the three-level model developed in Chapter 4, in a visionary organization employees may play a major role in assessing their own learning needs. You, as the reader, will need to reflect on how you can communicate to the people you work with from what you learn from this book about assessing learning needs.

Time for reflection

What happens in your organisation about LNAs? How often are they done?

Does the list of reasons for not carrying out needs assessments ring true with you?

5.5 Getting started with a learning needs assessment

Although there is limited academic research available about LNAs, there is significant practitioner-oriented literature. The approach here will draw on a three-level model often known as O-T-P, attributed to McGehee and Thayer,[21] but which has been developed by many others. This sees organisational objectives or goals as a starting point, which then need to be considered from the task perspective (what needs to be done), and then analysis of the person who needs to be trained (hence the O-T-P). This model is particularly appropriate for looking at the connection between strategic change and learning and fits well with the recursive abilities of the Viable System Model (VSM), which will be used as a framework for defining the content of learning required.

In line with the systems thinking approach used throughout this book, we will frame the LNA in systemic terms, turning the *situation* of interest, the need to develop a learning strategy, into a "*system* of interest". Peter Checkland offers the PQR way for defining a system of interest, to do P by Q in order to achieve R.²² Based on this structure, our starting point will be to develop:

> A system to ensure people within the organisation constantly enhance their knowing, skills and attitudes through learning activities to support the organisation achieving its vision of sustainability.

Astute readers will notice the use of the word "knowing" here, rather than the more familiar "knowledge". I think that it is a valuable word to use in this definition because the two terms express somewhat different ideas. "Knowledge" suggests something static, discrete and defined which can be acquired and possessed, possibly shutting off another understanding that what we are really talking about is a process, partly a process of acquiring "knowledge" certainly, but also *of practice* in order to deepen understanding. The organisational learning scholars Scott Cook and John Seely Brown describe knowing as "the epistemic work that is done as part of actual practice, like that done in the actual riding of a bicycle".²³ The bicycle analogy seems appropriate in the context of sustainability, and like riding a bicycle, learning about sustainability needs to be continuous—we have no defined endpoint where we can stop and say, "Yes, we are now sustainable and can stop doing what we are doing". Our system for learning therefore needs to ensure an ongoing commitment to knowing.

An LNA is essentially a process of making boundary decisions—who learns, what they learn, and how they learn—and, of course, how these decisions are made. The first stage in the analysis is reflecting on where you and your organisation are initially in terms of sustainability and learning: this will define your starting point for conducting the assessment. To do this we will use Werner Ulrich's framework for making boundary judgements, Critical Systems Heuristics, deployed in an ideal mapping mode, as described in Section 2.13.

We pull together these lines of thinking in Table 5.1, which presents the 12 Critical Systems Heuristics boundary judgement questions in the left-hand column, reworded to make them refer more specifically to our system of interest. Against each of these judgement questions are more detailed questions that are relevant to ask or reflect on at this initial stage in the analysis. Essentially, this process helps you to reflect on what underlying assumptions you and the organisation may have. These could possibly lead to subconscious initial boundary decisions—at this stage, for example, there may be little awareness of informal learning in your organisation, in which case building it into a learning strategy could be overlooked; working with external stakeholders such as community groups might never have been done before, so their perspective might not be sought.

Against each general question are four columns: as well as columns for the three elements of content, mechanisms and principles, there is one for judgements that cut across each of these. At this initial, pre-analysis stage, not all of the questions can be answered. What you are best able to think about at this stage is what Ulrich calls the sources of power and knowledge, in practical terms, you and your organisational context. As we progress through Chapters 5–8, we will develop the content of this table, so that we can conclude with a comprehensive set of questions that we will need to address during the LNA in order to feel reasonably confident that our learning strategy is as holistic as is practicable. However, note that this is not necessarily a sequential process of working through content then mechanisms then principles. Although developing clarity on content is an important first step, making judgements about mechanisms and principles may well fall out of this process.

The table that emerges from this process will form the basis for subsequent evaluation of the learning strategy, a process explored in Chapter 10.

Table 5.1 Baseline conditions for the LNA

Boundary judgement questions	Cross-cutting questions	Content-related	Mechanisms-related	Principles-related
1 Who should benefit from the learning strategy?				
2 What is the purpose of the learning strategy?		What is the overall aim of the learning strategy at this stage of understanding?		
3 What is the measure of success for the learning strategy?				
4 Who makes decisions about the strategy?	Who will make a decision about the learning strategy?			
5 What resources and constraints relevant to the strategy does the decision-maker control?	What is the tradition within the organisation about decision-making on learning? Who holds the budget for learning activities?		What mechanisms are generally used?	What principles are generally used?
6 What conditions of the strategy's operation are outside of the control of the decision-maker?	What are the drivers in the operational environment for social and environmental sustainability? What pressure is there from the workforce to adopt social and environmental sustainability strategies?			
7 Who should be involved in the design of the strategy?				
8 What expertise is needed to design the strategy?				
9 What guarantees of success do the sources of expertise offer?		What level of knowledge do you have or is available to you about sustainability?		
10 Who will represent the affected society and the natural environment?				

(Continued)

150 *Developing a learning strategy: what to learn*

Boundary judgement questions	*Cross-cutting questions*	*Content-related*	*Mechanisms-related*	*Principles-related*
11 What opportunity does the affected society and natural environment have to challenge the strategy?		What are the political possibilities for engaging with external representatives in discussing sustainability-focused learning?		
12 What is the worldview underlying the design of the learning strategy?	How does social and environmental sustainability sit within your organisation's culture and philosophy? What are your own perspectives on social and environmental sustainability? What is the organisational tradition for conducting the LNA process?			

Time for reflection

Spend a little while looking at the questions in Table 5.1, and see how many of them you can answer in some way now.

Think about what you need to do in order to develop a more complete set of answers.

5.6 Identifying the content for the learning strategy

Having established the context within which you will carry out your needs analysis, the first thing we will do is to think about the content that the learning strategy must cover. We will look at two different perspectives about content: the task requirements for sustainability, for which we will use the term competences; and the personal attributes which can contribute to sustainable practice, which we will describe as competencies. As will be discussed, the HR literature is inconsistent about the use of these two terms, but it is useful here to establish some clarity.

5.6.1 Competences, competencies and knowledge, skills and attitudes

The first confusion to deal with is between competence and competency. In general usage, there is little difference between the terms: the Oxford English Dictionary defines them both as "the quality or extent of being competent". Much academic writing also treats them as synonyms: for example, the text in Prahalad and Hamel's seminal paper on organisational core competences[24] uses the words competencies and competences quite indiscriminately. Here, for clarity, I will draw a clear distinction between the two, following Michael Armstrong's definitions of the terms in his authoritative text on HRM.[25]

Competence refers to a task which is done, without reference to the person doing it. This idea of competence emerged out of the ideas of scientific management and behaviourism. Generic, standardised training, such as much online learning, follows such behaviourist principles in assuming that all learners are the same. Prahalad and Hamel developed this idea of individual competence into that of an organisation's core competences, by noting that organisations may develop a specific competence in doing things such as designing video recorders or building cars and motorcycles.

In contrast, a competency refers to a person and their behaviours which contribute to a competent performance.[26] The American psychologist David McClelland first articulated this concept of a competency,[27] suggesting that assessment of individuals in occupational settings should pay attention to personality variables such as communication skills, patience and goal setting, which could be criterion-referenced against what would be required in any particular work setting. This idea was further developed by Richard Boyatzis, who suggested that three clusters of competencies can be identified:

- cognitive competencies related to areas such as systems thinking and pattern recognition
- emotional intelligence competencies related to such things as self-awareness and self-control
- social intelligence competencies, including social awareness, empathy and teamwork.[28]

Most organisations nowadays develop competency frameworks which can be used to help in HRM, but confusingly, these may be a hybrid of competences and competencies.

So, in summary, here competences will be used to refer to tasks and other activities relevant to sustainability, while competencies will refer to personal qualities that can contribute to satisfactory performance of such tasks and activities.

The second confusion arises in the literature relating to the design and development of learning programmes, and the use of the words knowledge, skill and, more problematically, attitude, ability or behaviour (Knowledge, Skills and Abilities (KSA) or KSB). Knowledge may be seen as having two requirements:

- An individual receives information in which they develop a "justified true belief" (a concept in the theory of knowledge which is satisfied if the information is true, the individual believes the information and has adequate justification for that belief[29]).
- The individual integrates this within their personal mental model.

Some readers may feel that such a definition of knowledge may be labouring a point, but when dealing with a contested and potentially politically charged concept such as sustainability, having a clear understanding of how information becomes knowledge is important. As discussed in Chapter 2, how each individual is socialised has a strong influence on what they understand as legitimate knowledge. For example, in respect of climate change, there are oppositional understandings about the role of human activity in levels of greenhouse gases in the atmosphere. The scientific consensus is that human activity is responsible for high levels of such gases, in other words, this is what we are taking to be true. If an individual believes this and accepts the available evidence which confirms it, then they can be said to have knowledge. However, if an individual does not believe this, or believes the alternative to be true, and can point to sources of information which justify their particular belief, can they be said to have knowledge in our terms? This is a deeply philosophical problem and points to the importance of thoroughly thinking through processes which will be followed in order to facilitate learning about a particular subject. For example, what preparation would you as a learning facilitator need to do in order to be able to challenge information disseminated by climate change deniers, should you need to do this?

The definition of skill is relatively straightforward, and we may rely on the dictionary definition of it being practical expertise or dexterity.

The third letter in the acronym is more problematic because different terms may be used depending on context. Within the learning design world, A for "attitude" is perhaps the most commonly used, where attitude is defined as a settled mode of thinking.[30] For consistency, we will therefore refer to KSA as meaning knowledge, skill and attitude.

So how do these terms link to each other? Figure 5.5 is a heuristic which can help thinking about this question. The technical requirements of the workplace determine the competence required, and this may be defined in terms of the knowledge and skill required. Competency, as an individual characteristic, contributes to skill and attitude. Both individual and organisational characteristics contribute to identity and the transfer climate is influenced by the organisational characteristics. These terms and their significance are examined in more detail in Chapter 6.

The heuristic shows the importance of thinking about effective performance as being the outcome of a complex relationship which includes the individual, the requirements of the task and the environment within which the task is carried out. Reductionist thinking about competences or competencies on their own will not help very much in thinking through how to support effective SFL.

5.6.2 Competences for sustainability

Competences are task-specific, and so will be unique to every organisation, but some taxonomies have been developed which can help with thinking about what is relevant to a particular situation. Although these have generally been defined with reference to

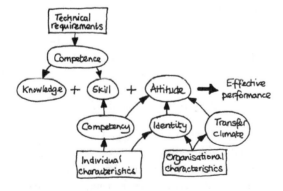

Figure 5.5 Relationships between competence, competency and KSA.

Developing a learning strategy: what to learn 153

environmental sustainability, they can be interpreted to help with our more holistic conception of SFL.

Deniz Ones and Stephan Dilchert have suggested what they call the "Green Five" behaviours.[31] These are as follows:

- Conserving, being frugal or thrifty with resources such as water, fuel and other natural resources. According to Ones and Dilchert, this is the most commonly seen category of pro-sustainability behaviour.
- Working sustainably, adapting working practices so that they have a more positive sustainability impact on the social or natural environments.
- Avoiding harm, working in a way to minimise damaging impacts on society or the natural environment.
- Influencing others, through sharing knowledge or taking part in conversations which can help other people to understand the importance of sustainability.
- Taking the initiative, doing things which challenge conventional norms but which contribute to better sustainability. This might be seen as empowerment, but could also extend into activism, where employees lobby senior management to improve existing practice.

Another way of looking at sustainable behaviour is by distinguishing between required and voluntary behaviours.[32] With required behaviours, employees follow agreed policies and procedures relating to sustainability, whereas voluntary behaviours go beyond these minimum requirements. Typically, these may reflect an individual's personal commitment to sustainability, with the person applying their own external values to what they do in the workplace. Clearly, this could extend to internal activism and could be seen as exemplified by the Project Maven incident in Google referred to earlier.

5.6.3 Competencies for sustainability

Competencies are person-specific, so in contrast to organisation-specific competences, we can make more progress in identifying generic personal qualities appropriate to sustainable working. A considerable amount of research has been done in this area under the general heading of Education for Sustainable Development (ESD), addressed in Sustainable Development Goal (SDG) 4, where Target 4.7 states:

> By 2030, ensure that all learners acquire the knowledge and skills needed to promote sustainable development, including, among others, through Education for Sustainable Development and sustainable lifestyles, human rights, gender equality, promotion of a culture of peace and nonviolence, global citizenship and appreciation of cultural diversity and of culture's contribution to sustainable development.[33]

Note that in the context of *Agenda 2030* and SDG 4, "learners" refers to *lifelong* learners, not just those in the educational system, so this target may be seen as relevant to learners in organisational settings as well. The emphasis in the target on social sustainability is also noteworthy.

As interest in ESD developed, various research efforts went into drawing up lists of what competencies it implied. UNESCO has consolidated much of this extensive research,[34] proposing eight key competencies relevant to sustainability which it sees as supplementing more context-specific competencies which may be defined within a competency framework. Cognitive sustainability competencies are:

- Systems thinking competency, the ability to recognise and understand relationships and complex systems.
- Integrated problem-solving competency, the overarching ability to apply different problem-solving frameworks to complex sustainability problems.
- Anticipatory competency, the ability to understand and evaluate multiple futures (which we might also think of as wisdom).
- Critical thinking competency, the ability to question norms, practices and opinions.

Social intelligence competencies include:

- Collaboration competency, the ability to learn from and respect the needs of others.
- Normative competency, the ability to understand and reflect on norms and values underlying action.
- Strategic competency, the ability to collectively develop and implement innovative actions.

Finally, there is a self-awareness competency, the ability to reflect on one's own role, which is an emotional intelligence quality.

A big question is, of course, the degree to which learning activities within the organisational setting can strengthen a competency as opposed to a competence. Cognitive competencies are probably most amenable to being strengthened through forms of directed learning, so that, for example, as a reader of this book, your competency in systems thinking may be strengthened after studying it. We can also strengthen systems thinking skills through formal training and through encouraging the use of systems thinking tools such as diagramming in team meetings and other settings. Formal learning programmes should be designed so that they strengthen these competencies: learning design centred around passive reading or listening will not achieve this. Learning strategies should contribute to higher-level problem-solving, anticipatory, reflection and critical thinking competencies, but these need further, ongoing workplace opportunities for real development. However, emotional and social intelligence competencies are less tractable to change in an organisational setting. Nevertheless, some of the techniques for transformative learning and critical thinking discussed in Chapter 7 may be able to play a part in opening up possibilities for change even with these.

Time for reflection

How do these competencies align with your own organisation's competency framework?

What do you do in your organisation to help people develop these competencies?

5.7 Using the Viable System Model to map content requirements

The previous section has outlined the competences needed to support the sustainability strategy in rather general terms and provided a fairly consistent set of competencies that we should look to develop in employees. We now need to try and be more specific in identifying where these competences and competencies might be relevant within typical organisational activity so that we can identify what learning needs exist.

To do this we will use VSM. This was introduced in Chapter 2, where we explained briefly how it provided a way of thinking about how information is used within an organisation rather than by examining structures. In Chapter 4, we developed a model proposing three levels at which an organisation could approach a sustainability strategy and considered some ideas about what implications these would have for organisational activities and management practice. We can now draw these separate strands of thinking together in order to create a framework that we can use for a sustainability-focused LNA. The recursive quality of VSM also means that we can use the same structure at organisational, team and individual levels.

We can therefore construct a series of tables (Tables 5.2–5.4) which bring together the five VSM systems, the O-T-P level of analysis, and level of sustainability relevant for an organisation (Figure 4.15), and into these map what competences are needed at each level. This mapping exercise draws on research into generic knowledge requirements for each system[35] and the various observations made in Chapter 4 and this chapter about the organisational implications of sustainability.

As a reminder of what each level of organisational sustainability means:

- Complier—the organisation follows regulatory requirements within the operational landscape, such as those imposed by national or international government regulations, or by trade bodies.
- Strategist—the organisation moves beyond compliance and looks for ways in which following sustainability strategies could provide some competitive advantage.
- Visionary—the organisation sees social and environmental sustainability as an end in itself and develops appropriate internal processes and policies.

Before looking at these tables, it is important to recognise some limitations. First, the three-level model is highly reductive, and in reality, no single organisation would be simply one or the other. Certain characteristics of each level may dominate, but it is most likely that different parts of an organisation or distinct processes could be seen to align with different levels. Similarly, there is no distinct cut-off between each of the levels, and each descriptor needs to be read somewhat loosely. A third issue is that, as the three-level model represents a progression towards a more complete approach to sustainable practice, each level tends to build on the preceding level, so that in general what is required by a complier organisation will also be a requirement for strategists and visionaries, but with additions and possible refinements. Finally, these competences are generic and need to be customised for your particular situation.

When carrying out your own LNA, use these tables as a thinking aid, not as prescriptive requirements. Every organisation's SFL strategy will be different, depending on where you are on the sustainability journey and what level of engagement with and understanding about sustainability your workforce has. Parts of the learning map will be more or less important, but the content of the tables will give you a solid, systemically-based starting point for thinking through your own specific requirements.

5.7.1 Tables of potential learning content

Table 5.2 Learning content at the organisational level for each VSM system

System	Function	Levels of sustainability strategy		
		Complier	Strategist	Visionary
		The organisation needs to have required levels of KSA to ensure:		
S1	Operations	Primary activities comply with all regulatory requirements.	Primary activities produce products and services which contribute to sustainability and improve organisational competitiveness.	Primary activities enhance social and environmental sustainability. Culture of innovation to strengthen sustainability.
S2	Coordination	Coordination activities ensure a consistent and compliant response to regulatory requirements.	Coordination activities strengthen overall organisational competitiveness.	Coordination activities support autonomy and promote cohesion and equity.
S3	Delivery	Policies and procedures are implemented and updated as necessary to ensure regulatory compliance. Capacity for compliance is maintained.	Policies and procedures are implemented and updated as necessary to ensure improved competitiveness. Strengthening of team members' sustainability competencies supported.	Policies and procedures promote eco-effective, closed loop principles. Participation by all in decision-making about policies and procedures. Strengthening of team members' sustainability competencies supported.
S3*	Monitoring	Information about non-compliance with regulatory requirements is communicated appropriately.	Information about competitiveness in sustainable marketplace disseminated.	Information about impact of organisational activities on social and natural environment is disseminated through organisation. Efficient and effective systems for employee feedback.
S4	Development	Awareness of developments in regulatory landscape and implications for internal control systems.	Awareness of developments in political economy characteristics, regulatory and business landscape and implications for internal control systems.	Awareness of developments in social and natural environment where the organisation could enhance sustainability. Strengthened cooperation and collaboration with business partners and external stakeholders in sustainability issues.
S5	Policy	Sustainability policy in line with regulatory requirements.	Organisational ethos which sees sustainability as a way to improve business performance. Sustainability policy competitive within operational landscape. Learning culture which links social and environmental sustainability with competitiveness. Integration of implications of SDGs, planetary boundaries and other key concepts.	Organisational ethos and culture which sees viability as a way to contribute to social and environmental sustainability. Sustainability policy covers social and environmental issues, is accepted by all employees and evolves constantly. Learning culture which emphasises adaptation to strengthen sustainable practice.

Table 5.3 Learning content at the team level for each VSM system

System	Function	Levels of sustainability strategy		
		Complier	Strategist	Visionary
		Teams need to have required levels of KSA to ensure:		
S1	Operations	Innovation to ensure compliance encouraged. Activities restricted to required pro-sustainability behaviours.	Operational procedures do not cause social or environmental harm. Innovation to strengthen market advantage encouraged.	Innovation culture within team promoted. Voluntary pro-sustainability actions encouraged.
S2	Coordination	Coordination ensures compliance.	Coordination increases operational efficiency and contributes to sustainability.	Coordination activities strengthen social and environmental sustainability. Ongoing sharing of information about sustainability-related issues.
S3	Delivery	Operational practices ensure regulatory compliance. Capacity for compliance is maintained.	Eco-efficient practices are followed. Workplace practices meet basic needs and improve social equity and cohesion.	Sharing of information which can contribute to improved sustainability. Developments to delivery systems enhance autonomy, cohesion and equity. Collaborative leadership style within teams.
S3*	Monitoring	Information about non-compliance with regulatory requirements is communicated appropriately.	Monitoring data are used to improve product or service competitiveness in terms of sustainability.	Non-standard ideas which can improve sustainability are encouraged. Monitoring data used to question assumptions within team as necessary to promote double loop learning.
S4	Development	Recognition of impact of products and services which may contravene regulatory requirements.	Recognition of impact of products and services which may affect competitiveness from a sustainability perspective.	Recognition of external threats to sustainability which could be addressed by changes to design or delivery of products and services.
S5	Policy	Team ethos of compliance with social and environmental regulatory requirements.	Team ethos focused on strengthening social and environmental sustainability of products and services in order to improve business.	Team ethos of individual empowerment and active awareness of social and environmental issues.

Table 5.4 Learning content at the individual level for each VSM system

		Levels of sustainability strategy		
		Complier	Strategist	Visionary
System	Function	Employees need to have required levels of KSA to ensure:		
S1	Operations	Innovation to ensure compliance.	Innovation to create market advantage.	Innovation to strengthen social and environmental sustainability.
S2	Coordination	Primary activities are coordinated to ensure compliance.	Coordination improves economic, social and environmental efficiency.	Coordination strengthens social and environmental sustainability of products and services. Continuous lifelong individual learning aimed at improving sustainability impact of products and services.
S3	Delivery	Operational practices ensure regulatory compliance.	Operational practices minimise the use of natural resources.	Operational practices optimised to strengthen social and environmental sustainability impact.
S3*	Monitoring	Information about non-compliance with regulatory requirements is communicated appropriately.	Employee feedback on product and service effectiveness sought during monitoring activities.	Non-standard ideas which can improve sustainability are encouraged. Employees regularly providing feedback about sustainability effectiveness of primary activities.
S4	Development	Recognition of impact of products and services which may contravene regulatory requirements.	Recognition of impact of products and services which may affect competitiveness from a sustainability perspective.	Recognition of external threats to sustainability which could be addressed by changes to design or delivery of products and services.
S5	Policy	Individual ethos recognising importance of compliance with social and environmental regulatory requirements.	Individual ethos recognises business importance of improving social and environmental sustainability of products and services. Awareness of significance of SDGs, planetary boundaries and other concepts.	Individual ethos recognises central importance of social and environmental sustainability.

Developing a learning strategy: what to learn 159

5.7.2 How to use these tables

There is a possibly daunting amount of content in these tables and integrating the recommendations across the three organisational levels may prove quite challenging.

Here are some thoughts about what you can do to make this process easier:

- Remember that working towards sustainability is an ongoing process, driven by the vision that your organisation holds for sustainability. Reflect on your vision and pick out content that seems to be immediately relevant to working towards this.
- Treat SFL as a journey which will take a long time. Thinking that all this content needs to be addressed in the next six months is guaranteed to induce unnecessary panic.
- Return to these tables regularly to think about where you are on the journey. As time goes by other topics may appear to be particularly important—integrate them appropriately.
- Avoid the temptation to think that all of this content needs to be covered by formal training. Much of it is not amenable to training and needs to be addressed through other learning mechanisms.
- When possible, integrate content about sustainability into existing learning programmes so that it becomes a natural part of "what we do around here". Avoid designing "bolt-on" programmes about sustainability, which serves to create the idea that sustainability is an optional extra.

Remember that these tables focus on competences, and that competencies cut across all KSA requirements. You will also therefore need to consider how learning can contribute to strengthening sustainability-related competencies, to the degree that this is possible.

5.8 Making decisions about content

The previous section has shown how VSM can be used to identify what content will be needed in an SFL strategy. By carrying out this process, we are making a number of boundary judgements about content aspects of the strategy, decisions about what people should or should not learn. We can therefore update our table of boundary judgement questions from earlier in the chapter (Table 5.1) to incorporate these new boundaries. Table 5.5 shows which boundary judgements we should now be able to examine with some degree of confidence—those updated or added as a result of this new stage in the process are shown in **bold** text.

5.9 Learning and the contested concept of sustainability

The aim of this chapter has been to shine some light on what subjects may need to be covered in an SFL strategy. To do this, we have drawn on and condensed the content from previous sections and used VSM to populate three tables with generic proposals for content. This highlights one of the main challenges in developing an SFL strategy, that the contested nature of sustainability makes it difficult to decide what people need

Table 5.5 Questions to ask about decisions on learning content

Boundary judgement questions	Cross-cutting questions	Content-related	Mechanisms-related	Principles-related
1 Who should benefit from the learning strategy? 2 What is the purpose of the learning strategy?		Who needs to learn about sustainability? What competences and competencies need to be addressed in the SFL strategy? What broader knowledge about sustainability is needed to underpin SFL?		
3 What is the measure of success for the learning strategy?		What are the desired learning outcomes for the relevant level of organisational sustainability? What are the criteria of success for the learning outcomes? What are other possible measures of success?		
4 Who makes decisions about the strategy? 5 What resources and constraints relevant to the strategy does the decision-maker control? 6 What conditions of the strategy's operation are outside of the control of the decision-maker?	Who will make a decision about the learning strategy? What is the tradition within the organisation about decision-making on learning? Who holds the budget for learning activities? What are the drivers in the operational environment for social and environmental sustainability? What pressure is there from the workforce to adopt social and environmental sustainability strategies?		What mechanisms are generally used?	What principles are generally used?

#	Question		
7	Who should be involved in the design of the strategy?		Who should be involved in the design: • Operational staff? • Supervisors? • Others?
8	What expertise is needed to design the strategy?		What expertise is needed to design learning that will meet the competence and competency requirements?
9	What guarantees of success do the sources of expertise offer?		How reliable is the knowledge about required aspects of sustainability that you have or is available to you? What consensus exists about required aspects of sustainability?
10	Who will represent the affected society and the natural environment?		Who can provide information from society or the natural environment to inform what content is needed?
11	What opportunity does the affected society and natural environment have to challenge the strategy?	What are the political possibilities for engaging with external representatives in discussing sustainability-focused learning?	What content from outside the organisation is needed to support the SFL strategy?
12	What is the worldview underlying the design of the learning strategy?	How does social and environmental sustainability sit within your organisation's culture and philosophy? What are your own perspectives on social and environmental sustainability? **What other worldviews on sustainability exist which should be considered?**	How can external perspectives on sustainability be taken into consideration?

162 Developing a learning strategy: what to learn

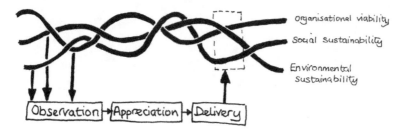

Figure 5.6 Appreciation of the flow of sustainability and its implications for learning.

to learn about. Every organisation will see sustainability differently, will identify different priorities for approaching social or environmental sustainability, and will have a different profile of employees in terms of how receptive they are to or knowledgeable about sustainability.

We can draw on Sir Geoffrey Vickers' concept of an appreciative system to see this graphically (Figure 5.6).[36] We represent the three dimensions of organisational sustainability as an entangled flux, constantly changing in time. At some point we make an observation of what is happening and "appreciate" its significance. We use this information to decide what form of learning is appropriate and then deliver it—at which point the flux of sustainability has moved on and the situation has changed—and our carefully thought-through learning solutions may no longer be relevant.

Although this makes learning about sustainability more problematic than with clearly defined and well-bounded subjects such as new products, processes or services, by using appropriate learning mechanisms or principles this apparent problem can become a rich source of learning. For example, sustainability can be presented as an example of a wicked problem, and learning can revolve around thinking about what are the interrelated issues which affect sustainability. Alternatively, the potential tension between viability and environmental sustainability could be used to generate a discussion about short-term and long-term issues for the organisation. Learning around dialectics such as this forces a constructivist approach to learning.

Drawing on systems thinking ideas could be very useful here, for example by pointing out and discussing multiple perspectives about what sustainability is, what interrelationships there may be between the different dimensions of sustainability, or what boundary judgements need to be made. There is more information about how to integrate systems thinking into learning activities and pedagogical principles to use in Chapter 7.

5.10 Key points in this chapter

Figure 5.7 summarises the key points in this chapter. Assessing learning needs is essentially a process of making boundary judgements about what is important in order to change behaviour and improve performance. A fundamental boundary judgement is in recognising that "traditional" approaches to learning through formal training are often based on unitarist assumptions, that the interests of the organisation and its employees can be easily aligned.

For this reason, a systems thinking approach to LNA can be very useful. Critical Systems Heuristics provides a set of 12 questions which can help to develop a SFL strategy in terms of the content required, the mechanisms that can be used, and the pedagogical principles that will be utilised.

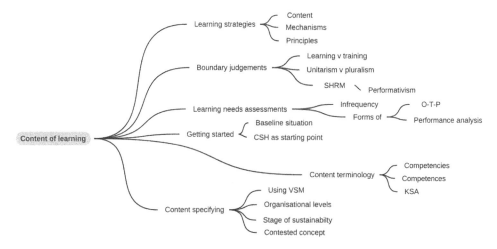

Figure 5.7 Key points in this chapter.

The content required for SFL can be expressed in terms of competences, and the attitudes that need to be developed are related to employees' competencies.

VSM provides a useful tool for developing a framework of what content is relevant in a learning strategy at organisational, team and individual levels. This assessment can be done for organisations in the three possible stages of transforming to sustainable practice.

Although sustainability is a contested concept and there is a considerable lack of clarity about what it means, this can provide a useful focus for learning activities.

Notes

1 H.A. Giroux, *Ideology, Culture and the Process of Schooling* (London: The Falmer Press, 1981), 29.
2 Kurt Kraiger and J. Kevin Ford, 'The Expanding Role of Workplace Training: Themes and Trends Influencing Training Research and Practice', in *Historical Perspectives in Industrial and Organizational Psychology*, ed. L. Koppes (New York: Psychology Press, 2007), 281–309.
3 Walter Dick, 'A History of Instructional Design and Its Impact on Educational Psychology', in *Historical Foundations of Educational Psychology*, ed. John Glover and Royce Ronning (London: Springer, 1987), 183–202; Robert A Reiser, 'A History of Instructional Design and Technology: Part II: A History of Instructional Design', *Educational Technology Research and Development* 49, no. 2 (2001): 57–67.
4 T. Keenoy, 'Human Resource Management', in *The Oxford Handbook of Critical Management Studies*, ed. Mats Alvesson, T. Bridgman, and Hugh Willmott (Oxford: Oxford University Press, 2011), 454–72; Michael Müller, 'Unitarism, Pluralism, and Human Resource Management in Germany', *Management International Review* 39, no. 3 (1999): 125–44.
5 W. Richard Scott and Gerald F. Davis, *Organizations and Organizing: Rational, Natural, and Open System Perspectives* (Abingdon, Oxon: Routledge, 2007).
6 David E. Guest, 'Human Resource Management and Industrial Relations', *Journal of Management Studies* 24, no. 5 (1987): 503–21; Müller, 'Unitarism, Pluralism, and Human Resource Management in Germany'.
7 Michael Armstrong, *Human Resource Management Practice*, 8th Edition (London: Kogan Page, 2001), 32.

8 Reid Bates, 'A Critical Analysis of Evaluation Practice: The Kirkpatrick Model and the Principle of Beneficence', *Evaluation and Program Planning* 27, no. 3 (2004): 341–47; Thomas N. Garavan and David McGuire, 'Human Resource Development and Society: Human Resource Development's Role in Embedding Corporate Social Responsibility, Sustainability, and Ethics in Organizations', *Advances in Developing Human Resources* 12, no. 5 (2010): 487–507; Kiran Trehan and Clare Rigg, 'Theorising Critical HRD: A Paradox of Intricacy and Discrepancy', *Journal of European Industrial Training* 35, no. 3 (2011): 276–90.
9 Jürgen Habermas, *The Theory of Communicative Action*, trans. Thomas McCarthy, vol. 2: Lifeworld and system: A critique of functionalist reason, 2 vols (London: Heinemann Educational Books, 1984).
10 Alexandre Ardichvili, 'The Role of HRD in CSR, Sustainability, and Ethics: A Relational Model', *Human Resource Development Review* 12, no. 4 (2013): 460.
11 Bates, 'A Critical Analysis of Evaluation Practice: The Kirkpatrick Model and the Principle of Beneficence'.
12 Ardichvili, 'The Role of HRD in CSR, Sustainability, and Ethics'; L. Bierema and M. D'Abundo, 'HRD with a Conscience: Practicing Socially Responsible HRD', *International Journal of Lifelong Education* 23, no. 5 (2004): 443–58; Tom L. Beauchamp and James F. Childress, *Principles of Biomedical Ethics* (Oxford: Oxford University Press, 2001); David McGuire, Christine Cross, and David O'Donnell, 'Why Humanistic Approaches in HRD Won't Work', *Human Resource Development Quarterly* 16, no. 1 (2005): 131–37; Garavan and McGuire, 'Human Resource Development and Society'.
13 Philip Mirowski, *Never Let a Serious Crisis Go to Waste: How Neoliberalism Survived the Financial Meltdown* (London: Verso Books, 2013), 59.
14 Trehan and Rigg, 'Theorising Critical HRD'; Russ Vince, 'The Future Practice of HRD', *Human Resource Development International* 6, no. 4 (2003): 559–63.
15 Elena Antonacopoulou, 'The Relationship between Individual and Organizational Learning: New Evidence from Managerial Learning Practices', *Management Learning* 37, no. 4 (2006): 455–73.
16 S. Turnbull and C. Elliott, 'Pedagogies of HRD: The Socio-Political Implications', in *Critical Thinking in Human Resource Development*, ed. C. Elliott and S. Turnbull (London: Routledge, 2005), 189–201.
17 Winfred Arthur Jr et al., 'Effectiveness of Training in Organizations: A Meta-Analysis of Design and Evaluation Features.', *Journal of Applied Psychology* 88, no. 2 (2003): 234; ATD, 'Needs Assessments: Design and Execution for Success' (Association for Talent Development, 2018); Jacqueline Reed and Maria Vakola, 'What Role Can a Training Needs Analysis Play in Organisational Change?', *Journal of Organizational Change Management* 19, no. 3 (2006): 393–407.
18 Eric A. Surface, 'Training Needs Assessment: Aligning Learning and Capability with Performance Requirements and Organizational Objectives', in *The Handbook of Work Analysis: The Methods, Systems, Applications and Science of Work Measurement in Organizations*, ed. Mark Alan Wilson et al. (London: Routledge, 2012), 437–62.
19 Elwood F. Holton III, 'Customer Service Is Not the Best Model for HRD Practice', *Human Resource Development Quarterly* 9, no. 3 (1998): 207; Elwood F. Holton III, 'On the Misapplication of Customer Service in HRD', *Human Resource Development Review* 2, no. 2 (2003): 103–5.
20 Nicholas Clarke, 'The Politics of Training Needs Analysis', *Journal of Workplace Learning* 15, no. 4 (2003): 141–53.
21 William McGehee and Paul W. Thayer, *Training in Business and Industry* (Chichester: John Wiley & Sons, 1961).
22 Peter Checkland, 'Soft Systems Methodology: A Thirty Year Retrospective', *Systems Research and Behavioral Science* 17 (2000): S28.
23 Scott D.N. Cook and John Seely Brown, 'Bridging Epistemologies: The Generative Dance between Organizational Knowledge and Organizational Knowing', *Organization Science* 10, no. 4 (1999): 387.
24 Coimbatore K. Prahalad and Gary Hamel, 'The Core Competence of the Corporation', *Harvard Business Review* 68, no. 3 (1990): 79–91.
25 Armstrong, *Human Resource Management Practice*, 301, 563.
26 Armstrong, 302.

27 David C. McClelland, 'Testing for Competence Rather than for "Intelligence"', *American Psychologist* 28, no. 1 (1973): 1.
28 Richard E. Boyatzis, 'Competencies in the 21st Century', *Journal of Management Development* 27, no. 1 (2008): 5–12.
29 Thomas W. Jackson, 'Applying Autopoiesis to Knowledge Management in Organisations', *Journal of Knowledge Management* 11, no. 3 (2007): 8.
30 Armstrong, *Human Resource Management Practice*, 148.
31 D.S. Ones and S. Dilchert, 'Employee Green Behaviors', in *Managing Human Resources for Environmental Sustainability*, ed. S.E. Jackson et al. (Chichester: John Wiley & Sons Ltd, 2012).
32 Thomas A. Norton et al., 'Employee Green Behavior: A Theoretical Framework, Multilevel Review, and Future Research Agenda', *Organization & Environment* 28, no. 1 (2015): 103–25.
33 United Nations, 'Transforming Our World: The 2030 Agenda for Sustainable Development' (New York: United Nations, 2015), 21, https://sdgs.un.org/2030agenda.
34 UNESCO, 'Issues and Trends in Education for Sustainable Development' (Paris: UNESCO, 2018).
35 J. Achterberg and D. Vriens, 'Managing Viable Knowledge', *Systems Research and Behavioral Science* 19, no. 3 (2002): 223–41; Jennifer Preece, 'Etiquette, Empathy and Trust in Communities of Practice: Stepping-Stones to Social Capital.', *Journal of Universal Computer Science* 10, no. 3 (2004): 294–302; Markus Schwaninger, 'Systemic Design for Sustainability', *Sustainability Science* 13, no. 5 (2018): 1225–34; Markus Schwaninger, 'Cyberstemic Education: Enabling Society for a Better Future', *Kybernetes* 48, no. 7 (2019): 1376–97.
36 G. Vickers, *The Art of Judgement: A Study of Policy-Making* (London: Harper & Row, 1983); P. B. Checkland and Alejandro Casar, 'Vickers' Concept of an Appreciative System: A Systemic Account', *Journal of Applied Systems Analysis* 13, no. 3 (1986): 3–17.

6 Developing a learning strategy 2
How people learn

6.1 What this chapter covers

Figure 6.1 outlines the structure of this chapter, which focuses on how learning happens. It starts by looking at different practical mechanisms for learning, in particular the distinction between formal and informal learning and related concepts, and then examines some ideas about learning from cognitive psychology and knowledge management studies. The chapter then continues by looking at factors which can affect the quality of what we are calling sustainability-focused learning (SFL).

6.2 Mechanisms for learning

6.2.1 Practical mechanisms for learning

There are many different mechanisms available to people learning within organisations, and as is often the case, these may be described in different ways. Before progressing, we need to look at what these different mechanisms may be and develop some consistent terminology.

Figure 6.2 is an attempt to show what these mechanisms are, but noting that distinctions between them are not necessarily clear-cut. One fundamental distinction is between formal and informal learning. Formal learning has been defined as learning which occurs within the boundaries of an activity explaining "canonical practice",[1] and as such is "... typically institutionally sponsored ... and highly structured".[2] Often described as training, this might be on- or off-the-job.

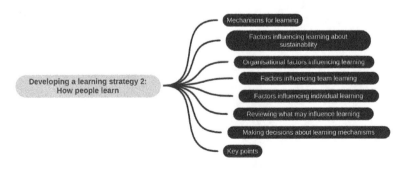

Figure 6.1 Map of Chapter 6.

DOI: 10.4324/9781003218296-7

Figure 6.2 Mechanisms for learning.

By way of contrast, informal learning can be characterised as integrated with daily routines, triggered by a specific incident, not highly conscious, influenced by chance, a process of reflection and action and linked to the learning of others.[3] However, this does not mean that just anything may be learnt: the scope of such learning is limited by the boundaries of everyday practice, for example, access to particular types of information will be more or less easy,[4] and organisational culture may define what is seen as legitimate to discuss.

Informal learning includes many possibilities. We have what may be called "incidental"[5] or accidental learning, which is the sort of knowledge sharing and reflective practice which might happen within teams or in chance conversations. Informal learning may also be more structured when individuals engage in workplace tasks where one specific desired outcome is learning. This category includes coaching and mentoring arrangements, organised reflective practice such as debriefings, and what are sometimes called "structured work extensions", which might include secondments, service learning, job shadowing, or taking part in specific projects. The effectiveness of these mechanisms depends on various factors: if the activities are temporary or short-term, or if the individuals are seen as outsiders in well-established teams, the opportunities for higher-order learning may be limited.

The third grouping in this informal learning categorisation includes individual and collective self-directed learning, which might occur where individuals or teams recognise a gap in their understanding of a situation and act autonomously to remedy this.

The term "workplace learning" is also sometimes used, but is ambiguous—is it formal learning conducted on-the-job or informal or incidental learning? This ambiguity highlights that it might be more useful to avoid seeing a clear distinction between formal and informal learning, and rather consider a spectrum of mechanisms.

> **Box 6.1**
>
> People often think 'I don't understand what I can do in my job about sustainability'. So what we are trying to do is to help people understand that they don't have to be doing big things about sustainability. There can just be an accumulation of lots of small things, so if they talk to other people, inspire them to do the same, it will make a difference along the line.
>
> Natalie Wilkinson, NG Bailey

As the quotation in Box 6.1 shows, the accumulation of small, everyday conversations and examples of sustainable behaviour can lead to big changes overall (in systems thinking terms, nonlinearity). Karl Weick wrote:

> The massive scale on which social problems are conceived often precludes innovative action because the limits of bounded rationality are exceeded and arousal is raised to dysfunctionally high levels. People often define social problems in ways that overwhelm their ability to do anything about them.[6]

"Small wins" can be more effective than major transformations because they do not arouse immediate fear or resistance, because people find they can make small changes without noticing them, because they are less likely to cause political reactions, and as Weick notes, small changes create an environment within which the big problem seems smaller and further positive changes more possible. Informal and incidental learning can create such small wins.

What is interesting to note about the distinction between formal and informal learning is that research has shown that people often think they only learn when taking part in formal training activities, and that developing new ways of doing things through everyday, on-the-job experience is not actually learning.[7] However, this may be changing as the practice of sharing and gathering knowledge through social media and looking for YouTube videos for specific information is increasingly normalised.

Note that Figure 6.2 also shows what I have called the "Environment for learning". This is the context within which all forms of learning seek to happen and is best described by the term "learning culture"—we will look at this in more detail in Section 6.4.2.

The 70:20:10 framework is one concept that has increased awareness about the importance of informal learning. The idea, which originated from research into learning about leadership[8] but has been widely extrapolated to other domains, proposes that 70% of workplace learning is through on-the-job experience, 20% through relationships and feedback and just 10% through formal training. Although the percentages and delineation of mechanisms for learning are not necessarily as clear as the snappy name suggests,[9] 70:20:10 has proved effective in raising consciousness in the learning and development practitioner community about the significance of informal learning.

Although popular in the corporate world, limited academic research has been done into its effectiveness. One study looking at how it was used in public service organisations in Australia criticised the distinction between "on-the-job experience" and

Developing a learning strategy: how to learn 169

"relationships", pointing out that all work experience involves relationships and hence social learning, and also noted that in the absence of some formalisation which integrated the three mechanisms, its effectiveness as a deliberate strategy could be limited.[10] The issue of formalising the informal is tricky—complexity theory and the edge of chaos concept reminds us of the importance of balancing the legitimate and shadow systems, so it is important that informal learning is not stifled or channelled in inappropriate specific directions. However, it is important that systems and structures for encouraging, integrating and institutionalising new knowledge and skills are enabled—clearly a field where Human Resource Development (HRD) has a major contribution to make.

6.2.2 Cognitive mechanisms of learning

In this section, we shall look at some ideas about learning which are particularly relevant to developing an SFL strategy.

As described previously, since the middle of the 20th century the idea of "training" has taken a central place in learning within organisations, and literature aimed at learning and development practitioners has been heavily influenced by cognitive psychology, in particular concepts such as behaviourism, constructivism, and experiential learning. How these are presented is often limited by an emphasis on the individual, and reliance on them means that, for example, we design training programmes around learning outcomes or objectives which include statements such as "At the end of this training programme the learner will be able to...". Such practices reinforce an idea that learning is for individuals and serve to obscure a reality that organisations are about people working together to achieve some common purpose. The emphasis on individual cognition means that social learning is a somewhat neglected field in the learning and development practitioner literature, so here we will also look at social and team learning in more detail.

Perhaps the most influential theory about individual learning in the HRD practitioner world is David Kolb's concept of the experiential learning cycle,[11] often represented by a diagram something like Figure 6.3.

We can start at any point in the cycle to explain the idea of experiential learning. Suppose we need to carry out a new procedure in our everyday work. We could start by just having a go (experience), after which we would reflect on what happened and then develop some sort of theoretical conceptualisation about what had happened and why. We would then plan how we might be able to perform the procedure more effectively

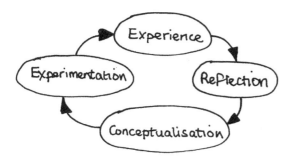

Figure 6.3 Kolb's experiential learning cycle.

or efficiently (experimentation). We can then repeat the experience, and through an ongoing cyclical experience start to become competent performers. A great strength of the experiential learning cycle is the way that it connects theory and practice, and so provides a useful way to develop an understanding of how praxis (theory-informed practice) is strengthened. As a result, the experiential learning cycle is referred to in many texts on learning in organisational settings. It has relevance in the design of formal learning interventions in that it encourages the integration of action into the learning design, and it is also relevant to thinking about how informal, ongoing and everyday learning works.

However, one of its limitations is its emphasis on the individual and a consequent implication that people do this alone. In reality, in an organisational setting away from formal, individualised training, people talk to each other about what they are doing, discuss problems and share information—all examples of shared reflection. This can be represented as in Figure 6.4.

Shared experiential learning opens up many more possibilities. For each individual learning becomes an open system, with participants now able to draw in energy (alternative reflections) from others, making it possible to avoid the otherwise inevitable increase in individual entropy which here would be manifested by running out of new ideas! After all, the amount of reflection that any one person can do on their own may be quite limited, and for one experience the experiential learning cycle could very quickly grind to a halt, whereas a shared, social reflection has the potential to open up many more different conceptualisations and experiments.

This idea of shared experiential learning may be seen as an example of social learning. Some caution is needed when using the term "social learning", because it can refer to either a process (how we have been using it here) or an outcome (what has been learnt in a social manner). The shift from individual to social learning also makes more outcomes possible. While individual learning emphasises cognitive outcomes, social learning introduces three other possibilities[12]:

- Normative outcomes occur when people change their values or worldviews.
- Relational outcomes are where learning has an impact on interrelationships, such as through improving understanding about how others think or value things, strengthening trust, or improving cooperation.
- Collective outcomes are where cognitive, normative and relational outcomes lead to collective action.

A thorough LNA should identify where these are desirable outcomes and recommend appropriate strategies.

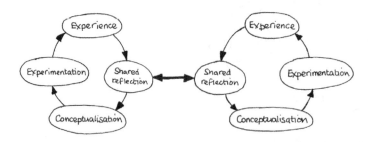

Figure 6.4 Shared experiential learning.

In our organisational setting, ideas about experiential and social learning feed into work on how groups, teams and even organisations learn. For example, in Figure 6.5 external pressure for sustainability forces organisational reflection, and this triggers a spiral dynamic of experiential learning as the pressure for and awareness of sustainability change.[13] Note the similarities between this process and that predicted by institutional theory in Chapter 4, Section 4.4.3, the dynamics of the European Corporate Sustainability Framework (ECSF) in Chapter 6, Section 6.4.1, and the individual levels of existence model in Chapter 6, Section 6.6.1.

We can now move on to look at some further ideas about mechanisms of team learning.[14] As a collection of individuals, learning happens inside the head of each member of the team, but this does not mean that team learning is a simple aggregation of what each person learns. Rather, we can see a team functioning as a system, where team members' interactions in sharing knowledge create an emergent property of new knowledge and behaviour shared by the team.[15] This is perhaps well explained by the idea of knowledge conversion[16] illustrated in Figure 6.6.

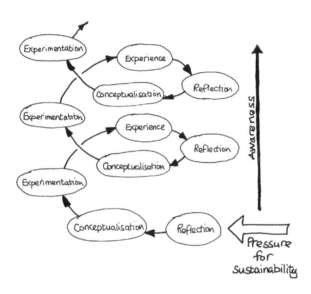

Figure 6.5 Experiential learning as a spiral of increasing awareness.

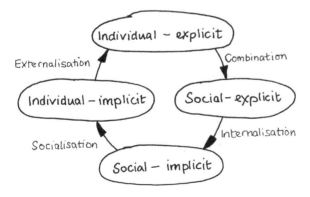

Figure 6.6 Knowledge conversion.

172 Developing a learning strategy: how to learn

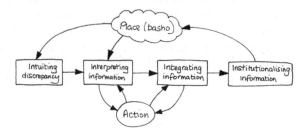

Figure 6.7 The 4I model with action and place.

We start with Individual–Implicit, the tacit knowledge that an individual has about a particular situation of interest. This understanding will have been acquired through prior socialisation and experience of possibly similar situations. When they enter into a conversation with someone else about this situation, they externalise this knowledge, sharing it with the other person and through discussion create new, combined "social-explicit" knowledge, which they can then internalise as being a socially implicit understanding of this situation (similar to Berger and Luckmann's social constructionism). This can create a constantly evolving cycle of knowledge creation.

An alternative explanation is the "4I" model (Figure 6.7).[17] In the core model, an individual or group of individuals "intuits" a discrepancy between what is happening and what should happen. This leads to a search for information about the situation which must be "interpreted" and then "integrated" in order to remove the discrepancy and achieve the desired outcome. Once proved successful, this new knowledge can be "institutionalised", a process which shows that individual learning has become true organisational learning.

We also need to consider action and place. Action reminds us of the importance of experiential learning, that as we interpret and integrate information by doing something, our understanding is enhanced. Place is important because, as Gestalt psychology tells us, discrepancies or inconsistencies in the world around us trigger discomfort, moving us to find ways to resolve these problems. So place informs the intuiting stage and initiates the whole process. It also has a place in interpreting information. Drawing on ideas from Japanese philosophy and the concept of *basho*, or place, Noam Cook and Hendrik Wagenaar write that:

> everything that exists does so in a particular location (a *basho*), and the social and physical history embodied in a given *basho* make possible and inform the activities that take place within it[18]

Place is also important because of the power that it generates. The French social theorist Michel Foucault talked about the idea of "disciplinary power",[19] the power that exists in any social situation created by the interaction of people who feel they may be being watched by others in the group. The particular configuration of place and team implicitly categorises some information as legitimate and others as not legitimate, so that team members will pay no attention to information that they think others will consider to be not legitimate. Box 6.2 shows how this may play out with the "not invented here" syndrome.

> **Box 6.2**
>
> We have all these people who are working on tough things. When I started my role, I thought that if in Ohio they have figured out how to do something the people in Iowa would want to know all about it. And they did, but I learned that sharing the news requires trust, and it would be like, 'Ohioans have figured out how to do what you were doing but way better, so maybe you should try doing what Ohio is doing'. But it turned out that people don't really like to be told that. It's not great news that we've been doing it wrong and there's a better way.
>
> Gail Francis, RE-AMP

Finally, the new knowledge is integrated back in the place, from where it can serve to inform future knowledge creation. This model provides valuable insights into both formal and informal learning. For formal learning interventions, it shows the structural weaknesses of training carried out "off the job" where place plays no part, so that transferring the new knowledge or skill to the *basho* may be harder. For informal learning, it highlights the value of it happening in a workplace context and explains some of the problems inherent in a "working from home" culture (at least, from the perspective of the organisation).

These models also assume that knowledge is created to fill a vacuum, but in practice, there is always some previous understanding which the new knowledge may challenge. Existing practices may therefore need to be "unlearnt",[20] and this may be problematic if new knowledge seems to challenge existing legitimate knowledge. Creating new knowledge and unlearning may therefore challenge existing power and control structures and encounter resistance.[21]

6.3 Factors influencing learning about sustainability

Much research about the effectiveness of learning within organisations is based on unitarist assumptions and assumes that the problem of aligning learner behaviours with required competences is largely technical. However, the value-based nature of sustainability means that it is important to consider a range of other factors which may have an impact.

Figure 6.8 is an influence diagram illustrating the interconnectedness of various factors. Difficulties caused by the contested nature of sustainability have been identified earlier (Section 5.9), so in this chapter, we will focus on the other three levels.

The contested nature and moral implications of sustainability have an influence on organisational and learning cultures, and also bear on individual social identities. In turn, organisational culture influences what is seen as relevant to the subject of sustainability. The sections that follow explore these factors and their interrelationships in more detail.

The diagram has also been drawn with the factors within loosely defined clouds to carry across the idea that these factors are not clearly defined or limited. You might therefore note that this system of interest has the characteristics of a wicked problem (Section 2.9), where, amongst other things, issues are not well defined, they are interconnected, and changes in one affect the whole system. There is also no finite set of

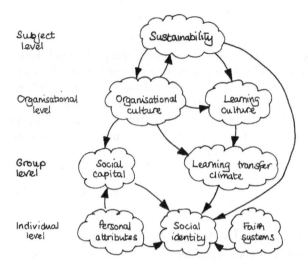

Figure 6.8 Factors influencing learning about sustainability.

clear right and wrong actions to take: all we can do is to try and make the situation better. We must therefore accept the reality that our SFL strategy will be a best guess and will need to be constantly reviewed and updated as time and circumstances develop.

6.4 Organisational factors influencing learning

6.4.1 Organisational culture

Perhaps the most fundamental factor at the organisational level which will have an influence on how effective SFL may be is the general level of openness of the organisation to the concept of sustainability, however this is understood. What this relationship is will be strongly influenced by what may be called organisational culture.

What do we mean by culture? Geert Hofstede defines culture as "collective programming of the mind that distinguishes the members of one group or category of people from others".[22] Again we may think back to the social constructionism of Berger and Luckmann (Section 2.5), that as we grow from infancy we observe the world around us and learn how things work and how we need to behave in order to become accepted. Culture is a manifestation of this aspect of learning.

Edgar Schein, one of the most influential writers on organisational culture, suggested that culture may be seen through three levels (shown in Figure 6.9).[23] The most visible level is that of artefacts, physical manifestations. For example, the football club Forest Green Rovers makes its environmental sustainability culture visible by being certified as the only carbon-neutral football club in the world, through only selling vegan food at its ground, and by plans to build an all-wood stadium.

The next level is of beliefs and values at different levels of visibility. For example, at a high level, an organisation invests resources in running a management development programme, believing that training programmes of this sort are effective in strengthening managerial skills. At a deeper level, there will be beliefs and values about such things as trustworthiness, respect, fairness and citizenship. As with Chris Argyris' concept of

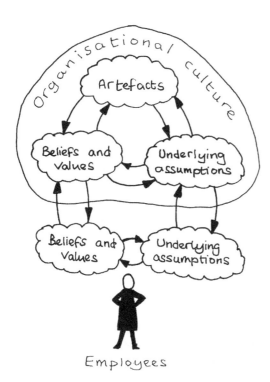

Figure 6.9 Elements of organisational culture and employee significance.

espoused theories and theories-in-use, the beliefs and values at an organisation espouse may not be consonant with what it does in practice. An organisation may espouse a belief that it is a good employer while maintaining discriminatory employment practices, or it may have an environmental sustainability policy while sending senior executives on long-haul flights for two-hour meetings. Beliefs and values also trigger what people see as significant in the world around them (their *basho*). Intuiting a discrepancy in the world around them is Crossan's first step in the 4I model, so from this perspective, anything which resonates, positively or negatively, with an individual's beliefs and values is potentially more likely to trigger the cycle of learning.

As people routinely draw on existing beliefs and values, they acquire the status of taken for granted, underlying basic assumptions, Schein's third level. As Berger and Luckmann suggest, anyone challenging such an assumption may cause high levels of anxiety amongst others or be dismissed as ignorant. Questioning basic assumptions within an organisation is very difficult and restricts learning to the single loop level.

The three levels are closely interrelated. As Schein noted, the "founders" of a group or organisation bring with them their assumptions, beliefs and values, and these lead to the initial creation of the group's artefacts. As time goes by, and the group expands, new employees will accept to a greater or lesser extent the beliefs and values of the existing group and may or may not become aware of underlying assumptions. However, they also bring their own beliefs and values which will in various ways contribute to those within the organisation. Through these dynamics the culture of the organisation may evolve as time goes by.

Every organisation develops its own, unique culture, but within an organisation it is not necessarily the same everywhere—particular divisions, groups or teams may have their own subcultures that exist in greater or less tension with the overall culture of the organisation.

Organisational culture manifests itself in different ways, such as in organisational identity, its conception of morality, and attitude to learning—we will look at the first two here, and at attitudes to learning in Section 6.4.2.

Organisational identity may be seen as how people within the organisation perceive, feel and think about where they work, and as such is a characteristic derived from the beliefs, values and assumptions which form the organisational culture.[24] Identity is an important organisational characteristic in the context of sustainability because it serves to legitimate the organisation in its operational landscape and provides a secure reference point for its employees. However, individuals also have an identity, and as we see in Section 6.6.2, there is the potential for conflict to occur as a result of a mismatch between organisational and individual identity.

Culture may also be seen in the organisation's moral compass, perceived in the ethical climate which defines ethical or unethical behaviour.[25] A multi-pronged approach to strengthening the ethical climate regarding sustainability will probably be needed to make it more likely that relevant ethical behaviour will be maintained.[26] A fundamental requirement is a clear definition of what the organisation's ethical values are, and this will need to be addressed by some form of formal training (how this may best be done is explored in more detail in Chapter 7). This would be necessary but not sufficient, and needs to be supported by policies and processes which, as far as is possible, ensure ethical behaviour. The third requirement is leadership which demonstrates, communicates and reinforces ethical behaviour.

The ethical culture of an organisation depends on the framework of values which are dominant within the organisation, and this exploration of values was at the heart of the grandly titled ECSF, developed as part of an EU research project in the early 2000s.[27] It took as a starting point a framework of individual values developed by the American psychologist Clare Graves,[28] looked at more closely in Section 6.6.1. The key idea underpinning the Graves framework and the ECSF is that individuals adopt a set of values which enables them to exist in harmony with their world. As conditions in this world change, an individual may realise that they need to adopt a new set of values in order to maintain a harmonious existence (a process similar to experiential learning). This may result in a trajectory upwards from a starting point of individual survival and domination-related values towards the highest level where their values are about interdependence and collectivity. Of course, what goes up may come down, and it is also possible for values to regress if external conditions create that pressure.

The ECSF recognises that, as shown in Figure 6.9, an organisational value framework is a dynamic relationship involving the interaction of individual employee values and the organisation's historical development of its own value framework. The ECSF proposed that six levels could be seen in an organisation's value framework (Figure 6.10).

How are the six levels seen in an organisational context?

- Energy and power—powerful, dominant leadership, impulsive and egocentric behaviour.

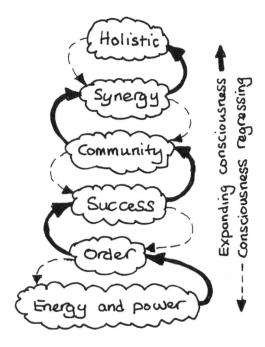

Figure 6.10 The European Corporate Sustainability Framework.

- Order—reliance on rules and regulations, obedience to rightful authority.
- Success—competition and result-driven, means serve the end, pragmatic.
- Community—tolerance, acceptance of difference, consensus and mutual growth.
- Synergy—self-development and environmental concern, learning and application of learning important, organisational structure flexible and relevant to the situation.
- Holistic—a broader view of working and living, recognising the unity of social and natural environmental issues, altruism.

Time for reflection

Think about this discussion of organisational culture. How does your organisational culture integrate social and environmental sustainability?

What are the artefacts which show that the organisation cares about sustainability?

What beliefs and values does it espouse which show its commitment to sustainability?

Where do you think your organisation sits within the ECSF? Particularly important, what are the underlying assumptions which drive the way the organisation functions and operates in the world?

6.4.2 Learning culture

The organisation's attitude to learning is another aspect of organisational culture. We might think about what a learning culture is using Schein's three levels:

- At an artefactual level there are such things as learning and development policies, training catalogues and learning management systems.
- At the beliefs and values level, there is the importance attached to learning as an essential strategy to ensure an organisation adapts to its operational environment.
- At the underlying assumptions level are those factors which constrain how learning is supported (for example, learning is about training) or implemented (learning is always a solution to a performance problem).

Subcultures are again important: attitudes to learning may be inconsistent across an organisation, with some divisions, departments or groups being more or less open to learning opportunities.

Schein offers a list of ten requirements[29] for a learning culture:

- A proactive approach to problem-solving, and confidence that this will lead to learning.
- There needs to be a commitment to "learning to learn", in terms of both how internal relationships may need to change and what the external environment demands.
- Leaders must have a positive attitude about their people, believing that they will learn if given opportunities and the psychological safety to try things out. This is arguably the most important of these requirements.
- A belief that challenges and difficulties that the organisation faces can be overcome or managed in some way.
- There must be a commitment to enquiry and dialogue that enables a mutual understanding of different perspectives.
- People must think about the future, far enough ahead to be able to think through systemic consequences of action, and near enough to be able to assess what is happening.
- There must be a commitment to open communication across the organisation.
- The organisation must embrace and utilise cultural diversity.
- People must be able to think systemically, abandoning simple linear causal logic and recognising the inherent complexity and nonlinearity of the world.
- There must be an ongoing reflection on the organisation's cultural practices in order to become aware of how change happens.

Such a learning culture may be seen in the concept of the "learning organisation", a term popularised by Peter Senge in his influential 1990 book *The Fifth Discipline*. According to Senge, this is an organisation:

> ... where people continually expand their capacity to create the results they truly desire, where new and expansive patterns of thinking are nurtured, where collective aspiration is set free, and where people are continually learning how to learn together.[30]

Senge proposed that five "disciplines" are needed within a learning organisation. The first four are personal mastery, mental models of how the world around an individual works, a shared vision of what the organisation stands for, and team learning, using dialogue and discussion to explore complex issues in order to create innovative, coordinated action. The fifth discipline is systems thinking (in Senge's presentation, system dynamics), which is a discipline for seeing wholes, a framework for looking at interrelationships rather than things and for observing patterns of change rather than snapshots.

One of the problems with the learning organisation concept is understanding just what one may look like, and you may wonder whether your own organisation can think of itself as one. As a way of providing some guidance, Victoria Marsick and Karen Watkins developed the Dimensions of the Learning Organization Questionnaire (DLOQ),[31] a tool for measuring the parameters which might indicate that an organisation is a learning organisation. This is based around nine constructs:

- Continuous learning opportunities, is learning designed into work, and are there opportunities for ongoing learning?
- Are enquiry and dialogue promoted?
- Are collaboration and team learning encouraged through work design and reward systems?
- Are systems in place to capture and share learning?
- Are people empowered, in terms of participation in establishing visions and in the ability to make decisions?
- Can people see how their work has an impact on the wider organisation, the external operational environment and communities within which they work?
- Is learning supported by leadership?
- Are the organisation's products and services enhanced by learning?

You will notice some clear parallels with Schein's principles above, notably the centrality of learning in everyday practice, the need for supportive leadership to encourage learning, and the ability to think systemically.

Creating the learning culture that is an essential requirement for a learning organisation is challenging. These constructs imply a pluralist approach to learning, and underlying assumptions in the organisational culture may be strongly unitarist. Learning is essentially about change, and many organisations resist this for a variety of reasons. At the workgroup level, change may threaten long-established status and power dynamics. The trend in many organisations towards remote working, part-time or short-term contract employment patterns makes it much harder to develop the continuity and commitment central to the learning organisation concept. Progress through the educational system inculcates an idea that learning is about individualism and the acquisition of certificates and qualifications, which can militate against the idea that learning is also about social engagement and participation in some form of learning community.[32]

The HRD function within an organisation must play a central part in promoting a strong learning culture. The fundamental importance of informal learning must be explicitly acknowledged in learning and development policies, along with a commitment to providing appropriate formal learning opportunities. Opportunities for learning need to be emphasised in performance management systems. HRD staff need to work closely with line management to provide advice on facilitating learning, and they need to develop the skills and confidence to support what may seem to be radical approaches to learning, such as transformative learning, action learning, critical thinking and systems thinking. This may all prove challenging—as discussed previously, the pressure of concepts such as SHRM has pushed HRD in a performative direction, arguably at the expense of more holistic conceptions of learning and development.

180 *Developing a learning strategy: how to learn*

Time for reflection

How do you see your learning culture? Take a look back at Schein's 10 requirements and the DLOQ questions, and evaluate your own organisation against these suggestions.

How does your learning culture align with the learning space triangle (Figure 5.4)?

How well do you come out of this activity?

What are things that you can do to address any shortcomings, now, quickly, or in the longer term?

6.5 Factors influencing team learning

6.5.1 Social capital

I mentioned earlier how much of the discussion around learning within organisations focuses on the individual and that this tends to underplay the importance of social learning. Social learning requires interrelationships between people, and the quality of these is usefully explored by the concept of social capital, described by one of the most influential writers on the subject, the American political scientist Robert Putnam, as "features of social organisation such as networks, norms and social trust that facilitate coordination and cooperation for mutual benefit".[33] It is characterised by trusting relationships between members of a community which can facilitate mutual support and collaboration.

In the context of social capital, interrelationships are often referred to as "ties". There are different types of tie, and they may be weak or strong. Consider Figure 6.11. Here

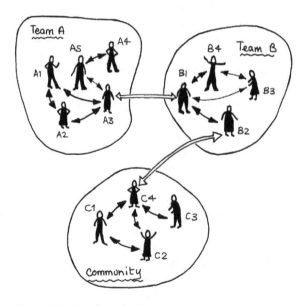

Figure 6.11 Bonding, bridging and bracing ties.

we have two teams within an organisation, and an external, community association. Looking at Team A, its members are connected by "bonding" ties. Ties can vary in strength (shown here by the thickness of the connecting lines), the strength being an emergent property determined by factors such as how long people have known each other, the strength of their emotional connection, levels of trust, how much they confide in each other and what services they offer each other.[34]

We can also see in Figure 6.11 that person A3 seems to be much better connected than other members of the team—they would be what is known as a "hub". We probably all know such people in our organisations who seem to know everything that is going on. There are many reasons why this may happen—experience, seniority, personality and others.

A3 is also connected to B1 in Team B: this is a "bridging" tie, as this connects two separate groups of people. Typically, but not necessarily, bridging ties are weaker because of the less intense contact between the individuals. People such as A3 and B1 are also sometimes known as "boundary spanners", and it is important to remember that they are not necessarily people who are well connected within their own group: a certain detachment from the group may make it easier for them to operate as a boundary spanner.[35]

Thirdly, we note the connection between B5 and C4, the latter being a member of an external, community association. Although we might classify this as a bridging tie, it may alternatively be called a "bracing" tie, as rather than working horizontally within the organisation, it provides a vertical, external connection, and so might be regarded as a form of "social scaffolding", connecting the organisation to its external environment.[36]

Ties clearly represent a potential conduit for exchanging information and sharing knowledge within and across a group. They strengthen a sense of identity within and solidarity across a group, and this can bring more material benefits such as better opportunities for promotion and people you can call on for favours. Being a hub with access to multiple sources of information can increase your influence within a group.

However, there are potential problems. The amount of information flowing through a highly connected network may overwhelm the ability of individuals to make use of it effectively,[37] and the identity engendered by a group's social capital may serve to delegitimise some potentially valuable information, particularly if it is seen as coming from outside the group (as with "groupthink"). This can have a negative impact on innovation, and it is therefore important to remember the potential "strength of weak ties",[38] bridging or bracing ties connecting separate groups: these are often important as sources of different information or perspectives.

As key conduits for information, hubs have a critical role and while they can facilitate information transfer, they may also reduce or prevent it, perhaps through being overloaded but also possibly because it serves their purpose to keep certain information to themselves.[39] Well-connected groups may also have "free riders" who take advantage of other people's activities.[40]

The relative significance of strong or weak, bonding, bridging or bracing ties will depend on the particular context: for example, organisational control mechanisms may influence how well information can be shared and used[41]; well-defined activities which are specific to a particular group will mean a greater emphasis on bonding ties, whereas if there is uncertainty and new knowledge is needed (as with exploration strategies) bridging and bracing may become more relevant.[42]

As with the earlier discussion about the mechanisms of knowledge creation, these ideas about bonding, bridging and bracing ties overlook the messy realities of everyday

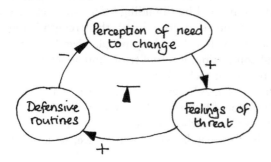

Figure 6.12 Defensive routines minimising the need to change.

life, issues which can be neatly subsumed under the heading of group dynamics. When people in the workplace first come together, they do not immediately start to function as a team—it takes time for them to work through the forming, storming and norming stages,[43] and the quality of team learning will vary dramatically through this process.

The role of trust in developing social capital is complex. It would seem that a lack of trust within a group impedes information sharing, but increasing levels of trust does not necessarily mean that more information will be shared.[44] Also, a certain amount of trust is needed in order to create a feeling of psychological safety,[45] which can open up the possibility for sharing potentially controversial information or trying to do something in a different way. Thinking about double loop learning, social dynamics within a team will be threatened if new ideas challenge existing norms, and there will be resistance unless the team is able to deal with the emotional consequences. Figure 6.12 illustrates how these defensive routines, manifested by such actions as denial or avoidance, may minimise the need to make any changes.[46]

Trust is an emotional connection between people, but in many organisations open discussion of emotions is seen as difficult, and this will limit the quality of communication, making it more likely that people will blame each other if things go wrong and people become cautious about trying anything new. Trust evaporates. Box 6.3 provides a vivid example of how important it is to understand how human emotions can stand in the way of learning.

Box 6.3

This was a highly educated group of folks and I would ask them what was the best way for you to learn? They would say, we want reports. So I would write reports and nobody read them. They would say that report is about another state, it's not relevant. Why was it so hard to get these highly educated people to learn? They were the most learning resistant group of people I had met, and I thought it was because they thought they already knew everything. But basically I hadn't built the trust, I hadn't taken the time to understand people and how I could help them engage. Fast forward 10 years, and I do everything totally different now.

Gail Francis, RE-AMP

Informal learning about the beliefs and values relevant to social and environmental sustainability is more likely to happen throughout the organisation if the organisational culture allows a high level of social capital. It is therefore useful to understand something about this in your organisation so that you can reflect about the likely effectiveness of informal learning.

Time for reflection

How would you assess the level of social capital in your organisation?

How could you use it to encourage more informal learning about sustainability?

Think particularly about ideas such as hubs (who might be useful for spreading the message) and bracing ties (for introducing external thinking).

6.5.2 Learning transfer climate

One factor that is particularly significant when thinking about learning from formal settings (for example, from training) is that of what is often known as "learning transfer". This refers to the way in which knowledge and skills from outside sources which are imparted in a formal learning activity are utilised in the real world of the workplace. This is seen as having two components: generalisation, where the knowledge and skills are generalised from the training activity into the workplace; and maintenance, where they continue to be used as time passes.[47]

The extensive research into learning transfer indicates that, broadly speaking, there are three main factors which influence how well generalisation and maintenance will take place: the quality of the training design, in terms of what mechanisms and pedagogic principles were deployed; the characteristics of the individuals undergoing training; and the environmental variables in the workplace. The significance of mechanisms and pedagogy are explored in the preceding and following chapters, and the relationship between individual variables and learning is covered in more detail in Section 6.6. In this section we will examine the significance of environmental variables, a factor often known as the "learning transfer climate".

A key factor in determining the quality of the learning transfer climate is the prevailing learning culture, as discussed previously. However, what seems to be of greatest significance is the culture prevalent in the particular department or other group setting where a learner needs to apply their new knowledge or skill, rather than any overarching organisation-wide learning culture.[48] At this level the learning culture is heavily influenced by leadership variables, such as quality of supervision and the degree to which supervisors allow or encourage people in their team to implement new skills or adopt different attitudes.[49] It is useful to remember the importance of nonlinearity in a system, that a small change can have a big effect: a supervisor or manager making a chance, negative comment about such things as new initiatives or a training programme can destroy people's positivity about them. Blame should not be put solely on supervisors' shoulders: peer group pressure may make it difficult for an individual to behave differently, a variable related to the social capital within the work group, and the (de) legitimation of certain behaviours or knowledge. This may be seen as an example of Foucault's disciplinary power in action.

Another significant factor is the immediate practical relevance of the new knowledge and skill—if an individual does not have the chance to apply what they have learnt it will seem less important and they will quickly forget. This is supported by the classic 19th-century research into forgetting by Ebbinghaus as well as more contemporary work.[50]

Time for reflection

What do you think the transfer climate will be for learning about sustainability in your organisation?

Do you think it will be receptive, questioning or rejecting?

How might it vary across different parts of the organisation?

What implications might that have for an SFL strategy, in terms of what learning mechanisms and principles you might need to employ?

6.6 Factors influencing individual learning

6.6.1 Individual characteristics

There is an extensive body of research looking at how an individual's specific characteristics may affect how much they learn from formal training activities.[51] This suggests that key variables are such things as cognitive ability and confidence in applying learning, but other factors such as age and personality type also seem to be significant.

These factors are givens, and when you are doing an LNA, it is important information to inform the design and implementation of a learning strategy. Within the learning process itself, techniques can be used to improve motivation, such as activities which develop individuals' self-efficacy, help them believe that the new knowledge and skills will be of value to them and the organisation, or that more senior managers encourage the learning, for example. These factors are also related to the variables of social capital and learning transfer climate discussed in previous sections.

Less research is available about individual characteristics and attitudes to sustainability, although more work has looked at environmental sustainability. Looking first at demographic characteristics, research into age and environmental concern provides a mixed picture. While it would seem that older workers practice more conserving and avoiding harm behaviours, younger workers are often better educated and more aware about environmental and social issues and as a result, show stronger pro-environmental attitudes. Age provides more opportunity for relevant life experiences, and people who have had more experience of outdoor life can have significantly stronger pro-environmental attitudes.[52]

Studies looking at the implications of gender and sustainability point towards a generally higher level of both environmental and social sustainability concerns among women, as might be expected from broader theories about gender and socialisation.[53] Interestingly, how such concerns are manifested seems to vary between men and women, with men engaging in more overt, public expressions of pro-environmental behaviour while women engage in less visible, private activities in terms of informing others and education about sustainability.[54]

Individual value frameworks are also important, as we saw when looking at the development of the ECSF (Section 6.4.1), which was based on the "levels of existence" model developed by Clare Graves (Figure 6.13).[55] Graves proposed that human behaviour is driven by values which we maintain because they seem to be appropriate in helping us to deal with the world within which we live, our conditions of existence. These value systems are not fixed, and as the conditions of existence change (for example, the organisational culture regarding sustainability or the social or environmental conditions in our community), then we feel the need to revise our personal set of values to one which is more appropriate to the new situation, so that we evolve "by saccadic, quantum-like jumps from one steady-state system to another".[56] Graves identified eight stages of evolution, from "Automatic", where awareness is limited to that which is needed to satisfy basic needs, through to the "Experientialistic", where all material needs are satisfied and we may value such things as reverence, humility, unity and poetic perceptions of reality. During this journey of expanding our consciousness, we would have to pass through Subsistence Level 6, the sociocentric stage, and this is perhaps the point at which we begin to be able to value social and environmental sustainability. At this level, we become concerned with our relationship with life and the total universe.

Graves' model has been picked up and developed by others, as by Laloux with the concept of the "teal organisation" (Section 4.6.2). Abigail Lynam suggests that as an

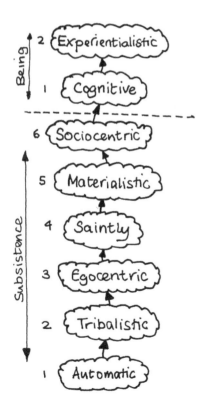

Figure 6.13 The Graves levels of existence model.

individual's consciousness develops they expand their worldview, bringing a wider perspective on their identity and relationship with the complexities of life around them. Their levels of prejudice and judgement decrease, and they become more comfortable at dealing with the uncertainty and ambiguity of the wicked problem of sustainability.[57]

A common theme across these models is that the journey of expanding consciousness is not something that we can do alone, but that we need help in recognising where we are and what our potentialities can be. It is also important to recognise the dialectic between the individual and the world in which they live. The process of expanding our individual consciousness depends on how we perceive the environment within which we live, so moving to a higher level is easier if that environment welcomes that correspondingly higher set of values. Encouraging people to adopt a more sustainability-related value framework through a learning strategy is therefore less about making people conscious of the need to make changes than through developing an organisational culture which embraces sustainability and a learning culture which makes such a change easier.

6.6.2 Social identity

The values that an individual holds are fundamental in defining their self-concept, or sense of identity as a person. Identity will therefore have an effect on how receptive people are to SFL and values that it implies. So let us look in more detail at what "identity" means.

Each person's self-concept comes from two sources, a personal identity which is derived from such things as their gender, age and physical characteristics, and their "social identity", which comes from characteristics of the social settings within which they are located.[58] As an individual becomes more aware of the salient features of their social setting, their social identity evolves so that they increasingly identify with others in that group, and see themselves as distinct from those who are not within it.[59] This is a process which has increasingly attracted media attention as people spend more time engaged with social media rather than through physical meetings, and hence find themselves located within a virtual bubble of like-minded people. Such virtual groupings may be seen as an example of a psychological in-group, where people develop a social identity through their life experience—other examples are being a member of a profession, as a parent, or, as in the author's life, a supporter of Sheffield Wednesday Football Club. There are also physical groupings which create a social identity, such as those which would be created for people who work within the same organisation or part of an organisation. Within any particular social identity, individuals will understand what behaviour and knowledge are legitimate and feel the effects of Foucault's disciplinary power, which will constrain their ability to display characteristics of alternative identities.

Of course, people's lives are complex, and they play a role in many different groups. This means that they will generally have multiple social identities, and the importance at any specific time attached to each identity will depend on their immediate context and salience. In the context of organisational life, this means that everyone will have social identities as an employee (where they are expected to align their interests with those of the organisation) and as a member of a societal environment (which will strongly influence the shape of the individual's lifeworld (see Chapter 5, Section 5.3.2)). This is illustrated in Figure 6.14.

This complexity is often not recognised in unitarist organisational theory: indeed, in Weber's rational systems conception of the bureaucracy, role holders are assumed to have no external social identity. In the open systems perspective on organisations that

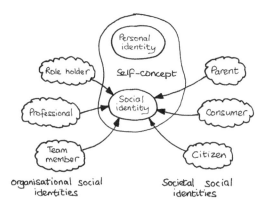

Figure 6.14 Multiple identities of an individual.

we are following here, these "societal social identities" may have a profound impact on how the organisation does or should interact with its operational environment, and we therefore need to pay careful attention to the social identity concept in thinking about how learning about sustainability may happen.

We can see the relevance of this in situations where, for example, someone works in a factory whose effluent pollutes local water supplies or air quality, or someone with concerns about greenhouse gas emissions has a job which requires extensive flying. Situations like this can create an "identity conflict", which can contribute to psychological discomfort resulting from the inherent cognitive dissonance.[60] If this happens, people can try to minimise the resulting stress in different ways, such as through minimising or denying one identity at the expense of another, pleading helplessness, suppressing one identity completely, alternating between different social identities or, if possible, by renegotiating the demands of one identity. An example of this latter strategy may be seen in the 2018 revolt at Google previously mentioned.

This also suggests that using formal learning activities to develop new organisational social identities as an organisation adopts a sustainability strategy may be problematic if people see this as conflicting with their societal social identities which do not have compatible value frameworks. In the absence of a thorough LNA top-down learning strategies can often fail to take this obstacle to learning into consideration.[61] On the other hand, encouraging a more social, informal learning culture may allow for the gradual development of a new group with a social identity whose values are more accepting of sustainability.[62]

Time for reflection

What are your thoughts about the social identities of people in your organisation?

How disparate might these be?

How open to ideas about social and environmental sustainability might people be?

6.6.3 Faith systems

The importance of taking individual value frameworks into consideration leads us into considering a major influence on values for many people around the world, what I shall call faith systems. I use this term rather than the word "religion", which is more commonly used in Western writing on the subject because it can be argued that the term "religion" is a relatively recent construct closely related to modern Protestant Christianity. As Karen Armstrong, an influential writer on the subject of faith, puts it, religion is:

> a coherent system of obligatory beliefs, institutions and rituals, centring on a supernatural God, whose practice is essentially private and hermetically sealed off from all 'secular' activities.[63]

On the other hand, as Armstrong continues, followers of other faith systems see their beliefs as vaguer and more encompassing, representing the totality of human existence captured in words such as the Arabic *din* and the Hindu and Buddhist *dharma*.

The following looks at how a number of important faith systems around the world view sustainability.

6.6.3.1 Daoism

Daoism (in older texts known as Taoism) is one of the main faith systems followed in China, other significant ones being Confucianism and Buddhism. Although Daoism has distinct characteristics, everyday reality throughout China is that these faith systems tend to become interwoven with both each other and local religious practices. Daoism has attracted interest from scholars interested in how it relates to an environmental ethic, but much writing centres around the challenges of interpreting concepts from canonical texts, in particular the *Dao-de jing*, written by (the possibly legendary) Lao-tzu in the 6th century BCE.

The core concept is *dao*, which translates simply as "the way", and which may be variously understood as the "shared context within which all things exist"[64] or as the order of the universe.[65] Many scholars understand Daoism to see humanity as part of nature, and so to be subject to its order. This may be seen in traditional Daoist art which shows the internal human body as comprising mountains, trees, rivers and other elements from the natural world.[66] Existing as part of nature, the correct way to behave is through practising *wu wei*, another concept open to many translations, but which from an environmental ethics perspective may be most usefully understood as doing things which are in accordance with nature.[67] This, of course, raises questions about how nature itself behaves, a difficulty which may be resolved by seeing *dao* as an abstraction, as a tool to help one visualise what action should be taken in order to achieve the best possible outcome within an environment which includes all of nature. The Daoist environmental ethic then suggests that humanity should act in a way which leads to a "... maximally coherent and superlative state of affairs",[68] a philosophy which proposes that the best way forward is not necessarily something that is ideal for everyone and everything concerned, but that which is the best possible compromise.

6.6.3.2 Buddhism

It can be hard to see a connection between Buddhism and an environmental sustainability ethic. There are several reasons why this is the case. Firstly, Buddhism is fundamentally a faith system about the individual, and there is little in its canonical texts about how followers should relate to the natural environment.[69] Secondly, people who have written most explicitly about the natural environment and Buddhism are often American rather than from the Asian heartland of Buddhism, which has led to their being open to charges of cultural appropriation,[70] and that they are selective about important aspects of Buddhism and have blended Buddhism with a "New Age religiosity".[71]

The core idea in Buddhism is that the individual is caught in an endless cycle of suffering and rebirth (*samsara*), but that there are things that can be done in order to break out of *samsara* and achieve enlightenment. A key concept is "emptiness", that while there is a real world out there, that what it actually is is a function of our relationship to it. Until we can come to accept that this external world is actually meaningless we will be attached to it, and this is the basis of our suffering. We can achieve this acceptance through "experiential knowing" of our own lives through techniques such as mindfulness and meditation.

The problem that this philosophy presents as regards an environmental ethic is that if the natural world is empty in this sense, it has no purpose and we cannot attach any importance to it. This does seem to present a major stumbling block to ecological Buddhism, but an alternative argument is presented by considering the personal qualities developed in someone who is following Buddhist principles as a way of easing their suffering. Such a person would display compassion to all other sentient beings who are travelling through *samsara* and would display humility as they seek to destroy feelings of pride about their attachments in the world. Through mindfulness they would be alert and aware about the world around them and would display a caring and attentive manner. This creates what may be seen as a *de facto* environmental ethic, one which is not created by the inherent purpose of Buddhism, but which works through predisposing a follower to environmentally sustainable behaviours.[72]

The concept of the *bodhisattva* in Mahayana Buddhism is also of interest if we view escaping suffering as a contribution to social sustainability. The *bodhisattva* is an individual who has worked towards enlightenment and the possibility of escaping *samsara*, but who then dedicates their existence to working for the enlightenment of all sentient beings.

6.6.3.3 Hinduism

At first sight, Hinduism would seem to be a religion highly attuned with environmental sustainability. Its canonical texts, such as the *Rig Veda* and the *Bhagavad Gita*, make constant references to the sacred nature of mountains and rivers, and to the importance of respecting the natural world. A central principle (as in a number of other Eastern faith systems) is *dharma*, a concept describing the importance of behaviours and duties which are needed in order to maintain cosmic order and balance. These canonical texts contain numerous explanations about how *dharma* includes respect for ecological order.

Karma is another concept within Hinduism that is central to other faith systems, such as Buddhism and Jainism. Within *karma* theory, all matter on the Earth is composed of souls trapped in the cycle of *samsara*. *Karma* accumulates during each cycle as the individual does what they do, and positive *karma* accrues if they follow the principle of non-harming (*ahimsa*). Although some writers on *karma* see it as being fatalistic and deterministic, many others stress the importance of free will: that while *karma* predisposes an individual to behave in a certain way, they can, if they wish, change and strengthen their practice of *ahimsa* to the natural world.[73] One way this can happen is through the practice of yoga, where concentration on the experience of bodily sensations strengthens awareness of our relationship with the physical world.

Despite the centrality of these ideas within Hindu thought, India suffers greatly from environmental degradation. Seemingly paradoxical, its most sacred river, the Ganges, is one of the most polluted waterways in the world. Vijaya Nagarajan suggests that this may be difficult to understand from a Western perspective of environmental sustainability but not necessarily from a Hindu worldview, where the sacrality of the river means that it is "… a divine being and therefore capable of cleaning herself…. The goddess transforms dirt, pollution, and sin to pure, clean and fresh natural substances".[74] Of course, as a Hindu faith system was emerging a long time ago, the population was much smaller, waste would have been organic and biodegradable, and rivers would indeed have seemed to possess a magical ability to eliminate impurity.

Although Hinduism creates what Nagarajan calls an "embodied ecology", she also suggests that the respect for sacrality may be intermittent, and that many rituals performed to respect the natural environment are apologetic, performed when sacrality needs to be overlooked. Economic development breaks the relationship between people and their natural environment, and that, along with intermittent sacrality, may account for the apparent enthusiasm with which an increasingly wealthy Indian middle class has embraced consumerism and its attendant environmental implications. The Hindu caste system may also play its part in allowing the affluent to ignore environmental degradation: dealing with waste and pollution is the responsibility of lower caste members of society, meaning that taking action to protect the environment becomes less of a pressing issue to people in power.[75] The operation of the caste system also challenges the ideas presented earlier about social sustainability, which are drawn from a Western perspective.

It is important to acknowledge the contribution of Mahatma Gandhi to the broader sustainability discourse. Gandhi wrote extensively about *ahimsa* and its implications for nonviolence towards all living things, declaring that non-human animals have the same moral value as humans. He was also a strong advocate of local industrialisation and criticised modern urban civilisation, where people are:

> … uncomfortably packed like sardines in boxes and finding themselves in the midst of utter strangers who would oust them if they could and whom they would, in their turn, oust similarly.[76]

Gandhi also objected strongly to mechanisation whose aim was to save labour, as he saw this leading to unemployment, to urban middle classes preying parasitically on working classes, and the concentration of wealth in the hands of a few.[77] These writings influenced Ernst Schumacher considerably, and Gandhi's views on economics and industrialisation contributed significantly to Schumacher's 1973 book *Small is Beautiful*, an important book in the sustainable development discourse emerging at that time.

6.6.3.4 Islam

The next three sections concern the three great monotheisms, Islam, Judaism and Christianity, faith systems which originated in the same area of the world at different times and which share certain canonical texts, but which have evolved in radically different directions. The degree of importance that each places on the wording of the canonical texts varies between and within each system, but is, in general much greater than in the Eastern faith traditions.

A central tenet of each system is that God created the world and that humanity has some form of stewardship responsibility for nature which implies an interdependency between humanity and nature and ascribes a responsibility to humans for looking after the created world.[78]

The concept of creation also leads to the idea that there was a *beginning* to time. Such a cosmology does not exist in Buddhism and Hinduism which see time as cyclical rather than linear, where the consequences of what we do today will come back to haunt us in a future existence.

Islam sees the world as having been created by a God, in Arabic, *Allah*. Considering sustainability, Nawal Ammar[79] notes that everything in the world reflects *Allah's* power and might, but must not be seen as sacred: only *Allah* is sacred, a central idea in Islam's fundamental principle of *tawheed*. Existence may be seen as a dualism comprising *Allah* and everything that *Allah* has created, which implies that humanity should be seen as on an equal level with the rest of nature, a perspective that Islam shares with deep ecology. However, *Allah* recognises that humans have special (not necessarily better) qualities which means that they are suited to protect the world, and that they can, as the *Koran* says, distinguish themselves by "better deeds". Although humanity has a responsibility to protect *Allah's* world, it is also enjoined to use and enjoy the bounties of the world. Ammar notes that the Prophet Mohammad instructed Muslims that they should "work in this world as though you are living for ever and work for the hereafter as though you are dying tomorrow",[80] a thought-provoking injunction for sustainable behaviour.

Islam also contains a number of practical instructions about how humanity's relationship with the world should be conducted. Waste is explicitly criticised, and people should see their relationship with the rest of nature as a partnership, using only what is a fair share. It also explores economic behaviour in some detail: business activities should respect fair ideas of value to avoid exploitation, and concepts such as charging higher prices based on supply and demand considerations are seen as usurious. Actions that individuals and businesses take should be judged by the benefit that they create to the public and should not be done for personal benefit.[81]

Muslims maintain strong feelings about history, and are very aware about contributions made to natural sciences by Islamic scholars: for example, Ammar[82] notes 10th-century writings (attributed to Jabir Ibn Hayyan but possibly the work of several scholars) concerned with the impact of pollution on human health. But by the same token, Ammar recognises that there is a strong contemporary feeling that the main contribution to the damage of the world has been carried out by Western, secular forces, leading to tensions about what appropriate responses to global environmental challenges should be.

6.6.3.5 Judaism

What is the Judaist perspective on sustainability? God created the world as part of a divine plan, so this determines the value, purpose and meaning of everything in nature. The canonical texts, the *Torah* and the *Talmud*, provide clear information about how humanity can use and respect nature that it needs for its existence but say little about nature that is outside the human community. Nature that is outside of the human community is of no interest to people and is God's responsibility.[83]

As is perhaps understandable for a faith system for a community seeking to develop in turbulent times and in an often difficult geographical setting, there is an emphasis on following prescribed ways to use nature, rather than spending time appreciating its aesthetic qualities.[84] Protection of the land is recognised in the concept of *shmita*, the sabbatical year, when land should be left to lie fallow—this is also recognised in Christianity as "Jubilee" (see below). However, reflecting the scars of the period of enslavement in Egypt, texts also contain injunctions about right behaviour to others, for example as in the Ten Commandments.

6.6.3.6 Christianity

This world tour of the relationship between faith systems and sustainability ends with Christianity. Christianity and Judaism both have the Old Testament of the Bible as canonical texts, and a number of key figures are also referred to in the Koran, so some of the concepts previously discussed are relevant here. For example, certain parts of the Bible discourage the ill-treatment of animals and refer to the importance of seeing nature as important in its own right.[85] In the New Testament, the parables told by Jesus often used nature as a metaphor for desirable human behaviour, showing a concern for stewardship of the environment.[86] The Judaic and Christian concept of "Jubilee" shows a concern for both society and the environment. Jubilee dictates that on every seventh day people and their animals should rest, land should be worked for six years and allowed to rest in the seventh year, and after seven cycles of seven years there is a Jubilee year, when:

> All the accumulated inequities of the past seven times seven years, between humans in debt, loss of land and enslavement, and to nature in overuse of land and animals should be rectified. All is to be restored to right balance.[87]

The influence of a linear cosmology may be of particular importance in Christianity, where it has helped to create "… an implicit faith in perpetual progress",[88] seen in its dynamic contribution to economic progress in the last two centuries.

However, as could be expected for texts which were written by different people over a long period of time, there are ambiguities and inconsistencies, and many of the critiques of Christianity and sustainability revolve around how certain passages should be understood. A key subject for various writers is the concept of "dominion", as seen in a key verse in Genesis:

> And God blessed them, and God said unto them, Be fruitful, and multiply, and replenish the earth, and subdue it: and have dominion over the fish of the sea, and over the fowl of the air, and over every living thing that moveth upon the earth.
> (Genesis, 1:28)

What does "dominion" mean? Does it mean governing as a benevolent ruler, or does it mean exercising total control? The notion that Christianity in practice has taken up the second definition was put forward in an influential 1967 paper with the provocative title "*The historical roots of our ecologic crisis*" by the mediaeval historian and practising Christian, Lynn White. White laid the blame for the developing environmental crisis at the door of the Christian church, writing that Christians, neo-Christians and post-Christians see themselves as "… superior to nature, contemptuous of it, willing to use it for our slightest whim".[89] White's anger is directed at a particular Western, deracinated Christian practice, where, as in Weber's Protestant ethic concept, material temptations have led to a particular interpretation of the Bible.

However, this is a criticism which could in contemporary times be levelled against elites of all faiths across the world, whose pursuit of material wealth at the expense of social and environmental sustainability is counter to concepts of equity and stewardship within their original faith. So it is important to remember that there are still many people whose interpretation of Christian (or other) faith means that they still firmly believe in principles of environmental stewardship and social justice. Melanie Campbell, Ordinand in the Church of England, expresses this well in Box 6.4.

Box 6.4

To me sustainability means to flourish in a way that doesn't cause any harm to anybody or anything, that actually promotes well-being, whether that is of the organisation or a church community or of individuals. It is coming from the premise that doing what is best for the world is also how we might serve God and this means to love our neighbour too, that's the kind of underpinning principle. Loving your neighbour means looking after relationships, communities, the infrastructures that help people to flourish and be well. At the same time this has to involve looking after the climate and looking after our planet, because these two are inseparable.

Melanie Campbell

6.6.3.7 Reflections on faith systems and sustainability

This brief review of how global faith systems view sustainability shows both a wide range of contrasting perspectives both across and within faiths, but also a considerable amount of commonality. As regards contrasts, the three monotheisms are all much more concerned with prescribing a code of social behaviour to promote a sustainable community than is, for example, Buddhism. The concept of dominion over nature varies from the highly anthropocentric Christian perspective to the Daoist perspective of *wu wei*. The circularity of time implied by a belief in *samsara* and the karmic implications of one's actions contrast strongly with the linearity of creation-based faith systems and their resultant implicit belief in progress and development.

All faith systems, however, seem to have some conceptualisation of what is called the Golden Rule, for example, "Do unto others as you would have them do unto you" (from the Gospel according to Luke), or "What is hateful to you, do not do to your fellow man" (from the *Talmud*). All faith systems seem to have some concepts of stewardship of nature, although the extent and clarity about what these entail vary considerably.

We can therefore see that perspectives on social and environmental sustainability across different faith systems are complex and not necessarily consistent. This is an important point to remember for us as learning professionals, seeking to influence the behaviour and attitudes of people so that they respect a principle of sustainability.

Time for reflection

Reflecting on a faith system that influences you, what do you think about this brief summary?

Are you aware of any other important aspects to consider that you think can contribute to learning about sustainability?

6.7 Reviewing what may influence learning

This chapter has introduced a range of ideas about may influence the effectiveness of an SFL strategy. Figure 6.15 is a concept map which may help to make some sense of what these factors are and how they may interrelate.

Time for reflection

Concept maps are very useful diagrams to help with reflecting on key subjects in something you are learning. This concept map is my own, and I have picked out what seems to be important to me.

What about you? What would you add or leave out?

Perhaps try drawing your own concept map to see what learning this creates?

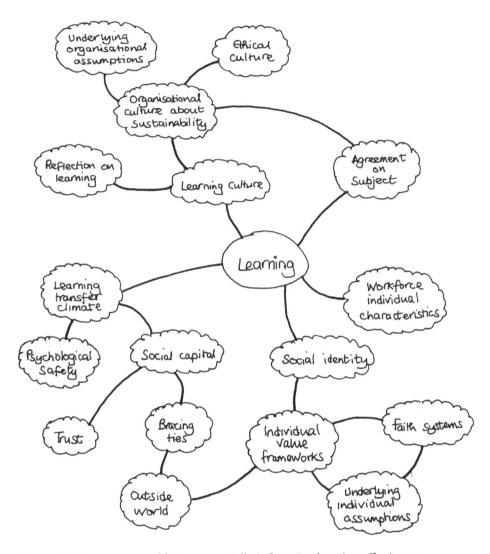

Figure 6.15 Concept map of factors potentially influencing learning effectiveness.

6.8 Making decisions about learning mechanisms

Having reflected on the possibilities and factors discussed in this chapter, we should now be in a position in our learning needs assessment to make some decisions about appropriate mechanisms to deploy or support an SFL strategy. We can therefore update our CSH boundary judgement table accordingly (Table 6.1).

Table 6.1 Questions to ask about decisions on learning mechanisms

Boundary judgement questions	Cross-cutting questions	Content-related	Mechanisms-related	Principles-related
1 Who should benefit from the learning strategy?		Who needs to learn about sustainability?	**Given decisions about who should benefit, what will appropriate learning mechanisms be?** What is known about the personal characteristics of people who will be required to learn about sustainability and what relevance that may have?	
2 What is the purpose of the learning strategy?		What competences and competencies need to be addressed in the SFL strategy? What broader knowledge about sustainability is needed to underpin SFL? What are the desired learning outcomes for the relevant level of organisational sustainability?	What mechanisms are appropriate, given the competences and competencies that need to be addressed?	
3 What is the measure of success for the learning strategy?		What are the criteria of success for the learning outcomes? What are other possible measures of success?	What mechanisms for learning are appropriate given the required success criteria?	
4 Who makes decisions about the strategy?	Who will make a decision about the learning strategy?		Who has good knowledge about how learning works within the organisation?	
5 What resources and constraints relevant to the strategy does the decision-maker control?	What is the tradition within the organisation about decision-making on learning? Who holds the budget for learning activities?		What can the decision-maker do to strengthen chosen mechanisms?	What principles are generally used?

6. What conditions of the strategy's operation are outside of the control of the decision-maker?

What are the drivers in the operational environment for social and environmental sustainability?

What pressure is there from the workforce to adopt social and environmental sustainability strategies?

What mechanisms for learning do people involved in the learning strategy use?

How do informal learning mechanisms operate in relevant parts of the organisation?

What knowledge sharing goes on within the organisation at the moment?

What is the quality of the learning transfer climate across the organisation?

What are the attitudes to sustainability amongst employees across the organisation?

7. Who should be involved in the design of the strategy?

Who should be involved in the design:
- Operational staff?
- Supervisors?
- Others?

Who can provide relevant information about factors relevant to learning in the target groups identified?

What should be the role of supervisors and others in thinking about mechanisms to utilise?

8. What expertise is needed to design the strategy?

What expertise is needed to design learning that will meet the competence and competency requirements?

What knowledge of group dynamics (levels of social capital, trust, organisational and social identity, etc.) relevant to learning do people involved in the design have, or should have?

What expertise is required in order to ensure that appropriate learning mechanisms are selected?

9. What guarantees of success do the sources of expertise offer?

How reliable about required aspects of sustainability that you have or is available to you?

What consensus exists about required aspects of sustainability?

How reliable is the information you have on group dynamics and learner characteristics?

(*Continued*)

Boundary judgement questions	Cross-cutting questions	Content-related	Mechanisms-related	Principles-related
10 Who will represent the affected society and the natural environment?		Who can provide information from society or the natural environment to inform what content is needed?	**Which external stakeholders can be engaged in the learning mechanisms deployed?**	
11 What opportunity does the affected society and natural environment have to challenge the strategy?	What are the political possibilities for engaging with external representatives in discussing sustainability-focused learning?	What content from outside the organisation is needed to support the SFL strategy? How can external perspectives on sustainability be taken into consideration?	**How can external stakeholders be engaged in the mechanisms used for SFL?**	
12 What is the worldview underlying the design of the learning strategy?	How does social and environmental sustainability sit within your organisation's culture and philosophy? What are your own perspectives on social and environmental sustainability? What other worldviews on sustainability exist which should be considered? What is the organisational tradition for conducting the LNA process?		What alternative worldviews may be identified as a result of engaging with external stakeholders?	

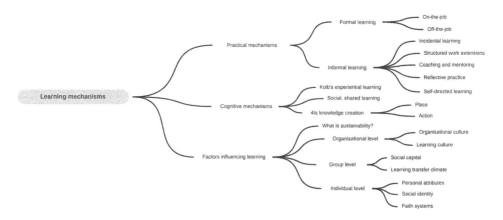

Figure 6.16 Key points in this chapter.

6.9 Key points in this chapter

The chapter has looked at the many different practical ways in which learning can happen, as shown in Figure 6.16. A basic, but often not clearly delimited, distinction is between formal and informal learning. Formal learning includes both on-the-job and off-the-job training. Informal learning includes incidental learning such as reflective practice and knowledge sharing, more formal informal learning occurs through structured work extensions, coaching and mentoring, and reflective practice, and may also occur through self-directed learning.

Kolb's experiential learning cycle for individual learning can be enhanced by including shared reflection on experience, and also can be used to help understand organisational learning as an adaptation to the requirements of sustainability. Learning can also be explained through considering how knowledge is created, recognising the importance of action and place on the process.

Many different factors can influence how well learning can take place. Organisational culture creates a context enabling or restraining many activities, including establishing an ethical culture which may be more or less welcoming to sustainability ideas. Within the organisational culture, a learning culture influences the degree to which new ideas and adaptation can take place. Social capital provides a way to understand how new ideas can flow through an organisation, and this plays a part in determining the learning transfer climate, of particular relevance to formal learning activities.

Individual characteristics are also significant, in particular the value frameworks that individuals hold, a variable associated with their social identity. This is also influenced by faiths to which individuals subscribe, and key global faith systems such as Daoism, Buddhism, Hinduism, Islam, Judaism and Christianity all establish principles relevant to social and environmental sustainability issues.

Notes

1 John Seely Brown and Paul Duguid, 'Organizational Learning and Communities-of-Practice: Toward a Unified View of Working, Learning, and Innovation', *Organization Science* 2, no. 1 (1991): 41.

2 Victoria J. Marsick and Karen Watkins, *Informal and Incidental Learning in the Workplace* (London: Routledge, 1990), 12.
3 Victoria J. Marsick and Karen E. Watkins, 'Informal and Incidental Learning', *New Directions for Adult and Continuing Education* 2001, no. 89 (2001): 28.
4 Stephen Billett, 'Workplace Participatory Practices: Conceptualising Workplaces as Learning Environments', *Journal of Workplace Learning* 16, no. 6 (2004): 312–24.
5 Marsick and Watkins, 'Informal and Incidental Learning'.
6 Karl E. Weick, 'Small Wins: Redefining the Scale of Social Problems', *American Psychologist* 39, no. 1 (1984): 40.
7 For example, Billett, 'Workplace Participatory Practices'.
8 M. M. Lombardo and R. W. Eichinger, *The Career Architect Development Planner*, 3rd Edition (Minneapolis, MN: Lominger Limited, 2000).
9 Harley Frazis, Maury Gittleman, and Mary Joyce, 'Determinants of Training: An Analysis Using Both Employer and Employee Characteristics' (Employer-provided training: Who pays? Who benefits?, Arlington, VA: Cornell University, 1998).
10 Samantha Jane Johnson, Deborah A. Blackman, and Fiona Buick, 'The 70:20:10 Framework and the Transfer of Learning', *Human Resource Development Quarterly* 29 (2018): 383–402.
11 David Kolb, *Experiential Learning: Experience as the Source of Learning and Development* (Upper Saddle River, NJ: Prentice Hall, 1984).
12 Robert-Jan Den Haan and Mascha C. Van der Voort, 'On Evaluating Social Learning Outcomes of Serious Games to Collaboratively Address Sustainability Problems: A Literature Review', *Sustainability* 10, no. 4529 (2018).
13 Mark G. Edwards, 'An Integrative Metatheory for Organisational Learning and Sustainability in Turbulent Times', *The Learning Organization* 16, no. 3 (2009): 189–207.
14 I will use the term 'team learning' rather than 'group learning' because the word team adds the implication of working to a common purpose to the basic concept of group.
15 Alma McCarthy and Thomas N. Garavan, 'Team Learning and Metacognition: A Neglected Area of HRD Research and Practice', *Advances in Developing Human Resources* 10, no. 4 (2008): 509–24.
16 Ikujiro Nonaka and Hirotaka Takeuchi, *The Knowledge-Creating Company: How Japanese Companies Create the Dynamics of Innovation* (Oxford: Oxford University Press, 1995); J. C. Spender, 'Making Knowledge the Basis of a Dynamic Theory of the Firm', *Strategic Management Journal* 17, no. S2 (1996): 45–62.
17 Mary M. Crossan, Henry W. Lane, and Roderick E. White, 'An Organizational Learning Framework: From Intuition to Institution', *Academy of Management Review* 24, no. 3 (1999): 522–37.
18 S.D. Noam Cook and Hendrik Wagenaar, 'Navigating the Eternally Unfolding Present: Toward an Epistemology of Practice', *The American Review of Public Administration* 42, no. 1 (2012): 24.
19 Foucault's writing is discussed in Stephen D. Brookfield, *The Power of Critical Theory for Adult Learning and Teaching* (Maidenhead: Open University Press, 2005), 118–48.
20 Eric W.K. Tsang, 'How the Concept of Organizational Unlearning Contributes to Studies of Learning Organizations: A Personal Reflection', *The Learning Organization* 24, no. 1 (2017): 39–48.
21 Mike Pedler and Shih-wei Hsu, 'Regenerating the Learning Organisation: Towards an Alternative Paradigm', *The Learning Organization* 26, no. 1 (2019): 97–112.
22 Geert Hofstede and Gert Jan Hofstede, *Cultures and Organizations: Software of the Mind* (New York: McGraw-Hill, 2005), 5.
23 Edgar H. Schein, *Organizational Culture and Leadership*, 5th Edition (Chichester: John Wiley & Sons Ltd, 2016).
24 Mary Jo Hatch and Majken Schultz, 'Relations between Organizational Culture, Identity and Image', *European Journal of Marketing* 31, no. 5/6 (1997): 356–65; David A. Whetten, 'Albert and Whetten Revisited: Strengthening the Concept of Organizational Identity', *Journal of Management Inquiry* 15, no. 3 (2006): 219–34.
25 Anke Arnaud and Marshall Schminke, 'The Ethical Climate and Context of Organizations: A Comprehensive Model', *Organization Science* 23, no. 6 (2012): 1767–80; Muel Kaptein, 'Developing and Testing a Measure for the Ethical Culture of Organizations: The Corporate Ethical Virtues Model', *Journal of Organizational Behavior* 29, no. 7 (2008): 923–47.

26 Mark S. Schwartz, 'Developing and Sustaining an Ethical Corporate Culture: The Core Elements', *Business Horizons* 56, no. 1 (2013): 39–50; Linda Klebe Treviño, Kenneth D. Butterfield, and Donald L. McCabe, 'The Ethical Context in Organizations: Influences on Employee Attitudes and Behaviors', *Business Ethics Quarterly* 8, no. 3 (1998): 447–76; Kaptein, 'Developing and Testing a Measure for the Ethical Culture of Organizations'.
27 Marcel Van Marrewijk and Marco Werre, 'Multiple Levels of Corporate Sustainability', *Journal of Business Ethics* 44, no. 2–3 (2003): 107–19.
28 Clare W. Graves, 'Levels of Existence: An Open System Theory of Values', *Journal of Humanistic Psychology* 10, no. 2 (1970): 131–55.
29 Schein, *Organizational Culture and Leadership*.
30 P. M. Senge, *The Fifth Discipline: The Art and Practice of the Learning Organization* (London: Century Business, 1993), 3.
31 Victoria J. Marsick and Karen E. Watkins, 'Demonstrating the Value of an Organization's Learning Culture: The Dimensions of the Learning Organization Questionnaire', *Advances in Developing Human Resources* 5, no. 2 (2003): 132–51.
32 Victoria J. Marsick and Karen E. Watkins, 'The Learning Organization: An Integrative Vision for HRD' (Academy of Human Resource Development Conference Proceedings, San Antonio, Texas, 1994), 129–34; Anna Sfard, 'On Two Metaphors for Learning and the Dangers of Choosing Just One', *Educational Researcher* 27, no. 2 (1998): 4–13.
33 Robert D. Putnam, 'Bowling Alone: America's Declining Social Capital', *Journal of Democracy* 6, no. 1 (1995): 66.
34 Mark S. Granovetter, 'The Strength of Weak Ties', *American Journal of Sociology* 78, no. 6 (May) (1973): 1360–80.
35 Paul S. Adler and Seok-Woo Kwon, 'Social Capital: Prospects for a New Concept', *Academy of Management Review* 27, no. 1 (2002): 17–40; Mark Dodgson, 'Learning, Trust, and Technological Collaboration', *Human Relations* 46, no. 1 (1993): 77–95; Granovetter, 'The Strength of Weak Ties', 1973.
36 Yvonne Rydin and Nancy Holman, 'Re-Evaluating the Contribution of Social Capital in Achieving Sustainable Development', *Local Environment* 9, no. 2 (2004): 123.
37 Indre Maurer, Vera Bartsch, and Mark Ebers, 'The Value of Intra-Organizational Social Capital: How It Fosters Knowledge Transfer, Innovation Performance, and Growth', *Organization Studies* 32, no. 2 (2011): 157–85.
38 Mark Granovetter, 'The Strength of Weak Ties: A Network Theory Revisited', *Sociological Theory* 1 (1983): 201–33; Granovetter, 'The Strength of Weak Ties', 1973.
39 Melissa A. Schilling and Christina Fang, 'When Hubs Forget, Lie, and Play Favorites: Interpersonal Network Structure, Information Distortion, and Organizational Learning', *Strategic Management Journal* 35, no. 7 (2014): 974–94.
40 Adler and Kwon, 'Social Capital'.
41 Maurer, Bartsch, and Ebers, 'The Value of Intra-Organizational Social Capital'.
42 Morten T. Hansen, 'The Search-Transfer Problem: The Role of Weak Ties in Sharing Knowledge across Organization Subunits', *Administrative Science Quarterly* 44, no. 1 (1999): 82–111.
43 Bruce W. Tuckman, 'Developmental Sequence in Small Groups', *Psychological Bulletin* 63, no. 6 (1965): 384–99.
44 Marloes Bakker et al., 'Is Trust Really Social Capital? Knowledge Sharing in Product Development Projects', *The Learning Organization* 13, no. 6 (2006): 594–605.
45 Amy Edmondson, 'Psychological Safety and Learning Behavior in Work Teams', *Administrative Science Quarterly* 44, no. 2 (1999): 350–83.
46 Chris Argyris, *Reasoning, Learning, and Action: Individual and Organizational* (San Francisco, CA: Jossey-Bass, 1982).
47 Timothy T. Baldwin and J. Kevin Ford, 'Transfer of Training: A Review and Directions for Future Research', *Personnel Psychology* 41, no. 1 (1988): 63–105; Brian D. Blume et al., 'Transfer of Training: A Meta-Analytic Review', *Journal of Management* 36, no. 4 (2010): 1065–105.
48 Toby Marshall Egan, 'The Relevance of Organizational Subculture for Motivation to Transfer Learning', *Human Resource Development Quarterly* 19, no. 4 (2008): 299–322.
49 For example, see Blume et al., 'Transfer of Training: A Meta-Analytic Review'; Lisa A. Burke and Holly M. Hutchins, 'Training Transfer: An Integrative Literature Review', *Human Resource Development Review* 6, no. 3 (2007): 263–96.

50 H. Ebbinghaus, *Memory: A Contribution to Experimental Psychology* (New York: Columbia University, 1885); Winfred Arthur Jr et al., 'Factors That Influence Skill Decay and Retention: A Quantitative Review and Analysis', *Human Performance* 11, no. 1 (1998): 57–101; Xiaoqian Wang et al., 'Factors Influencing Knowledge and Skill Decay after Training: A Meta-Analysis.', in *Individual and Team Skill Decay: The Science and Implications for Practice*, ed. Eric Anthony Day (London: Taylor & Francis, 2013), 68–116.
51 For example, see Raymond A Noe, 'Trainees' Attributes and Attitudes: Neglected Influences on Training Effectiveness', *Academy of Management Review* 11, no. 4 (1986): 736–49; Jason A Colquitt, Jeffrey A LePine, and Raymond A Noe, 'Toward an Integrative Theory of Training Motivation: A Meta-Analytic Path Analysis of 20 Years of Research.', *Journal of Applied Psychology* 85, no. 5 (2000): 678.
52 Gregor Torkar, 'Learning Experiences That Produce Environmentally Active and Informed Minds', *NJAS-Wageningen Journal of Life Sciences* 69 (2014): 49–55.
53 For example, Carol Gilligan, *In a Different Voice: Psychological Theory and Women's Development* (Cambridge, MA: Harvard University Press, 1982).
54 R.M. Klein, S. D'Mello, and B.M. Wiernik, 'Demographic Characteristics and Employee Sustainability', in *Managing Human Resources for Environmental Sustainability*, ed. S.E. Jackson et al. (Chichester: John Wiley & Sons Ltd, 2012).
55 Graves, 'Levels of Existence'.
56 Graves, 133.
57 Abigail Lynam, 'How Worldview Development Influences Knowledge and Beliefs about Sustainability', in *Encyclopedia of Sustainability in Higher Education*, ed. Walter Leal Filho (London: Springer, 2019), 899–909.
58 Blake E. Ashforth and Fred Mael, 'Social Identity Theory and the Organization', *Academy of Management Review* 14, no. 1 (1989): 20–39; Henri Tajfel, 'Social Psychology of Intergroup Relations', *Annual Review of Psychology* 33, no. 1 (1982): 1–39.
59 John C. Turner, 'Social Identification and Psychological Group Formation', in *The Social Dimension: European Developments in Social Psychology*, ed. Henri Tajfel, vol. 2, 2 vols (Cambridge: Cambridge University Press, 1984), 518–38.
60 Blake E. Ashforth, Spencer H. Harrison, and Kevin G. Corley, 'Identification in Organizations: An Examination of Four Fundamental Questions', *Journal of Management* 34, no. 3 (2008): 325–74; Leon Festinger, *A Theory of Cognitive Dissonance* (Stanford: Stanford University Press, 1957).
61 Russell F. Korte, 'A Review of Social Identity Theory with Implications for Training and Development', *Journal of European Industrial Training* 31, no. 3 (2007): 166–80.
62 Stanton Wortham, 'The Interdependence of Social Identification and Learning', *American Educational Research Journal* 41, no. 3 (2004): 715–50; Etienne Wenger, 'Communities of Practice: Learning as a Social System', *Systems Thinker* 9, no. 5 (1998): 2–3.
63 Michael Armstrong, *Human Resource Management Practice*, 8th Edition (London: Kogan Page, 2001), 2.
64 Karyn L. Lai, 'Conceptual Foundations for Environmental Ethics: A Daoist Perspective', in *Environmental Philosophy in Asian Traditions of Thought*, ed. J. Baird Callicott and James McRae (Albany: State University of New York Press, 2014), 178.
65 R.P. Peerenboom, 'Beyond Naturalism: A Reconstruction of Daoist Environmental Ethics', in *Environmental Philosophy in Asian Traditions of Thought*, ed. J. Baird Callicott and James McRae (Albany: State University of New York Press, 2014), 150–72.
66 James Miller, 'Ecology, Aesthetics and Daoist Body Cultivation', in *Environmental Philosophy in Asian Traditions of Thought*, ed. J. Baird Callicott and James McRae (State University of New York Press, 2014), 225–43.
67 Peerenboom, 'Beyond Naturalism: A Reconstruction of Daoist Environmental Ethics'.
68 Lai, 'Conceptual Foundations for Environmental Ethics: A Daoist Perspective', 189.
69 Ian Harris, 'Causation and "Telos": The Problem of Buddhist Environmental Ethics', in *Environmental Philosophy in Asian Traditions of Thought*, ed. J. Baird Callicott and James McRae (Albany: State University of New York Press, 2014), 117–29.
70 Christopher K. Chapple, 'Toward an Indigenous Indian Environmentalism', in *Purifying the Earthly Body of God: Religion and Ecology in Hindu India*, ed. Lance Nelson (Albany: State University of New York, 1998), 13–37.

71 Simon P. James, 'Against Holism: Rethinking Buddhist Environmental Ethics', in *Environmental Philosophy in Asian Traditions of Thought*, ed. J. Baird Callicott and James McRae (Albany: State University of New York Press, 2014), 99–115.
72 Harris, 'Causation and "Telos": The Problem of Buddhist Environmental Ethics'.
73 Harold Coward, 'The Ecological Implications of Karma Theory', in *Purifying the Earthly Body of God: Religion and Ecology in Hindu India*, ed. Lance Nelson (Albany: State University of New York, 1998), 39–49.
74 Vijaya Rettakudi Nagarajan, 'The Earth as Goddess Bhu Devi: Toward a Theory of "Embedded Ecologies" in Folk Hinduism', in *Purifying the Earthly Body of God: Religion and Ecology in Hindu India*, ed. Lance Nelson (Albany, NY: State University of New York, 1998), 277.
75 Chapple, 'Toward an Indigenous Indian Environmentalism'.
76 Quoted in Bart Gruzalski, 'Gandhi's Contributions to Environmental Thought and Action', in *Environmental Philosophy in Asian Traditions of Thought*, ed. J. Baird Callicott and James McRae (Albany: State University of New York Press, 2014), 58.
77 Thomas Weber, 'Gandhi, Deep Ecology, Peace Research and Buddhist Economics', *Journal of Peace Research* 36, no. 3 (1999): 349–61.
78 Susan S. Case and Edward Chavez, 'Guiding Lights for Morally Responsible Sustainability in Organizations: Revisiting Sacred Texts of Judaism, Christianity, and Islam', *Journal of Organizational Psychology* 17, no. 2 (2017): 35–49.
79 Nawal Ammar, 'Islam and Deep Ecology', in *Deep Ecology and World Religions: New Essays on Sacred Ground*, ed. David Landis Barnhill and Roger S. Gottlieb (Albany: State University of New York Press, 2001), 193–211.
80 Ammar, 201.
81 Abbas J. Ali, *Business Ethics in Islam* (Cheltenham: Edward Elgar Publishing, 2014), 202.
82 Ammar, 'Islam and Deep Ecology', 205.
83 Eric Katz, 'Faith, God and Nature: Judaism and Deep Ecology', in *Deep Ecology and World Religions: New Essays on Sacred Ground*, ed. David Landis Barnhill and Roger S. Gottlieb (Albany: State University of New York Press, 2001), 153–67.
84 Erhun Kula, *History of Environmental Economic Thought* (London: Taylor & Francis Group, 1998).
85 Kula, *History of Environmental Economic Thought*, 171.
86 Susan S. Case and Edward Chavez, 'Faith, God and Nature: Judaism and Deep Ecology', *Journal of Organizational Psychology* 17, no. 2 (2017): 42.
87 Rosemary Radford Ruether, 'Deep Ecology, Ecofeminism, and the Bible', in *Deep Ecology and World Religions: New Essays on Sacred Ground*, ed. David Landis Barnhill and Roger S. Gottlieb (Albany: State University of New York Press, 2001), 235.
88 Lynn White, 'The Historical Roots of Our Ecologic Crisis', *Science* 155, no. 3767 (1967): 1205.
89 White, 'The Historical Roots of Our Ecologic Crisis', 1206.

7 Developing a learning strategy 3
Designing formal learning

7.1 What this chapter covers

Figure 7.1 shows how this chapter is organized. While Chapters 5 and 6 looked at what might be regarded as "neutral" aspects of a learning strategy for organisational sustainability (sustainability-focused learning (SFL)), in this chapter, we move on to what may be more challenging, how to design formal learning in a way which, in Habermasian terms, addresses technical requirements but also recognises the way in which the emancipatory aspects of a learner's lifeworld may affect the effectiveness of formal learning. What we look at here may be challenging because it moves beyond what may be seen as a conventional explanation of pedagogies for organisational learning to exploring in more detail what might be seen as 'critical' approaches, approaches which encourage people to question values.

Although some of these ideas may appear challenging in organisational settings, I think that it is important to introduce them to the world of learning and development in organisations. Approaches such as transformative learning and critical thinking are increasingly being used in educational settings, particularly at higher education level, but there is little evidence that they are being adopted in organisational life. This is perhaps because they ask people to reflect on challenging issues, such as the often unitarist assumptions that underlie organisational behaviour, on the dominant political economy of the last half-century, and of the implications these have for how we think that organisations must function. Sustainability represents a new paradigm for how we exist in the world, and if we in the learning and development world continue to think within a 20th-century paradigm, we will not be able to develop learning and development practices that are relevant for the 21st century as it matures.

7.2 Principles for designing formal learning

Conventional approaches to designing formal learning generally have roots in the behaviourist thinking dominant in the 1950s, out of which emerged the discipline of

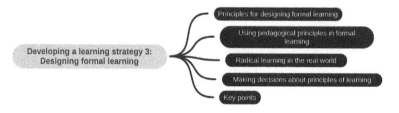

Figure 7.1 Map of Chapter 7.

DOI: 10.4324/9781003218296-8

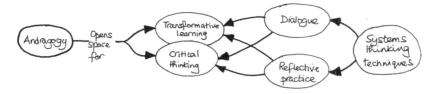

Figure 7.2 Principles of adult learning.

Instructional Systems Design (ISD). However, even with the adoption of more constructivist ideas about learning design in the 1970s and 1980s, there remain strong unitarist assumptions in much writing about the design of formal learning.

ISD and its derivatives can provide a reliable way to design and deliver performative learning experiences, and be effective at communicating important principles and technical knowledge, and there is consequently a comprehensive literature available about how to design and implement formal learning from such a perspective so we will not consider this in detail here.

However, it is useful to recognise the difference between learners conforming and committing: performative learning may make people conform, but effective and enduring transfer of learning relies on people committing, particularly with regard to sustainability practices which they may find meaningless, which do not conform with their identity or value framework, or which, in, a word popular as I write, they find 'woke'.

Thinking back to our discussion in Chapter 5 about recognising pluralist perspectives and the insights provided by Jürgen Habermas' critical philosophy, we will devote much of this chapter to looking at pedagogical principles which may be able to move learners from merely conforming towards committing to sustainability—andragogy, transformative learning and critical thinking, and the associated skills of dialogue and reflective practice. We can also see how some of the ideas within systems thinking that we have used throughout this book may be of use.

Figure 7.2 provides a way of understanding how these subjects relate to each other. I have shown transformative learning and critical thinking as overlapping, because, as will be seen below, there are strong connections between the two approaches.

7.2.1 Andragogy

The first to consider is andragogy, a concept associated with the American educator Malcolm Knowles in the 1970s.[1] However, it was not a radically new idea: andragogy was being written about in 1830s Germany and it had existed as a discipline in parts of continental Europe since that time.[2] It was, however, a novel concept in the United States of the late 20th century, and attracted a significant amount of criticism for proposing that adults and children learn differently.

The distinction that Knowles was making centres around the idea of dependency. In his opinion, the educator of children, the pedagogue, maintains a relationship characterised by those learning depending on the pedagogue, whereas the adult educator, the andragogue, should seek to help people move from dependency towards being more self-directed. This is because adults have their own experience and sense of identity, and therefore approach learning with some degree of scepticism which the andragogue needs to acknowledge and overcome. In Knowles' terms, adult learners therefore often have attitudes which may be described as ambiguous and contradictory.

The practical principles of andragogy-influenced learning have evolved somewhat since Knowles' first articulation, but may be summarised as emphasising:

- the learner as self-directed rather than dependent
- the learner as a resource for learning
- the importance of experience in the learning process
- the importance of an intrinsic motivation to learn rather than because of an extrinsic reward.

These conditions mean that the learning process should be collaborative and consensual, involve participative decision-making in terms of deciding what learning is needed and how it should be assessed, be structured according to the learner's needs and readiness rather than to an external curriculum, and be based around real-world projects and experimentation.

Several of the ideas presented in this book lend support to the value of recognising these andragogical principles:

- Stakeholder theory points to the importance of involving all stakeholders in a situation of interest in key decision-making: from that perspective, learners need to be consulted about aspects of learning on which they can provide an informed opinion.
- Complexity theory and the concept of variety highlight that learners will often have the most relevant knowledge about what issues they face in the workplace and where they need help in managing their variety. Andragogy therefore contributes to bringing the legitimate and shadow systems into balance at an edge of chaos.

While andragogy may be seen as providing a framework for how learning should take place, ideas such as transformative learning and critical thinking provide ways to show how it might be implemented. Andragogy therefore can play a part in strengthening social equity as regards learning within the organisation and may therefore contribute to internal social sustainability.

7.2.2 Transformative learning

In most organisations transitions towards sustainable practice may require significant shifts in policies, practices and underlying assumptions about how decisions are made. In Chapter 4 we introduced the perhaps abstract idea that we can question and change such assumptions through double loop learning—transformative learning is an approach to pedagogy which can enable this at the individual level.

Transformative learning was developed by the American educationalist Jack Mezirow[3] as a way to help people deal with a situation which challenges their understanding of how the world works (in Mezirow's language a "disorienting dilemma"), and which may require them to change this understanding. Mezirow drew inspiration for his ideas from a number of sources, including Jürgen Habermas whom we have already discussed, and the Brazilian educator Paulo Freire who saw improving literacy as a key tool in societal development.

Transformative learning also draws on the idea of social constructionism that we looked at in Chapter 2, that our understanding of how the world around us works comes from our socialisation as we grow up. Mezirow calls this understanding our "frame of reference", and it is built from the various legitimated political, cultural, religious, moral-ethical and so on ideas and practices that we experience in life. It shapes our perceptions of the world around us, contributes to our understanding of how it works and influences our feelings. Our frame of reference then gives us a "point of view" which is our interpretation of any situation we are facing.

Box 7.1

I was on a call the other day with some people talking about a couple of meetings, and one of them talked about a meeting I had run in 2018. She said 'almost nothing has changed my life more than that meeting.' Another person talked about a meeting about access to clean energy as a human right. They said 'That meeting has probably informed four different policies. It has brought me a lens I didn't have before and now I use that lens on everything'. It wasn't because I delivered a lot of content. I delivered a little content and got people talking to each other and using their own experiences to metabolise that content.

Gail Francis, RE-AMP

Box 7.1 provides a good example of how we might see the results of transformative learning. To understand the relevance of transformative learning in SFL let us think about where it might come into play. Your organisation might decide to introduce a new travel policy aimed at reducing carbon dioxide emissions by asking all employees to use public transport where possible and to cycle to work. This might be seen as a rather radical change and could invoke varying levels of resistance and even hostility. We can think about people's alignment with organisational policies on a spectrum moving from conformity (I do it because I have to do it) to commitment (I do it because I want to do it).[4] Relying on conformity is unhealthy because it contributes to resentment and anomie in the workforce, something that is contrary to good internal social sustainability, and does not guarantee in any way that the learning will "stick". Transformative learning provides a way of making commitment a more likely outcome.

Transformative learning follows a number of stages. First, our learner is confronted with the disorienting dilemma. In our example, the new policy represents something sudden, but it could also be a steadily growing awareness of a problem. This could also be relevant here, with employees seeing ever more evidence in the media about the damage caused by carbon emissions. When this happens the individual starts to reflect on what this all might mean, referring to their frame of reference to try and make sense of it. For example, their frame of reference might include beliefs that climate change is not the result of carbon dioxide emissions, or that they have a right to travel to work using whatever means of travel they want. These beliefs could produce a point of view that such a travel policy is pointless and infringes their personal rights. Referring back to Habermas, this is their emancipatory interest, in tension with the technical interest of the travel policy.

At this point, the aim of transformative learning is to help the person to reflect on their frame of reference. This is a process which someone can do on their own, but which generally works more effectively if supported or facilitated by someone else. The essential point at this stage is that the individual needs to be able to enter into a dialogue about the situation where, according to Mezirow, they would have accurate and complete information, be free from coercion, be open to alternative points of view, they would look at everything objectively, and could test assumptions. Again, referring back to Habermas, such a process relies on strong communicative knowledge. Patricia Cranton[5] recommends three areas to work on in this process of reflection:

- Content of the dilemma—what is the problem here, how do I feel about this situation, what is the change that I am being asked to make?
- Process by which the dilemma came about—how did this situation arise, what prompted the change in policy, how did I come to believe what I believe?
- Premise, why the problem is a problem to me—why is changing travel arrangements difficult for me, what are the obstacles to me changing?

It is the third area here, the premises behind a frame of reference, which is the most challenging to explore but also the most important, as this is the one which relates to each individual's value framework. Transformative learning can occur if the individual reflects on these values and how they relate to the dilemma, critically considers the assumptions that they are based on, and as a result changes their frame of reference. The carbon emissions issue in our example is particularly interesting because of the often polarised nature of the conversation around climate change and the prevalence of information challenging the scientific consensus that it is a serious problem. So, for example, an individual's frame of reference might be that climate change is a myth, that human activity does not contribute to rising levels of carbon dioxide in the atmosphere, or that what any individual can do is insignificant. Questions to help someone critically reflect on this premise might include:

- What are your reasons for thinking that climate change is a myth?
- Where has your information come from?
- How reliable is that information?
- What makes that source of information more significant than what most scientists are saying?

As the individual answers such questions, it is useful to look out for common problems that we all have in constructing our frames of reference, such as[6]:

- relying on fake experts, people who do not have adequate knowledge or qualifications about a subject
- using logically flawed arguments to arrive at conclusions
- saying that climate change is only a theory and that there is no proof, showing a lack of understanding about how science works
- cherry-picking, selecting one or two possibly unrepresentative stories in order to make generalisations
- conspiracy theories, asserting that the scientific consensus is a result of some hidden global conspiracy.

The important thing here is not to say that the person is wrong and that your ideas are correct, because you may then be making the same sort of fallacious claim (are you a real expert, are you part of the global conspiracy, etc.), and also because transformative learning seeks to avoid indoctrination. What you are looking to do is to unsettle the individual's attachment to their frame of reference and to encourage them to reconsider what it means. If done well, through effective, authentic discussion with a facilitator or friends and colleagues whom they respect, the individual may eventually come to think that there probably is a connection between driving a car, carbon dioxide emissions, and climate change, and also that exercising their own right to drive has an impact on other people's rights to enjoy clean air or for future generations to enjoy a stable climate.

At that point the individual can start to live their life incorporating this new frame of reference, trying out what its consequences are and integrating it into their everyday existence. Once that has happened we can say that the process of learning has been completed.

Although Mezirow's original conceptualisation of transformative learning applied to individuals, its principles are also relevant for group learning. Various ways in which this can be done are explored later in this chapter.

There are some important points to note about this process. Perhaps the most important is that it must not be coercive: the facilitator in a transformative learning process must not try to manipulate or indoctrinate the learner. Their role is to engage in a process which helps the individual to reflect on their assumptions in the light of the dilemma, to ask and answer questions which help the individual understand the situation more fully and clearly so that they can come to a free and fully informed decision to change their frame of reference. The organisation's culture needs to be sufficiently open to create the psychological safety for the individual to try out new points of view.

Second, developing the ability to critically self-reflect is a very valuable skill for all adults, and having practised it in a situation such as this they may be able to incorporate it into other aspects of their lives to become an authentic, autonomous person.

Time for reflection

Try your own transformative learning exercise. Think about a disorienting dilemma that you have recently faced.
How did this challenge your frame of reference?
For what reasons did this dilemma prove challenging?
Has this led to a change in your point of view? If so, how did this happen?

7.2.3 Critical thinking

Transformative learning has a strong focus on enabling individuals to change, and presentations about it often do not discuss in detail the context for the change, particularly where they are associated with issues of power and its potential for preventing change. This issue is addressed by critical thinking, an approach to pedagogy which may be seen as integrating critical theory (introduced in Section 5.3) with the principles of transformative learning.

At the heart of transformative learning lies making changes to our frame of reference, and with critical thinking close attention is paid to the origins of the frame—what is the social and political context which has led to the frame of reference acquiring a particular quality, in terms of what knowledge it legitimates, what beliefs it creates, or how individuals communicate?

A central concept in critical thinking is that of questioning hegemony. In our context, hegemony is seen as the network of beliefs and assumptions that inform our everyday lives, pervade our existence and which create what we think to be "common sense".[7] So, for example, we might see it as common sense that people who go to private schools should have the best jobs, or that people should work and live in completely different parts of a city. Because hegemonic ideas like this are seen as common sense, we need to be able to look at situations from a completely different frame of reference, such as might come from Marxism (the most common alternative perspective in critical theory) or from one of sustainability. The most well-known writer about Marxist perspectives on hegemony was the Italian Antonio Gramsci,[8] who made the point that the beauty of hegemony lies in its ability to have individuals in society willingly accept structures and systems which are not necessarily in their best interests. For example, neoliberal economics promotes a culture which encourages consumption which, while creating some satisfaction, also leads to a wide range of social and environmental problems. The pervasiveness of hegemonic thought also makes it very difficult to identify its sources and challenge it. Referring back to Habermas' concept of the lifeworld, hegemony represents a situation where our lifeworld has been totally colonised by the external system.

Hegemony emerges out of a dominant ideology, accepted "... values, beliefs, myths, explanations, and justifications that appear self-evidently true, empirically accurate, personally relevant, and morally desirable to a majority of the populace".[9] In our contemporary world, our dominant ideology is that of neoliberal economics, which, as we saw in Chapter 3, has proved particularly successful at insinuating itself into everyday lives, and hence influencing how we can approach sustainability. The starting point for critical thinking is therefore to challenge dominant ideologies and contest associated hegemonic assumptions. It is then necessary to unmask the power which maintains the ideology and identify how it is being exercised and then to explore ways in which people can lead more fulfilling and authentic lives.

Although this explanation of hegemony suggests that it operates at a state level, we can also see hegemonic thinking in action within organisations, as represented by cultural practices and organisational identity, standard operating procedures, and the invisible underlying assumptions which drive everyday practice—for example, unitarist assumptions underlying the design of formal learning programmes, the constant pressure in organisations to just get things done and work long hours, or that there is no time to stop and reflect on what is being done, aspects of organisational culture which have become reified. Critical thinking is therefore relevant to Argyris and Schön's double loop learning, as discussed in Chapter 4. Practising a critical pedagogy therefore provides a practical way to implement double loop learning when needed. So how can a critical pedagogy be implemented?

First, because there is a need to draw a learner's attention to the hegemonic water that they are swimming in, a facilitator is needed, or as Patricia Cranton describes the role,[10] a provocateur. While in many learning-related activities it is sufficient for someone to facilitate the process and to not intervene in content matters, the role of the provocateur is to help people become aware of and challenge their existing belief systems. Stephen Brookfield, a key writer about critical thinking, observes that in everyday life most people have little opportunity to take part in what Habermas calls an "ideal speech" situation,[11] where, as described in Chapter 5, they have access to trusted and reliable information, they are free from coercion, are open to alternative points of view, can look at everything objectively, and can test assumptions. The role of the provocateur is to provide access to such information and create a learning environment which allows ideal speech to emerge.

This raises one of the major criticisms of critical thinking, that in creating a situation where people can think about the power that is affecting them, that the provocateur substitutes a new form of power, potentially trying to create a new hegemony. Critical thinking may therefore potentially be seen as elitist, or as having the potential to create distrust within a community.[12]

Second, critical pedagogy needs to be based around a process of critical reflection on social, political and cultural factors relevant to the situation of interest,[13] and to promote reflexivity, the awareness of each individual's role in creating or maintaining these factors.[14] This is why a competency in systems thinking is so important in SFL, as it draws learners' attention to the multiple perspectives, interrelationships and boundary judgements inherent in every situation.

Thirdly, the provocateur needs to reflect on what is likely to be the most effective balance of content and method in a critical learning activity. For example, should there be an emphasis on exposing learners to radical content (which could be, for example, the principles of deep ecology and its implications for organisational practice), or using a radical method, asking challenging questions and deliberately moving people some way out of their comfort zone? Or both? Or being much softer in terms of content and method? This is not an easy question to answer and is why being a critical thinking provocateur in an organisational setting may be very difficult, and few HRD practitioners may be confident about taking this on.

So far we have talked about critical pedagogy as a group activity, but individual critical thinking is also possible. The provocateur may provide someone with radical content or they may access suitable material online, and they then take themselves away from conformist pressures within their community to reflect.[15]

Almost inevitably attempts to stimulate critical thinking will meet with resistance (think back to the discussion about defensive routines in Chapter 6). It might be expected that reflecting on and finding problems with perhaps long-held, comfortable assumptions about how we operate in the world will be uncomfortable, and resistance would be a normal response. A way to minimise defensiveness and make engagement more likely may be to engage with sustainability challenges at a human level, for example to reflect on implications about how what we are doing may have an impact on our own children or grandchildren.

We may also find it easier to relate the complexity of sustainability to more easily grasped, everyday issues that are closer to everyday experience rather than try to explain it with reference to global climate changes which people feel have not affected them.[16]

> **Box 7.2**
>
> When I started, science was the only value people ascribed to, but now if you say why are you really doing this, people say 'Well, I look at my four-year old son', or 'I look at my community', and now they are not just talking about molecules, but why it really matters. And when they do that, other people are invited into their value framework, and say 'You just showed me a picture of your community and we can share its values.'
>
> Gail Francis, RE-AMP

Box 7.2 recounts Gail Francis' experience of helping people in her social impact network to move from the scientific perspective to one of personal impact and value. In Gail's story, the four-year-old son and the community may be seen as examples of a 'boundary object', something (not necessarily a physical object) which has a different meaning to two groups of people. Beverley Hawkins and others[17] looked at attitudes to sustainability in a dairy and found that initially, the owners of the business were not interested in minimising their carbon footprint. However, this changed when they agreed a contract with a supermarket for whom sustainability and carbon footprint was an important part of their organisational identity. The contract therefore became a boundary object which forced them to review their attitudes to sustainability and accept that they needed to address their own carbon footprint.

Organisational life will be full of such boundary objects if we look for them. For example, a company may decide to convert part of its staff car park to bicycle stands as part of a strategy to encourage people to cycle to work. However, this will reduce the amount of parking available, and the bicycle stands become a boundary object, a focus for discussion. Although a relatively small issue in practical terms, facilitating a discussion about this part of the policy following a critical thinking approach has the potential to create a wide-ranging discussion about social and environmental matters. Another boundary object could be the availability of female toilets in a building (as discussed in Chapter 4), a critical examination of which could lead to an examination of assumptions regarding the status of women within an organisation.

7.2.4 Dialogue

We now turn to the first of the two practical skills that play an integral part in transformative learning and critical thinking, dialogue. According to the midwife of the learning organisation concept, Peter Senge, dialogue is a key requirement of his fourth discipline, team learning.[18] Unfortunately, it is a word which is often not understood clearly: we may associate it with "monologue", one person talking, and assume that it simply means two people talking. However, the "dia" does not mean "two" (which would be 'di') but "through", and in the organisational learning context refers to the manner in which a group of people converse, as "a sustained collective inquiry into the processes, assumptions, and certainties that compose everyday experience".[19] Senge talks about the connection with "discussion" and the difference between the two concepts: in discussion different views are presented and decisions are made, whereas in dialogue different views are presented in order to discover new views and develop a better understanding of complex issues. In a group learning context about how to address sustainability matters more effectively, there will therefore need to be a dance in and out of the two styles of conversation. In Habermasian terms, dialogue uses communicative skills to explore emancipatory concerns of participants in order to work towards a consensual outcome.

Senge and others at Massachusetts Institute of Technology (MIT) suggest a number of key steps needed in a process of dialogue.[20] It starts with a conversation about the situation of interest. As this unfolds people start to become aware that opinions expressed are informed by underlying assumptions, and this is a key moment. These assumptions now need to be, in MIT language, "suspended", or what I think is a useful metaphor, hung out on the washing line for all to see. Discussion now turns into dialogue, as more assumptions appear on the washing line and it becomes possible to ask questions such as which are true and which are false,[21] as when reflecting on premises which inform our frames of reference (Section 7.2.2). William Isaacs talks about this as being a moment where there is a "crisis of suspension",[22] as participants reflect on what previously seemed to be common sense no longer being common. At this point, if the group is willing to do so, the conversation can open up and flow in a new direction where there are new levels of understanding.

Dialogue therefore opens up the possibility that people may not only question underlying assumptions but help them to recognise ways in which they can do this, perhaps through different learning activities or different approaches to pedagogy. As such, this metacognition takes the questioning assumptions of double loop learning to another level, and is sometimes described as "triple loop learning".[23]

Many factors can contribute to effective dialogue. It needs a facilitator to manage the process, but also requires a group with positive dynamics of openness and a motivation to discuss new ideas, trust between participants and a sufficient sense of psychological safety to be open about personal frames of reference. Diversity within the group will also help to contribute to a range of perspectives being expressed.[24] Wals and Schwarzin[25] point out the value of participants having appropriate personal competencies, particularly those associated with sustainability (Section 5.6.3). However, as is crucial with all aspects of organisational culture, there needs to be strong encouragement by leaders within the organisation that this form of self-analysis can take place.

Think about dialogue as if it were an example of a complex adaptive system (CAS). Dialogue has the potential to change the rules by which actors in the CAS operate. There is diversity to open up alternative perspectives, and interactions between participants make it possible that the dialogue will shift the system to a new attractor. It may just be talking, but it can have a big impact.

7.2.5 Reflective practice

Reflection plays a key part in both transformative learning and critical thinking, so it is worth exploring it in more detail. We reflect when we deliberately and consciously think about our existence, perhaps as "reflection in practice", where we think about what we are doing when we do it, or "reflection on practice", where we think about something we are going to do or have done.[26] We can reflect at different levels—we might reflect on making a mistake and think about how we can avoid doing this in the future (single loop learning) or we might reflect more deeply about how we understand this mistake or what underlying assumptions are involved in what we are doing (double loop learning). Recognising assumptions means that we have to consider alternative perspectives on the situation—as such, reflection is a core part of systems thinking.

Thinking about sustainability, if we are manufacturing widgets we might reflect on the *means* by which we make them in order to make the process more socially or environmentally sustainable. However, if we were to look deeper and reflect on the *ends* of what we are doing, why widgets are important, we are shifting from single loop to double loop learning and are starting to practice critical reflection. As explored in Section 7.2.3, critical reflection means that we seek to question hegemonic ideas that are driving us, for example, why is profit maximisation more important than improving social cohesion within the organisation, or why is protecting intellectual property so important in commercial organisations?

Critical reflection is never easy. In our personal lives, it forces us to question who we are and our identity, and in an organisational setting it can be deeply threatening: the growing research literature about critical reflection acknowledges this difficulty. However, we cannot ignore power and hegemonic thinking completely if we are to think seriously about effective SFL, so it is useful to remember that the first part of critical reflection, to recognise the existence of power around us which delimits our thinking is very important in itself and may be as much as we in organisational learning and development can realistically achieve.[27]

7.2.6 Systems thinking techniques

In this book, I have used systems thinking at several different levels—to help make sense of situations of interest relevant to sustainability, and as a methodology for developing an SFL strategy. However, we might also choose to use it at the level of a pedagogical principle, integrating the ideas outlined in Chapter 2 into formal learning activities.

For example, we could ask individuals or groups to draw:

- a rich picture (Figure 2.2) of a situation of interest to see what this might reveal
- a system map (for example, Figure 2.3) to identify actors relevant to the situation
- an influence diagram (Figure 2.7) to show how people perceive power relationships operating within the situation
- causal flow diagrams (as in Section 2.11) to show perceptions of dynamic relationships within the situation and how these might unfold over time
- a concept map (as in Figure 6.15) to identify topics of significance.

Visual activities such as these can be powerful ways to encourage both critical reflection and, in a group setting, dialogue. For example, as the drawing progresses, ask the questions:

- What is included in the diagram and what is being left out (boundary judgements)?
- What does the relative position or size of different elements in the diagram mean (multiple perspectives, interrelationships)?
- What was drawn first and what was added later? Why (multiple perspectives, interrelationships)?
- What relationships (information flows, influence) are indicated, and what has been missed (interrelationships, boundary judgements)?

Often the process of drawing tells us as much about how we view a situation as what we actually draw.

In Chapter 10 we will also see how we can use diagramming to help with the process of evaluating SFL.

Time for reflection

In the introduction to this chapter, I provided a "health warning" about the challenges involved in using ideas such as transformative learning and critical thinking in an organisational setting.

Do you think that caution is necessary? Would you feel confident about using these ideas in your organisation's formal learning about sustainability? Perhaps you already do!

7.3 Using pedagogical principles in formal learning

In this section, we shall look at some practical ways in which ideas about pedagogy can be used in an organisational setting. First, we will look at what is probably the default pedagogy for formal learning activities, what I call a performative approach, and will then move on to consider some particular methods which can be used which can draw in the principles of transformative learning and critical thinking within the potential constraints of an organisational setting.

7.3.1 Performative approaches

In this section, I will briefly look at what is probably the default pedagogy for formal learning within organisations. This follows from a unitarist, managerialist philosophy about how an organisation operates, that the content and method to be used for delivering formal learning is determined by specialist management functions and is essentially a top-down activity based on a management-determined performance requirement (as discussed in Section 5.3). It will consequently focus on delivering formal learning which furthers the aims of the organisation as defined by senior management. This can be done in a variety of ways ranging from trainer-centred face-to-face events to online learning designed using a content delivery perspective.

Using the learning space triangle to relate it to Habermas' knowledge interest concept, we might position performative approaches as in Figure 7.3, where there is a strong emphasis on technical knowledge at the possible expense of communicative and emancipatory knowledge. If the training facilitator were to adopt more participatory or constructivist approaches, the contribution to communicative knowledge might be greater (as shown by the possible extension to the learning space).

There is nothing intrinsically "bad" about this. As identified in Chapter 5, much of the content within an SFL strategy may be technical in nature, and there will be a regular demand for formal learning aimed at improving people's abilities to work

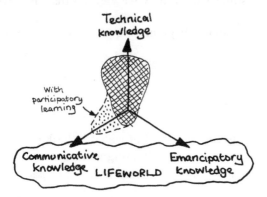

Figure 7.3 The learning space triangle with unitarist learning approaches.

in environmentally sustainable ways and to follow working practices which are non-discriminatory, for example. However, in the context of sustainability, conventional, performative training approaches may have limitations:

- They represent a top-down approach, where the content and the pedagogical principles deployed have been identified and decided on by more senior management or experts elsewhere, and thus may not necessarily take full account of what learners see as important or meaningful (their emancipatory interest). In complexity and systems thinking terms, this makes it more difficult to arrive at the edge of chaos or achieve requisite variety.
- The complex, multi-dimensional nature of sustainability makes it problematic to reduce the subject to a simple technical problem. It runs the risk of not allowing learners to contribute their own specific understanding of the situation to the process of learning. Without opening up the learning activity to the learners' lifeworlds by using andragogic principles, the whole activity may fail to engage participants.

7.3.2 Action learning

Action learning is an approach developed by Reg Revans based on the idea that the people best placed to find solutions to a problem within organisations are those dealing with the problem (in other words, those in the shadow system), and that the solutions may be found through collaborative action. The basic approach is that a group of people come together to form an "action learning set", agree on a particular challenge to address, and usually with the help of a facilitator over a period of time develop responses to the challenge. Within that basic structure, there are a wide variety of possibilities: participants may be from the same or different organisations, they may be at similar or different levels within hierarchies, and they may be more or less familiar with the issue to be discussed. However, the issue that they will work on needs to be something that they can relate to, that they are responsible for it, able to do something about it, and ideally should be able to implement solutions identified. Being empowered to find their own solutions to an organisational challenge, means that we can see action learning as embracing both a technical and emancipatory interest.[28]

Developing a learning strategy: formal 217

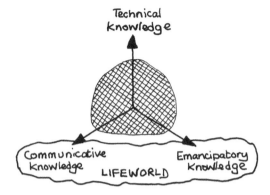

Figure 7.4 The learning space for action learning.

Using our learning space diagram again, we might see action learning as represented by Figure 7.4, where the emphasis is on technical knowledge contributed to by emancipatory knowledge and where the collaborative processes within the set can contribute to communicative knowledge.

Action learning may therefore be a useful approach to follow to address sustainability-related challenges, for example:

- What are the sustainability-related challenges we face in our organisation?
- What can we do to make our products more environmentally sustainable?
- How can we learn to recognise problems with internal social sustainability?

The list is probably endless.

Mike Pedler identifies a number of key processes crucial to make action learning effective.[29] Set members have a chance to describe their perspective of the challenge they are facing, drawing on their own practical awareness of the situation. There need to be ground rules addressing such things as confidentiality and respecting everyone's opinions to create the necessary psychological safety, for example. Set members need to be supportive in helping all to understand ideas and different perspectives. The set needs to have a questioning attitude so that it is able to develop insights. It needs to recognise that there will be a process of development, as people get to know each other and agree on how to work together. It also needs to be able to review progress and question its internal processes to make sure they are working effectively. It is beyond the scope of this book to provide guidance on how to manage an action learning set, but the further reading section at the end of the chapter provides some suggestions for more information.

There are many different ways in which the principles of action learning can be applied. In Box 7.3, Rob Hubbard, CEO of the certified B Corp LearningAge Solutions, explains how he runs 'design jams' with his team of learning design experts, software engineers and graphic designers. Rob sees working in this way as well aligned to the ethos of being a B Corp. Everyone has an opportunity to contribute to design decisions, bringing in perspectives from their own varied social identities: as Rob puts it, "Outside of LAS our team are musicians, authors, videographers, poets and carers. Some run clothing labels and publish books. We benefit from their wider interests in the creativity, perspective and ideas they bring to LAS".

> **Box 7.3**
>
> We'll run a design jam if we come up against a challenge where we need new thinking. We invite anyone from LAS to come along, whatever their role. We brief them in advance, then in the jam; explain the challenge, take questions and brainstorm ideas for an hour or so. We keep the jam open for about three days so that people can come back with further ideas and builds that they think of later. Doing it this way works well for the extroverts who generate ideas off-the-cuff and also for reflective introverts, who have time and space for the ideas to crystallise. When all the ideas are in, we then apply the project constraints to prioritise them and move forward.
>
> Rob Hubbard, LAS

One potential difficulty with action learning which is relevant to an SFL strategy is that conventional ways of implementing it may not address issues of power, both within the set and externally with the rest of the organisation.[30] While a set's ground rules may nominally say that each member is equal, in practice the power relations that come from such things as their gender or function within the organisation may subconsciously influence how the set works. Externally, how effective the set can be will depend on the power that it has within the organisation: Revans himself suggests a 12-point scale for the perceived power that an action learning set may have,[31] ranging from "carte blanche confidence", where senior management expresses full confidence in the work that it is doing, down to "defensive rationalisation", where any idea put forward by the set is dismissed—in such situations agreeing to the action learning process may be tokenism, or worse, be a strategy to legitimate a predetermined senior management decision.

To address such potential problems, critical theory can be introduced into the action learning process to try and ensure that power, however it is manifested, is recognised and addressed appropriately. As described previously in Section 7.2.3, the facilitator in a critical action learning process becomes even more important: as well as ensuring that the set functions effectively, they will have a role in helping the participants to critically reflect on where power may be having an effect on internal group dynamics and on the power of the set within the organisation. For example, they may need to point out where hegemonic assumptions may be limiting what the set is prepared to discuss.

7.3.3 Games and simulations

Games and simulations are valuable tools to deploy in formal aspects of an SFL. There are overlaps between games and simulations: a simulation may have the characteristics of a game, but a game is not necessarily a simulation. Simulation-based training is necessarily close to reality, and has been defined as a "... synthetic practice environment that is created in order to impart... competencies... that will improve a trainee's performance".[32] On the other hand, a game is some form of rule-based interactive activity where someone takes action and experiences feedback related to what they do in a situation which is related to reality but not necessarily realistic. In the "serious games" associated with learning in organisations, the primary purpose of the action-feedback loop is learning rather than entertainment.[33]

Neither games nor simulations need be complex. A simple form of simulation is the role play, where learners act out some version of reality in order to develop a competence or competency. A simple form of game used to help people understand the idea of exponential growth is to just fold a sheet of paper in half repeatedly—they discover how quickly this becomes impossible, and this can open up a discussion about the impossibility of sustained economic growth. At the other end of the complexity spectrum lie computer simulations with varying degrees of fidelity to reality where the learner makes decisions and sees what effect these have within the simulated reality (for example, as in a flight simulator). These have some of the qualities of a game in that there are no real consequences and that the learner is emotionally engaged with what they are doing.

Serious games can have a number of different purposes. They can help individuals to become more aware of how they think or behave in a particular situation, and as such can help to surface hidden assumptions and hence contribute to a double loop learning process. Games can help to strengthen communication and collaboration between team members, and games of this sort are a common staple of organisational team-building events. Thirdly, games (or what might be called here a simulation) can help people learn how a complex system operates: these might vary from "playing with" how an organisation's internal processes function through to moving entire armies across a continent.[34]

The relevance of these three different outcomes to SFL means that games and simulations can play an important part in a formal learning strategy, and there is an ever-increasing catalogue of books and online information available suggesting possibilities (albeit with something of an emphasis on environmental rather than social sustainability). For example, *The Climate Change Playbook*[35] describes 22 games based around systems thinking ideas which are designed to improve understanding of environmental sustainability issues. One of its games is "Harvest", where four or more players use paper and coins to explore fishery management issues. An essential part of the game is the debriefing activity, where participants are encouraged to think about whether they behaved aggressively or cooperatively, how they cooperated with each other (or not), and how simple interactions create complexity and unpredictable outcomes. There is also the sophisticated game/simulation "Sustainable Delta",[36] where teams of players using a computer model make decisions about how to manage a water resource, balancing a variety of needs and trying to avoid floods or droughts.

Although there are a great variety of possible designs for a game or simulation, certain common principles are important if they are to be effective and valuable in an SFL context. First, there needs to be a clear and relevant context for the activity—it might be difficult to engage employees in a retail chain with a simulation of river management, for example. Second, and in line with principles of Knowles' andragogy, they should be problem-solving, demanding that learners apply knowledge in order to achieve something which is meaningful and important in practical terms to them.[37] Also, by exposing learners to unpredictability and uncertainty they can force them to surface and question assumptions in order to encourage critical thinking. This also implies that learners need to be in control throughout over what decisions they make and the actions they take.

The most important aspect of learning through a simulation or serious game may be the role of a facilitator.[38] An actively engaged facilitator helps to increase enthusiasm for the activity and is there to provide support if people need help or something goes wrong. They also play an important part in perhaps the most essential part of the activity, the debrief. A facilitator should think about asking participants questions such as these once the activity has been completed[39]:

- What did I learn about myself, my behaviour and my values during the game?
- What did I learn about the behaviour of others taking part?
- What did I learn about communication during the game?
- What was new to me?
- What did I know but not do?
- What did I not know but now can do?

So far we have talked about games generally, so these observations might apply to any sort of game, whether it involves throwing dice or turning over cards. But an area of growing interest in formal learning within organisations is that of computer-based serious games. One of the United Kingdom's most respected serious games designers, Helen Routledge, says that well-designed games draw people in on an emotional journey, engaging them in a "core loop" of simple actions, repeated over and over in different settings, but which require them to think carefully about what decisions they could or should make. The great advantage of computer gaming is that the computer makes no moral judgements about you as a game player—you can try things out with no finger wagging if you make dubious decisions! Helen's story in Box 7.4 provides a perfect example of how a computer-based serious game can create a space for discussion about potentially sensitive subjects.

Box 7.4

There was a problem in the bank with diversity training. It was hours long and everybody thought it was patronising. So we designed a game based on a space station, where the characters were all aliens with stereotypes. Some aliens looked old, but were not. There was a big muscular blue alien who you might assume was quite domineering, but was actually quite gentle.

So because you had never seen these characters before, every assumption you made about these characters was coming from your unconscious assumptions about what people looked like. The game setting gave everyone a safe place to start talking about how what people looked like shaped what kind of person we thought they were. It worked really well.

Helen Routledge, Totem Learning

As another example, Helen designed a game for a paint manufacturer which allowed players to make different decisions about what ingredients to use, drawing on information about where they came from and what their environmental advantages or disadvantages were. Players' decisions influenced not only the profitability of the paint but its health and environmental impact. Making the game available during the manufacturer's Global Sustainability Day, employees around the world were able to develop a much better understanding of the social and environmental consequences of what they did every day.

There are some key principles to follow in designing computer-based serious games. Start from the learners and the world that they understand. Create a game environment which is close to reality but is sufficiently different so that players recognise that it is not reality. Take them on a journey: the classic storyline of the heroine/hero's journey works well, where someone has to go on a quest to achieve something but is confronted with problems along the way that they must overcome. Provide choices about what to do, and when someone makes a choice give them quick feedback, with a simple reward for making a good decision. Repeat the core loop of decision-making related to the purpose of the game to build up confidence as different and more complex challenges are introduced.

Well-designed and implemented serious games and solutions can be very effective at imparting the knowledge and skills and influencing the attitudes needed for social and environmental sustainability. Games can expose learners to hegemonic ideas in a way that does not necessarily provoke an immediate negative reaction, as by leaving reality 'common sense' may be safely suspended. They can offer a risk-free environment for trying out new ideas, can provide complex and realistic simulations of reality, provide a way of helping learners engage with complex and ambiguous situations, and are not necessarily expensive to develop or run. Perhaps most importantly in terms of promoting social sustainability, they provide a way to accelerate social learning: through collapsing time and space and bringing people with different experiences and expertise together in order to experiment with doing things in different ways changes that might take weeks or months informally or incidentally can be achieved in hours.

Time for reflection

How would you draw the learning space diagram for a computer-based serious game?

What would you include within the game to strengthen the communicative and emancipatory knowledge aspects?

7.3.4 Debating

Debating is often an activity associated with an expensive education and posh universities, and perhaps because of these associations, it has largely been overlooked as a pedagogical tool for learning within organisations. However, I have included it several times in training of trainers workshops that I have run (even though I did not have an expensive education), and have found that it works very well.

What do I mean by a debate? Here we mean a formal, structured discussion about a specific proposition. The classic way to launch a debate is to state a 'motion', sometimes using the somewhat archaic phraseology of "This house believes that…". The most important thing for the motion is that it expresses an opinion which may be readily contested. For example, we might start a debate with a motion that "This house believes that human activity is responsible for climate change" or "This house believes that automation will lead to more employment".

Having developed the motion, there is a specific way in which a debate runs. In its simplest form, you convene a group of people and from the group identify two people to present arguments supporting the motion and two people to oppose it. These people may be volunteers or chosen at random (the latter meaning that they may have to support a motion with which they disagree which could be a valuable opportunity for transformative learning). Alternatively, you could have a team of four or five people on each side of the debate. You may run the debate as a face-to-face activity, where it might take about an hour, or you could do it online with the arguments for and against being presented on successive days. There are many possibilities, but the important thing is to follow the general process.

Here is a summary of the process you need to follow (assuming two pairs of presenters):

1. Present the motion to the group.
2. Find out who will argue for and against the motion (volunteers or chosen).
3. Allow each pair about five minutes to prepare their arguments. Explain that they:
   - will have just five minutes each to present their case to the group
   - must decide how they will present their arguments and who should do this
   - should think about what their opponents may say and plan how they will argue against this
4. Invite the first person from the team arguing in support of the motion to speak. They should present the main arguments for or against the motion. Make sure that they do not speak for more than their allowed five minutes.
5. Invite the first person from the team arguing against the motion to speak. They will challenge the arguments presented by the other team's first speaker, and will summarise their own position. Keep them within their five minutes.
6. Allow the audience to ask questions. Try to make sure that this takes no longer than about 15 or 20 minutes.
7. Invite the second person arguing in support of the motion to speak. They should challenge any arguments presented against the motion and summarise their own position. Keep them within five minutes.
8. Invite the second person arguing against the motion to speak. Keep them within five minutes.
9. Vote by asking people to raise their hands to see whether people agree or disagree with the motion.
10. Bring the debate to a close by announcing "By a vote of [x] to [y], this house agrees (or disagrees) with the motion that (state the motion)".
11. Finish off the activity by asking everyone what they feel they have learned from the debating process.

Developing a learning strategy: formal 223

Running a debate to discuss a sustainability-related topic brings several potential advantages.[40] As the structure forces participants to look at different perspectives to the motion, think about the strength of an argument and challenge it, it develops critical thinking. The structure means that people must gather information, assess what that means for their argument, and communicate it clearly to others, an important generic skill. The process also means that participants must learn to "think on their feet", a valuable skill in all situations, and particularly so for issues relating to sustainability where people may unexpectedly find themselves having to justify a particular decision. The "controlled confrontation" of a debate can stimulate a considerable amount of energy and enthusiasm, and this can continue well after the final vote is taken.

However, it should be recognised that taking part does not necessarily mean that someone thinks deeply about the motion. Also, depending on the number of participants, many people may be quite unengaged with the process.

Time for reflection

I have just provided ideas about three methods that could be used in a formal learning approach to sustainability. What other methods do you know of that could be utilised?

For example, you might include the SWOT (Strengths, Weaknesses, Opportunities, Threats) analysis technique as something that could be valuable here. Think about others that might be of use.

7.4 Radical learning in the real world

The previous sections have explored various ideas about how SFL might be delivered, ideas which have ranged from what is perhaps normal or conventional within organisations (the performative approach) through to the radical, where learners are encouraged to reflect on, perhaps uncomfortable, hegemonic norms of political economy. Designing and delivering formal learning activities which incorporate critical thinking may be challenging, and perhaps even impossible, in many organisations, particularly those in a Level 1 or 2 model of sustainability. Apart from top-down resistance, critical thinking may also cause discomfort and unhappiness amongst learners to the extent that transformative learning may become impossible.

The reality is that transformative learning and critical thinking approaches are probably easier to use in an educational environment, particularly at higher education level. Indeed, Ralph Stacey questions whether such radical techniques are feasible in organisational settings and suggests that the prospect of changing beliefs and values through dialogue and exploring assumptions is a "highly idealised notion".[41]

> **Box 7.5**
>
> We are demonstrating that sustainability is integral to our business operations. Our policies encompass environment, carbon, social value and circular economy principles and we consistently reinforce these commitments across our organisation to ensure our people are clear about our vision and values.
>
> Fozia Parveen, ISG Ltd

Nevertheless, it is important to be aware of some of the principles which underlie these more radical ideas. As Box 7.5 suggests, that while an organisation's leadership can develop sustainability-related policies, the challenge is instilling it in employees so that they commit rather than just conform. First, it is useful to be able to think about how everyone's understanding of the world around them is socially constructed, based on what they have experienced in their lives. As such, these understandings are not immutable—they can be influenced. Second, in any group of people, there will be scepticism and resistance, as well as cognitive dissonance as people reflect on the inconsistencies in their own lives. Even in a "conventional" training session being run on performative principles you may encounter resistance: being able to draw on some of the ideas of transformative or critical thinking may be useful. For example, you might be able to ask a person raising an issue what is the basis for their objection, where has their scepticism come from, how reliable is that source of information, and so on. Note also the central importance of reflection within each of these techniques. It is therefore useful to be aware of the basic ideas about transformative learning and critical thinking so that you can draw on them as necessary.

Even in visionary organisations driven by sustainable values, we should not fall into the unitarist trap, that what is good for the organisation is good for its employees. Every individual's lifeworld and its attendant values should be respected and while there may well be a higher percentage of socially and environmentally aware employees in such an organisation, the contested nature of sustainability means that there will always be the potential for different points of view.

Performative learning will be useful in many organisational settings, but care must be taken to make sure that communicative and emancipatory interests are respected. Transformative learning and critical thinking may need to be given more attention in situations where employee engagement with sustainability is lower. Embedding critical thinking challenges within ostensibly "lighter" learning activities such as debates or serious games may be one way to encourage people to reflect on hegemonic assumptions in their frames of reference without feeling overly threatened.

7.5 Making decisions about principles of learning

Having considered various possibilities for alternative pedagogies, we can now update our table of boundary judgements (Table 7.1).

Table 7.1 Questions to ask about decisions on principles for formal learning

Boundary judgement questions	Cross-cutting questions	Content-related	Mechanisms-related	Principles-related
1 Who should benefit from the learning strategy?		Who needs to learn about sustainability?	Given decisions about who should benefit, what will appropriate learning mechanisms be? What is known about the personal characteristics of people who will be required to learn about sustainability and what relevance that may have?	**What is known about attitudes to sustainability?**
2 What is the purpose of the learning strategy?		What competences and competencies need to be addressed in the SFL strategy? What broader knowledge about sustainability is needed to underpin SFL? What are the desired learning outcomes for the relevant level of organisational sustainability?	What mechanisms are appropriate, given the competences and competencies that need to be addressed?	**How does the strategy need to change levels of engagement about sustainability within the organisation?**
3 What is the measure of success for the learning strategy?		What are the criteria of success for the learning outcomes? What are other possible measures of success?	What mechanisms for learning are appropriate given the required success criteria?	**How can we assess changes in the levels of commitment to sustainability?**
4 Who makes decisions about the strategy?	Who will make a decision about the learning strategy? What is the tradition within the organisation about decision-making on learning?		Who has good knowledge about how learning works within the organisation?	**Who can provide advice about suitable pedagogical strategies to use?**
5 What resources and constraints relevant to the strategy does the decision-maker control?	Who holds the budget for learning activities?		What can the decision-maker do to strengthen chosen mechanisms?	**What resources for formal learning are available?**

(Continued)

Boundary judgement questions	Cross-cutting questions	Content-related	Mechanisms-related	Principles-related
6 What conditions of the strategy's operation are outside of the control of the decision-maker?	What are the drivers in the operational environment for social and environmental sustainability? What pressure is there from the workforce to adopt social and environmental sustainability strategies?		What mechanisms for learning do people involved in the learning strategy use? How do informal learning mechanisms operate in relevant parts of the organisation? What knowledge sharing goes on within the organisation at the moment? What is the quality of the learning transfer climate across the organisation? What are the attitudes to sustainability amongst employees across the organisation?	
7 Who should be involved in the design of the strategy?		Who should be involved in the design: <ul><li>Operational staff?</li><li>Supervisors?</li><li>Others?</li></ul>	Who can provide relevant information about factors relevant to learning in the target groups identified? What should be the role of supervisors and others in thinking about mechanisms to utilise?	**Who should be involved in the pedagogical design of the formal learning activities?**
8 What expertise is needed to design the strategy?		What expertise is needed to design learning that will meet the competence and competency requirements?	What knowledge of group dynamics (levels of social capital, trust, organisational and social identity, etc.) relevant to learning in the design do people involved in the design have, or should have? What expertise is required in order to ensure that appropriate learning mechanisms are selected?	**What expertise in facilitating critical and transformative learning approaches is available?**

9 What guarantees of success do the sources of expertise offer?	How reliable is the knowledge about required aspects of sustainability that you have or is available to you? What consensus exists about required aspects of sustainability?	How reliable is the information you have on group dynamics and learner characteristics?	How confident are you about the effectiveness of pedagogical strategies that you will use in achieving the desired learning outcomes?
10 Who will represent the affected society and the natural environment?	Who can provide information from society or the natural environment to inform what content is needed?	Which external stakeholders can be engaged in the learning mechanisms deployed?	Who can provide alternative perspectives which challenge hegemonic thinking?
11 What opportunity does the affected society and natural environment have to challenge the strategy?	What content from outside the organisation is needed to support the SFL strategy? How can external perspectives on sustainability be taken into consideration?	How can external stakeholders be engaged in the mechanisms used for SFL?	What part can external stakeholders play in pedagogical strategies?
12 What is the worldview underlying the design of the learning strategy?	What are the political possibilities for engaging with external representatives in discussing sustainability-focused learning? How does social and environmental sustainability sit within your organisation's culture and philosophy? What are your own perspectives on social and environmental sustainability? What other worldviews on sustainability exist which should be considered? What is the organisational tradition for conducting the LNA process?	What alternative worldviews may be identified as a result of engaging with external stakeholders?	What underlying hegemonic assumptions are influencing the design of the SFL strategy?

228 *Developing a learning strategy: formal*

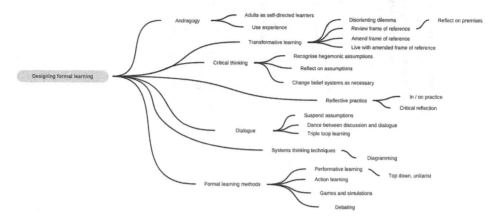

Figure 7.5 Key points in this chapter.

7.6 Key points in this chapter

Figure 7.5 outlines key points from this chapter. The ideas of Jürgen Habermas provide a way to think about different pedagogical strategies for SFL. Malcolm Knowles' andragogy sees learners as self-directed and with their experience as a resource to be used, so they should have influence within the learning process.

Jack Mezirow's transformative learning suggests that when confronted by a disorienting dilemma, people will think about their frame of reference for understanding the world and associated point of view. With the right support, they can amend their frame of reference in order to change their point of view about such dilemmas.

Critical thinking draws attention to the constructed nature of common sense, describing it as hegemonic thinking. With strong connections to transformative learning, if the individual recognises that their frame of reference and point of view may not actually be in their best interest, they may decide to change their understanding.

Dialogue can happen within a discussion when people taking part become aware of and suspend their assumptions so that they can be questioned. This makes it possible to change assumptions and potentially conduct a more constructive discussion.

Reflective practice may occur within or after doing something and opens up the possibility for doing things differently. With critical reflection, the individual thinks about the hegemonic assumptions which may be influencing their behaviour.

Systems thinking provides a set of tools and principles which may be of use in pedagogical practices.

Conventionally, formal learning within organisations uses performative approaches, which are often based on unitarist assumptions. Alternative formal learning techniques, such as action learning, serious games and debating increase the opportunities for learning through communication and addressing emancipatory concerns.

Notes

1 Malcolm Knowles, 'Adult Learning Processes: Pedagogy and Andragogy', *Religious Education* 72, no. 2 (1977): 202–11.
2 Joseph W.M. Kessels, 'Andragogy', in *The Routledge Companion to Human Resource Development*, ed. Rob F. Poell, Tonette S. Rocco, and Gene L. Roth (London: Routledge, 2014), 13–20.
3 Jack Mezirow, 'Perspective Transformation', *Adult Education* 28, no. 2 (1978): 100–10; Jack Mezirow, 'Transformative Learning: Theory to Practice', *New Directions for Adult and Continuing Education* 1997, no. 74 (1997): 5; Jack Mezirow, 'Transformative Learning as Discourse', *Journal of Transformative Education* 1, no. 1 (2003): 58–63; Jack Mezirow, 'An Overview on Transformative Learning', in *Contemporary Theories of Learning: Learning Theorists in Their Own Words*, ed. Knud Illeris (London: Routledge, 2008), 90–105.
4 Gregory M. Henderson, 'Transformative Learning as a Condition for Transformational Change in Organizations', *Human Resource Development Review* 1, no. 2 (2002): 186–214.
5 Patricia Cranton, *Understanding and Promoting Transformative Learning: A Guide for Educators of Adults*, 2nd Edition (San Francisco, CA: Jossey Bass, 2006).
6 John Cook et al., *America Misled: How the Fossil Fuel Industry Deliberately Misled Americans about Climate Change* (Fairfax, VA: Center for Climate Change Communication, George Mason University, 2019), https://www.climatechangecommunication.org/america-misled.
7 Stephen D. Brookfield, *The Power of Critical Theory for Adult Learning and Teaching* (Maidenhead: Open University Press, 2005), 93–97.
8 A. Gramsci, *Selections from the Prison Notebooks of Antonio Gramsci*, trans. Q. Hoare and G. Nowell Smith (London: Lawrence & Wishart, 1971).
9 Brookfield, *The Power of Critical Theory*, 41.
10 Cranton, *Understanding and Promoting Transformative Learning: A Guide for Educators of Adults*.
11 Stephen D. Brookfield, *The Power of Critical Theory for Adult Learning and Teaching* (Maidenhead: Open University Press, 2005).
12 Michael Reynolds, 'Towards a Critical Management Pedagogy', in *Management Learning: Integrating Perspectives in Theory and Practice*, ed. John G. Burgoyne and M. Reynolds (London: SAGE Publications, 1997), 312–28.
13 Reynolds.
14 Kate Kearins and Delyse Springett, 'Educating for Sustainability: Developing Critical Skills', *Journal of Management Education* 27, no. 2 (2003): 188–204.
15 Brookfield, *The Power of Critical Theory for Adult Learning and Teaching*.
16 Eugene Sadler-Smith, 'Communicating Climate Change Risk and Enabling Pro-Environmental Behavioral Change through Human Resource Development', *Advances in Developing Human Resources* 17, no. 4 (2015): 442–59; Eugene Sadler-Smith, 'Making Sense of Global Warming: Designing a Human Resource Development Response', *European Journal of Training and Development* 38, no. 5 (2014): 387–97.
17 Beverley Hawkins, Annie Pye, and Fernando Correia, 'Boundary Objects, Power, and Learning: The Matter of Developing Sustainable Practice in Organizations', *Management Learning* 48, no. 3 (2017): 292–310.
18 P. M. Senge, *The Fifth Discipline: The Art and Practice of the Learning Organization* (London: Century Business, 1993).
19 William N. Isaacs, 'Taking Flight: Dialogue, Collective Thinking, and Organizational Learning', *Organizational Dynamics* 22, no. 2 (1993): 25.
20 Senge, *The Fifth Discipline: The Art and Practice of the Learning Organization*; Edgar H. Schein, 'On Dialogue, Culture, and Organizational Learning', *Organizational Dynamics* 22, no. 2 (1993): 40–51; Isaacs, 'Taking Flight'.
21 Isaacs, 'Taking Flight'.
22 Isaacs, 36.
23 Isaacs, 30.
24 Schein, 'On Dialogue, Culture, and Organizational Learning'; Arjen E.J. Wals, *Beyond Unreasonable Doubt: Education and Learning for Socio-Ecological Sustainability in the Anthropocene* (Wageningen: Wageningen University, 2015).

25 Arjen E.J. Wals and Lisa Schwarzin, 'Fostering Organizational Sustainability through Dialogic Interaction', *The Learning Organization* 19, no. 1 (2012): 11–27.
26 Donald A. Schön, *The Reflective Practitioner: How Professionals Think in Action* (New York: Basic Books, 1983).
27 Linda Perriton, 'A Reflection of What Exactly? Questioning the Use of "Critical Reflection" in Management Education Contexts', in *Organizing Reflection*, ed. M. Reynolds et al. (London: Routledge, 2004), 131.
28 John Edmonstone, 'Beyond Critical Action Learning? Action Learning's Place in the World', *Action Learning: Research and Practice* 16, no. 2 (2019): 136–48.
29 Mike Pedler, *Action Learning for Managers* (Aldershot: Gower Publishing Ltd., 2012).
30 Russ Vince, 'The Contradictions of Impact: Action Learning and Power in Organizations', *Action Learning: Research and Practice* 9, no. 3 (2012): 209–18; Davide Nicolini et al., 'In Search of the "Structure That Reflects": Promoting Organizational Reflection Practices in a UK Health Authority', in *Organizing Reflection*, ed. M. Reynolds et al. (London: Routledge, 2004), 95–118.
31 Reginald W. Revans, *ABC of Action Learning* (Aldershot: Gower Publishing Ltd., 2011).
32 Eduardo Salas, Jessica L. Wildman, and Ronald F. Piccolo, 'Using Simulation-Based Training to Enhance Management Education', *Academy of Management Learning & Education* 8, no. 4 (2009): 560.
33 Robert-Jan Den Haan and Mascha C. Van der Voort, 'On Evaluating Social Learning Outcomes of Serious Games to Collaboratively Address Sustainability Problems: A Literature Review', *Sustainability* 10, no. 4529 (2018).
34 The 1983 wargame "Operation Able Archer" appeared so realistic to the Soviet Union that it thought that NATO was about to launch a nuclear strike and mobilised its own nuclear weapons in readiness.
35 Dennis Meadows, Linda Booth Sweeney, and Gillian Martin Mehers, *The Climate Change Playbook: 22 Systems Thinking Games for More Effective Communication about Climate Change* (Hartford, VT: Chelsea Green Publishing, 2016).
36 Deltares, 'Sustainable Delta Game', Deltares, accessed 4 June 2021, https://www.deltares.nl/en/software/sustainable-delta-game/.
37 Jiafang Lu, Philip Hallinger, and Parinya Showanasai, 'Simulation-Based Learning in Management Education: A Longitudinal Quasi-Experimental Evaluation of Instructional Effectiveness', *Journal of Management Development* 33, no. 3 (2014): 218–44.
38 Salas, Wildman, and Piccolo, 'Using Simulation-Based Training to Enhance Management Education'; Hans Dieleman and Don Huisingh, 'Games by Which to Learn and Teach about Sustainable Development: Exploring the Relevance of Games and Experiential Learning for Sustainability', *Journal of Cleaner Production* 14, no. 9–11 (2006): 837–47.
39 Dieleman and Huisingh, 'Games by Which to Learn and Teach about Sustainable Development', 846–47.
40 Jessica Hennessey, 'Motivating a Productive Discussion of Normative Issues through Debates', *The Journal of Economic Education* 45, no. 3 (2014): 225–39; Ruth L. Healey, 'The Power of Debate: Reflections on the Potential of Debates for Engaging Students in Critical Thinking about Controversial Geographical Topics', *Journal of Geography in Higher Education* 36, no. 2 (2012): 239–57.
41 Ralph D. Stacey, *Strategic Management and Organisational Dynamics: The Challenge of Complexity*, 6th Edition (Prentice Hall: Financial Times, 2011), 211.

8 Developing a learning strategy 4

Informal learning and the learning environment

8.1 What this chapter covers

Figure 8.1 shows how this chapter is structured. It has three main sections. Section 8.2 continues from the previous three chapters by looking at how the learning needs assessment process can take account of informal learning possibilities. Then, in Section 8.3, we will take a look at what might be regarded as the systemic environment for both formal and informal learning, the organisational culture, and consider the role that Human Resources functions generally, human resource development (HRD) and human resource management (HRM), can play in creating an environment conducive to sustainability-focused learning (SFL).

We are then in a position to complete our table of boundary judgements for the SFL strategy, and in Chapter 9, we will see how to convert that into a written strategy.

8.2 Supporting informal learning

In Chapter 6, we looked at various mechanisms through which informal learning may happen and attempted to summarise these in Figure 6.2. Almost by definition, informal learning is not organised in a formal sense, but some of the mechanisms identified can be supported and encouraged. The amorphous nature of informal learning also means that it is difficult to classify and define particular forms of informal learning. It is possible to apply a label to some particular forms of informal learning, and in this section, we will look at four of these, communities of practice, coaching and mentoring, after-event reviews and service learning. However, it is important to think carefully about the principles that these labels embody and to recognise that the techniques can be used flexibly.

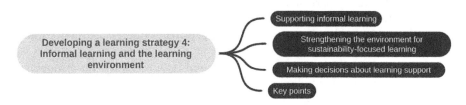

Figure 8.1 Map of Chapter 8.

DOI: 10.4324/9781003218296-9

8.2.1 Communities of practice

In Section 6.2.2, we looked at the relevance of social learning in the context of teams constructing knowledge. Social learning may manifest itself as a "community of practice" (CoP) a term popularised by Jean Lave and Etienne Wenger in the 1990s,[1] which describes a group of people coming together to share knowledge and learn from each other. Philosophically, Lave and Wenger's idea of the CoP was important as it stresses the idea of learning as participation, as an ongoing process, where people enter the community on a trajectory towards becoming more knowledgeable. This distinguishes it from formal learning and "courses", which are based on the idea that knowledge is something we acquire and demonstrate through some form of certification, creating the risk that once we have acquired it we no longer feel the need to continue learning. As such, the concept of the CoP therefore is highly relevant to SFL as contributing to the sustainability journey.

Communities of practice can be physical, with people meeting to share ideas, or virtual, where questions are asked and knowledge is shared online—hybrid versions are also quite possible. They can be internal, within one organisation, or interorganisational, bringing representatives from organisations together in a spirit of knowledge sharing around a particular aim. An example is the "generative social impact network", a form of CoP which comes together to achieve some social goal—RE-AMP[2] is a good example of this.

In an organisational setting what participants in a CoP want to learn is generally driven by the demands of work, so what knowledge it generates usually comes from the bottom up, and in this way contributes to establishing requisite variety and, in complexity terms, moves practice towards an edge of chaos between the shadow and legitimate systems.

A CoP may be seen as successful "when its members exchange specific knowledge, practices and/or experiences that contribute to developing a practice in a specific field".[3] So if CoPs focusing on sustainability seem like a useful strategy to support, what are the success factors? Research suggests a range of issues to consider[4]:

- The balance between top-down control and autonomy can have an impact on the form of knowledge generated, and this needs to be monitored.
- CoPs need a clear knowledge domain to address, but related subtopics will always appear.
- Some form of governance and facilitation is needed, to keep the momentum going, demonstrate good practice, monitor for problems, and so on.
- Occasional inputs from external experts help to provide energy (preventing the build-up of entropy (Section 2.8)).
- Community members need to sense excitement and energy from the CoP and feel that they are really part of a community, through such things as a steady flow of new questions and alternative (synchronous and asynchronous) modes of working.
- Access to other, related, networks can help provide interest and news sources of information.
- Mechanisms for dealing with problems caused by hierarchies, for example, senior managers shutting down discussion, even if unintentionally.
- The need for proof of effectiveness, for senior management who may be funding the CoP and to participants.
- A feeling of trust amongst community members is essential.

The ease with which a CoP focusing on SFL can be brought into existence will depend on how organisational culture views sustainability and the level of engagement of employees. Providing some form of technical infrastructure and/or facilitating early physical meetings may be an important part of encouraging the emergence of a CoP to support an SFL strategy.

8.2.2 Coaching and mentoring

The related mechanisms of coaching and mentoring occupy a position somewhere between formality and informality: they are formal in that they have some structure and may be planned, but are informal in that they do not necessarily have a particular agenda and may happen only when necessary.

Although there are differences between the two mechanisms, there are also important similarities. Both depend for their effectiveness on the quality of the relationship between two people, and researchers reflect on the similarities between coaching and mentoring and therapy.[5] Both have proved to be difficult to define, and the literature about each boasts several dozen different definitions.[6]

Coaching is probably the more varied practice. Broadly speaking, we can talk about two forms of coaching. Although the terminology is inconsistent, executive coaching is where a coach works with a senior manager, often working on personal development aimed at improving the executive's effectiveness. Workplace or managerial coaching occurs at lower levels in the organisation and describes the process where a supervisor or someone with specific skills helps an individual to improve in a specific area. Explained this way, there are clear parallels between coaching and training, and indeed, research into the effectiveness of coaching shows that it is influenced by similar factors, such as self-efficacy, motivation, feedback and supervisory support, amongst others (as in Section 6.5.2).[7] One factor that is different is the importance of establishing a "coaching culture".[8] Megginson and Clutterbuck suggest that this culture needs to evolve through four stages: "nascent", where there is no commitment to coaching and it is abandoned if other priorities appear; "tactical", the value of coaching is recognised but it is a problem for human resources (HR); "strategic", coaching is an accepted strategy and is considered in performance management discussions; and "embedded", where coaching occurs formally and informally throughout the organisation, and senior managers may even be mentored by less senior staff.

While coaching has a short-term tactical quality, mentoring is usually seen to be a long-term strategic activity, with a relationship between an often older, experienced person (the mentor) and someone generally younger (the protégé), who looks to the mentor for advice and wisdom. Mentoring may be formal, where the relationship is set up by a third party (sometimes described as a "blind date" mentoring arrangement), or informal, where the protégé seeks out someone they respect. The United Kingdom's Institute for Corporate Responsibility and Sustainability (ICRS) operates a mentoring scheme for its members, where the ICRS matches a mentor to someone looking for longer-term professional relationship.[9] There is research to show that informal mentoring is often more effective than formal mentoring.[10]

So what can coaching and mentoring bring to an SFL strategy? At its simplest level, it might be useful in the same way as for any other organisational knowledge or skill requirement. However, if operating sustainably is seen to be something of uncharted territory for an organisation or particular members of senior management, an external coach or mentor with the necessary interpersonal skills and a deep understanding of the complexity of sustainability could prove very valuable.

An interesting concept is that of "reverse mentoring",[11] where a technically junior individual, internal or external, provides mentoring support to a senior manager: again, this could be useful where the mentor has specific, valuable experience or knowledge.

Given the long-term commitment that sustainability requires and the probable challenges to be encountered along the way, mentoring in particular may be an important strategy to pursue, particularly for senior managers who have less knowledge of or experience with its implications.

8.2.3 After-event reviews

An after-event review (AER) is a meeting in which people gather to review and learn from a recent event. With roots in military practice, they are sometimes also called after-action reviews or debriefs and are used in many different settings—in the military, in healthcare and in aviation, as well as in general organisational practice.

They have a range of purposes, ranging from information sharing, process improvement, individual and team learning and development, as well as in exploring what might have gone wrong in a particular situation. As such, effective AERs can bring benefits at individual, team and organisational levels.

There is sometimes an assumption that an AER is only really needed after something goes wrong, as this is a primary opportunity for learning.[12] It is true that reflecting on mistakes made or failure is important so that necessary changes can be made, but reviewing success is also important to make sure that people do not become complacent and overlook complexities which on another occasion could cause failure.

Although various terms are used to describe the process of an AER, there are generally three stages to the process[13]:

- Observation and explanation—participants describe what happened.
- Developing an understanding about what happened, a process of sense-making where we look at what has happened to develop a plausible explanation.
- Feedback on what happened with a discussion about what might need to be done differently in the future.

The effectiveness of an AER can be explained from a systems perspective: that a process creates an output which does not conform with expectations, identifying a need for change. Referring again to Argyris and Schön's concept of single and double loop learning, the AER process needs to examine which level is appropriate, and the degree to which participants' mental models need to be examined and changed. These mental models may incorporate various forms of bias which we all carry around with us, for example: fundamental attribution, where we attribute success to our own personal qualities and failure to external factors; confirmation bias, where we pay more attention to factors which we initially think are significant; and hindsight bias, where outcomes affect our ability to judge what has gone before.[14]

AERs have to be carefully planned if they are to be effective. First, create structure, possibly through a skilled, non-judgemental facilitator who can guide the process of reflection and help to create a useful action plan, or alternatively use a pre-designed checklist outlining the process to be followed and questions to be asked.[15] Brief participants appropriately so that they know what will happen and what they are expected to do. There needs to be a strong feeling of psychological safety[16] within the group, which will be influenced by the facilitator, pre-existing trust, and particularly important, the organisational culture and its approach to mistakes.[17]

As with the concept of the coaching culture discussed previously, an organisational culture which sees AERs as a normal way of doing things can help to position them as an important part in an SFL strategy. In a sense, as sustainability is always something that an organisation is working towards and can never fully achieve, there is always something more that can be done, so the AER process will always be of value.

8.2.4 Service learning

One particularly amorphous category of informal learning is the 'structured work extension', which we explained as including such things as secondments, job shadowing or working on specific projects. Such initiatives can help to promote SFL if suitable opportunities are available within the organisation, but it may be that individuals need to venture outside to gain useful or appropriate experience about sustainable practice.

A more well-defined example of such activity is what is often known as "service learning". This may be described as learning occurring when individuals take part in community activities with the intention of promoting their learning and development.[18] It may be seen as an example of experiential learning, and has been described as learning with "head, hands and heart".[19]

Exactly how service learning happens can vary considerably. One form which has been researched is "international service learning", where organisations send employees overseas (often to low-income countries) to work on specific community projects. A pioneer in this respect is PricewaterhouseCoopers, but others such as IBM, Unilever and Novo Nordisk also have similar programmes.[20] The format for all is somewhat similar: a period of preparation with an extensive briefing on what will happen, the in-service experience itself, and a debrief period where an attempt is made to "make sense" of the experience. In many respects the debrief seems to be the most important part of the process, as without a structured attempt to make sense of what happened, the experience remains just an experience. To this end, participants are often asked to keep a journal of their experience, and during the debriefing process to recount stories about what happened, and through dialogue with others, to reflect on their learning and show how their understanding of problems they encountered has deepened.[21]

Studies have shown that service learning can bring various benefits to the learners, for example, being better able to grapple with complex, real-world problems, developing a sense of civic responsibility and strengthening understanding about such things as cultural differences, morality and ethical dilemmas.[22]

Of course, international service learning is expensive, and companies may attach it to a CSV policy, where the overseas experience also aims to strengthen the parent organisation's supply chain in some way. However, it is not unreasonable to think that similar experiences could be gained locally to where people work, for example as an initiative organised or sponsored by the employer, or self-motivated as a volunteer working in, for example, a homeless shelter or being active in an environmental group. A good example of this is provided by the UK engineering and services business, NG Bailey, who actively support local service learning opportunities (see Box 8.1). A key issue would be to make sure that the altruism is supplemented by a structured process of reflection which helps to strengthen learning, and even for those taking part to find ways to share their experience and learning with others in the organisation.

Box 8.1

There has always been a real focus on trying to inspire people to make positive change, whether that be at work, through their work, or just in their personal lives. So, for example, NG Bailey will support its employees in their own charitable giving outside of work, so we offer volunteering days to all our employees to use as they wish. If you give up your time freely outside of work, let's say you volunteer as a governor at your children's school, the business can support you in taking the time to attend those meetings but can also make a donation to those organisations in your name. So we go beyond transactional sustainability, and try to encourage people to take steps in their personal life as well.

Natalie Wilkinson, NG Bailey

Even if service learning as described is not relevant to your situation, staff may take part in internal structured work extensions such as secondments or project assignments. If so, the principles of preparation and an effective debrief remain relevant to ensure that learning happens.

Time for reflection

This section has suggested a few examples of how informal learning which is more easily accessible to HRD may be implemented.
    What are your thoughts about the suggestions?
    What could be implemented in your organisation?

8.3 Strengthening the environment for sustainability-focused learning

In Chapter 6, we looked at the range of mechanisms through which learning in organisations can happen and considered various factors which can influence its effectiveness. In systems thinking terms, these factors are what we can call the "environment for SFL", being elements which affect the system of learning but which are not controlled by it. The characteristics of this environment for SFL will have a particularly pronounced effect on informal learning: a hostile environment has the potential to restrict or even shut down valuable informal learning opportunities. However, many of these factors can potentially be influenced by organisational policies and practices, and the HR function through both HRD and the more organisational development-oriented HRM can have an important part to play in this.

The degree to which this is possible depends very much on how both the organisation and HR professionals see its role. One fundamental issue is that traditionally HR occupies a weak position in power structures, being seen as a service function rather than being operational. Gender issues may also be significant: the proportion of women working in HR is often higher than in other organisational functions,[23] and this can be significant in male-dominated hierarchical structures.[24] Other factors contributing to a lack of power may be the complex network of stakeholders who all have some degree of interest in how HR works,[25] and the difficulty HRD in particular has in demonstrating its value to the organisation.[26] More generally, HR is also something of a "weak" profession, as it does not have a clearly defined external body of scientific knowledge of professions as do medicine or engineering, and connections between the body of academic knowledge that does exist and practice are often limited.[27]

Nevertheless, the potential for playing a significant part in necessary changes is there, and the particular characteristics of the sustainability *zeitgeist* may give HR a unique opportunity to play a significant role in any transition towards sustainability. Thinking about the network of factors presented in Figure 6.7, at the highest level we have the contested concept of sustainability itself. HR practitioners, familiar with the challenges of grappling with the wicked problems presented by human behaviour, may find themselves competent in using the kinds of thinking tools needed for dealing with the complex, interdisciplinary nature of social and environmental sustainability concerns.

Organisational culture, being a manifestation of beliefs and values which prevail within an organisation, could be amenable to change through a carefully considered programme of learning and communication designed and delivered by HR.[28] An organisational culture has many facets, one of which is the ethical culture which prevails, and the resultant moral compass visible within the organisation. Traditionally, the HRM side of HR has been responsible for the morality of how organisations relate to their employees, but the performative focus in HRD in recent decades has led to criticisms that learning and development may have lost something of this broader moral focus (see Section 5.3), and this focus may need to be reclaimed.

Learning culture is another facet of organisational culture. While HR clearly has an important part to play in this, of fundamental importance is the example set by senior management—to what degree do they demonstrate commitment to learning, through creating space in allocating resources for learning activities, through tolerating mistakes as a route to learning, or through demonstrating their own fallibility and learning needs? HR will have a role to play in seeking to influence upwards to open up changes that may be necessary. As the example in Box 8.2 shows, opening up a space for people to talk about issues that are important to them can be very powerful.

> **Box 8.2**
>
> We have developed a programme of 'lunch and learn' sessions, which give people from the business a chance to talk about any issues of concern. This calendar of activities has been a great success and is very popular. We had one person talk about their MS as a hidden disability. She was very open about it, and it opened up conversations about what disabilities like that mean.
>
> Fozia Parveen, ISG Ltd

As we continue through the network of factors affecting learning, HRD also has an important part to play in influencing such things as social capital and the learning transfer climate, for example through delivering formal learning and supporting informal learning activities which foster interpersonal communication and collaboration and which engender trust. It would be important to develop a good understanding of the quality of networking within the organisation and the strength of the learning transfer climate in different parts of the organisation.

Thinking about the individual level, HRM may be seen to have an important part to play.[29] One of its roles is to make sure that legislation protecting minimum levels for conditions of employment is enforced and should, in principle, seek to make sure that even higher standards are observed. HRM is involved in reward and compensation schemes and can seek to make sure that these influence socially and environmentally sustainable activities. It plays a part in identifying and establishing work design to facilitate flexible employment patterns, working from home or remotely to help with work-life balance and to minimise commuting obligations. It manages the recruitment process, to try and make sure that people who join the organisation embrace a sustainability ethos. And amongst other things it manages the performance management process, where it can try to ensure that learning becomes an integral part of what people do and that working to improve social and environmental sustainability, inside and outside the organisation, is given due importance and is appropriately rewarded.

Time for reflection

What are your thoughts about these suggestions?
What other initiatives might be useful in your organisation?

8.4 Making decisions about learning support

We can now finalise the boundary judgement table with some observations relevant to supporting informal learning and the role of the learning environment (Table 8.1).

Table 8.1 Questions to ask about decisions on informal learning

Boundary judgement questions	Cross-cutting questions	Content-related	Mechanisms-related	Principles-related
1 Who should benefit from the learning strategy?		Who needs to learn about sustainability?	Given decisions about who should benefit, what will appropriate learning mechanisms be? What is known about the personal characteristics of people who will be required to learn about sustainability and what relevance that may have?	
2 What is the purpose of the learning strategy?		What competences and competencies need to be addressed in the SFL strategy? What broader knowledge about sustainability is needed to underpin SFL? What are the desired learning outcomes for the relevant level of organisational sustainability?	What mechanisms are appropriate, given the competences and competencies that need to be addressed?	How does the strategy need to change levels of engagement about sustainability within the organisation?
3 What is the measure of success for the learning strategy?		What are the criteria of success for the learning outcomes? What are other possible measures of success?		
4 Who makes decisions about the strategy?	Who will make a decision about the learning strategy?		What mechanisms for learning are appropriate given the required success criteria? Who has good knowledge about how learning works within the organisation?	How can we assess changes in the levels of engagement about sustainability?
5 What resources and constraints relevant to the strategy does the decision-maker control?	What is the tradition within the organisation about decision-making on learning? Who holds the budget for learning activities?		What can the decision-maker do to strengthen chosen mechanisms?	Who can provide advice about suitable pedagogical strategies to use? What resources for formal learning are available? **What resources for supporting informal learning are available?**

(*Continued*)

Boundary judgement questions	Cross-cutting questions	Content-related	Mechanisms-related	Principles-related
6 What conditions of the strategy's operation are outside of the control of the decision-maker?	What are the drivers in the operational environment for social and environmental sustainability? What pressure is there from the workforce to adopt social and environmental sustainability strategies?		What mechanisms for learning do people involved in the learning strategy use? How do informal learning mechanisms operate in relevant parts of the organisation? What knowledge sharing goes on within the organisation at the moment? What is the quality of the learning transfer climate across the organisation? What are the attitudes to sustainability amongst employees across the organisation?	**What tradition does the organisation have for supporting informal learning practices such as communities of practice, coaching, mentoring, after-event reviews and service learning? What does HRM do to promote a learning culture? What does HRM do to strengthen internal social sustainability?**
7 Who should be involved in the design of the strategy?		Who should be involved in the design: • Operational staff? • Supervisors? • Others?	Who can provide relevant information about factors relevant to learning in the target groups identified? What should be the role of supervisors and others in thinking about mechanisms to utilise?	Who should be involved in the pedagogical design of the formal learning activities? **Who can provide guidance on the strength of the learning culture within the organisation?**
8 What expertise is needed to design the strategy?		What expertise is needed to design learning that will meet the competence and competency requirements?	What knowledge of group dynamics (levels of social capital, trust, organisational and social identity, etc.) relevant to learning do people involved in the design have, or should have? What expertise is required in order to ensure that appropriate learning mechanisms are selected?	What expertise in facilitating critical and transformative learning approaches is available? **What expertise in developing communities of practice and facilitating other forms of informal learning is available?**

9	What guarantees of success do the sources of expertise offer?	How reliable is the knowledge that you have or is available to you about required aspects of sustainability? What consensus exists about required aspects of sustainability?	How reliable is the information you have on group dynamics and learner characteristics?	How confident are you about the effectiveness of pedagogical strategies that you will use in achieving the desired learning outcomes? **What do previous experiences of using informal learning approaches have to say for this strategy?**	
10	Who will represent the affected society and the natural environment?	Who can provide information from society or the natural environment to inform what content is needed? What content from outside the organisation is needed to support the SFL strategy? How can external perspectives on sustainability be taken into consideration? **How can external stakeholders be involved in informal learning activities?**	Which external stakeholders can be engaged in the learning mechanisms deployed? How can external stakeholders be engaged in the mechanisms used for SFL?	What part can external stakeholders play in pedagogical strategies?	
11	What opportunity does the affected society and natural environment have to challenge the strategy?	What are the political possibilities for engaging with external representatives in discussing sustainability-focused learning?			
12	What is the worldview underlying the design of the learning strategy?	How does social and environmental sustainability sit within your organisation's culture and philosophy? What are your own perspectives on social and environmental sustainability? What other worldviews on sustainability exist which should be considered? What is the organisational tradition for conducting the LNA process?	What alternative worldviews may be identified as a result of engaging with external stakeholders?	What underlying hegemonic assumptions are influencing the design of the SFL strategy? **What worldviews shape the organisation's culture and associated learning culture?**	

242 *Developing a learning strategy: informal*

8.5 Key points in this chapter

Figure 8.2 summarises the key points for this chapter. Many of the ways in which informal learning can happen are amenable to external support. Communities of practice bring people together to share ideas and develop knowledge. While the exact content should be driven by participants, the organisation, perhaps HRD, can provide an infrastructure to help it work and governance to maintain its progress.

Coaching and mentoring are two activities which rely on interpersonal relationships, perhaps focused on strategic issues or for developing specific knowledge and skill. They may also have a longer-term focus in helping individuals to develop personally.

After-event reviews can happen in many different settings, but the basic process is to discuss what has happened in a particular situation, make sense of what happened and why, and to draw lessons about what can be done more effectively in the future.

Service learning is where an individual contributes to some sustainability-related initiative outside the organisation. To be of maximum benefit it is important that they reflect on what they have learnt and report this back to their organisation so that others can benefit.

HRD and HRM both have a part to play in strengthening the environment for learning within the organisation. This can help to make informal learning work more effectively.

8.6 Further reading

The following books are useful for more information about action learning.

ABC of action learning, Reg Revans, Gower Publishing, 2011: an accessible text by the key name in the subject.

Action learning for managers, Mike Pedler, Gower Publishing, 2012: a valuable book by one of the key figures in contemporary action learning.

Action learning: A practical guide, Krystyna Weinstein, Gower Publishing, 1999: a useful practical guide to how to run action learning programmes.

A general guide to HRD and sustainability is *Embedding environmental sustainability in your organisation: A guide for HR professionals*, guidance for practitioners issued by the Chartered Institute for Personnel and Development in 2021, available at https://www.cipd.co.uk/Images/sustainability-guide_tcm18-98576.pdf.

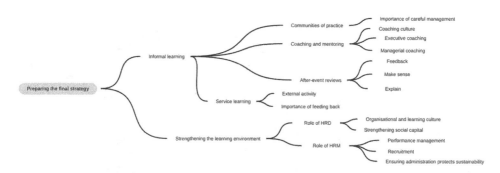

Figure 8.2 Key points in this chapter.

Notes

1 Jean Lave and Etienne Wenger, *Situated Learning: Legitimate Peripheral Participation* (Cambridge: Cambridge University Press, 1991).
2 https://www.reamp.org/.
3 Gilbert Probst and Stefano Borzillo, 'Why Communities of Practice Succeed and Why They Fail', *European Management Journal* 26, no. 5 (2008): 337.
4 Retna K.S. and Tee Ng P., 'Communities of Practice: Dynamics and Success Factors', *Leadership & Organization Development Journal* 32, no. 1 (2011): 41–59; Probst and Borzillo, 'Why Communities of Practice Succeed and Why They Fail'; Stefano Borzillo and Renata Kaminska-Labbé, 'Unravelling the Dynamics of Knowledge Creation in Communities of Practice Though Complexity Theory Lenses', *Knowledge Management Research & Practice* 9, no. 4 (2011): 353–66; Alexandre Ardichvili, 'Learning and Knowledge Sharing in Virtual Communities of Practice: Motivators, Barriers, and Enablers', *Advances in Developing Human Resources* 10, no. 4 (2008): 541–54.
5 Shirley C. Sonesh et al., 'The Power of Coaching: A Meta-Analytic Investigation', *Coaching: An International Journal of Theory, Research and Practice* 8, no. 2 (2015): 73–95.
6 Andrea D. Ellinger, 'Coaching and Mentoring', in *The Routledge Companion to Human Resource Development*, ed. Rob F. Poell, Tonette S. Rocco, and Gene L. Roth (London: Routledge, 2014), 258–71.
7 Gil Bozer and Rebecca J. Jones, 'Understanding the Factors That Determine Workplace Coaching Effectiveness: A Systematic Literature Review', *European Journal of Work and Organizational Psychology* 27, no. 3 (2018): 342–61; Ellinger, 'Coaching and Mentoring'; Sonesh et al., 'The Power of Coaching'.
8 David Megginson and David Clutterbuck, 'Creating a Coaching Culture', *Industrial and Commercial Training* 38, no. 5 (2006): 232–37.
9 https://icrs.info/cpd/mentoring. by "https://icrs.info/mentoring-programme/, accessed 11 February, 2022."
10 Ellinger, 'Coaching and Mentoring'; Paul W. Coombs, 'Mentoring: Perpetuated on a Myth?', in *Handbook of Human Resource Development*, ed. N. Chalofsky, Tonette S. Rocco, and M.L. Morris (San Francisco, CA: Pfeiffer, 2014), 425–37.
11 Ellinger, 'Coaching and Mentoring'.
12 Shmuel Ellis and Inbar Davidi, 'After-Event Reviews: Drawing Lessons from Successful and Failed Experience', *Journal of Applied Psychology* 90, no. 5 (2005): 857; Shmuel Ellis, Rachel Mendel, and Michal Nir, 'Learning from Successful and Failed Experience: The Moderating Role of Kind of after-Event Review', *Journal of Applied Psychology* 91, no. 3 (2006): 669.
13 Joseph A. Allen et al., 'Debriefs: Teams Learning from Doing in Context', *American Psychologist* 73, no. 4 (2018): 504; Ellis and Davidi, 'After-Event Reviews'.
14 Ellis and Davidi, 'After-Event Reviews'.
15 Allen et al., 'Debriefs'.
16 Amy Edmondson, 'Psychological Safety and Learning Behavior in Work Teams', *Administrative Science Quarterly* 44, no. 2 (1999): 350–83.
17 Allen et al., 'Debriefs'.
18 Nicola M. Pless and Markéta Borecká, 'Comparative Analysis of International Service Learning Programs', *Journal of Management Development* 33, no. 6 (2014): 526–50.
19 Yona Sipos, Bryce Battisti, and Kurt Grimm, 'Non-Traditional Pedagogies in Advanced Education: Engaging Head, Hands & Heart for Environmental and Educational Benefit', *International Journal of Sustainability in Higher Education* 9, no. 1 (2008): 69–86.
20 Nicola M. Pless, Thomas Maak, and Günter K. Stahl, 'Promoting Corporate Social Responsibility and Sustainable Development through Management Development: What Can Be Learned from International Service Learning Programs?', *Human Resource Management* 51, no. 6 (2012): 873–903.
21 Holly H. Brower, 'Sustainable Development through Service Learning: A Pedagogical Framework and Case Example in a Third World Context', *Academy of Management Learning & Education* 10, no. 1 (2011): 58–76; Pless, Maak, and Stahl, 'Promoting Corporate Social Responsibility and Sustainable Development through Management Development'.
22 Brower, 'Sustainable Development through Service Learning'; J. Haddock-Millar, M. Müller-Camen, and D. Miles, 'Human Resource Development Initiatives for Managing

Environmental Concerns at McDonald's UK', in *Managing Human Resources for Environmental Sustainability*, ed. D. S. Jackson et al. (Chichester: John Wiley & Sons, 2012), 341–61; Pless and Borecká, 'Comparative Analysis of International Service Learning Programs'; Pless, Maak, and Stahl, 'Promoting Corporate Social Responsibility and Sustainable Development through Management Development'.

23 For example, in the United Kingdom, 64% of HR employees are women (2017), and in the United States 71% of HR managers are women; ONS, 'EMP04: Employment by Occupation - Office for National Statistics', 2020, https://www.ons.gov.uk/employmentandlabourmarket/peopleinwork/employmentandemployeetypes/datasets/employmentbyoccupationemp04; BLS, 'Employed Persons by Detailed Occupation and Age', Bureau of Labor Statistics, 2017, https://www.bls.gov/cps/cpsaat11b.htm.

24 Laura Guillén, Margarita Mayo, and Natalia Karelaia, 'Appearing Self-Confident and Getting Credit for It: Why It May Be Easier for Men than Women to Gain Influence at Work', *Human Resource Management* 57, no. 4 (2018): 839–54; Laura L. Bierema, 'Critiquing Human Resource Development's Dominant Masculine Rationality and Evaluating Its Impact', *Human Resource Development Review* 8, no. 1 (2009): 68–96; Mary Shapiro et al., 'Making Sense of Women as Career Self-Agents: Implications for Human Resource Development', *Human Resource Development Quarterly* 20, no. 4 (2009): 477–501; Lynda Hanscome and Ronald Cervero, 'The Impact of Gendered Power Relations in HRD', *Human Resource Development International* 6, no. 4 (2003): 509–25.

25 R. Poell and F. van der Krogt, 'Why Is Organizing Human Resource Development so Problematic? Perspectives from the Learning-Network Theory (Part I)', *The Learning Organization* 24, no. 3 (2017): 180–93; S.A. Sambrook and M. Cseh, 'Critical HRD', in *Handbook of Human Resource Development*, ed. N. Chalofsky, Tonette S. Rocco, and M.L. Morris (San Francisco, CA: Pfeiffer, 2014), 145–63; Bierema, 'Critiquing Human Resource Development's Dominant Masculine Rationality and Evaluating Its Impact'; Reid Bates, 'A Critical Analysis of Evaluation Practice: The Kirkpatrick Model and the Principle of Beneficence', *Evaluation and Program Planning* 27, no. 3 (2004): 341–47.

26 Kay J Bunch, 'Training Failure as a Consequence of Organizational Culture', *Human Resource Development Review* 6, no. 2 (2007): 142–63.

27 Claretha Hughes and Matthew Gosney, *Bridging the Scholar-Practitioner Gap in Human Resource Development* (Hershey, PA: IGI Global, 2016).

28 Alexandre Ardichvili, 'The Role of HRD in CSR, Sustainability, and Ethics: A Relational Model', *Human Resource Development Review* 12, no. 4 (2013): 456–73; Eugene Sadler-Smith, 'Communicating Climate Change Risk and Enabling Pro-Environmental Behavioral Change through Human Resource Development', *Advances in Developing Human Resources* 17, no. 4 (2015): 442–59; Jan Maskell, *Embedding Organisational Sustainability in Your Organisation: A Guide for HR Professionals* (London: Chartered Institute of Personnel and Development, 2021).

29 For example, see guides produced by professional bodies, such as Elaine Cohen, Sully Taylor, and Michael Muller-Camen, 'HRM's Role in Corporate Social and Environmental Sustainability', SHRM Foundation's Effective Practice Guidelines Series (Alexandria, VA: Society for Human Resource Management, 2012); Maskell, 'Embedding Organisational Sustainability in Your Organisation: A Guide for HR Professionals'.

9 Preparing the final strategy

9.1 What this chapter covers

This is a very short chapter but is on its own because the process of pulling together the information from the previous chapters, in terms of identifying content, appropriate mechanisms for learning and deciding on suitable pedagogical principles to adopt is a discrete but important activity.

9.2 Writing the strategy

We have now gathered all the data needed for writing the learning strategy. In Chapter 5, we used the Viable System Model (VSM) to give us an extensive set of ideas about the different subjects that need to be included within a programme of learning. This covered three different levels, organisational, team and individual, and from that you should be able to identify the information relevant to the scale at which your learning strategy will cover.

From Chapter 5 onwards, we built up a Critical Systems Heuristics (CSH) table of boundary judgements (decisions) that need to be made as regards content, mechanisms for learning and principles to apply. This now gives us a comprehensive framework of questions that will give us confidence that our sustainability-focused learning (SFL) strategy is as comprehensive as is possible.

Table 9.1 has boiled down the questions from previous tables and presented them as a set of straightforward guidance as to what to include in a written strategy which could be presented to stakeholders. As mentioned above, this is scalable, so the final wording should reflect the scope of the learning intended. The sequencing of the statements is also flexible, and you should organise the content of the strategy so that the final document appears coherent and logical. For example, it might be logical to present a statement of the organisation's worldview (Q12) about sustainability at the beginning of the strategy, followed by the purpose (Q2) and then the measures of success (Q3).

However, note that boiling down reduces detail, so it is important to go back to these earlier tables and check the exact questions, whenever necessary.

This strategy document will provide important baseline data in any subsequent evaluation of the strategy or programme, so we will return to this in the final chapter, Chapter 11.

Table 9.1 Translating boundary judgements to strategy statements

Boundary judgement questions	Strategy implications
1 Who should benefit from the learning strategy?	Define who will be involved in formal and informal learning activities.
2 What is the purpose of the learning strategy?	State the overall aims of the programme and specific required learning outcomes and any requirements for underpinning knowledge about sustainability.
3 What is the measure of success for the learning strategy?	Define the success criteria for the strategy. State the organisation's vision for operating sustainably, and explain how these criteria can contribute to this. Explain the contribution of the strategy to the Sustainable Development Goals (SDGs).
4 Who makes decisions about the strategy?	State who will make decisions about the learning strategy.
5 What resources and constraints relevant to the strategy does the decision-maker control?	State the budget available for the strategy or programme, and list resources which are available to help in the design and delivery.
6 What conditions of the strategy's operation are outside of the control of the decision-maker?	Summarise external factors which are driving the need for social and environmental sustainability by the organisation. Summarise internal pressures for sustainability. Describe the characteristics of the organisation's culture, ethical climate, learning culture and characteristics of the workforce which will be relevant to the effectiveness of the strategy. Describe other initiatives that can reinforce formal and informal learning activities.
7 Who should be involved in the design of the strategy?	List people who need to be involved in the design and implementation of the strategy.
8 What expertise is needed to design the strategy?	Describe the different types of expertise which will be needed in order to develop an effective strategy.
9 What guarantees of success do the sources of expertise offer?	Explain how the people to be involved in the project and the expertise that they bring in terms of understanding sustainability, learning and pedagogical ideas will contribute to the overall success of the strategy.
10 Who will represent the affected society and the natural environment?	State which representatives of external communities or other organisations will be involved in the design and implementation of the learning strategy.
11 What opportunity does the affected society and natural environment have to challenge the strategy?	Explain how external representatives will be involved in the design and implementation of the strategy.
12 What is the worldview underlying the design of the learning strategy?	Describe philosophies relevant to the organisation's vision of sustainability and learning which are informing the strategy's design and implementation, for example worldviews about political economy and sustainability, and about the process of learning needs assessment itself.

10 Evaluating learning about sustainability

10.1 What this chapter covers

Figure 10.1 shows what this chapter covers about the evaluation of learning in organisations. I have long thought this subject presents something of a paradox. First, as a theory-informed practice it seems quite detached from the mainstream study of evaluation, a progressive discipline incorporating a wide and growing set of ideas about how to conduct evaluations: instead, "training evaluation" seems ever synonymous with the name Kirkpatrick, author of a framework for thinking about learning within organisations in the 1950s, a long-gone age. It is also paradoxical because Kirkpatrick's ideas, although providing a useful classification of how training may have an impact on learners and their employers, have not provided human resource development (HRD) practitioners with a tool that gives the sort of results that reliably inform decision-makers in organisations. As a result, evaluation of HRD activity tends to be a sporadic and inconsistent activity, leading to often unpersuasive reporting. This is largely because of the wicked nature of the situation that training evaluation seeks to judge—as discussed previously, examining a complex situation requires tools that can cope with complexity.

So in this chapter, we will look at some fundamental challenges associated with evaluating learning in organisations, and then briefly explore some of the specific criticisms that have been made of the Kirkpatrick and associated approaches to evaluation.

Then, we will look at how concepts and tools from systems thinking and related ideas can help to strengthen the practice of evaluating sustainability-focused learning (SFL).

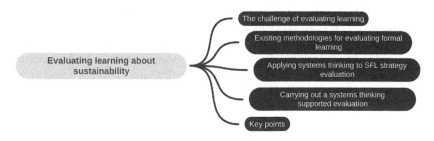

Figure 10.1 Map of Chapter 9.

DOI: 10.4324/9781003218296-11

10.2 The challenge of evaluating learning

10.2.1 Ambiguity about the purpose of evaluation

The first challenge to explore is why we evaluate learning. One authoritative definition of "evaluation" is that it is "the systematic assessment of the worth or merit of an object".[1] In the context of learning within organisations, what do we mean by "worth" and "merit"? According to leading writers in the field of evaluation, Daniel Stufflebeam and Anthony Shinkfield, merit may be seen as an intrinsic quality whereas worth is an extrinsic quality, rated by the perceived value of the object to someone who might use it.[2] So, we may have a training course with considerable merit, with well-designed objectives and accurate content, but which has little worth if it does not meet the needs of the target group.

There are two main purposes for evaluating learning programmes, for improvement and for accountability to stakeholders. The problem is that these purposes may be in conflict. For example, an evaluation which focuses on improvement will identify areas of weakness and will suggest how design or delivery could be improved in the future, but because of internal power dynamics and the politics of HRD, it may be deemed unwise to reveal these to senior managers.[3] This tension may drive evaluators to focus their attention on hard data, such as emphasising the number of "bums on seats" for people completing training rather than gathering qualitative data about perceptions of quality and effectiveness. The problem does not necessarily go away if an independent, third-party evaluator is commissioned: although professionalism should ensure an unbiased evaluation, commercial pressures may mean that even independents may be "economical with the truth". Evaluation may also identify issues which need to be addressed but which are regarded as "sacred cows" within the organisation, what has been done in the past must always be done in the future, and an evaluation report which proposes changes challenging organisational culture may be unacceptable. In this context, there is a danger that evaluation reporting simply becomes an exercise to keep the customer satisfied.

These tensions are made worse by the increasing importance attached to calculating the return on investment of formal learning, an activity which seeks to reduce the complexity of social dynamics to the relative simplicity of capital investment in new machinery by trying to attribute a "42"-style answer to a much more complex problem.

10.2.2 Limitations of objective-based evaluation

The evaluation of formal learning emerged as a discipline in its own right only in the 1950s. As discussed in Chapter 5, standardised approaches to training started to be developed during World War II, and this led to the emergence of "training" as a discrete activity to be carried out by professionals. Up until this time evaluation of training had not really been seen to be necessary: the relatively limited scope of industrial activity until the 1950s had meant that promotion up a hierarchy came through being an expert in what the organisation did, meaning that supervisors knew more than subordinates and consequently would have a good idea about how well they were learning. Training as a specialist function broke this connection and increasing specialisation in what people do as a result of technological development further highlighted the need for a way to evaluate learning within organisations.

As with how to design training, early training evaluators looked to prevailing ideas about educational psychology for guidance and drew on then-dominant ideas of behaviourism. As a result, the basis for evaluating training became the objectives identified for the training, and this remains recommended practice.[4] Stufflebeam and Shinkfield observe that objective-based evaluations are common in all fields of evaluation, but comment that although there is an inherent common sense in the approach:

> such studies lead to terminal information that is neither timely or pertinent to improving a programme's process, that information often is far too narrow to constitute a sufficient basis for judging the object's merit and worth, that the studies do not uncover positive and negative side-effects, and that they may credit unworthy objectives.[5]

These criticisms are all relevant to the evaluation of training. As regards timeliness, in Figure 5.6 we thought about Vickers' idea of the appreciative system, that we study a system of interest, decide what is relevant at that moment, use that to define objectives and hence design formal learning, and then deliver the learning—by which time the flux of sustainability has changed, meaning that our objectives may well be irrelevant. Defining objectives is also a highly reductive process, where we attempt to capture the complexity of a real-world wicked problem in a series of carefully crafted statements, clearly an impossibility. Objectives create a sense that there is a "completion", a point at which we know what there is to know and hence need know no more. This fits well with a culture where we "acquire" knowledge as a means to an end but can run counter to the participation ethos of social learning and of the idea of "knowing" as opposed to knowledge. This also creates the idea that evaluation happens at the end of a learning intervention making it less likely that constructive recommendations can be usefully deployed. Evaluating against objectives also means that we may miss the unintended consequences of what our formal learning does both inside and outside of the organisation and, as well as drawing our attention away from the potentially much greater significance of informal learning. Finally, the objectives may be unworthy, often the case where a careful learning needs assessment (LNA) has not been done and where objectives are consequently based on hunches or best guesses.

A fundamental problem is that objectives may make perfect sense in the clearly delineated world of education where the requirements for a learning programme concluded by an examination and certification may be relatively easy to define, but this is not the case in learning in an organisational setting where the situation is more complex, as we are looking for outcomes at individual, team and organisational levels embracing knowledge, skills and attitudes, and when considering sustainability, also have to take into account outcomes at a societal or environmental level.

10.2.3 Inadequacies of learning needs assessment process

We noted in Section 5.4 common weaknesses in the LNA process, and that LNAs are done infrequently and often not adequately. However, as Figure 10.2 shows, needs assessment and evaluation should be integral parts of a system for learning.

In this loop, the needs assessment informs the design and delivery of the strategy, and the evaluation should be something of a report on the effectiveness of the needs assessment. If the needs assessment is non-existent or inadequate, this reporting back

250 *Evaluating learning about sustainability*

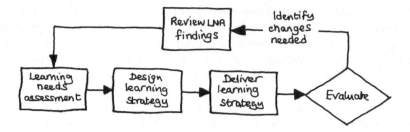

Figure 10.2 Learning needs assessment and evaluation as a feedback mechanism.

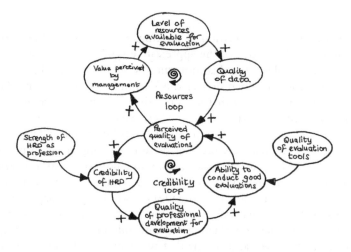

Figure 10.3 Causal flow diagram showing organisational constraints on evaluation.

loses significance. It is also harder to identify the degree to which the learning strategy is effective because baseline data captured in the needs assessment will not be available.

Effective evaluations therefore rely heavily on thorough needs assessments.

10.2.4 Organisational constraints

Research suggests that a complex web of interrelated factors conspire to weaken the extent to which formal learning in organisations is evaluated, and that when it does happen it is not done particularly effectively. Data collected over many years by organisations such as the Association for Talent Development consistently shows that while the great majority of organisations (for example, 88% in 2016[6]) collect evaluation data at the very simplest level of reaction to learning, barely a third (35%) try to assess if formal learning contributes to better organisational performance.

Quite a few different, but interconnected, reasons have been suggested as to why this may happen. To help explain this and explore the connectedness, it would be useful to use system dynamics and a causal flow diagram (Figure 10.3).

We will start with the problem of how the quality of learning evaluation is perceived (at the heart of this diagram) and explore what I have called the "Resources" loop. The reliance on superficial measures such as reactions to learning (we liked it) and the lack of credible information connecting learning to organisational performance means that evaluation reports are not necessarily highly valued by senior management. This has a direct impact on the level of resources made available for evaluation: gathering data about performance levels months after people have attended a training programme requires considerable effort, and operational functions with little confidence in the evaluation process may be reluctant to cooperate, so necessary data is difficult to gather. Pressure from stakeholders to deliver quick evaluation results may also mean that the process may be carried out too hastily, not allowing for the true long-term effects of training to become apparent.[7] Poor data has a further direct and negative effect on evaluation quality, so a vicious circle is completed.

Turning to the "Credibility loop", the perceived poor quality of evaluation directly affects the credibility of the HRD function, which is often problematic for other reasons, as previously discussed (Chapter 8, Section 8.3): as it is particularly relevant here, we highlight the weakness of HRD as a profession. This may mean that opportunities for HRD staff to undertake professional development in evaluation are limited, so that it is difficult to improve the quality of evaluations.[8] This is also affected by the quality of available tools. We therefore have another vicious circle compounding the perception of formal evaluation as of limited value.

The challenge with reinforcing loops as we have here is to reverse the direction, to find ways in which the reinforcing effect is virtuous rather than vicious. To do that we look for points of leverage, external inputs which can change things. Clearly strengthening HRD as a profession would be highly desirable, but that is beyond the scope of this book. Another point of leverage is the quality of evaluation tools that are available. As we shall see in the following section, there is a reliance in HRD on a limited set of tools for evaluating learning, tools which have some major weaknesses. We shall therefore look at how these may be strengthened as a way of providing an effective point of leverage in a system for evaluating formal learning. Another point of leverage may be to seek to change the perceptions about evaluation as a burden, and to consider ways in which the evaluation process could contribute to better performance: how we might be able to do this is explored in Section 10.5.4.

Time for reflection

Do you recognise these observations about evaluating formal learning?

How valid do you think they are, generally or in your organisation?

10.3 Existing methodologies for evaluating formal learning

The "... bellwether for evaluation decision-making in practice"[9] and what "... is acknowledged by many practitioners as the standard in the field"[10] is a framework developed in the 1950s[11] and attributed to Donald Kirkpatrick.[12] The framework proposes four levels for evaluation:

- Level 1: Reaction to the training
- Level 2: Learning of new knowledge, skills and attitudes
- Level 3: Behaviour changes in the workplace
- Level 4: Results in terms of workplace performance.

Despite its pre-eminence with practitioners, the Kirkpatrick framework receives a considerable amount of criticism from researchers on a number of different grounds. Although it is acknowledged that it is a useful taxonomy for looking at different levels where formal learning may have an impact,[13] it cannot be seen as a model for explaining the causality of impact as it is not theory-based[14] and provides "... an oversimplified view of training effectiveness that does not consider individual or contextual influences".[15]

The limitations with the framework occur when we try to make causal assumptions, that a positive reaction leads to learning, that this leads to behaviour change, and this contributes to organisational results. Although Kirkpatrick's own writings are not clear on the matter, they do suggest that there are causal linkages between the successive levels: for example, he claims "If training is going to be effective, it is important that trainees react favourably to it".[16] Unfortunately, a significant amount of research suggests that these causal relationships cannot be reliably and consistently established,[17] as many factors play a part in the complex relationship connecting formal learning and organisational change. For example, at the reaction level, learning is about changing existing ways of doing things, and this may not be a comfortable experience (as when learning is transformative); hence, reaction may be negative even though valuable learning results.

It is important to note that Kirkpatrick's definition of learning is not altogether the same as the one I have used in this book to date. His definition is an educational "... extent to which participants change attitudes, improve knowledge, and/or increased skill",[18] whereas I have been using the organisational learning understanding as it being about adaptation to new demands, a definition which brings Kirkpatrick's learning and behaviour change together. The difficulty is that changing attitudes, improving knowledge and increasing skill during a learning activity does not necessarily mean that behaviour in the workplace will change—in Chapter 6, we looked at a wide variety of factors which influence how well learning may be transferred to the workplace. Linking learning to behavioural change is also harder because many training evaluations rely on how people have performed in end of course tests as a measure of learning, and these are often conducted using tests of declarative (factual) knowledge rather than tests of procedural knowledge (proving how to apply what has been learnt).[19] And, of course, by the time we reach the end of the chain of causality, so many other factors can influence organisational impact that it is very difficult to ascribe changes to individuals' formal learning activities.

The criticisms also apply to other models which are based on Kirkpatrick's framework, in particular the so-called "fifth level" of return on investment (Jack Phillips' ROI).[20]

Although many organisations attach significant levels of importance to ROI calculations, the methodology is problematic. For example, while changes at organisational level may be quantifiable for activities such as reducing the level of customer complaints or levels of wastage in an industrial process, for many sustainability-related concerns, particularly those in the not-for-profit sector, financial implications are very difficult to quantify reliably. Also, the process relies on making assumptions about the level of impact of learning at each stage in the chain of causality, again a highly problematic activity, especially where learners are asked to self-assess. Although it is possible to show attractively high rates of return for formal learning activities, a focus on ROI as a measure of the value of learning runs the risk of strengthening the importance attached to performative learning which satisfies shareholders at the expense of the professional development of employees or learning where the potential return is over a much longer timescale, as with SFL.[21]

A further criticism with both the Kirkpatrick and ROI approaches is the internal focus, with no interest being paid to the external consequences of formal learning. Kaufman and Keller's Organisational Elements Model (OEM) was an attempt to address this weakness through a fifth level which requires organisations to:

> ... consider the societal consequences and payoffs of their actions. Every organization exists as part of a larger system with which it has mutually dependent relationships... [and organisations]... are increasingly being called to account for unintended societal consequences such as increases in pollution and lack of safety.[22]

However, OEM seems to be little used in practice.

Time for reflection

What do you think about this critique of the Kirkpatrick approach to training evaluation?

What experience does your organisation have of ROI evaluations? Have they proved reliable and useful?

10.4 Applying systems thinking to SFL strategy evaluation

Having outlined some limitations of existing approaches to evaluating learning within organisations, we need to propose an approach which may be more effective for SFL. Throughout the book, I have mentioned the importance of recognising that organisational sustainability is not like implementing a new product or service, but that it represents a new way of being, and is therefore an ongoing and never-ending process. One of the touchstones in systems thinking is a theorem put forward by Roger Conant and Ross Ashby in 1970, that "every good regulator of a system must be a model of that system".[23] For example, a central heating boiler heats water until a house reaches a certain temperature, as measured by the thermostat (a regulator). This allows the boiler to operate until it senses that the house temperature reaches the desired value, at which point it switches off the boiler—how the thermostat works models the boiler. As I have mentioned several times, sustainability is an ongoing process, so from the Conant-Ashby Theorem SFL must also be a process centred around ongoing learning and "knowing" rather than discrete, "run it once and forget about it" formal learning. Similarly, learning evaluation, as a regulator of the learning itself, needs to be ongoing and seen as a process rather than as a one-off event.[24]

Systems thinking has been another constant throughout the book, both as a competency for understanding sustainability and also as a methodology for thinking about SFL strategies. Using systems thinking ideas in evaluation fits comfortably with this need to adopt a process-oriented evaluation approach. In evaluation thinking generally, interest in systems thinking approaches has risen and fallen during recent decades,[25] but at the time of writing at least, it is in an ascendancy, and contemporary research particularly emphasises the value of using systemic approaches in the evaluation of sustainability-related activities.[26] Systems thinking ideas have been used by a number of influential people in the evaluation field, generally as aids within conventional approaches to evaluation.[27] Here we will retain the objective-based approach of Kirkpatrick and its derivatives but strengthen them with systems thinking-based concepts and tools.

To date, there seems to have been limited application of systems thinking ideas to the evaluation of learning within organisations, so what I am proposing here represents a synthesis of my own professional practice of using systems thinking concepts and the substantial amount of research that does exist into systems thinking-based evaluation in general. We have based the development of our SFL strategy around the 12 Critical Systems Heuristics (CSH) questions which Werner Ulrich identified as being necessary to clarify boundary judgements about a system of interest. The scalability of systems thinking ideas means that we can draw on the same set of questions irrespective of the level we are examining, in other words, whether or not we are evaluating the overall SFL strategy or a specific learning intervention. Bear this in mind as you read below, and be prepared to adapt what you ask appropriately.

10.5 Carrying out a systems thinking supported evaluation

10.5.1 Clarifying the theory of change

Through Chapters 5–8, we have followed a systematic process for developing the SFL, and this represents what we might call a theory of change. The final stage in the process is the evaluation, and we can present the complete theory in the flowchart shown in Figure 10.4.

In Stage 1, we conducted the LNA, and from that identified what content would be appropriate, what mechanisms for learning should be implemented or supported, and decided what pedagogical principles would be most effective. We established these by asking a series of boundary judgement questions and recorded our answers in a series of tables which culminated in Table 8.2, where we showed how to translate these answers into a learning strategy (Stage 2). Although the 12 CSH questions do not map exactly

Evaluating learning about sustainability 255

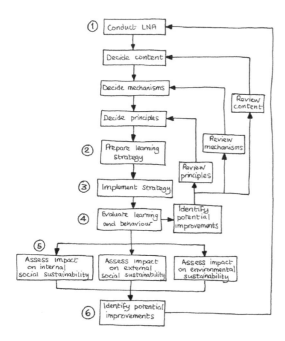

Figure 10.4 A logic model for SFL theory of change.

into our content, mechanisms and principles classification, we can broadly identify which ones are relevant for each:

- Content—CSH Q1, Q2, Q3, Q10, Q11
- Mechanisms—CSH Q1, Q4, Q5, Q6, Q7, Q8, Q9, Q11
- Principles—CSH Q6, Q7, Q8, Q9, Q12.

Recognising this mapping will be useful at Stage 4 in the evaluation process, where we look to evaluate learning which has happened and behaviour changes which have resulted.

10.5.2 Assessing the implementation of the strategy (Stage 3)

The first aspect of the evaluation should be to establish the extent to which the requirements of the learning strategy were implemented. The CSH process means that we should have 'swept in' to the strategy as much as is realistically possible for it to be effective as a system for enabling SFL. If any of these requirements are not addressed, it is possible that the effectiveness of the strategy will be reduced.

If you are evaluating your own SFL strategy, you will have control over what and how you carry out the evaluation. However, if the evaluation is to be carried out by a third party, the requirements for the evaluation will need to be defined in some form of 'terms of reference'. These will normally define such things as the aims of the evaluation, suggestions for a process to follow, the objectives or outcomes for the learning activities, and who key stakeholders will be.

If you are a systems thinking practising evaluator reviewing terms of reference that you have been given, you should first reflect on the degree to which they have actually swept in all systemic factors. Drawing on our CSH questions, we can identify some questions which you should ask at this stage to establish how the learning strategy was designed and implemented (Table 10.1). Recognising systemic weaknesses at this stage will be invaluable in helping you to identify if important boundary judgements have not been optimal. There are some points to note:

- Customise questions, based on the exact context of the evaluation.
- This is a long list of questions, and it may well be impractical to ask them all, particularly during one meeting.
- The questions do not need to be asked in the sequence shown. For example, it may be more logical to ask about the aim of the learning before asking who was involved.
- Think about getting answers to these questions as an iterative process, so that you ask the questions to appropriate people and at appropriate times as the evaluation progresses.
- Triangulate your information gathering by asking the same questions to different people.
- Use the questions to stimulate your own thinking about better, more contextually appropriate questions.
- Be prepared for people to find some questions challenging!

Table 10.1 Evaluation questions for clarifying high-level decisions

Boundary judgement questions	Evaluation questions to ask
1 Who should benefit from the learning strategy?	Who has been involved in the learning activities? Who was not involved, and why were they not included?
2 What is the purpose of the learning strategy?	What has been the overall aim of the learning? Based on experience, could that be improved or altered in any way?
3 What is the measure of success for the learning strategy?	What were the defined outcomes/objectives for the learning in terms of learning, behaviour change and impact on sustainability measures? How do these relate to content that was included in the strategy? How do these relate to the organisation's vision for sustainability? Based on experience, do you think these outcomes/objectives should have been expressed differently?
4 Who makes decisions about the strategy?	Who made decisions about the learning, for example, content, objectives/outcomes, modes of delivery, pedagogical strategies, etc? Was that the right person for making such decisions? Should others have been involved?
5 What resources and constraints relevant to the strategy does the decision-maker control?	What budget and other resources were available for developing the learning? Were these adequate for what was intended? What compromises, if any, had to be made because of resource limitations?

6 What conditions of the strategy's operation are outside of the control of the decision-maker?	What are the drivers for sustainability for your organisation? How would you describe the commitment to sustainability amongst the workforce in the organisation? How would you describe the organisational culture as it relates to sustainability? How would you describe the learning culture within the organisation? How do you see learning happen? What HRM processes exist to encourage learning and how effective are they?
7 Who should be involved in the design of the strategy?	Who was involved in the design of the learning? Was there anyone who was not involved, but should have been?
8 What expertise is needed to design the strategy?	What expertise was needed to design the learning? Was there any additional expertise which should have been used?
9 What guarantees of success do the sources of expertise offer?	What was your justification for using these particular people in the design and delivery of the learning? To what extent has your confidence in these people been confirmed?
10 Who will represent the affected society and the natural environment?	Did people or groups from outside your organisation contribute in any way to the implementation of the learning? (For example, trades unions, community groups, environmental groups). Who were these people or groups? Based on experience, do you think anyone else should have been involved?
11 What opportunity does the affected society and natural environment have to challenge the strategy?	How were people or groups from outside the organisation involved in the learning? Were there any ways in which their contribution could have been strengthened?
12 What is the worldview underlying the design of the learning strategy?	How would you describe the worldview within your organisation as it relates to learning and sustainability? For example:

- How do you think learning happens in your organisation?
- What do you think the purpose of your organisation is with respect to society and the environment?
- How would you describe your organisation's responsibility for ensuring that its employees have a good life?
- What do you think a good life is?

10.5.3 Assessing causality and contribution

At two points in the evaluative process, between learning and behaviour change, and between behaviour change and impact (at stages ④ and ⑤ in Figure 10.4), we need to try and draw some conclusions about causal connections. The biggest challenge with evaluating a situation such as the impact of learning on what an organisation does is the complexity of factors which are also involved in the system. This means that we can never confidently say that A caused B: all we can realistically say is that it seems likely, on the balance of evidence available, that A contributed to B.

258 *Evaluating learning about sustainability*

This is the basis of John Mayne's contribution theory.[28] Mayne proposes a logic chain which is needed if we are to be able to make a valid 'contribution claim':

1 Our learning strategy must be based on a reasoned theory of change: our rigorous and systematic use of Viable System Model (VSM) and CSH can help us feel confident that this is the case.
2 The requirements of the theory of change must have been implemented. This is the purpose of the series of questions we asked in Section 10.5.2.
3 The theory of change worked in practice. The learning strategy has been implemented, but we need to confirm how well.
4 External factors influencing learning have been identified and their effects are taken into consideration (the purpose of CSH Q6 and as explored in Chapter 6).

Figure 10.5 shows how data collection should progress. After collecting initial evidence, we see if we can make an assessment about contribution, but may need to go back and gather additional evidence if we cannot do this confidently. Once we have gathered enough evidence, we should be in a position to finalise any claim for contribution.

10.5.4 Connecting learning and behavioural changes (Stage 4)

The first of the causality assessments is the connection between learning and behaviour, what a 'classical' training evaluation focuses on. Here the Kirkpatrick framework

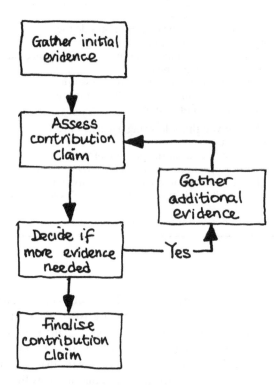

Figure 10.5 Reviewing the evidence for making a contribution claim.

becomes useful, as it provides a structure within which we can organise data collection. We will focus on Levels 2, 3 and 4, and not consider Level 1, reaction, as, while having some value[29] its causal connection with subsequent levels is insufficiently meaningful.

There is an extensive literature covering how to gather data about reaction, learning, behaviour and results, so we will not examine that here.[30] We should also remember that our learning strategy should include support for informal and incidental learning activities, which are not considered within the classic Kirkpatrick framework. Rather, we will look at how systems thinking can potentially offer some support to the more problematic issue of how we can make sense of the data collected by shining some light on the causal connections which may (or may not) link learning to changes in behaviour and organisational sustainability.

One initial issue to consider is that of emergence, that complex systems create outcomes that cannot be predicted from a simple aggregation of individual actions. Even the most carefully designed set of learning outcomes will lead to unpredictable consequences, some positive, some negative. This was one reason why the influential evaluator Michael Scriven pointed out the value of "goal-free evaluations",[31] where the evaluator simply looks for any change that may be attributed to the intervention. By purposefully staying ignorant about official objectives, the evaluator becomes more alert to unintended consequences, and should, if the intervention has been successful, identify the objectives anyway. It is also possible that after initially working in ignorance of official goals, that the evaluator finds out what they are and continues the evaluation process.

There are a number of key questions which need to be answered at this stage, for clarity grouped into several general categories.

Questions about learning:

- What are the key things that people seem to have learnt from what they have done?
- How do these things relate to the intended learning outcomes?
- What were the most useful things relating to sustainability to emerge out of the learning that they did?
- Were there any aspects of the learning that they would change in any way?
- Has the learning strategy meant that people think differently about what is important to them in their work or personal lives as regards social and environmental sustainability?
- To what extent did learning activities consider the learner's personal value framework?

Questions about behaviour:

- What working practices did they change as a result of the learning?
- Were there any changes they made in their working practices which were unexpected in any way?
- What aspects of the learning strategy were most effective in helping them to change working practices?

Questions about learning transfer climate:

- What factors in their working environment helped with using the results of the learning?

- What factors in their working environment made it harder to use the results of the learning?
- How could you describe the learning culture in the organisation?
- Are there any ways in which the learning culture is changing?

These are generally standard questions used in evaluating learning strategies and represent what may be called a "first-order" approach to evaluation: you as the evaluator are an observer of a fixed, objective world, and your responsibility is to gather data in order to arrive at some conclusions for the evaluation. This is a somewhat scientific way of carrying out an evaluation which relies to a large extent on the ability (and willingness) of the objective world to provide solid data. This is sometimes possible for certain aspects of the data collection, for example, in terms of quantifiable outputs, but often it is not, particularly where the learning seeks to address some form of a wicked problem and where what happens is subjective and cannot be quantified easily. It also makes the evaluation *extractive*, where the actions of the evaluator are oriented towards satisfying the commissioner of the evaluation, but do not necessarily help the people who contribute to the data collection. As discussed in Section 10.2.4, one reason why evaluations of learning are difficult to carry out is that operational staff and supervisors do not necessarily see any benefit to them in cooperating—rather, it is a drain on their pressured time.

An alternative approach is to shift to a "second-order" mode of evaluation, where you use the process of evaluation to not only gather data but to contribute in some way to how people understand or utilise the learning that they have been involved in.[32] In a second-order evaluation, the evaluator becomes part of the system of interest and *contributes* to how well it functions, which may create an effective point of leverage (see Figure 10.3). How might that work?

Let us think about the classic learning evaluation problem of identifying a causal connection between learning and changes of behaviour. With first-order thinking, we might ask learners or their supervisors the simple question, "How much do you think the learning contributed to changes in your working practice?" Experienced researchers know well that the answers to such questions can be completely unreliable for all sorts of reasons, which ultimately makes it much harder to justify conclusions that we draw about the effectiveness of a learning strategy, as we saw with Figure 10.3.

The second-order alternative is to put ourselves *in* the system for learning and work with people to develop a shared understanding of what factors contribute to learning effectiveness. For example, to gather information about how well learning contributed to a change in behaviour, we might work with people to explore an idea called the Behaviour Engineering Model (BEM), an idea for process improvement developed by Tom Gilbert.[33] Gilbert proposed that satisfactory performance in a job is influenced by three primary factors, the effectiveness of information about the performance needed, quality of the equipment needed to perform and desire to perform well. We can represent the BEM as in Figure 10.6.

Gilbert suggested that each of these three factors was influenced from two directions: the supporting environment, what was available to the individual; and their "repertory of behaviour", each individual's characteristics. Figure 10.6 shows the influences connecting these. For example, the effectiveness of information is determined not only by the fact that it is available and expressed clearly (perhaps through informal learning channels) but also by a person's understanding of the information (a key aspect of what formal learning seeks to achieve). Similarly, equipment must be available and suitable,

Evaluating learning about sustainability 261

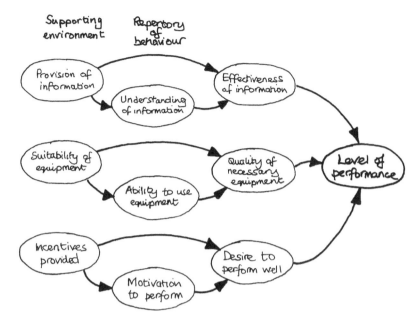

Figure 10.6 The Behaviour Engineering Model as an influence diagram.

and a person needs to be able to use it (another aspect of learning). The desire to perform well is influenced by incentives provided and the degree to which someone responds positively to these incentives (our discussion of conforming and commitment (Section 7.2.2) is relevant here). We can see the Knowledge, Skills and Abilities (KSA) framework embodied here.

How is this relevant here? Rather than the easy to ask but hard to answer question "How much did the learning contribute to your change of behaviour?" the evaluator could (ideally) facilitate a diagramming exercise where people draw their own ideas about what they think contributes to good performance. They could then compare their own understanding of the situation with Gilbert's model and see what they think about that. Asking the question about the significance of learning in changing behaviour then becomes much more informed. People have a better idea about what might be going on in their situation, could provide some suggestions about the relative importance of the different influences, and even take some ideas away which could help them to strengthen learning transfer possibilities. If drawing such a diagram does not seem realistic given the circumstances, the "official" BEM (as in Figure 10.6) could be used to spark a discussion about the local situation.

An alternative way to present the BEM might be as a causal flow diagram (Figure 10.7). Depending on the ability of participants in the conversation to draw or understand such diagrams, this might be jointly constructed, or again, it could be presented and explained as something for discussion. Discussion points here might be:

- The main reinforcing loop is about motivation to perform well. What are your thoughts about that?

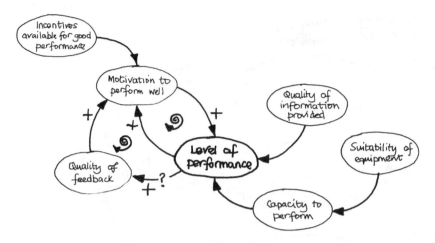

Figure 10.7 The Behaviour Engineering Model as a causal flow diagram.

- Motivation can be strengthened by getting quality feedback. Does that happen here?
- What do you think about the quality of information provided about the performance (for example, training provided)?
- What do you think about the equipment or tools that you have to do your work? How helpful are they?

As with all systems thinking diagrams, the accuracy of the diagram is not crucial: what people see as mistakes or weaknesses in a diagram can provide valuable sources of learning.

Again, an evaluator who encourages discussion about issues such as these can gather better quality data about the effectiveness of learning and also stimulate learning about the subject itself as well as the overall effectiveness of learning transfer.

A third possibility for diagramming might be a joint construction of a rich picture (as in Figure 2.2). The same possibilities for opening up discussions about learning apply here.

I have used the BEM here as an example of how diagramming with participants in a learning programme can shine more light on the strengths and limitations of the programme. Sometimes the abstract generality of the BEM might be relevant, but on other occasions it might be useful to develop influence diagrams, causal flow diagrams or rich pictures based on specifics within the evaluation. For example, in an evaluation looking at the effectiveness of leadership training on strengthening sustainability, you might encourage participants to draw diagrams which illustrate the importance of factors such as managerial culture, the constraints of the organisation's hierarchy, the difficulty of getting any new ideas accepted, the frustrations of being micro-managed, and so on.

By using an appropriate blend of first- and second-order evaluation techniques, we should be able to pull together a picture which shows the degree to which our learning strategy has led to learning and influenced desirable changes in behaviour. This will also give us ideas about which aspects of the learning strategy should be strengthened, such as by introducing additional content or leaving out material which does not seem

Evaluating learning about sustainability 263

to be relevant, changing the balance of learning mechanisms used in the strategy, and reflecting on principles which have been used. In Figure 10.4, we see this as the negative feedback loops asking us to review these three factors.

Having collected the data, the next stage is to assess any causality connecting learning and behaviour change. As in Figure 10.5, we gather and review evidence, and then consider the following[34]:

- Did behaviour change?
- Have we assessed the significance of all factors that we think would have an influence on changes in behaviour (see Chapter 6)?
- Have we identified any other factors which may influence behaviour change?
- Have we accounted for any other factors which could influence behaviour change?

At this point, we may need to go back and collect additional evidence, but once we are satisfied that we can answer these questions, then we can claim (or not) that it is likely that, to some degree (which we may be able to quantify in some way), learning contributed to the change in behaviour. The vagueness of the word "contributed" is important: in a complex system of human behaviour, there will be many different reactions to learning which may contribute to an overall change in behaviour.

10.5.5 Connecting behavioural change and impact on sustainability (Stage 5)

The second causal connection to consider is the relationship between behavioural change and the impact on the organisation's social and environmental sustainability. To do this, we follow exactly the same process as outlined in Section 10.5.3, but this time the information on which we base contribution assessments is different.

Exactly what information is needed will depend on the criteria for success defined in the learning strategy (CSH Q3 in Table 8.2). You may be able to find data for this in reports developed for external sustainability accreditation such as Global Reporting Initiative (GRI) or B Corp, or in triple bottom line reporting that your organisation does. You may also be able to collect data internally for evaluating the impact on internal social sustainability, either through any employee satisfaction surveys that have been done or through your own specially designed survey. As before, we can try using first-order methods, although here other techniques may be possible: for example, for quantifiable data we may be able to use a trendline analysis and see if there is any correlation between this data and the implementation of the learning strategy, or there may be control groups, people who have not taken part in learning. However, second-order ideas are also possible, such as working with stakeholders to draw diagrams exploring the network of factors which may be contributing to organisational changes in addition to learning.

It is also important to collect data on the external impact on sustainability, Kaufman and Keller's OEM fifth level. Again, some of this data may be available through GRI or B Corp reporting standards, but it may be necessary to venture outside with your own data collecting. What that means will depend on the size of the organisation, what it does, where it operates and other variables (and, of course, the willingness of the organisation to solicit external perspectives).

With all of these sources of data, it is important to remember the importance of baseline data, what was the starting point? Statements of this baseline data should be found within the LNA report.

You can then follow the same process as described previously for coming to a conclusion about contribution. Repeating the questions above:

- Did organisational sustainability change?
- Have we assessed the significance of all factors that we think would have an influence on changes in organisational sustainability (see Chapter 4)?
- Have we identified any other factors which may influence sustainability?
- Have we accounted for any other factors which could influence sustainability?

As in the previous section, if we can answer all the questions confidently, then we can claim (or not) that it is likely that, to some degree (which we may be able to quantify in some way), that the change in behaviour contributed to changes in the organisation's social and/or environmental sustainability performance.

10.5.6 Drawing evaluative conclusions (Stage 6)

This section has shown that there are essentially two stages to the evaluation: to confirm that high-level boundary judgements were considered in the implementation of the learning strategy, and then to gather data and assess contribution claims for the causal connections between learning and behaviour, and behaviour and impact on sustainability.

From this process, we can then, with more or less confidence, conclude that it is likely (or not) that learning did (or did not) contribute to improvements in social and environmental sustainability.

If we can conclude that learning has contributed, our journey here is complete.

But, of course, the quest for sustainability never ends. The idea that the quest for sustainability is a never-ending process means that our SFL strategy will never be retired. Rather, we will need to continually identify ways in which we can strengthen the strategy in order to respond to new developments in the social and natural environments. In Chapter 1 I presented the original World Commission on Environment and Development (WCED) definition of sustainable development, and now paraphrase it to define SFL and close this chapter:

> An effective sustainability-focused learning strategy is one which meets the needs for social and environmental sustainability of present and future generations of the organisation and its stakeholders.

Time for reflection

What are your thoughts about this approach to evaluation?
 In particular, what do you think about the idea of the first- to second-order shift?
 How useful do you think it would be to use the evaluation of learning as an opportunity to strengthen learning?

10.6 Key points in this chapter

Figure 10.8 summarises the key points in this chapter. There are a number of challenges associated with evaluating learning. There is often a tension between evaluating in order to improve and in order to show value. Although objectives are necessary in order to develop a learning strategy, evaluating solely against objectives can be limiting, and lead to unintended consequences being missed. LNAs are often not carried out thoroughly, and there are a number of different practical, organisational constraints which can affect how well an evaluation can be carried out.

Commonly used methodologies for evaluating formal learning, such as the Kirkpatrick framework and the Phillips ROI approaches, suffer from various weaknesses which make them difficult to use effectively and can lead to unreliable conclusions.

Various systems thinking concepts and tools can be used to supplement existing methodologies for evaluating learning. It is important to have used a rigorous LNA process to develop a learning strategy which addresses the various boundary judgements relevant to any system: this effectively forms a theory of change.

The first step in the evaluation process is to ensure that high-level boundary judgements defined in the learning strategy have been implemented and to see what lessons have been learnt from this. We can then look in detail at what learning has taken place, what behaviours have changed and what impact there has been on social and environmental sustainability. Using systems thinking tools, particularly diagramming, can help to make causality clearer and can contribute to the learning of people involved in the evaluation process. Applying the principles of contribution theory can help in making final conclusions as to whether or not learning has contributed to changes in sustainability.

10.7 Further reading

Evaluating training programs: The four levels, Donald Kirkpatrick, Berrett Koehler, 1994: the foundational text for evaluating training courses.

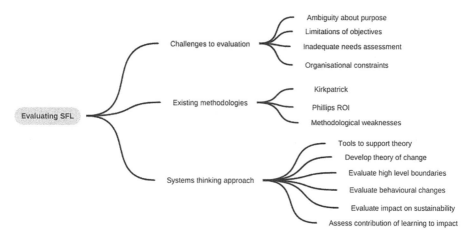

Figure 10.8 Key points in this chapter.

How to measure training results, Jack Phillips and Ron Stone, McGraw-Hill, 2002: key text for learning more about calculating the ROI of training.

Evaluation theory, models, and applications, Daniel Stufflebeam and Anthony Shinkfield, John Wiley & Sons, 2007: an encyclopaedic look at theories of evaluation and how they are applied.

Learning and performance, Bryan Hopkins, Routledge, 2017: an examination of how different systems thinking concepts and tools can be used for learning needs assessment and evaluation.

Notes

1 Joint Committee on Standards for Educational Evaluation, The Program Evaluation Standards (Thousand Oaks, CA: Corwin Press, 1994), 3.
2 Daniel L. Stufflebeam and Anthony J. Shinkfield, *Evaluation Theory, Models, and Applications* (San Francisco, CA: Jossey-Bass, 2007), 9.
3 Angela Everitt, 'Developing Critical Evaluation', Evaluation 2, no. 2 (1996): 173–88.
4 Eduardo Salas et al., 'The Science of Training and Development in Organizations: What Matters in Practice', *Psychological Science in the Public Interest* 13, no. 2 (2012): 74–101; Robert A Reiser, 'A History of Instructional Design and Technology: Part II: A History of Instructional Design', *Educational Technology Research and Development* 49, no. 2 (2001): 57–67.
5 Stufflebeam and Shinkfield, Evaluation Theory, Models, and Applications, 161.
6 ATD, 'Evaluating Learning: Getting to Measurements That Matter' (Alexandria, VA: Association for Talent Development, 2016).
7 Perri Estes Kennedy et al., 'Training Professionals' Usage and Understanding of Kirkpatrick's Level 3 and Level 4 Evaluations', *International Journal of Training and Development* 18, no. 1 (2014): 1–21; Rosalie T. Torres and Hallie Preskill, 'Evaluation and Organizational Learning: Past, Present, and Future', *The American Journal of Evaluation* 22, no. 3 (2001): 387–95.
8 Herman Aguinis and Kurt Kraiger, 'Benefits of Training and Development for Individuals and Teams, Organizations, and Society', *Annual Review of Psychology* 60 (2009): 451–74; Torres and Preskill, 'Evaluation and Organizational Learning: Past, Present, and Future'.
9 K. Kraiger and S.S. Culbertson, 'Understanding and Facilitating Learning: Advancements in Training and Development', in *Handbook of Psychology, Industrial and Organizational Psychology*, ed. I.B. Weiner et al. (Chichester: John Wiley & Sons, 2012), 253.
10 Elwood F. Holton III, 'The Flawed Four-Level Evaluation Model', *Human Resource Development Quarterly* 7, no. 1 (1996): 5.
11 It has been noted that three years before Kirkpatrick published his original paper in 1959, Raymond Katzell published a paper outlining a hierarchy of four steps, which are almost identical to Kirkpatrick's levels, to be considered in training evaluation. Katzell's original contribution is largely forgotten. See Cynthia J. Lewis, 'A Study of the Impact of the Workplace Learning Function on Organizational Excellence by Examining the Workplace Learning Practices of Six Malcolm Baldrige National Quality Award Recipients' (D.Ed., San Diego, CA, University of San Diego, 2011).
12 D. L. Kirkpatrick, *Evaluating Training Programs* (San Francisco, CA: Berrett-Koehler, 1994).
13 Holton III, 'The Flawed Four-Level Evaluation Model'.
14 Holton E.F. and S. Naquin, 'A Critical Analysis of HRD Evaluation Models from a Decision-Making Perspective', *Human Resource Development Quarterly* 16, no. 2 (2005): 275.
15 Reid Bates, 'A Critical Analysis of Evaluation Practice: The Kirkpatrick Model and the Principle of Beneficence', *Evaluation and Program Planning* 27, no. 3 (2004): 342.
16 Kirkpatrick, Evaluating Training Programs, 27.
17 George M. Alliger and Elizabeth A. Janak, 'Kirkpatrick's Levels of Training Criteria: Thirty Years Later', *Personnel Psychology* 42, no. 2 (1989): 337.
18 Kirkpatrick, Evaluating Training Programs, 22.
19 Kurt Kraiger, J. Kevin Ford, and Eduardo Salas, 'Application of Cognitive, Skill-Based, and Affective Theories of Learning Outcomes to New Methods of Training Evaluation', *Journal of Applied Psychology* 78, no. 2 (1993): 311.

20 J. J. Phillips, *Return on Investment in Training and Performance Investment Programs* (Woburn, MA: Butterworth-Heinemann, 1997); Jack Phillips and Ron Stone, *How to Measure Training Results: A Practical Guide to Tracking the Six Key Indicators* (New York: McGraw Hill Professional, 2002).
21 L. Bierema and M. Cseh, 'A Critical, Feminist Turn in HRD: A Humanistic Ethos', in Handbook of Human Resource Development, ed. N. Chalofsky, Tonette S. Rocco, and M.L. Morris (Pfeiffer, 2014); Kiran Trehan and Clare Rigg, 'Theorising Critical HRD: A Paradox of Intricacy and Discrepancy', Journal of European Industrial Training 35, no. 3 (2011): 276–90; Darlene Russ-Eft and Hallie Preskill, 'In Search of the Holy Grail: Return on Investment Evaluation in Human Resource Development', Advances in Developing Human Resources 7, no. 1 (2005): 71–85; Robin Kramar, 'Beyond Strategic Human Resource Management: Is Sustainable Human Resource Management the next Approach?', The International Journal of Human Resource Management 25, no. 8 (2014): 1069–89.
22 Roger Kaufman and John M. Keller, 'Levels of Evaluation: Beyond Kirkpatrick', *Human Resource Development Quarterly* 5, no. 4 (1994): 377.
23 Roger C. Conant and W. Ross Ashby, 'Every Good Regulator of a System Must Be a Model of That System', *International Journal of Systems Science* 1, no. 2 (1970): 89.
24 Richard Hummelbrunner, 'Learning, Systems Concepts and Values in Evaluation: Proposal for an Exploratory Framework to Improve Coherence', *IDS Bulletin* 46, no. 1 (2015): 17–29.
25 Barbara Schmidt-Abbey, Martin Reynolds, and Ray Ison, 'Towards Systemic Evaluation in Turbulent Times — Making a Second-Order Practice Shift', *Evaluation* 26, no. 2 (2020): 205–26.
26 Andy Rowe, 'Sustainability-Ready Evaluation: A Call to Action', *New Directions for Evaluation* 2019, no. 162 (2019): 29–48.
27 Emily F. Gates, 'Learning from Seasoned Evaluators: Implications of Systems Approaches for Evaluation Practice', *Evaluation* 23, no. 2 (2017): 152–71.
28 John Mayne, 'Contribution Analysis: Coming of Age?', *Evaluation* 18, no. 3 (2012): 270–80.
29 Kenneth G Brown, 'An Examination of the Structure and Nomological Network of Trainee Reactions: A Closer Look at "Smile Sheets".', *Journal of Applied Psychology* 90, no. 5 (2005): 991.
30 For example, see B. Hopkins, *Learning and Performance: A Systemic Model for Analysing Needs and Evaluating Training* (Abingdon: Routledge, 2017), 207–11.
31 Michael Scriven, 'Evaluation Perspectives and Procedures', in *Evaluation in Education*, ed. W.J. Popham (Berkeley, CA: McCutchan Publishing Corp, 1974), 68–84.
32 Richard Hummelbrunner, 'Systemic Evaluation in the Field of Regional Development', in *Systems Concepts in Evaluation: An Expert Anthology*, ed. B. Williams and I. Imam (Washington, DC: American Evaluation Association, 2006), 161–80; Schmidt-Abbey, Reynolds, and Ison, 'Towards Systemic Evaluation in Turbulent Times — Making a Second-Order Practice Shift'.
33 Thomas F. Gilbert, *Human Competence: Engineering Worthy Performance* (Silver Spring, MD: International Society for Performance Improvement, 2007).
34 Mayne, 'Contribution Analysis: Coming of Age?'

11 Reflecting on learning about learning

11.1 What this chapter covers

Figure 11.1 explains the structure of this chapter. In a book about learning about learning, it is perhaps inevitable that it should end with some reflection, given that the word "reflect" or a derivative has been used over 200 times in the text. We will reflect on reflection in two different ways; first by thinking about key subjects that have been explored within the book; and second, by thinking about the importance of the process of reflection itself.

11.2 Reflection on what we have learnt

So what are the key issues we have considered?

Clearly what sustainability means is of fundamental importance, and we have seen how difficult it is to develop a clear definition that meets all needs. The idea of sustainability having three dimensions provides some help, but this introduces its own difficulties because of the complex and often contradictory implications of seeking to achieve sustainability in all three dimensions. I have tried to relate the United Nations' Sustainable Development Goals (SDGs) to the three dimensions as they apply to organisational activities and highlighted the importance of crosschecking sustainability-focused learning (SFL) activities with these.

Whatever understanding of sustainability we have, the reality is that embracing social and environmental sustainability will force greater or lesser changes onto what organisations do and onto our lifestyles. This will present major challenges to what we all see as "normal" and to what we value in our lives. For that reason, a recurring theme throughout the book has been how learning can help people review their value framework and come to welcome sustainability rather than see it as a hair shirt.

The contested nature of what sustainability means could, on first consideration, present serious challenges to developing a learning strategy, but by drawing on a range of ideas inspired by perspectives such as social constructionism and critical philosophy we were able to see how many different possible approaches to learning could be integrated

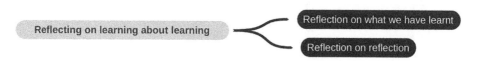

Figure 11.1 Map of Chapter 11.

DOI: 10.4324/9781003218296-12

into a strategy which could balance the technical requirements of learning about sustainability with respect for the personal values of learners.

Social constructionism appears throughout the book, helping us to realise that the system of political economy within which we live and which are contributing to the environmental crisis and social problems that we are experiencing is just a set of ideas, and that we can, if we find the political will, change it to something that gives us a better chance of sustainability. I have also pointed out the socially constructed nature of human resource development (HRD), again with the aim of highlighting that how it works and what its function is within an organisation is not an immutable object—it can be changed.

Organisations themselves are social technologies, and their role in society and the environment is also negotiable. To make the infinite range of possible alignments with sustainability manageable, we looked at three different approaches to organisational sustainability. Wherever your organisation is, it could aim to be visionary.

Another subject of central importance has been the use of systems thinking as the basis of a systematic process for developing a learning strategy. The systems thinking approach offers a number of considerable advantages for developing a learning strategy.

First, it avoids the Cartesian trap of thinking that we can identify one or two discrete subjects or methods which will give us the results that we need. Because Cartesian reductionism ignores the interrelationships between the many factors relevant to learning, it can never reliably provide a comprehensive solution to a wicked problem such as learning.

Second, the emphasis on exploring different perspectives means that we avoid making unitarist assumptions about what should be included in a programme and how this should be addressed. Rather, we develop a pluralist concept of what is needed in a learning programme, so that it takes into consideration not just the technical requirements for the organisation but also the emancipatory interests of learners. This reminds us of the need to involve a range of stakeholders in the design of the learning strategy—importantly this may also need to include people from outside the organisation who will be affected by what it does. This should help to contribute towards a programme where the learning transfers more effectively.

Because systems thinking revolves around models of interrelationships and boundary judgements it is scalable, meaning that we can use it to think at macro or micro levels and anywhere in between. We can therefore use the process to identify the content, mechanisms and principles relevant for a learning programme about a small, clearly defined subject, or for an organisation-level learning and development policy about a specific subject or about learning in general.

However, it is essential to remember that systemic must be combined with the systematic.[1] As we follow a systematic process for developing an SFL strategy we need to regularly look up and remember where we are within a system, to make sure that we are taking different perspectives into account, that we are recognising how interrelationships are affecting what we are doing, and that we are making appropriate boundary judgements about what is important about learning. By doing this, we can be confident that our final strategy is as holistic as is practically possible, sweeping in the content that is relevant, using a range of mechanisms to suit the specific situation of our learners, and adopting the principles that can help people to understand the reasons why sustainability is so vital.

270 *Reflecting on learning*

We have made extensive use of both systems thinking principles and of various tools based on these. Such a central use of systems thinking tools in HRD is unusual and my hope is that this contributes in some way to a paradigm shift in how learning and development is conceived.

A final point to remember in this brief summary is that sustainability is something that organisations need to build into everything they do and accept that this will be a permanent reality. As the evidence presented in this book has shown, we cannot continue as we have been doing since the dawn of the Industrial Revolution. Embracing sustainability in organisational practice now may mean that my grandchildren can live a long and fulfilling life on a stable Spaceship Earth.

Time for reflection

What are the key points you have picked up from this book?
What changes do you think this may make to your practice?
What have you disagreed with, and why?
How can you learn from these things you disagree with?

11.3 Reflection on reflection

To conclude, we should reflect on the importance of reflection itself. Arguably, reflection is the most important part of the whole process of learning. In cybernetic terms, it is the negative feedback we receive on everything we do: we act, realise that we have not achieved exactly what we want to do, so we make changes in how we act. Without this, there is no learning. We looked at this in terms of both single loop learning where we simply make changes to what we do, and double loop learning where we think about the assumptions (or, in different terms, our mental models or frames of reference) that are guiding our decisions about what to do.

Reflection is so fundamental in the learning process that we often do not notice that we are doing it. Even though most learning and development professionals will know all about Kolb's experiential learning cycle and its reflective stage, in my experience of developing organisational learning programmes reflection is something that is very often overlooked: in the rush to deliver information or instruction and see changes in behaviour and an organisational impact, allowing or creating space for reflection is often deemed unimportant. But not always, and there are voices pointing out the value of structured reflection through the use of tools such as reflective learning journals.[2] I have tried to emphasise the importance of reflection in this book through the regular "Time for reflection" slots, which have asked you to think about how the preceding content relates to your own experience, or the degree to which you might agree or disagree with what I have written. I hope they have proved useful.

I write these final words in September, a month which, for me, marks the end of warm days and long, light summer evenings, and a time for reflection about what the year has brought so far and what may happen in the coming darker days of winter. That may be, but hopefully not for the sake of our children and grandchildren, metaphorical for humanity on a global timescale. An SFL strategy which emphasises the importance of reflection and being mindful about the fragility of our existence may play a part in creating, in the words of Christine Wamsler, "... a fundamental shift in the way we think about, and ultimately act on, local and global economic, social, and ecological crises".[3]

Notes

1 Ison R., *Systems Practice: How to Act in Situations of Uncertainty and Complexity in a Climate-Change World*, 2nd ed. (London: Springer, 2017).
2 Travor Brown, Martin McCracken, and Paula O'Kane, '"Don't Forget to Write": How Reflective Learning Journals Can Help to Facilitate, Assess and Evaluate Training Transfer', *Human Resource Development International* 14, no. 4 (2011): 465–81.
3 Christine Wamsler, 'Mind the Gap: The Role of Mindfulness in Adapting to Increasing Risk and Climate Change', *Sustainability Science* 13, no. 4 (2018): 1122.

Index

Note: **Bold** page numbers refer to tables; *italic* page numbers refer to figures and page numbers followed by "n" denote endnotes.

3BL *see* triple bottom line
4I 172, 175
70:20:10 168

accidental learning *see* incidental learning
Acker, Joan 122
action learning 8, 179, 216–18, 228, **242**
adaptive management 58, 69
AER *see* after-event review
after-event review 8, 231, 234–35, **240**, **242**
age: in attitudes to sustainability 184; discrimination 105, 123; in identity 186; in training 184
Agenda 2030 13, 23, 153
Agenda 21 12, 20, 36
agnotology 15; *see also* denial
ahimsa 190
AI *see* artificial intelligence
AMOC *see* Atlantic Meridional Overturning Circulation
andragogy 8, 205–6, 219, 228
Anthropocene 17
anthropocentric 6, 49, 116, **130**, 136, 194; definition of 47; *see also* ecomodernism
appreciative system 162, 249
Argyris, Chris 50, 62, 70, 124–25, 174, 210, 234
Armstrong, Michael 151
artificial intelligence 119
Ashby, Ross 63, 253–54
assumptions: in culture 175, 179; in dialogue 212–13; in single and double loop learning 124–29, 136; in unitarist thinking 162; *see also* boundary judgment; dialogue; hegemony; pluralist thinking; unitarist thinking

Atlantic Meridional Overturning Circulation 22
attractor 57, 213
automation 119–20

B Corp 123, 133–34, 217, 263
basho 172, 175
Beck, Ulrich 17–18, 92, 107
Beer, Stafford 50–51, 63–64
Behaviour Engineering Model 260–62
behaviourism 159, 169, 204, 249
BEM *see* Behavior Engineering Model
Benefit Corporation 133
Berger, Peter 3, 46, 56, 91, 125, 172, 174, 175
Blueprint for Survival 13–14
bonding ties 132, 180–81
boundaries, planetary *see* planetary boundaries
boundary judgement: in evaluation 254, **256–57**, 264–65; explanation of 6–8, 35, 38, 41, 48–49, 50, 66–67, 68; in open systems 89, 99–100; as pedagogical method 214; for reflection 269; in strategy writing **246**; in sustainability assessment 131; use in learning needs assessment 143, 148, **149–50**, 159–60, 162, 195, 195–98, 211, 224–27, 238–**41**
boundary object 212
boundary spanner 181
Boyatzis, Richard 151
bracing ties 180–81, 183
bridging ties 132, 180–81
Brookfield, Stephen 211
Brown, John Seely 174
Buddhism 14, 15, 188–91, 194, 195
bureaucracy 99, 122–23, 128, 186
butterfly metaphor 57

Capital see Marx, Karl
capitalism 28, 74–81, 89, 93, 99, 106, 116; in crisis 18; and growth 83, 85, 87; Marxist critique 12, 47–48
carbon, social cost of *see* social cost of carbon
Carson, Rachel 2, 12, 15
Cartesian thinking: limitations of 54, 269; meaning of 36; and systems thinking 68
CAS *see* complex adaptive system
Catholic Social Tradition 119
causal flow diagrams *see* diagramming
Checkland, Peter 39, 148
Christakis, Alexander 16, 22
Christianity 188, 192–93, 199
Churchman, Charles West 48, 66
circular economics 7, 86–87, 90, 94, 117, 128, 224
closed systems 52, 68, 89, 101
Club of Rome 14, 16
coaching 167, 199, 231, 233–34, **240, 242**
cognitive: ability and learning 184; competencies 151, 154; ideas about learning 169–73
cognitive dissonance 187, 224
commitment: to employer 110, 113, 122; ethical 104, 110; to learning 148, 178, 237; social 18, 104, 107; to sustainable practice 126, 134, 153, 177–79, 205, 207, 224, **225**, 234, **257**, 260; *see also* conforming
communicative knowledge 3, 8, 66, 144–45, 208, 215, *216*, 217, 224
Community Interest Company 133
community of practice 232–33, **240, 242**
competence 124, 173, 219; definition of 150–53, 154; for sustainable practice 156–61, 163
competency *152*, 219; definition of 150–53; for sustainable practice 153–54, **161;** in systems thinking 6, 37, 211, 254
competitive advantage 108, 110–11, 127–28, **130**, 155
complex adaptive system 56, 69, 89, 122, 130, 213
complexity theory 6, 35, 55–58, 69, 145, 169, 206
complier (organisation) 127, 129, **130–31**, 136, 155–58
concept maps *see* diagramming
conforming (to learning) 205, 207, 261
constructionism, social *see* social constructionism
constructivism 169

contested concept: examples of 18–19, 27, 54, 131, 159, 163, 237; meaning of 18
contribution theory 258, 265
Cook, S.D.N. 148, 172
corporate responsibility *see* Corporate Social Responsibility; organisational sustainability
Corporate Social Responsibility: definition 102; history of 101–3; *see also* organisational sustainability
COVID-19 1, 2, 14, 17, 18, 42, 43, 79, 90, 92, 93, 105, 121
cradle-to-cradle 117, 128
cradle-to-grave 117, 128
Cranton, Patricia 208, 211
Creating Shared Value 102, 115–16, 135, 235
Critical Systems Heuristics 36; explanation of 66–68; use in LNA 148, **149–50, 160–61, 196–98, 225–27**, 239–40; *see also* boundary judgements
critical theory 210: *see also* critical thinking; pluralist thinking; unitarist thinking
critical thinking 8, 48, 145, 179, 204, 205, 206, 209–12, 215, 228; challenges in doing 223–24; in reflective practice 213; in serious games 219; as sustainability competency 154; *see also* hegemony
Crutzen, Paul 17
CSH *see* Critical Systems Heuristics
CSR *see* Corporate Social Responsibility
CSV *see* Creating Shared Value
culture: components of 174–76; definition of 174; socio-economic 109, 121, 144, 153; *see also* learning culture; organisational culture
cybernetics 6, 45, 63, 270

Daly, Herman 28, 81, 85
Danone 134
Daoism 188–89, 199
Dasgupta Review 28
debating 221–23
debrief *see* after-event review
deep ecology 47, 191, 211
deep sustainability 47
Deep Thought 131
Deepwater Horizon 83
denial: of climate change 15, 17; as psychological defence 182
Descartes, René 36
development, sustainable 12, 19, 153; *see also* sustainability; Sustainable Development Goals
dharma 188, 190

diagramming: causal flow diagrams 6, 59–62, 69, 70, 214, 250, 261, 262; concept maps 194–95, 214; influence diagrams 43–44, 68, 77, 80, 173–74, 214, 261, 262; rich pictures 39, 42, 214, 262; system maps 40–41, 44, 51, 68, 80–81, 89–90, 104, 105–6, 108–9, 214

dialectic: for learning 50, 90–92, 103, 130, 162; meaning of 91, 186

dialogue 205, 228, 235: cf. discussion 213; principles of 212–13; in transformative learning 208; value of 109, 178–79

Dimensions of the Learning Organization Questionnaire 179–80

disciplinary power *see* power; disciplinary

discounting, economic 78, 113

DLOQ *see* Dimensions of the Learning Organization Questionnaire

do no harm 118–19

double loop learning 7, 8, 125–28, 130, 136, **157**, 182; in after-event reviews 234; in dialogue 213; in reflective practice 214, 270; in serious games 219; in transformative learning 206, 210

doughnut economics 7, 87–89, 90, 94

Dow Jones Sustainability Index 134

Ebbinghaus, Hermann 184

ecocentric 6, 49, 116, 117, **130**, 136; definition of 47

ecoconsciousness 47

eco-effectiveness 128, **131**, 155

eco-efficiency 117, 128, **131**, **157**

ecofeminism 47

ecological ethos 66

Ecologist, The 13

ecomodernism 47, 78, 81, 84, 90, 116

Ecomodernist Manifesto, The 47

economic sustainability *see* sustainability, economic

economics *see* political economy

ecosocialism 47; *see also* Marxism

ecosystem services: cost of 90; definition of 22

ECSF *see* European Corporate Sustainability Framework

edge of chaos 57–58, 63, 69, 122, 169, 206, 216, 232

Education for Sustainable Development 36–37, 153

Elkington, John 132–33

emancipatory knowledge 144–45, 204, 207, 213, 215–17, 224, 228

emergence (within a system) 56–57, 99, 171, 181, 259

emotional intelligence 151, 154

entropy 68, 135: definition of 51–52; implications for learning 170, 232; implications for organisations 52, 56, 81, 100–1; implications for political economy 84–85, 87

environmental sustainability *see* sustainability, environmental

ESD *see* Education for Sustainable Development

espoused theory 50, 124–25, 175

ethical climate 66, 176, *195*

ethics: in neoliberal political economy 80; *see also* ethical climate; organisational culture

European Corporate Sustainability Framework 171, 176–77, 185; *see also* levels of existence

evaluation *see* learning evaluation

experiential learning 169–71, 176, 199, 235, 270

exploitation (change strategy) 126–27

exploration (change strategy) 126–27

externalities 65, 78, 79, 82, 93, 104, 113, 114, 132

Extinction Rebellion xix, 17

Fairtrade 128

faith systems *174*, 188–94, *195*

feedback: general principles 37, 38, 45, 56, 59; in institutional theory 107; in learning strategy **156**, **158**, 168, 233, 234, 250, 262, 263, 270; in organisations 63–65, 68, 100; in serious games 218, 219, 221

feminism: in organisational theory 122, **130**; in sustainability perspectives 47

Fifth Discipline, The 59, 61, 178–79

financialisation 79–80

Forest Stewardship Council 128

formal learning 7, 8, 142, 154, 232; definition of 166; design considerations 170, 173, 183, 187, 199, 204–5, 210, 214, 223, 224–27; modes of 167, 219, 220; role of HRD 179, 238–40, **242**; *see also* learning evaluation

Forrester, Jay 14

Foucault, Michel 172, 184, 186, 200n

frame of reference 5, 207–10, 213, 224, 228; *see also* mental model; worldview

Framework for Strategic Sustainable Development 58, 130

Friedman Doctrine 42, 51, 78, 104

Friedman, Milton 133

FSC *see* Forest Stewardship Council
FSSD *see* Framework for Strategic Sustainable Development
FTSE4GOOD Index 134

games, serious 218–21, 228
Gandhi, Mahatma 14, 190–91
GDP 82, 83
gender: attitudes to sustainability 184–85; and HRD 237; in organisation theory 105, 122–23; and power 218, 237; in SDGs 26, 29, 153
Gestalt 172
gig economy 120
Gilbert, Tom 260–61
Gilligan, Carol 123, 128
Giroux, Henry 91, 142
Global Compact 134
globalisation 17, 76, 92, 105
Global Reporting Initiative 133, 263
goal-free evaluation 259; *see also* learning evaluation
Golden Rule, the 194
Google 105, 153, 187
Gramsci, Antonio 91, 210
Graves, Clare 176, 185
Great Acceleration 1, 3, 7, 16, 17, 75, 93, 101
Green Five 153
green jobs 86, 117
Green New Deal 7, 85–86, 90, 93, 94
greenwash 87, 102, 115, 133
GRI *see* Global Reporting Initiative
groupthink 181; *see also* hegemony
growth: criticism of 19, 82–85, 93, 219; organisational **130**; of population 14–15; in SDGs 13, 23, 26, 29; cf. Steady state economics 7, 85; sustainable 17
Gulf Stream *see* Atlantic Meridional Overturning Circulation

Habermas, Jürgen 3, 8; in Critical Systems Heuristics 66; in learning design 204–8, 210–11, 213, 215, 228; theory of communicative action 144–46
Hardin, Garrett 22, 61
Hart, Stuart 110
Hayek, Friedrich 75
hegemony: definition of 91–92; in economic thought 108; in learning design 145, 214, 218, 221, 223–24, **227**, **241**; in organisational theory 123

Hinduism 15, 189–91, 199
hockey stick curve 1
homeostasis 47, 100
HR *see* Human Resources
HRD *see* Human Resource Development
HRM *see* Human Resource Management
hub, in social network theory 181, 183
Human Resource Development: challenges from sustainability 211, 236–38, **242**; history of 143–44; practice within 3, 8, 144–46, 147, 179, 247, *250*, 251
Human Resource Management 102, 143–45, 151, 237–42, **257**
Human Resources: history of 144
human rights 25, 88, 105, 115, 153

ICRS *see* Institute for Corporate Responsibility and Sustainability
ideal speech 211
ILO *see* International Labour Organization
incidental learning 8, 167–68, 199, 259
influence diagrams *see* diagramming
informal learning 8, 57–58, 148, 199, 249: definition of 167–69; importance of 121, 122, 173, 179, 260; support for 169, 183, 187, 197, **226**, 231–36, 239, **240**, **241**, **246**
institutional landscape 2, 74, 106, *107*, 122, 124, 127–28, 135, 155, 156; and organisational identity 176; *see also* institutional theory
institutional theory 106–9, *111*, 171
Instructional Systems Design 205
intellectual property 79, 88
International Labour Organization 46, 117
International Union for the Conservation of Nature 19
interrelationships: in diagramming 214; in social learning 170, 180; in sustainability 17, 30, 131, 133, 162; in systems thinking 38, 43–45, 49, 59, 68, 179, 211, 269
IPCC 1
ISD *see* Instructional Systems Design
Islam 191–92, 199
ISO 14000 12, 114, 134
isomorphism 108, 122
IUCN *see* International Union for the Conservation of Nature

Jevons Paradox 114
job shadowing 167, 235
jubilee 192
Judaism 192, 199
just transition 20, 117

Kanter, Rosabeth Moss 122
karma 190
Kirkpatrick, Donald 247, 252: critique of evaluation framework 252–54, 258, 265, 266n11
knowledge conversion 171
knowledge creation 172–73, 181
knowledge sharing *167*
Knowles, Malcolm 205–6, 219, 228
Kolb, David 169, 199, 270
Kramer, Mark 115
KSA 152
Kuhn, Thomas 3
Kuznets curve: inequality 76–77; environmental 77, **78**
Kuznets, Simon 76

Laloux, Frederic 128, 185; *see also* teal organisation
Lave, Jean 232
learning culture 8, 168, 173, *174*, 178–80, 183, 186, 187, *195*, 198, 199, **246**, **257**, 259; for coaching 233, 235; role of HR 237, **240**
learning evaluation 143, 245, 247–67; critique of methods *250*, 252–53; definition of 248; difficulties with 248–51; and systems thinking 7, 8, 44, 55, 58, 67, 147, 149, 260–61
learning, formal *see* formal learning
learning, informal *see* informal learning
Learning Needs Assessment: as boundary judgements 148; framework for 147–50, **160–61**, **196–98**, **225–27**, **239–42**; reasons why not done 146–47
learning organisation 178–79, 212
learning transfer climate 8, *174*, 183–84, *195*, 197, 199, **226**, 238, **240**, 259–260
legitimate system 57, 122
levels of existence 171, 185
Life Cycle Assessment 114
lifeworld 145, 186, 204, 210, *216*, *217*, 224
Limits to Growth, The 14–17, 20, 22, 36, 58–60
LNA *see* Learning Needs Assessment
Luckmann, Thomas 3, 46, 56, 91, 125, 172, 174, 175

machine learning 119
Marsick, Victoria 179
Marxism 12, 91, 210
Marx, Karl 11–12, 17, 28, 133
Massachusetts Institute of Technology 14, 213
Mayne, John 258

McClelland, David 151
mental model 151; *see also* frame of reference; worldview
mentoring 167, 199, 233–34, **240**, **242**
metabolic rift 12, 17, 28
Mezirow, Jack 206–9
Millennium Ecosystem Assessment 22
Mill, John Stuart 11, 85
Mirowski, Philip 76, 145
MIT *see* Massachusetts Institute of Technology
ML *see* machine learning
Monbiot, George 25, 92
Mont Pèlerin Society 75, 91
moral compass, in organisations 3, 176, 237
motivation (for learning) 184, 206, 213, 233, 261, 262
MSCI ACWI Sustainable Impact Index 134

New Economics Foundation 86, 94
North, Douglass 106
Novo Nordisk 114, 235

objectives: in evaluation 248–49, 255–56, 259, 265; in learning design 55, 67, 169; in learning needs assessment 147
OEM *see* Organisational Elements Model
offshoring 121
on-the-job learning 167–68
on-the-job training 167, 199
open systems: definition of 51–52, 56, 68: in learning 170; organisation as 81, 100–1
organisational culture 7, 108, 109, 119, 128, 129, 132, 144, 150, **161**, 173, *174*, *175*, 185, 199, 210, 213, **227**, 262; creation of **156–57**, 174–77; ethical 176, 237; impact on learning 167, 209, 235, **241**, **246**, 248, **257**; *see also* organisational identity
Organisational Elements Model 253, 263
organisational identity 176
organisational learning: as adaptation towards sustainability 106, 124–30, 252; as integration of individual learning 99, 172; and systems thinking 51, 63, 89; *see also* double loop learning; single loop learning
organisational sustainability, economic 112–18; external 114; internal 113
organisational sustainability, environmental 116–18
organisational sustainability, social 118–24; external 120; internal 120–24
organisations: commitment to sustainability 126–29; definition of 98; as systems 99–101

Orlitzky, Marc 104
O-T-P 147, 155
Our Common Future 2, 12, 31, 102
Ozbekhan, Hasan 14

performative (as pedagogical principle) 8, 144–45, 179, 205, 215–16, 223–24, 228, 237, 253
personality 151, 181, 184
perspectives: on sustainability 47; in systems thinking 6, 36, 45–48
philanthropy 101–3, 115, 120, 135
Phillips, Jack 252, 265
Piketty, Thomas 78
planetary boundaries 21, 24, 86, 89, 94, 117–18, 136, **156, 158**
pluralist thinking: in learning 48, 179, 269; as organisational culture 144, 205
Polanyi, Karl 27
political economy: as landscape **112**; neoclassical 7, 13, 42, 74, 76, 80–82, 90–91, 93, 104; neoliberal 76–81, 89–94, 108, 109, 113, 120, 144, 210; sustainable 81–90
Porter hypothesis 108–9
Porter, Michael 108, 115, 116, 128
POSIWID *see* purpose of a system
power (in organisations) 66–68, 126, 129, 148, 179, 214; disciplinary 172, 184, 186; and HRD 237, 248; implications for learning 209–12, 218
PQR 148
practical knowledge *see* communicative knowledge
Predicament of Mankind, The 14
profit: fair profit 113–14, 214; importance for private sector 51, **130–31**; for viability 133; *see also* financialisation
Project Maven 105, 153, 187
Protestant ethic 75
psychological safety 178, 182, *195*, 209, 213, 217
purpose: of a business 50–51, 104, 114; of a system 48, 56
Putnam, Robert 25, 101, 180

Quakers 119

Raworth, Kate 87–88
RBV *see* resource-based view
recursion 65
reflection: critical 214, 228; importance in learning 8, 154, 170, 208, 234, 268–71; reflective practice *167*, 213–14

regenerative 18, 87, 88, 89, 117, **131**
religion *see* faith systems
Requisite Variety, Law of 63, 216, 232
resilience: cf. economic efficiency 79, 90, 93; in SDGs 26; as sustainability 18, 42–43, 86, 114
resource-based view 110–11
return on investment (as evaluation criterion) 252–53, 265, 266
Revans, Reg 216, 218, **242**
rich pictures *see* diagramming
risk society 17, 107
Rittel, Horst 52, 53, 54
Rockström, Johan 21, 89
ROI *see* return on investment
Royal Dutch Shell 107

samsara 189–90, 194
SCC *see* social cost of carbon
scepticism *see* agnotology
Schein, Edgar 174–75, 178–80
Schön, Donald 50, 124–25, 210, 234
Schumacher, Ernst 2, 14, 82, 84, 191
scientific management 99, 123
Scott, Richard 98–99, 123
Scriven, Michael 259
SD *see* System Dynamics
SDG *see* Sustainable Development Goals
secondments 167, 235, 236
self-directed learning 8, 167, 199, 205, 206, 228
self-efficacy 184, 233
Senge, Peter 59, 61, 178–79, 212–13
serious games *see* games, serious
service learning 167, 231, 235–36, **240, 242**
SES *see* socio-environmental system
SFL *see* sustainability-focused learning
shadow system 57, 69, 122, 145, 169, 206, 216
Sheffield City Council 6, 38, 39, 45, 49, 54
SHRM *see* Strategic Human Resource Management
Silent Spring 2, 12
simulations *see* games, serious
single loop learning 125–26, 136, 175, 213, 214, 270
Small is Beautiful 2, 14, 82, 191
Smith, Adam 11, 85
social capital: concept of 180–82; importance for learning 8, *174*, 181–83, 184, *195*, 197, 199, **226**, 238, **240**; in social sustainability 28, 87, 113, 121, **130**, 132
social cohesion 25, 76–77, 120, 121, 122, 136, 214

social constructionism: in complexity theory 56; creating perspectives 45–48, 268, 269; in knowledge creation 91, 172, 174; *see also* frame of reference; mental model; worldview
social contract theory 105–6, *111*
social cost of carbon 28
social enterprise 105, 128
social equity 4, 7; in learning content **157**, 206; in organisations 120, 122, 136; in political economy 76–77; in social sustainability 24–25
social identity *174*, 186–87, *195*
social impact network 212, 232
social intelligence 151, 154
social learning: meaning of 169–71; outcomes of 171; in serious games 221; and social capital 180; *see also* community of practice
Social Network Analysis 132
Social Return on Investment 114
social technology 28–29, 74, 144
social value 108–9, 113–15, 127, 224
socio-environmental system 27, 42, 79
Spaceship Earth 83–84, 101, 270
spiral dynamics 106–8, 171
Stacey, Ralph 55, 57, 69, 223
stakeholder theory 109–10, *111*, 206
Stern Review, The 78
stewardship: of products 111, 116–17, **130**, 136; theological 191–94
stockholder theory 104, *111*
Stockholm Resilience Centre 21
Stoermer, Eugene 17
Strategic Human Resource Management 144–45, 179
strategist (organisation) 127, 129, 136, 155–58
structured work extensions 167, 199, 235, 236
subak 22
sustainability: definition of 18–19; history of term 10–18
sustainability, assessment 131–34
sustainability, economic 27–30
sustainability, environmental 20–24
sustainability-focused learning: meaning of 166, 264; questions to ask 238–41; strategy writing 245–46
sustainability, organisational *see* organisational sustainability, economic; organisational sustainability, environmental; organisational sustainability, social
sustainability, social 24–27
Sustainable Development Goals: and economic sustainability **29**; and environmental sustainability **23**; and organisational learning 106, 114, 115, 116, 118, 130, 153–54, **156–58**; origin of 13; and social sustainability **26**
system: definition of 37
System Dynamics 58–62; *see also Limits to Growth, The*
system maps *see* diagramming
systems theory 38
systems thinking: and adult learning *205*, 214–15; first-order 37, 260; meaning of 36–37, second-order 38, 260–61

tacit knowledge 172
Tainter, Joseph 15, 52, 62, 69
Taylor, Frederick 99, 122, 123
TBL *see* triple bottom line
teal organisation 128, 185
technical knowledge: in performative learning 204; in theory of communicative action 215, 217
technocentric *see* ecomodernism
theoecocentrism 47
theory-in-use 50, 124–25
theory of action 124
Thermodynamics, Second Law of 51–52, 83, 87
ties (in social network theory) 180–81
time (linear and cyclical conceptions) 194
Tragedy of the Commons, The 22, 61
transformative learning 125, 154, 179, 205, 206–9
triple bottom line 5, 132, 263
triple loop learning 213
trust: and double loop learning 126; and HRD 238; in SFL strategy **226**, **240**; in social learning 170, 173, *195*, 213, 232, 235; in teams 130, 132, 180–82

Ulrich, Werner 48, 50, 66, 148, 254
UNCED *11*, 12, 13
UNCHE *11*, 12
UNCSD *11*, 13
UNEP 12, 20, 86–87
UNESCO 153
unitarist thinking: in learning 162, 179, 205, 210, 216, 224, 228, 269; as organisational culture 48, 144, 173, 186, 204, 215,
unlearning 173

values: importance in sustainability 3, 8, 14, 16, 111, 185–86; of individuals 45–47, 56, 122, 126, 153, *195*, 269; and learning 170, 183, 186–87, 204, 208, 210, 220, 223;

organisational 65–66, 113, 119, 127, 128, **130**, 133, 136, 174–78, 224, 237; in political economy 92, 106; in SDGs 23; *see also* frame of reference; mental models; social identity; worldview

variety 57, 58, 63, 65, 108, 216, 232

viability (financial in organisations) 101, 113, 116, 129, 131, 132, 133, 136, **156**, 162; *see also* Viable System Model

Viable System Model: explanation of 63–66; use in LNA 155–59

Vickers, Geoffrey 162

visionary (organisation) 128–30, 147, 155–58, 224, 269

VSM *see* Viable System Model

VUCA 54

Wagenaar, Hendrik 172

Watkins, Karen 179

WCED *see* World Commission on Environment and Development

Webber, Melvin 52, 53, 54

Weber, Max 75, 99, 122–23, 128, 186, 193

Weick, Karl 168

Weltanschauung see worldview

Wenger, Etienne 232

WFH *see* working from home

wicked problems 6, 35; explanation of 52–55, 68–69; and learning 162, 173, 237, 247, 249, 260, 269; and sustainability 87, 186

working from home 121, 173, 238

workplace learning 144, 167, 168

World Commission on Environment and Development 12, 18, 264

World Conservation Strategy 19

worldview: in CSH 49, 67, **150**, **161**, 198, **227**, **241**; definition of 47; in learning evaluation **257**; in SFL strategy 245, **246**; significance of 6, 18, 22, 28, 54, 170; and sustainability 47, 186, 190; *see also* frame of reference, mental model

wu wei 188, 194

zoonotic disease 17